Software Quality Assurance

Software Quality Assurance

In Large Scale and Complex Software-Intensive Systems

Edited by

Ivan Mistrik
Heidelberg, Germany

Richard Soley
Object Management Group, Needham, MA, USA

Nour Ali
University of Brighton, Brighton, UK

John Grundy
Swinburne University of Technology, Hawthorn, VIC, Australia

Bedir Tekinerdogan
Wageningen University, Wageningen, The Netherlands

AMSTERDAM • BOSTON • HEIDELBERG • LONDON
NEW YORK • OXFORD • PARIS • SAN DIEGO
SAN FRANCISCO • SINGAPORE • SYDNEY • TOKYO

Morgan Kaufmann is an imprint of Elsevier

Acquiring Editor: Todd Green
Editorial Project Manager: Lindsay Lawrence
Project Manager: Priya Kumaraguruparan
Cover Designer: Maria Inês Cruz

Morgan Kaufmann is an imprint of Elsevier
225 Wyman Street, Waltham, MA 02451, USA

ISBN: 978-0-12-802301-3

British Library Cataloguing-in-Publication Data
A catalogue record for this book is available from the British Library.

Library of Congress Cataloging-in-Publication Data
A catalog record for this book is available from the Library of Congress.

For Information on all Morgan Kaufmann publications
visit our website at www.mkp.com

Working together
to grow libraries in
developing countries

www.elsevier.com • www.bookaid.org

Contents

*Padmalata V. Nistala, Kesav V. Nori, Swaminathan Natarajan,
Nikhil R. Zope and Anand Kumar*

List of Contributors

Alain Abran
Ecole de Technologie Supérieure (ETS), Montréal, Canada

Nour Ali
University of Brighton, Brighton, UK

Maurício Aniche
University of São Paulo (USP) Department of Computer Science,
São Paulo/SP-Brazil

Paris Avgeriou
Department of Mathematics and Computing Science, University of Groningen,
Groningen, The Netherlands

Luis Azevedo
Department of Computer Science, University of Hull, Hull, UK

Jim Buckley
Lero, University of Limerick, Ireland

Luigi Buglione
Engineering Ingegneria Informatica SpA, Rome, Italy; Ecole de Technologie
Supérieure (ETS), Montréal, Canada

J.J. Collins
Lero, University of Limerick, Ireland

Maya Daneva
University of Twente, Enschede, The Netherlands

Barry Demchak
University of California, San Diego, La Jolla, CA, USA

Michael English
Lero, University of Limerick, Ireland

Claudiu Farcas
University of California, San Diego, La Jolla, CA, USA

Emilia Farcas
University of California, San Diego, La Jolla, CA, USA

I. Fleming
SQA.net, USA; SugarCRM Inc., Cupertino, CA, USA

William G. Griswold
University of California, San Diego, La Jolla, CA, USA

John Grundy
Swinburne University of Technology, Hawthorn, VIC, Australia

Eduardo Guerra
National Institute of Space Research (INPE), Associated Laboratory for
Computing and Applied Mathematics, São José dos Campos/SP-Brazil

Andrea Herrmann
Herrmann & Ehrlich, Stuttgart, Germany

Sohag Kabir
Department of Computer Science, University of Hull, Hull, UK

Marouane Kessentini
Department of Computer and Information Science, University of Michigan-
Dearborn, Dearborn, MI, USA

Ingolf Krueger
University of California, San Diego, La Jolla, CA, USA

Anand Kumar
Tata Consultancy Services, TCS Innovation Labs—Tata Research Development
and Design Centre, Pune, Maharashtra, India

Zengyang Li
Department of Mathematics and Computing Science, University of Groningen,
Groningen, The Netherlands; International School of Software, Wuhan
University, Wuhan, People's Republic of China

Peng Liang
State Key Lab of Software Engineering, School of Computer, Wuhan University,
Wuhan, People's Republic of China; Department of Computer Science, VU
University Amsterdam, Amsterdam, The Netherlands

Doji Samson Lokku
Tata Consultancy Services, Hyderabad, Telangana, India

Bruce R. Maxim
Department of Computer and Information Science, University of Michigan-
Dearborn, Dearborn, MI, USA

Massimiliano Menarini
University of California, San Diego, La Jolla, CA, USA

Ivan Mistrik
Heidelberg, Germany

Swaminathan Natarajan
Tata Consultancy Services, TCS Innovation Labs—Tata Research Development
and Design Centre, Pune, Maharashtra, India

Padmalata V. Nistala
Tata Consultancy Services, Hyderabad, Telangana, India

Kesav V. Nori
International Institute of Information Technology, Hyderabad, Telangana, India

Yiannis Papadopoulos
Department of Computer Science, University of Hull, Hull, UK

David Parker
Department of Computer Science, University of Hull, Hull, UK

Kevin Patrick
University of California, San Diego, La Jolla, CA, USA

Fred Raab
University of California, San Diego, La Jolla, CA, USA

Septavera Sharvia
Department of Computer Science, University of Hull, Hull, UK

Richard Soley
Object Management Group, Needham, MA, USA

Ioannis Sorokos
Department of Computer Science, University of Hull, Hull, UK

Bedir Tekinerdogan
Information Technology Group, Wageningen University, Wageningen, The Netherlands

Martin Walker
Department of Computer Science, University of Hull, Hull, UK

Yan Yan
University of California, San Diego, La Jolla, CA, USA

Celal Ziftci
University of California, San Diego, La Jolla, CA, USA

Nikhil R. Zope
Tata Consultancy Services, Andheri (E), Mumbai, Maharashtra, India

Biography

Ivan Mistrik is a researcher in software-intensive systems engineering. He is a computer scientist who is interested in system and software engineering (SE/SWE) and in system and software architecture (SA/SWA), in particular: life cycle system/software engineering, requirements engineering, relating software requirements and architectures, knowledge management in software development, rationale-based software development, aligning enterprise/system/software architectures, value-based software engineering, agile software architectures, and collaborative system/software engineering. He has more than 40 years' experience in the field of computer systems engineering as an information systems developer, R&D leader, SE/SA research analyst, educator in computer sciences, and ICT management consultant. In the past 40 years, he has been primarily working at various R&D institutions in the United States and Germany and has done consulting on a variety of large international projects sponsored by ESA, EU, NASA, NATO, and UN. He has also taught university-level computer sciences courses in software engineering, software architecture, distributed information systems, and human—computer interaction.

He is the author or coauthor of more than 90 articles and papers in international journals, conferences, books, and workshops, most recently a chapter Capture of Software Requirements and Rationale through Collaborative Software Development, a paper Knowledge Management in the Global Software Engineering Environment, and a paper Architectural Knowledge Management in Global Software Development.

He has written a number of editorials, most recently for the book on Aligning Enterprise, System, and Software Architecture and the book on Relating System Quality and Software Architecture.

He has also written over 120 technical reports and presented over 70 scientific/technical talks. He has served in many program committees and panels of reputable international conferences and organized a number of scientific workshops, most recently two workshops on Knowledge Engineering in Global Software and Development at the International Conference on Global Software Engineering 2009 and 2010 and IEEE International Workshop on the Future of Software Engineering for/in the Cloud held in conjunction with IEEE Cloud 2011.

He has been the guest-editor of IEE Proceedings Software: A special Issue on Relating Software Requirements and Architectures published in 2005 and the lead-editor of the book Rationale Management in Software Engineering published in 2006. He has been the coauthor of the book Rationale-Based Software Engineering published in May 2008. He has been the lead-editor of the book Collaborative Software Engineering published in 2010, the book on Relating Software Requirements and Architectures published in 2011, and the lead-editor of the book on Aligning Enterprise, System, and Software Architectures published in 2012.

He was the lead-editor of the Expert Systems Special Issue on Knowledge Engineering in Global Software Development and the coeditor of the JSS Special Issue on the Future of Software Engineering for/in the Cloud, both published in 2013. He was the coeditor for the book on Agile Software Architecture published in 2013. He was the lead-editor for the book on Economics-driven Software Architecture and the book on Relating System Quality and Software Architecture, both published in 2014.

Nour Ali is a Principal Lecturer at the University of Brighton, UK. She holds a PhD in Software Engineering from the Polytechnic University of Valencia-Spain for her work in Ambients in Aspect-Oriented Software Architecture. She is Fellow of UK Higher Education Academy (HEA). Her research area encompasses service-oriented architecture, software architecture, model-driven engineering, adaptive software, and distributed and mobile systems. In 2014, the University of Brighton granted her a Rising Stars award in Service Oriented Architecture Recovery and Consistency. She is currently leading the Knowledge Transfer Partnership project for migrating legacy software systems using architecture centric approach. She has also been the Principal Investigator for an Enterprise Ireland Commercialization Project in Architecture Recovery and Consistency and coinvestigator in several funded projects. Dr. Ali is the Applications Track Chair for 2015 IEEE International Conference on Mobile Services (MS 2015) and serves on the Programme Committee for several conferences (e.g., ICWS, ICMS, HPCC, etc.) and journals (e.g., JSS, or JIST). She has cochaired and co-organized several workshops such as the IEEE International Workshop on Engineering Mobile Service Oriented Systems (EMSOS) and the IEEE Workshop on Future of Software Engineering for/in the Cloud. She was the coeditor of the JSS Special Issue on the Future of Software Engineering for/in the Cloud published in 2013 and Agile and lean service-oriented development: foundations, theory, and practice published in 2012. Her personal Web site is: http://www.cem.brighton.ac.uk/staff/na179/.

John Grundy is Dean of the School of Software and Electrical Engineering and Professor of Software Engineering at the Swinburne University of Technology, Melbourne, Australia. He has published nearly 300 refereed papers on software engineering tools and methods, automated software engineering, visual languages and environments, collaborative work systems and tools, aspect-oriented software development, user interfaces, software process technology, and distributed systems. He has made numerous contributions to the field of software quality assurance and software engineering including developing a number of software architecture modeling and quality analysis tools; developing several performance engineering techniques and tools; analytical tools for software processes, designs and code; project management tools; and numerous software design tools. He is particularly interested in the modeling of quality concerns and implementing appropriate analytical techniques to ensure these are met. He has focused much research on model-driven engineering techniques and tools to ensure repeatability of process and quality. He is an Associate Editor in Chief of IEEE Transactions on Software Engineering and Associate Editor of IEEE Software and Automated Software Engineering. He has been Program Chair of the IEEE/ACM Automated Software Engineering conference, the IEEE Visual Languages and Human-Centric Computing Conference, and has several times been a PC member for the International Conference on Software Engineering. He is a Fellow of Automated Software Engineering and Engineers Australia.

Richard Mark Soley is Chairman and Chief Executive Officer of OMG®, Executive Director of the Cloud Standards Customer Council, and Executive Director of the Industrial Internet Consortium. As Chairman and CEO of OMG, Dr. Soley is responsible for the vision and direction of the world's largest consortium of its type. Dr. Soley joined the nascent OMG as Technical Director in 1989, leading the development of OMG's world-leading standardization process and the original CORBA® specification. In 1996, he led the effort to move into vertical market standards (starting with healthcare, finance, telecommunications, and manufacturing) and modeling, leading first to the Unified Modeling Language™ (UML®) and later the Model Driven Architecture® (MDA®). He also led the effort to establish the SOA Consortium in January 2007, leading to the launch of the Business Ecology Initiative in 2009. The Initiative focuses on the management imperative to make business more responsive, effective, sustainable and secure in a complex, networked world, through practice areas including Business Design, Business Process Excellence, Intelligent Business, Sustainable Business, and Secure Business. In addition, Dr. Soley is the Executive Director of the Cloud Standards Customer Council, helping end-users transition to cloud computing and direct requirements and priorities for cloud standards throughout the industry. In 2014, Dr. Soley helped found the Industrial Internet Consortium and (IIC) serves as a Executive Director of the organization. The IIC was formed to accelerate the development, adoption and wide-spread use of interconnected machines and devices, intelligent analytics, and people at work. The members of the IIC catalyze and coordinate the priorities and enabling technologies of the Industrial Internet.

Dr. Soley also serves on numerous industrial, technical and academic conference program committees, and speaks all over the world on issues relevant to standards, the adoption of new technology and creating successful companies. He is an active angel investor, and was involved in the creation of both the Eclipse Foundation and Open Health Tools. Previously, Dr. Soley was a cofounder and former Chairman/CEO of A. I. Architects, Inc., maker of the 386 HummingBoard and other PC and workstation hardware and software. Prior to that, he consulted for various technology companies and venture firms on matters pertaining to software investment opportunities. Dr. Soley has also consulted for IBM, Motorola, PictureTel, Texas Instruments, Gold Hill Computer and others. He began his professional life at Honeywell Computer Systems working on the Multics operating system. A native of Baltimore, MD, USA, Dr. Soley holds bachelor's, master's, and doctoral degrees in Computer Science and Engineering from the Massachusetts Institute of Technology.

Bedir Tekinerdogan is a full professor and chair of the Information Technology group at Wageningen University in The Netherlands. He received his MSc degree (1994) and a PhD degree (2000) in Computer Science, both from the University of Twente, The Netherlands. From 2003 until 2008, he was a faculty member at University of Twente, after which he joined Bilkent University until 2015. At Bilkent University, he has founded and led the Bilkent Software Engineering Group which aimed to foster research and education on software engineering in Turkey. He has more than 20 years of experience in software engineering research and education. His main research includes the engineering of smart software-intensive systems. In particular, he has focused on and is interested in software architecture design, software product line engineering, model-driven development, parallel computing, cloud computing, and system of systems engineering. Much of his research has been carried out in close collaboration with the industry. He has been active in dozens of national and international research and consultancy projects with various large software companies whereby he has worked as a principal researcher and leading software/system architect. As such, he has broad experience in software engineering challenges of various different application domains including finance and banking, defense, safety-critical systems, mission critical systems, space systems, education, consumer electronics, and life sciences. He has served on the Program Committee of many different software engineering conferences. He also organized more than 50 conferences/workshops on important software engineering research topics to initiate and trigger important developments. He is the initiator and steering committee chair of the Turkish Software Architecture Design Conferences which have been organized since 2005. He is a member of the scientific advisory committee of the Integrated Software Excellence Research Program ERP that aims to establish research cooperation frameworks between researchers from universities in Europe and IT companies in Turkey. He has reviewed more than 100 national and international projects and is a regular reviewer for around 20 international journals. He has graduated around 40 MSc students and supervised/graduated more than 10 PhD students. He has developed and taught more than 15 different academic software engineering courses and has provided software engineering courses to more than 50 companies in The Netherlands, Germany, and Turkey.

Deployability

In recent years, the time it takes for code to get into production after a commit by a developer has come under scrutiny. A movement known has DevOps has advocated a number of practices intended to reduce this time. If we call the time to get code into production after a commit the *deployment* time, we have defined a new quality attribute for complex systems—deployability.

Two factors affect the deployment time of code. First is the coordination time that is required among various stakeholders prior to actually realizing the code. The second is the processing of the new code through a tool chain into production.

RELEASE PLAN

A common source of problems when new code goes into production is inconsistency between the new code and the code that depends on it or on which it depends. Another common source for problems is that the environment into which the code is deployed is not suitable for one reason or another. For these reasons, among others, many organizations have a formal deployment process. The goals of such a process are (http://en.wikipedia.org/wiki/Deployment_Plan)

- Define and agree release and deployment plans with customers/stakeholders
- Ensure that each release package consists of a set of related assets and service components that are compatible with each other
- Ensure that integrity of a release package and its constituent components is maintained throughout the transition activities and recorded accurately in the configuration management system
- Ensure that all release and deployment packages can be tracked, installed, tested, verified, and/or uninstalled or backed out, if appropriate
- Ensure that change is managed during the release and deployment activities
- Record and manage deviations, risks, issues related to the new or changed service, and take necessary corrective action
- Ensure that there is knowledge transfer to enable the customers and users to optimize their use of the service to support their business activities
- Ensure that skills and knowledge are transferred to operations and support staff to enable them to effectively and efficiently deliver, support and maintain the service, according to required warranties and service levels.

The key goal for our purposes is the second which specifies that all assets must be compatible with each other. In practice, this means that development teams must synchronize prior to generating a deployable release. This synchronization does not only involve the development of new code but also involves synchronizing on the technologies that are used, down to the versions. Suppose, for example, that one development team is using version 1.3 of a support library and another is using version 1.4. Between these two versions of the library, interfaces could have changed, features could have been added, or other changes could have occurred that affect the clients of the library. Now which version of the support library should be used in the integration of the two? This decision must be made and the development team using the rejected version must now test and possibly correct their code to work with the selected version.

Now consider that a reasonable size system may depend on dozens of different support libraries or external systems. Also consider that multiple development teams must coordinate over these support libraries, not just the two in our example. The amount of coordination among teams grows exponentially with the number of teams and the number of items to coordinate over. Many organizations have a position called "Release Engineer" whose role it is to coordinate the many activities that go into preparing a release.

MOVING THROUGH THE TOOL CHAIN

Deployment time has a number of constituents.

1. the time to build a testable version of the system,
2. the time to test the system using integration tests,
3. the time to move the system into a staging or user acceptance test environment,
4. the time to test the system in the staging environment,
5. the time for a gatekeeper to decide that the system is suitable for production,
6. the time to deploy a portion of the system into a "canary test," i.e., limited production,
7. the time to decide that the canary test has been successful,
8. the time to deploy the remainder of the system,
9. the time to rework and retest any errors discovered.

Furthermore, each of these actions may be preceded by time in a queue waiting for resources or dependent portions of the system to become available.

TRADE-OFFS

With all of these potential sources of delay, it is understandable why organizations concerned with time to market, that is, almost all organizations, have begun to focus on deployment time. As with all other quality attributes, time to market is one concern that must be balanced with others. The primary trade-offs that are made with deployability are with reliability and with organizational structure. The trade-offs with reliability are because many of the delays are intended to reduce the number of errors that creep into production. The trade-offs with organization structure are intended to reduce the necessity for coordination among different development teams and different portions of the organization concerned with managing the system once it has gone into deployment.

GENERAL SCENARIOS AND TACTICS

As with other quality attributes, deployability can be characterized by a collection of general scenarios and has a collection of architectural tactics that will improve the deployability of code. The general scenarios all have the same stimulus—a developer commits code to a version control system and the same response—the code is placed into production. The measures for the scenarios are the amount of time spent in each station enumerated above and the amount and time for rework caused by errors in a deployment.

In addition, also as with other quality attributes, there is a collection of architectural tactics intended to improve the deployability of code. These tactics reduce the coordination requirements among development teams or improve the performance of automated tests.

- Improving the performance of automated tests can be done by making components small. A small component is easier to test since it has less functionality that must be tested.
- Having components communicate only by message passing reduces the requirement for using the same support libraries. We elaborate on this tactic just below.
- Controlling the activation of features through special switches in each component allows features that span multiple components to be activated or deactivated simultaneously and independently of the order of deployment of the components.

MICROSERVICES

In response to the time taken up in coordination, Amazon, among other organizations, has adopted policies that dramatically reduce the amount of time teams spend coordinating. In particular, if each team packages their code as a standalone service communicating only through message passing, then the version of support libraries that other teams are using becomes irrelevant. As a team, you choose your base technologies, your languages, and your support systems and package them all together behind a service boundary. Any other team that wishes to use your service needs to know your interface but does not need to know and is unaffected by your choice of technology. This has led to an architectural style called microservices (Newman, 2014) where each team produces a service, each service is independent, and the action of a complicated system is governed by the interactions between the services. Microservices are an extension of the Unix notion of composable pieces, each of which does only a single function.

CONTINUOUS DEPLOYMENT

Continuous deployment is a development practice that results from automating all deployment steps after a commit by developer. It is one practice that is included in the collection of practices known as DevOps. DevOps, its associated practices, and the architectural tactics used to achieve the practices are described by Bass et al. (2015).

A key concept in understanding continuous deployment is that of an environment. An environment consists of a system, a dataset, a set of configuration parameters and a set of external entities with which the system interacts. Viewing each of the steps that a system goes through on its path to production as being in a different environment is a means of organizing continuous deployment.

Each step consists of the following steps:

1. Create an environment appropriate for that step.
   a. Set up the dataset for the environment. At integration test, the data being used for the test is a replica of a subset of real data. The system accesses its data through a configuration parameter that points to the test dataset
   b. Ensure that external systems are either provided or mocked up for the environment
   c. Set up the configuration parameters for the system
   d. Move the system into the environment.
2. Execute the system with its tests within the environment.
3. If the tests are passed promote the system to the next stage in the continuous deployment process. If the tests fail, then inform the developer.

Repeating these steps for different environments, each with its own set of configuration parameters, test data, and external systems will move the system into production.

ROLL BACK

Even with all tests passed, it is still possible that errors can creep into production systems. Once an error is discovered two possible options are to roll back—return to a prior version—or to roll forward—fix the error in a subsequent version.

There are tactics that support rolling back, just as there are tactics that support installing a new version—rolling forward. The choice between rolling back and rolling forward depends on the severity of the error, the organizational preferences, and what state may have been corrupted by the error.

THE NUMBER OF QUALITY ATTRIBUTES IS GROWING

Historically, the most important quality attributes were performance, reliability, security, and modifiability. As the field has matured and as organizations have learned how to achieve these four quality attributes, the number of other qualities that have become important has grown. The latest list of standard qualities (ISO 25010) has a breathtaking number of qualities and subqualities to consider.

For the purposes of this volume on Assuring Quality in Complex Systems, my message is that the breathtaking number of qualities that must be achieved in order to have a successful system is still increasing and that deployability is one of the new qualities that architects must consider.

Len Bass
NICTA, Sydney, Australia

REFERENCES

<http://en.wikipedia.org/wiki/Deployment_Plan>.
Bass, L., Weber, I., Zhu, L., 2015. DevOps: A Software Architect's Perspective. Pearson Publishing.
Newman, S., 2014. Building Microservices: Designing Fine-Grained Systems. O'Reilly Media.

Foreword

In recent decades we have seen enormous increases in the capabilities of software intensive systems, resulting in exponential growth in their size and complexity. Software and systems engineers routinely develop systems with advanced functionalities that would not even have been conceived of 20 years ago. This observation was highlighted in the Critical Code report commissioned by the US Department of Defense in 2010, which identified a critical software engineering challenge as the ability to deliver "software assurance in the presence of...architectural innovation and complexity, criticality with respect to safety, (and) overall complexity and scale" (National Research Council of the National Academies, 2010).

Advances in software engineering have brought us incredible successes such as the Mars exploration missions, automated surgical robots, and autonomous cars which utilize artificial intelligence to maneuver through traffic without the need for human drivers. On the other hand there are numerous accounts of software projects which failed dramatically due to inability of the project team to handle complexity. For example, the FBI's Virtual Case File project failed after multiple attempts and at significant costs to the US tax payers, primarily because project stakeholders seemed incapable of taming the essential complexity of the requirements (Goldstein, 2005). In 1991, 28 soldiers were killed when the software in the US Patriot Missile Defense System exhibited an error in its global clock and therefore failed to intercept an incoming Scud missile that struck military barracks. In January 1990, a previously unexecuted sequence of code unearthed a flaw in the software and caused malfunctions of 114 switching centers across the United States and 65 million unconnected calls. In 2005, the FDA recalled three different pacemaker models developed by Guidant based on a malfunction which they determined could lead to a "serious life-threating event." More recently, we have observed the debacle of the US Healthcare.gov project (Cleland-Huang, 2015). The development team was tasked with delivering a hugely complex software system which needed to integrate data securely across multiple heterogeneous insurance providers while scaling up to support 60,000 users—a number that grossly underestimated the reality of 250,000 simultaneous users that logged on following the go-live date. The result was lethargic response times, alarming security breaches of personal data, and failure to deliver basic functionality. In hindsight we see that political pressures dictated aspects of the solution and its delivery timeline, and this set the project up for failure.

So why do some highly complex systems succeed, while others fail? To answer this question we need to explore the notion of complexity itself. In 1996, Dietrich Dorner, a cognitive psychologist, defined complexity as "the label we give to the existence of many interdependent variables in a given system—the more variables and the greater their interdependence, the greater that system's complexity" (Dorner, 1996). More recently the IEEE standard dictionary defined it as "the degree to which a system or component has a design or implementation that is difficult to understand and verify" (IEEE, 2010). Both definitions point to the extent to which we are able, or not able, to comprehend the breadth and depth of a system. As humans, we typically address complexity by organizing systems into palatable views—often by devising classification schemes, proposing theorems, or by decomposing complex behaviors into subsystems and viewpoints.

We see such strategies at work across multiple domains including social and natural sciences as well as the full gamut of engineering disciplines. Take astronomy for example. Black holes fascinate us—for the very reason that we cannot fully comprehend them. Nevertheless, we describe their basic behavior to an extent commensurate with our individual knowledge of physics or astronomy, using scientific terms such as "mass," "event horizon" or "gravitational singularity." In this way, extremely complex phenomenon can be described in at different levels of abstraction, according to individual skills, knowledge, and communication purposes.

Whereas we are mere observers of black holes, we are entirely responsible for devising, designing, engineering, controlling, and evolving software intensive systems. Instead of seeking pinpricks of understanding into vastly complex natural phenomenon—we find ourselves stretched to fully comprehend our own human-made socio-technical solutions. It turns out that we can apply many of the same strategies that are used successfully to describe complex scientific behaviors. By constructing functional, behavioral, and crosscutting views of the system we are able to decompose it into cognitively palatable chunks. Furthermore, to ensure that the system possesses desired qualities, we measure and control its development and its runtime behaviors.

The question addressed by this book is how software quality can be delivered and even assured in the face of such complexity. Defined by NASA as "the planned and systematic set of activities that ensures that software life cycle processes and products conform to requirements, standards, and procedures" (NASA, n.d.), software quality assurance includes numerous subareas such as software quality engineering, software quality assurance, software quality control, software safety, software reliability, V&V (verification and validation), and IV&V(independent V&C). A quality software system is one that meets users' needs and expectations and for which the delivered solution and the adopted process meet specified requirements.

In practice, the means by which software quality is achieved and assured are diverse. They include defined processes such as the Capability Maturity Models (e.g., CMMI) (Herbsleb, 1997) and ISO 9000, and also individual software engineering activities designed to build quality assurance into each and every phase of the software system. For example, during the requirements phase, engineers must ensure that requirements are correct, valid, sufficiently unambiguous, free of conflicts, testable, and complete (Robertson, 2013). During architectural design, architects must ensure that the planned solution is fit for purpose—that it satisfies fault-tolerance, scalability, adaptability, and security requirements specified by the project stakeholders, or at least balances them in ways that are satisfactory (Len Bass, 2012). Developers are then responsible for writing correctly functioning code and testing it to ensure that it delivers the desired functionality at specified levels of quality. Furthermore, Software Quality Assurance activities reach across every aspect of the software development process—influencing not only the requirements, architectural design, and code, but also software traceability, maintenance, evolution, safety-analysis and other such activities.

Ask any IT professional about the need for quality—and for the most part they will agree to its essentiality. It is far less likely that they will agree upon how such quality can or should achieved.

Scott Ambler, renowned agilest, argued in an article entitled "Quality in an Agile World" that "common agile software development techniques...lead to software that proves in practice to be of much higher quality than what traditional software teams usually deliver" (Ambler, 2005). He claimed that agilists are "quality infected" and that by following key practices such as keeping the code clean through refactoring, test-driven development, and replacing formal requirements with test cases, high quality solutions will be produced.

On the other hand, Dan Dvorak, Chief Architect of NASA's review board, stressed the importance of carefully defining requirements all the way from the system level down to the subsystem and components level (Mirakhorli and Cleland-Huang, 2013). The domain of complex cyber-physical systems in which Dvorak works—calls for a different flavor of development practices than those prescribed by Ambler. While practices such as Test driven development, refactoring, and incremental exploration of architecture and requirements can be effective across diverse projects, other activities designed to deliver and assure high quality software are driven by the characteristics and requirements of the domain.

The challenges are vast! Almost as soon as we learn to tame complexity for one type of system at certain degrees of scale, technology evolves and introduces new possibilities and challenges. The increasing ubiquity of self-adapting systems requires software to respond to changes in the environment—scaling up and down upon demand, thwarting security breaches, and even dynamically reconfiguring to deliver new functionality (Nelly Bencomo, 2014). Over time, existing systems, designed for a single purpose, pool their capabilities and resources into systems of systems to deliver new and complex functionality which surpasses that of their constituent parts. Further, as society's reliance on such systems grows, there is an increasing demand for systems to reliably detect and thwart security threats, operate safely and correctly in the face of adversity, scale up to support peak usage patterns and even unexpected traffic spikes, provide greater interactivity, integrate multimedia, provide social collaboration, maintain performance, tolerate faults, and dynamically push new features to users while constantly improving the user experience.

This book describes fundamental principles and solutions to address this difficult quest. Covering topics that include eliciting and analyzing quality concerns, measuring and predicting system qualities, tool support for quality assessment and management, and industrial case studies—it deals head-on with issues of Software Quality Assurance within the context of complex cutting-edge software systems. The editors, have collected and shaped an excellent collection of articles which establish foundations, vision, and practical guidelines for delivering reliable solutions even in the presence of significant complexity.

Twenty-five years ago we would never have even imagined the extent to which software would pervade our society today, and the extent to which it has driven innovation—despite some of the mishaps along the way. While we can only speculate about what the next generation of software products might look like—it is our responsibility as today's engineers to lay solid foundations that infuse qualities such as reliability, scalability, security, adaptability, and longevity into future products, thereby paving the way for future endeavors.

Jane Cleland-Huang

REFERENCES

Ambler, S., 2005. Quality in an agile world. Softw. Qual. Prof.

Cleland-Huang, J., 2015. Don't fire the architect! Where were the requirements? IEEE Softw..

Dorner, R., 1996. The Logic of Failure: Recognizing and Avoiding Error in Complex Situations. Perseus Books, Cambridge, MA.

Goldstein, H., 2005. Who killed the virtual case file? IEEE Spectr.

Herbsleb, J.D., D.Z., 1997. Software quality and the capability maturity model. Commun. ACM 40, 6.

IEEE, 2010. Standard ISO/IEC/IEEE 24765:2010. IEEE.

Len Bass, P.C., 2012. Software Architecture in Practice. Addison-Wesley.

Mirakhorli, M., Cleland-Huang, J., 2013. Traversing the twin peaks. IEEE Softw.

NASA, n.d. Software Assurance Definitions. National Aeronautics and Space Administration.

National Research Council of the National Academies, 2010. Software Producibility for Defense. The National Academies Press, Washington, DC.

Nelly Bencomo, R.B., 2014. *Models@run.time*—Foundations, Applications, and Roadmaps (Dagstuhl Seminar 11481). Lecture Notes in Computer Science 8378. Springer.

Robertson, S.R., 2013. Mastering the Requirements Process. Pearson Education.

Preface

Software Quality is a critically important yet very challenging aspect of building complex software systems. This has been widely acknowledged as a fundamental issue for enterprise, web, and mobile software systems. However, assuring appropriate levels of software quality when building today (and tomorrow's) adaptive, software-intensive and highly diverse systems is even more of a challenge. How to ensure appropriate levels of quality in agile-based processes has become a topical concern. The implications of large-scale, highly adaptive systems on quality is critical, especially with the likely emergence of the Internet of Things. In this book we collect a range of recent research and practice efforts in the Software Quality Assurance domain, with a particular focus on emerging adaptable, complex systems. We aim for this book to be useful for researchers, students and practitioners with an emphasis on both practical solutions that can be used now or in the near future but with a solid foundation of underpinning concepts and principles that will hold true for many years to come.

INTRODUCTION

According to Webster's Dictionary, "quality" is "a degree of excellence; a distinguishing attribute." That is, quality is the degree to which a software product lives up to the modifiability, availability, durability, interoperability, portability, security, predictability, and other attributes that a customer expects to receive when purchasing this product. These quality attribute drivers are the key to ensuring the quality of software-intensive systems.

Ever since we started to develop "programs" for the very first computer systems, quality has been both a laudable goal but also a very challenging one to actually obtain. Software, by its very nature, is complex and multi-faceted. Systems are used in a very wide range of contexts, by a very wide range of people, for a very wide range of purposes. Thus system requirements—including quality requirements—vary tremendously. Quality may come at significant cost to build-in and maintain. However, substandard quality may come with far greater costs: correcting defects, fixing up business data or processes gone wrong, and sometimes very severe, even life-threatening consequences of lack of appropriate quality.

Defining quality is challenging. Typically a system or system architecture is thought to have a range of quality attributes. These are often termed non-functional requirements. A great range has been developed over many decades in systems engineering. Commonly considered system quality attributes ones include safety, availability, dependability, standards compliance, scalability, and securability. When considering the design and implementation of systems, we often think in terms of reusability, modifiability, efficiency, testability, composability, and upgradability, among many others. Users of software systems are often concerned with usability, along with associated quality issues of performance, robustness and reliability. Developmental processes wish to ensure repeatability, efficiency and quality of the process itself. As software-intensive systems get larger, more complex, and more diverse, many if not all of these quality attributes become harder to ensure. With cloud-based and adaptive systems, many are "emergent," that is, quality expectations and requirements change as a system is deployed, integrated with new systems, user requirements evolve, and systems of systems result.

With the large interest and focus on complex software architectures over the past two decades, describing and ensuring software quality attributes in architecture models has become of great interest. This includes developing quality attribute metrics to enable these attributes to be measured and assessed, along with trade-off analysis where ensuring a certain level of quality on one dimension may unintentionally impact others. Again, this is especially challenging in new domains of complex mobile applications, multitenant cloud platforms, and highly adaptive systems. From a related viewpoint, how design decisions influence the quality of a system and its software architecture are important. It has been well-recognized that requirements and architecture/design decisions interplay, especially in domains where the actual deployed system architecture, components and ultimately quality attributes are unknown, or at least imprecise.

There is strong demand to better align enterprise, system, and software architecture from the point of view of ensuring total quality of resultant software-intensive systems. Each of these perspectives interact in terms of desired quality goals, constraints that come with particular technologies and third party systems, and regulatory environments. In safety-critical domains, and increasingly in security-critical domains, demonstrable compliance with best practices and standards are essential.

Many diverse methods and processes have been developed for evaluating quality in software processes, architectures and implementations. To make them practical, almost all require some degree of tool support to assist in defining quality expectations, taking appropriate measures of process / system / architecture / implementation, and complex analysis of this data. Software testing methods and tools are a critical component applied at varying levels of software artefacts and at various times. Robust empirical validation of quality has become an important research and practice activity.

There has been strong demand for effective quality assurance techniques to apply to legacy systems and third party components and applications. As these very often come with "pre-defined" quality measures, understanding these and their impact on other components—and wider system quality—is often critical in engineering effective composite systems. However, many quality constraints and sometimes compromises may need to be made. Understanding and balancing these is critical.

Finally, many new emergent technological domains have quickly gained interest in the software engineering and wider systems engineering communities, as well as with end users. The emergence of enterprise, cloud-enabled and mobile applications has resulted in much more volatile enterprise system platforms where new services and apps are dynamically deployed and interacted with. There is growing interest in engineering context-aware systems that incorporate diverse knowledge about role, task, social, technological, network, and platform information into ensuring quality systems. The rapidly emerging "Internet of Things" will bring with it increasing need to ensure the quality of a great many interconnected and interacting software systems.

It is not just the new focus on implementation architectures, particularly embedded and distributed implementation architectures, that increases the demand for software quality, but the integration of software engineering into systems of systems—electrical engineering, civil engineering, product lifecycle management, asset management, service management techniques—that has increased the call for software quality techniques to respond in the way that manufacturing quality techniques responded to the quality call over the last fifty years.

Interestingly, though nearly all software quality techniques in widespread use (and even most of those discussed in this book) focus primarily on increasing software quality by managing the *process* used to deliver software, it is useful and instructive to review what happened to the quality movement in the manufacturing world. There, process quality techniques (lean manufacturing, total quality management, six sigma techniques and so forth) rule the roost; every large, complex systems manufacturer (and most small and medium ones too) not only use these techniques to improve product quality, but insist on the use of matching techniques throughout their supply chains (and generally service chains too) to increase the probability of providing products that work, that deliver customer satisfaction. Nevertheless, they *all* also continue to use part and subassembly acceptance testing when suppliers bring them parts; in general, nothing goes into the system that has not been at least statistically tested.

This is happening in the software quality world too, with creeping adoption of software *artifact* testing along with software *process* improvement. Obviously both approaches are valid, and in fact even support each other--a software process that delivers poor part quality is obviously flawed, and part testing results can inform software process improvement. Standards are even being launched, as they were years ago in the software process improvement space (like CMMI)—look out for software artifact quality (both security-focused and performance-focused) to improve and focus over the coming years. This book will help speed that process.

WHY A NEW BOOK ON SOFTWARE QUALITY

Software Quality Assurance is an established area of research and practice. However, recently software has become much more complex and adaptable due to the emergence of globalization and the emergence of new software technologies, devices, and networks. Traditional Software Quality Assurance techniques and methods have to be extended, adapted, and all-new techniques developed in order to cope with these fast-moving changes.

Many software quality attributes are discussed in the seminal work on Software Architecture in Practice by Bass, Clements and Kazman. The authors use the key concept of architecture-influencing cycles. Each cycle shows how architecture influences, and is influenced by, a particular context in which architecture plays a critical role. Contexts include technical environment, the life cycle of a project, an organization's business profile, and the architect's professional practices. Quality attributes remain central to their architecture philosophy. Rozanski and Woods in their book Software Systems Architecture show why the role of the architect is central to any successful information-systems development project, and, by presenting a set of architectural viewpoints and perspectives, provide specific direction for improving organization's approach to software systems architecture. In particularly, they use perspectives to ensure that an architecture exhibits important qualities such as performance, scalability, and security. The Handbook of Software Quality Assurance by Schulmeyer and McManus serves as a basic resource for current SQA knowledge. It emphasizes the importance of CMMI and key ISO requirements and provides the latest details on current best practices and explains how SQA can be implemented in organizations large and small. It also includes updated discussion on the American Society for Quality SQA certification program. In Software Quality Assurance, David Galin provides an overview of the main types of Software Quality Assurance models. This includes reviewing the place of quality assurance in several software process models and practices. An emphasis is on metrics as these are crucial to permitting an objective assessment of a project's system quality as well as progress.

This new book makes a valuable contribution to this existing body of knowledge in terms of state of the art techniques, methodologies, tools, best practices and guidelines for Software Quality Assurance and point out directions for future software engineering research and practice. We invited chapters on all aspects of Software Quality Assurance, including novel and high-quality research related approaches that relate the quality of software architecture to system requirements, system architecture and enterprise-architecture, or software testing.

We asked authors to ensure that all of their chapters will consider the practical application of the topic through case studies, experiments, empirical validation, or systematic comparisons with other approaches already in practice. Topics of interest included, but were not limited, to: quality attributes of system/software architectures; aligning enterprise, system, and software architecture from the point of view of total quality; design decisions and their influence on the quality of system/software architecture; methods and processes for evaluating architecture quality; quality assessment of legacy systems and third party applications; lessons learned and empirical validation of theories and frameworks on architectural quality; empirical validation and testing for assessing architecture quality.

BOOK OUTLINE

We have divided the book into five key parts, grouping chapters by their link to these key themes. Part I examines the fundamentals of Software Quality Assurance. Here two chapters provide a broad outline of the area of Software Quality Assurance.

Software quality is more than ensuring that a completed software product conforms to its explicitly stated requirements. Meeting customer expectations (both implicit and explicit) are an important aspect of Software Quality Assurance. The news media is filled with reports of failed software systems. Most of these failures can be traced to defects that could have been detected if software engineers paid better attention to the management of software quality as the products were being developed. Users have high expectations regarding the reliability and security elements found in modern software products. Pressure to produce software systems faster has never been greater and agile methods have been proposed to accommodate uncertain and changing user requirements. It is clear that quality cannot be added to an evolving software system just before its release. Chapter 2, by Bruce Maxim and Marouane Kessentini, provides an introduction to Software Quality Assurance concepts. This chapter focuses on Software Quality Assurance practices that are capable of accommodating change and while providing developers with some control over the quality of the resulting software products.

Chapter 3, by Ian Fleming, examines three popular software characterization models in order to assist practitioners in understanding, measuring, and improving process effectiveness. Today, Agile practices are perceived to mitigate the inherent risks of misunderstood or invalid software requirements as well as project cost and time overruns. That being said Agile is not a goal unto itself and this fact is embodied in the last of the 12 Agile principles. At regular intervals, the team reflects on how to become more effective, then tunes and adjusts its behavior accordingly. The issue with measuring process effectiveness within the software arena is one that has consistently engaged the minds of academics and practitioners alike, regardless of the software production process being followed. In order to measure the effectiveness of any process the output of the process needs to be characterized and measured.

Four chapters make up Part II of this book, all focusing on managing the Software Quality Assurance process. Chapter 4, by Nikhil Zope, Kesav Vithal Nori, Anand Kumar, Doji Samson Lokku, Swaminathan Natarajan, and Padmalatha Nistala, discusses issues of Quality Management and Software Process Engineering. Currently, testing practices and enabling technologies support Software Quality Assurance. CMMI has prescribed processes and managerial practices for software development, while contributing to managerial practices with respect to quality assurance. However, these practices do not provide guidance on how software process can be engineered so that different role players can know how they are contributing to software quality and how it can be assured through related activities and design. The authors present a new approach for Software Quality Assurance. First, they present their notion of processes in which we highlight that a process is not just about steps (represents responsibility towards meeting expected requirements) but also about qualities associated with each step and constraints within which the steps need to be performed. Next, they bring out the difference between quality control and quality assurance (primarily supported by engineering the process for qualities to be delivered through it). Later, they discuss how localization of focus on quality can aid in engineering the process followed by discussion on software life-cycle models where they touch upon different ways processes can progress in terms of quality achievement. Finally, the authors discuss the contextual constraints which processes must satisfy to determine the feasible options during engineering the process. They believe that their approach can allow one to confidently assert that Software qualities are delivered.

Chapter 5 is by Zengyang Li, Peng Liang, and Paris Avgeriou and proposes a framework for systematically documenting architectural technical debt (ATD). This framework is comprised of six architecture viewpoints related to ATD (ATD viewpoints in short): the ATD Detail viewpoint, the ATD Decision viewpoint, the ATD Stakeholder Involvement viewpoint, the ATD Distribution viewpoint, the ATD-related Component viewpoint, and the ATD Chronological viewpoint. Each viewpoint frames one or more stakeholders' concerns about ATD that were systematically collected from a literature review on technical debt. The ATD viewpoints help related stakeholders to get a comprehensive understanding of ATD in a software system, thereby providing support for architecture decision-making and supporting maintainability and evolvability. To evaluate the effectiveness of the ATD viewpoints in documenting ATD, the authors conducted an industrial case study on a complex system in a large telecommunications company. The results of the case study show that the documented ATD views can effectively facilitate the documentation of ATD. Specifically, the ATD viewpoints are relatively easy to understand; it takes an acceptable amount of effort to document ATD using the viewpoints; and the documented ATD views are useful for stakeholders to understand the ATD in a software project.

Increasingly, software systems design, development and usage have to deal with evolving user needs, increased security threats, many interacting systems, emergence of new technologies and multiple channels of communications. This increased complexity and scale of software systems present difficult challenges in design and development and in asserting software quality. It has been observed that software service organizations which develop and maintain software systems on an industrial scale, have huge challenges in addressing software product quality concerns in terms of identifying a comprehensive set of software quality goals and ways to achieve them in spite of adoption to industry standard quality systems and processes. Chapter 6, by Padmalata Nistala, Nikhil Zope, Kesav Vithal Nori, Swaminathan Natarajan, and Anand Kumar, proposes a product quality engineering approach that addresses these quality challenges by connecting the generic software processes defined at organization level to specific product quality concerns through quality engineering techniques. The chapter outlines a new approach realized through a set of principles that identifies product quality requirements in a comprehensive manner. It starts with the ISO 25010 standard, maps principles to a solution space with associated quality patterns, assures compositional traceability, and finally builds process—product correlation for the software product. Each principle focusses on systematic achievement of a specific quality engineering concern and contributes to quality assurance of software systems in a consistent manner.

Part III of this book includes three chapters that discuss the role of metrics, prediction and testing in Software Quality Assurance. Chapter 7, by Luigi Buglione, Alain Abran, Maya Daneva, and Andrea Herrmann, describes a way to Improve Requirements Management for Better Estimates. Poor application of requirements management is often detrimental to the estimation of project time and costs. Various problems grounded in requirements elicitation and specification lead to under-estimation or an estimation error larger than expected. To tackle the number and the severity of such issues and to improve the overall management of a project, the authors propose a solution based on a "fill the blank" exercise. Their proposed solution proposes an update of a Quality Function Deployment (QFD) tailoring, namely QF^2D (Quality Factor through Quality Function Deployment) using the latest ISO standards and empirical evidences from industry practices. The aim is to achieve effective Software Quality Assurance for any project within an organization, by reinforcing the Requirements Management discipline. Such a revised QF^2D focuses on requirements based on measurable entities (e.g., on organization, project, resources, process, product levels). The chapter illustrates the application of the solution to one of the ISO 25010 characteristics, namely *portability*. The chapter ends with a discussion of the approach, a calculation example for making visible the way the technique works and can give added value, and its implications for research and practice.

Chapter 8 is by Michael English, Jim Buckley, and J.J. Collins and describes an investigation of software modularity using class and module level metrics. The authors identify that the traditional approach of assessing modularity at the class level is inadequate for very large systems, which benefit from a module-level focus. However, the definition of a module is varied and techniques to capture high-level module metrics at differing levels of abstraction are needed. The authors review current techniques described in the literature and embodied in commercial and research tool sets. They describe an empirical study they have carried out to explore the use of new module-level metrics definitions and capture. They investigate the modularity of an open source software system, Weka, a data mining toolkit. They show that they can characterize the module structure of Weka using various techniques and that finding relationships between metrics at differing levels of abstraction is promising.

Chapter 9, by Eduardo Guerra and Mauricio Aniche, discusses Quality on Software Design Through Test-Driven Development. Test-driven development

(TDD) is a technique for developing and designing software where tests are created before production code in short cycles. There is some discussion in the software engineering community on whether TDD can really be used to achieve software quality. Some experiments were conducted in the last years comparing development by using TDD with one creating tests after the production code. However, these experiments always have some threats to validity that prevent researchers from reaching a final answer about its effects. This chapter, instead of trying to prove that TDD is more effective than creating tests after, investigates projects where TDD was successfully used, and presents recurrent and common practices applied to its context. A common mistake is to believe that just by creating tests before production code will make the application design "just happen." As with any other technique, TDD is not a silver bullet, and while it certainly helps to achieve some desirable characteristics in software, such as decoupling and separation of concerns, other practices should complement its usage, especially for architecture and design coherence. In this chapter, we dive deep into TDD practice and how to perform it to achieve quality in software design. The authors also present techniques that should be used to setup a foundation to start TDD in a project and to refine the design after it is applied.

Part IV includes three chapters that discuss models and tools needed to realize Software Quality Assurance. Chapter 10 is by Bedir Tekinerdogan. Software systems are rarely static and need to evolve over time due to bug fixes or new requirements. This situation causes the so-called *architectural drift* problem which defines the discrepancy between the architecture description and the resulting implementation. A popular approach for coping with this problem is *reflexion modeling* which usually compares an abstract model of the code with the architecture model to identify the differences. Although reflexion modeling seems to be relatively popular the architecture model for it has been remained informal. In this paper the author proposes to enhance existing reflexion modeling approaches using architecture viewpoints. For this the author introduces an architecture reflexion viewpoint that can be used to define reflexion model for different architecture views. The viewpoint includes both a visual notation and a notation based on design structure matrices. The design structure reflexion matrices (DSRMs) that have been defined provide a complementary and succinct representation of the architecture and code for supporting qualitative and quantitative analysis, and likewise the refactoring of the architecture and code. For this a notion of *design structure reflexion matrices* (DSRM) and a generic reflexion modeling approach based on DSRMs are introduced. Finally the author discusses the key challenges in this novel approach and aims to pave the way for further research in DSM-based reflexion modeling.

Driving Design Refinement is the topic of Chapter 11, by Ioannis Sorokos, Yiannis Papadopoulos, Martin Walker, Luis Azevedo, and David Parker. The success of a project is often decided early in its development. Decisions on architecture have a large impact on the cost and quality of the final system and are often irreversible without incurring redevelopment costs and time delays. There is increasing agreement that design processes should provide control over quality attributes, such as dependability, from the start. Towards this end, recent work on model-based development has examined how progressively refined models of requirements and design can drive development and verification of complex systems. In this chapter, we explore this issue in the aerospace domain, where system level safety requirements, expressed as Development Assurance Levels (DALs), are allocated to architectural elements to meet the overall system requirements. DALs lie at the heart of the safety assessment process advocated in the ARP4754-A set of guidelines for commercial aircraft, allowing decomposition of software quality requirements to safety-critical elements. The authors propose a novel method of automatically allocating DALs across an aircraft's architecture by extending the established reliability analysis tool HiP-HOPS in conjunction with a metaheuristic optimization technique, Tabu Search, to allocate DALs optimally with respect to the development costs they incur. They present the case study of an aircraft wheel braking system to demonstrate the method's effectiveness. The method can be generalized to apply towards other types of software quality requirements.

Model-based Dependability Analysis is the topic of Chapter 12, authored by Septevera Sharvia, Sohag Kabir, Martin Walker, and Yiannis Papadopoulos. Over the past two decades, the study of model-based dependability analysis has gathered significant research interest. Different approaches have been developed to automate and address various limitations of classical dependability techniques to contend with the increasing complexity and challenges of modern safety-critical system. Two leading paradigms have emerged. The first is Failure Logic Synthesis and Analysis, which constructs predictive system failure models from component failure models compositionally using the topology of the system. The other is Behavioral Fault Simulation, which utilizes design models—typically state automata—to explore system behavior through fault injection. In this chapter, the authors review a number of prominent techniques from both of these two paradigms and provide an insight into their working mechanisms, applicability, strengths, and challenges. Failure Logic Synthesis and Analysis techniques discussed include FPTN, FPTC, Component Fault Trees, State Event Fault Trees, HiP-HOPS, and AADL; Behavioral Fault Simulation approaches covered include FSAP-NuSMV, Altarica, SAML, and DCCA. The authors discuss recent developments within the field and describe the emerging trends towards integrated approaches and advanced analysis capabilities. Lastly, the authors outline the future outlook for model-based dependability analysis.

Finally, Part V provides two chapters with industrial case studies reporting Software Quality Assurance experiences for two different domains of software-intensive systems. Chapter 13, by Emilia Farcas, Massimiliano Menarini, Claudiu Farcas, William Griswold, Kevin Patrick, Ingolf Krueger, Barry Demchak, Fred Raab, Yan Yan, and Celal Ziftci, examines the Influences of Architectural and Coding Choices on CyberInfrastructure Quality. CyberInfrastructures (CIs) are socio-technical-economical systems supporting the efficient delivery, processing, and visualization of data across different communities. E-Health CIs are patient-centric community-serving systems, which have particular regulations for information security, governance, resource management, scalability, and maintainability. The authors have developed multiple successful E-Health interdisciplinary CIs. In this chapter, they compare these CIs and use a common framework to analyze their requirements and measure their quality characteristics. They analyze the different tradeoffs and architectural decisions and how they impact the resulting software quality, focusing on maintainability aspects. From this analysis, the authors devise a series of recommendations for improving the quality of future CIs. The main contributions in this work are twofold: (1) The analysis and comparison of quality characteristics for E-Health CIs—the authors believe that this analysis has a general appeal and can be readily applied to other domains to identify architectural decisions that influence the overall quality of resulting software in a specific domain. (2) A set of recommendations to improve the overall quality of E-Health CIs.

Chapter 14, by Ian Fleming, describes ways of exploiting the synergies between SQA, SQC and SPI in order to facilitate CMMI® adoption. Government regulations, such as the Sarbanes−Oxley Act of 2002, have caused a significant increase in the number of software professionals performing audits and inspections in order to ensure regulatory compliance. Whilst adherence to such regulations requires a company to invest in a significant quality assurance capability, there is no requirement in these regulations to improve the overall effectiveness and efficiency of the underlying processes. The opportunity (and challenges) to leverage compliance Software Quality Assurance professionals, for software process improvement, is the motivation and subject of this chapter. By examining the traditional roles of quality assurance, quality control, and process improvement, synergies and overlaps can be identified and exploited in order to utilize compliance-focused personnel within a continuous software process improvement framework and strategy based on CMMI®.

**John Grundy, Ivan Mistrik, Nour Ali,
Richard M. Soley, Bedir Tekirerdogan**

Quality concerns in large-scale and complex software-intensive systems

1

Bedir Tekinerdogan[1], Nour Ali[2], John Grundy[3], Ivan Mistrik[4] and Richard Soley[5]

*[1]Wageningen University, Wageningen, The Netherlands [2]University of Brighton, Brighton, UK
[3]Swinburne University of Technology, Hawthorn, VIC, Australia [4]Heidelberg, Germany
[5]Object Management Group, Needham, MA, USA*

1.1 INTRODUCTION

Since the days of ENIAC (the first computer), computer system developers and their end users have been concerned with quality issues of the resultant systems. Quality comes in many guises and it manifests in many ways. To some, quality relates to the system itself, for example, can it be understood, maintained, extended, scaled, or enhanced? For others, the process of producing the system is their focus, for example, can it be delivered on time, to budget, does it follow best practices and/or relevant standards, and is the process used to develop the system itself of a suitable quality and appropriate for required software quality achievement? Finally, customers, stakeholders, end users and the development team themselves are all concerned, in different ways, whether the system meets its requirements, whether it has been sufficiently verified and/or validated, and does—and can keep on doing—what it was intended to do. A lack of software quality is almost always seen to be highly problematic, again from diverse perspectives.

Nowadays, systems have become very software-intensive, heterogeneous, and very dynamic, in terms of their components, deployment, users, and ultimately their requirements and architectures. Many systems require a variety of mobile interfaces. Many leverage diverse, third-party components or services. Increasingly, systems are deployed on distributed, cloud-based platforms, some diversely situated and interconnected. Multi-tenant systems require supporting diverse users whose requirements may vary, and even change, during use. Adaptive systems need to incorporate various deployment environment changes, potentially including changes in diverse third-party systems. Development processes such as agile methods, outsourcing, and global software development add further complexity and change to software-intensive systems engineering practices.

1

Increasingly, software applications are now "systems of systems" incorporating diverse hardware, networks, software services, and users.

In order to achieve these demanding levels of software quality, organizations and teams need to define and implement a rigorous software quality process. A key to this is defining, for the project at hand, what are the software quality attributes that allow the team, organization, and stakeholders to define quality and required quality levels that must be achieved and maintained. From these attributes, a set of quality requirements for the target system can be defined. Some relate to the functional and non-functional characteristics of the system. Some relate to its static properties, for example, its code, design. Other its run-time properties, for example, behavior, performance, security. Overall system quality must be achieved not only at delivery, but during operation and as the system—and its environment—evolve over time. Quality must be assessed to determine proactively when system quality attributes may fall under a desired threshold and thus quality requirements fail to be met. Mitigations must be applied to ensure these quality requirements are maintained.

Many different kinds of quality challenges present when engineering such systems. Development processes need to incorporate appropriate quality assurance techniques and tools. This includes quality assessment of requirements, architecture, design and target technologies, code bases, and deployment and run-time environments. Software testing has traditionally been a mainstay of such quality assurance, though many other quality management practices are also needed. Testing has become much more challenging with newer development processes, including agile methods, and more complicated, inter-woven service architectures. Because today's complex software-intensive systems are almost invariably composed of many parts, many being third-party applications running on third-party platforms, testing is much more difficult. Adaptive systems that enable run-time change to the software (and sometimes platform) are even more challenging to test, measure quality attributes, and ensure appropriate quality attributes continue to be met. Multiple tenants of cloud applications may each have different requirements—and different views of what "quality" is and how it should be measured and evaluated. Different development teams collaborating explicitly on global software engineering projects—and implicitly on mash-up based, run-time composed systems—may each have differing quality assurance practices, development processes, architectures, technologies, testing tools, and maintenance practices.

A very challenging area of software quality assurance (SQA) is security and privacy. Software-intensive, cloud-hosted, large-scale distributed systems are inherently more vulnerable to attack, data loss, and other problems. Security breaches are one area where—even if all other quality concerns with a software system are met—massively damaging issues can result from a single, severe security problem.

Some software-intensive systems are manifestly requiring of very high levels of quality assurance in software, process, verification and validation, and ongoing maintenance and evolution. Safety-critical systems such as transport (air, rail, in-vehicle), health, utility (power, gas, water), and financial systems all require very high degrees of holistic SQA practices. These must work in cohesion to ensure a suitable level of quality is able to be achieved at all times.

In this chapter we provide an overview of the SQA domain, with a view to how the advent of software-intensive, large-scale, distributed, complex, and ultimately adaptive and multi-tenant systems have impacted these concepts and practices. Many quality concerns of course remain the same as ever. In many cases, however, achieving them—measuring, assessing, and even defining them— have become much more challenging to software engineers.

The chapter is organized as follows. In Section 1.2 we provide a general discussion on software quality management (SQM) and define the context for SQA. Section 1.3 presents the basic concepts related to software quality models and provides a conceptual model that defines the relation among the different concepts. Section 1.4 discusses the approaches for addressing software quality. Section 1.5 elaborates on assessing system qualities. Section 1.6 presents the current challenges and future directions regarding SQA. Finally, Section 1.7 concludes the chapter.

1.2 SOFTWARE QUALITY MANAGEMENT

Early after the introduction of the first computers and programming languages software became a critical for many organizations. The term "software crisis" was coined at the first NATO Software Engineering Conference in 1968 at Garmisch, Germany. Typically the crisis manifests in different ways including projects exceeding the estimated costs for development, the late delivery of software, and the low quality of the delivered software. Currently, software continues to be a critical element in most large-scale systems and many companies have to cope with a software crisis. To manage the challenges of software development and to ensure the delivery of high quality software, considerable emphasis in the research community has been directed to provide SQM.

SQM is the collection of all processes that ensure that software products, services, and life cycle process implementations meet organizational software quality objectives and achieve stakeholder satisfaction (Galin, 2004; Schulmeyer, 2007; Tian, 2005). SQM comprises three basic subcategories (Figure 1.1): software quality planning (SQP), software quality assurance (SQA), and software quality control (SQC). Very often, like in the Software Engineering Body of Knowledge (Guide to the Software Engineering Body of Knowledge, 2015), software process improvement (SPI) is also described as a separate sub-category of SQM, although it could be included in any of the first three categories.

SQA is an organizational quality guide independent of a particular project. It includes the set of standards, regulations, best practices and software tools to produce, verify, evaluate and confirm work products during the software development life cycle. SQA is needed for both internal and external purposes

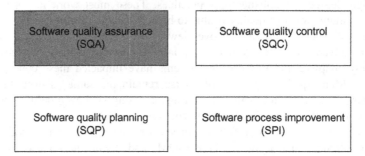

FIGURE 1.1

Context of SQA within the overall SQM process.

(Std. 24765) (ISO/IEC/IEEE 24765:2010(E), 2010). Internal purposes refer to the need for quality assurance within an organization to provide confidence for the management. External purposes of SQA include providing confidence to the customers and other external stakeholders. The IEEE standard (IEEE Std 610.12-1990, 1991) provides the following definitions for *SQA*:

1. a planned and systematic pattern of all actions necessary to provide adequate confidence that an item or product conforms to established technical requirements
2. a set of activities designed to evaluate the process by which products are developed or manufactured
3. the planned and systematic activities implemented within the quality system, and demonstrated as needed, to provide adequate confidence that an entity will fulfill requirements for quality
4. part of quality management focused on providing confidence that quality requirements will be fulfilled.

A SQP is defined at the project level that is aligned with the SQA. It specifies the project commitment to follow the applicable and selected set of standards, regulations, procedures, and tools during the development life cycle. In addition, the SQP defines the quality goals to be achieved, expected risks and risk management, and the estimation of the effort and schedule of software quality activities. A SQP usually includes SQA components as is or customized to the project's needs. Any deviation of an SQP from SQA needs to be justified by the project manager and be confirmed by the company management who is responsible for the SQA.

SQC activities examine project artifacts (e.g., code, design, and documentation) to determine whether they comply with standards established for the project, including functional and non-functional requirements and constraints. SQC ensures thus that artefacts are checked for quality before these are delivered. Example activities of SQC include code inspection, technical reviews, and testing.

SPI activities aim to improve process quality including effectiveness and efficiency with the ultimate goal of improving the overall software quality. In practice, an SPI project typically starts by mapping the organizations' existing processes to a process model that is then used for assessing the existing processes. Based on the results of the assessment an SPI aims to achieve process improvement. In general, the basic assumption for SPI is that a well-defined process will on its turn have a positive impact on the overall quality of the software.

1.3 SOFTWARE QUALITY MODELS

The last decades have shown a growing interest and understanding of the notion of SQA and software quality in general. In this context, a large number of definitions of software quality have emerged. Many of these definitions tend to define quality as conformance to a specification or meeting customer needs. The IEEE ISO/IEC/IEEE 24765 "Systems and software engineering vocabulary" provides the following definition for *quality* (ISO/IEC/IEEE, 2010):

1. the degree to which a system, component, or process meets specified requirements
2. ability of a product, service, system, component, or process to meet customer or user needs, expectations, or requirements
3. the totality of characteristics of an entity that bear on its ability to satisfy stated and implied needs
4. conformity to user expectations, conformity to user requirements, customer satisfaction, reliability, and level of defects present (ISO/IEC 20926:2003)
5. the degree to which a set of inherent characteristics fulfills requirements
6. the degree to which a system, component, or process meets customer or user needs or expectations.

To structure the ideas and provide a comprehensive framework several software quality models have been introduced. A software quality model is a defined set of characteristics, and of relationships between them, which provides a framework for specifying quality requirements and evaluating quality (ISO/IEC 25000:2005) (ISO/IEC, 2011). Usually, software quality models aim to support the specification of quality requirements, to assess existing systems or to predict the quality of a system.

One of the first published quality models is that of McCall (McCall et al., 1977). McCall's model was developed for the US Air Force and is primarily focused on the system developers and the system development process. This model aims to reduce the gap between users and developers by focusing on software quality factors that are important for both users and developers. McCall's quality model adopts three major perspectives for defining software quality: *product revision*, *product transition*, and *product operations*. Product revision relates to the ability to undergo changes, product transition to the ability to adapt to new environments, and product operations to the operation characteristics of the software. These three types of major perspectives are further decomposed and refined in a hierarchy of 11 quality factors, 23 quality criteria and quality metrics. The main idea of this model is the hierarchical decomposition of quality down to a level at which we can measure and, as such, evaluate quality. In McCall's model, quality factors are defined which describe the external view of the software as defined by the users. Quality factors in turn include quality criteria that describe the internal view of the software as seen by the developer. Finally, for the identified quality criteria the relevant quality metrics are defined to support their measurement and evaluate software quality.

A similar hierarchical model has been presented by Barry W. Boehm (Boehm, 1978) who focuses on *the general utility* of software that is further decomposed into three high-level characteristics including *as-is utility*, *maintainability*, and *portability*. These high-level quality characteristics have in turn seven quality factors that are further decomposed into the metrics hierarchy. Several variations of these models have appeared over time, among which the FURPS that decomposes quality into functionality, usability, reliability, performance and supportability.

The International Organization for Standardization's ISO 9126: Software Product Evaluation: Quality Characteristics and Guidelines for their Use-standard, was inspired by McCall and Boehm models, and also classifies software quality in a structured set of characteristics and sub-characteristics. ISO 9126 has later been revised by ISO/IEC 25010, which now includes ISO25010, and has 8 product quality characteristics and 31 sub-characteristics. The ISO/IEC Standard 9126 and its successor ISO/IEC Standard 25000 (ISO/IEC, 2011) decompose software quality into process quality, product quality, and quality in use.

In the IEEE 24765 Systems and Software Vocabulary the terms software quality factor and software quality attribute are defined as follows:

Software quality factor:

1. A management-oriented attribute of software that contributes to its quality.
2. Higher-level quality attribute.

Software quality attribute:

1. Characteristic of software, or a generic term applying to quality factors, quality sub-factors, or metric values.
2. Feature or characteristic that affects an item's quality.
3. Requirement that specifies the degree of an attribute that affects the quality that the system or software must possess.

To provide a quantitative measure for quality the notion of *metric* is defined:

1. A quantitative measure of the degree to which an item possesses a given quality attribute.

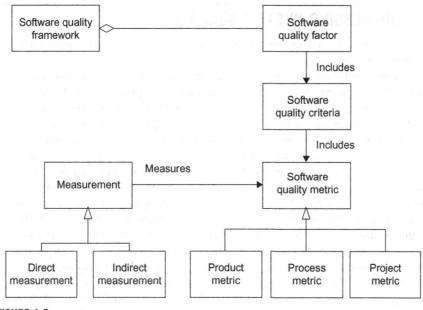

FIGURE 1.2

Conceptual model for SQA.

2. A function whose inputs are software data and whose output is a single numerical value that can be interpreted as the degree to which the software possesses a given quality attribute.

A distinction is made between direct metrics and indirect metrics. A direct metric is "a metric that does not depend upon a measure of any other attribute" (Fenton and Pfleger, 1998). Software metrics are usually classified into three categories: product metrics, process metrics, and project metrics. Product metrics describe the characteristics of the product such as size and complexity. Process metrics describe the characteristics of the software development process. Finally, project metrics describe the project characteristics and execution.

Related to metric is the concept of measurement which is defined as follows:

1. "Measurement is the process by which numbers or symbols are assigned to attributes of entities in the real world in such a way as to characterize them according to clearly defined rules" (Fenton and Pfleger, 1998).
2. "Formally, we define measurement as a mapping from the empirical world to the formal, relational world. Consequently, a measure is the number or symbol assigned to an entity by this mapping in order to characterize an attribute" (Fenton and Pfleger, 1998).

Figure 1.2 shows a conceptual overview of the relations of the above concepts.

1.4 ADDRESSING SYSTEM QUALITIES

SQA can be addressed in several different ways and cover the entire software development process.

Different software development lifecycles have been introduced including waterfall, prototyping, iterative and incremental development, spiral development, rapid application development, and agile development. The traditional waterfall model is a sequential design process in which progress is seen as flowing steadily downwards (like a waterfall) through the phases of Analysis, Design, Implementation, Testing, and Maintenance. The waterfall model implies the transition to a phase only when its preceding phase is reviewed and verified. Typically, the waterfall model places emphasis on proper documentation of artefacts in the life cycle activities. Advocates of agile software development paradigm argue that for any non-trivial project finishing a phase of a software product's life cycle perfectly before moving to the next phases is practically impossible. A related argument is that clients may not know exactly what requirements they need and as such requirements need to be changed constantly.

It is generally acknowledged that a well-defined mature process will support the development of quality products with a substantially reduced number of defects. Some popular examples of process improvement models include the Software Engineering Institute's Capability Maturity Model Integration (CMMI), ISO/IEC 12207, and SPICE (Software Process Improvement and Capability Determination).

Software design patterns are generic solutions to recurring problems. Software quality can be supported by reuse of design patterns that have been proven in the past. Related to design patterns is the concept of anti-patterns, which are a common response to a recurring problem that is usually ineffective and counterproductive. Code smell is any symptom in the source code of a program that possibly indicates a deeper problem. Usually code smells relate to certain structures in the design that indicate violation of fundamental design principles and likewise negatively impact design quality.

An important aspect of SQA is software architecture. Software architecture is a coordination tool among the different phases of software development. It bridges requirements to implementation and allows reasoning about satisfaction of systems' critical requirements (Albert and Tullis, 2013). Quality attributes (Babar et al., 2004) are one kind of non-functional requirement that are critical to systems. The Software Engineering Institute (SEI) defines a quality attribute as "a property of a work product or goods by which its quality will be judged by some stakeholder or stakeholders" (Koschke and Simon, 2003). They are important properties that a system must exhibit, such as scalability, modifiability, or availability (Stoermer et al., 2006).

Architecture designs can be evaluated to ensure the satisfaction of quality attributes. Tvedt Tesoriero et al. (2004), Stoermer et al. (2006) divide architectural evaluation work into two main areas: pre-implementation architecture evaluation, and implementation-oriented architecture conformance. In their classification, pre-implementation architectural approaches are used by architects during initial design and provisioning stages, before the actual implementation starts. In contrast implementation-oriented architecture conformance approaches assess whether the implemented architecture of the system matches the intended architecture of the system. Architectural conformance assesses whether the implemented architecture is consistent with the proposed architecture's specification, and the goals of the proposed architecture.

To evaluate or design a software architecture at the pre-implementation stage, tactics or architectural styles are used in the architecting or evaluation process. Tactics are design decisions that influence the control of a quality attribute response. Architectural Styles or Patterns describe the structure and interaction between collections of components affecting positively to a set of quality attributes but also negatively to others. Software architecture methods are encountered in the literature to design systems based on their quality attributes such as the Attribute Driven Design (ADD) or to evaluate the satisfaction of quality attributes in a software architectural design such as the Architecture Tradeoff Analysis Method (ATAM). For example, ADD and ATAM follow a recursive process based on quality attributes that a system needs to fulfill. At each stage, tactics and architectural patterns (or styles) are chosen to satisfy some qualities.

Empirical studies have demonstrated that one of the most difficult tasks in software architecture design and evaluation is finding out what architectural patterns/styles satisfy quality attributes because the language used in patterns does not directly indicate the quality attributes. This problem has also been indicated in the literature (Gross and Yu, 2001 and Huang et al., 2006).

Also, guidelines for choosing or finding tactics that satisfy quality attributes have been reported to be an issue in as well as defining, evaluating, and assessing which architectural patterns are suitable to implement the tactics and quality attributes (Albert and Tullis, 2013). Towards solving this issue Bachmann et al. (2003), Babar et al. (2004) describe steps for deriving architectural tactics. These steps include identifying candidate reasoning frameworks which include the mechanisms needed to use sound analytic theories to analyze the behavior of a system with respect to some quality attributes (Bachmann et al., 2005). However, this requires that architects need to be familiar with formal specifications that are specific to quality models. Research tools are being developed to aid architects integrate their reasoning frameworks (Christensen and Hansen, 2010), but still reasoning frameworks have to be implemented, and tactics description and how they are applied has to be indicated by the architect. It has also been reported by Koschke and Simon (2003) that some quality attributes do not have a reasoning framework.

Harrison and Avgeriou have analyzed the impact of architectural patterns on quality attributes, and how patterns interact with tactics (Harrison and Avgeriou, 2007; Harrison and Avgeriou). The documentation of this kind of analysis can aid in creating repositories for tactics and patterns based on quality attributes.

Architecture prototyping is an approach to experiment whether architecture tactics provide desired quality attributes or not, and to observe conflicting qualities (Bardram et al., 2005). This technique can be complementary to traditional architectural design and evaluation methods such as ADD or ATAM (Bardram et al., 2005). However, it has been noted to be quite expensive and that "substantial" effort must be invested to adopt architecture prototyping (Bardram et al., 2005).

Several architectural conformance approaches exist in the literature (Murphy et al., 2001; Ali et al.; Koschke and Simon, 2003). These check whether software conform to the architectural specifications (or models). These approaches can be classified either by using static (source code of system) (Murphy et al., 2001; Ali et al.) or dynamic analysis (running system) (Eixelsberger et al., 1998), or both. Architectural conformance approaches have been explicit in being able to check quality attributes (Stoermer et al., 2006; Eixelsberger et al., 1998) and specifically run-time properties such as performance or security (Huang et al., 2006). Also, several have provided feedback on quality metrics (Koschke, 2000).

1.5 ASSESSING SYSTEM QUALITIES

Sections 1.2−1.4 defined concepts and a plan of how we can realize system quality. In this section, we define some of the metrics relating to system quality and how these are monitored and tracked throughout the software development life cycle. The purpose of using metrics is to reduce subjectivity during monitoring activities and provide quantitative data for analysis, helping to achieve desired software quality levels. In this section we focus on approaches for assessing different quality attributes and suitable metrics relevant to the assessment of these quality attributes.

As discussed above, a huge range of software quality attributes have been identified, ranging from low-level code quality issues to overarching software procurement, development, and deployment processes. Each class of quality attribute has a set of metrics that can be used to assess differing quality dimensions of the software system. Metrics need to be assessed to determine whether the software is meeting—or likely to meet—the required quality thresholds set by stakeholders. The thresholds may vary considerably depending on software size, cost, nature of team, software process being used, software quality framework being used, and so on. With modern, complex software-intensive systems, quality requirements may even vary depending on changes to deployment scenario and end users.

1.5.1 ASSESSMENT PROCESSES

The IEEE Software Quality Metrics Methodology (Huang et al., 2006) is a well-known framework for defining and monitoring system-quality metrics and analysis of measurements gathered through the implementation of metrics. Key goals of the framework are to provide organizations a standard methodology to assess achievement of quality goals, establish quality requirements for a system, establish acceptance criteria, detect anomalies, predict future quality levels, monitor changes in quality as software is modified, and to help validate a metrics set. A software quality metrics framework is provided to assist achieving these goals.

The first step of the methodology is to establish a set of software quality requirements. This includes identifying possible requirements, determining the requirements to use, and determining a set of metrics to use to measure quality. A set of metrics—an approved metrics set—is then established, including a cost−benefit analysis of implementing and monitoring the metrics and a process of commitment to the established metrics set. The metrics are then implemented on the software project. This includes data collection procedures, a measurement process established, and metric computation from measures. An analysis phase is used to interpret the results from the metrics capture, identifying the levels of software quality being achieved against the requirements targets. Predictions can be made to assist project management and a quality requirements compliance process is implemented to ensure the project is on target. A final step is validating the quality metrics to ensure they provide a suitable set of product and process metrics to predict desired quality levels. A set of validity criteria are used in the assessment of the metrics set and the results are documented and periodically re-validated.

A range of complementary and alternative approaches have been developed to support the software quality assessment process. CMMI (Bardram et al., 2005) includes several components relating to SQM that incorporate aspects of the assessment of quality attributes. In particular, PPQA (product and process quality assurance) and related PMC (project monitoring and control) and MA (measurement and analysis). Higher levels of quality assurance organization include QPM (quantitative project management) and CAR (causal analysis and resolution). Various agile development processes incorporate quality assessment processes. These include several efforts to develop an agile maturity model (AMM) (Patel and Ramachandran, 2009), complementary in many ways to CMMI but incorporating agile concepts of rapid iteration, on-site customer, pair programming and other agile practices, and minimal investment as in spikes and refactoring as and when needed. The move to many cloud-based applications has increased interest in suitable quality assessment processes and techniques for such nontraditional applications where systems are composed from disparate services, many from different providers.

Key issues with any quality assessment processes include:

- Cost vs. benefit of carrying out the assessment—this includes cost to capture suitable measurements, cost to implement, cost to analyze vs. benefit gained in terms of monitoring quality compliance, and predictive quality assessment
- Team adoption and training—including integrating assessment into the development process, ensuring data can be suitably collected and analyzed, and the team can act on problematic quality assessments

- Evolution of both requirements and system—particularly challenging in the context of cloud-based systems and autonomic systems, where new stakeholders and/or deployment environment conditions can dramatically impact overall system quality metrics
- Lack of mitigations if quality requirements are not being met—if the project is failing to meet one or more quality targets, or likely will fail to meet these, suitable actions must be available to address the issue or the project is at risk of failure.

1.5.2 METRICS AND MEASUREMENTS

A set of metrics are required by which quality attributes can be assessed, and metrics have a set of measurements that need to be periodically taken in order to make judgements about the state of product and process quality. Quality assessment requires the following:

- Definition of appropriate metrics/measures to use—how quality attributes will be assessed
- Definition of a set of expected measurement targets—these can be simple thresholds or very complicated calculations based on a number of measurements taken
- A data collection process put in place to periodically take required measurements, including suitable data collection tools identified and deployed on the project
- Data analysis conducted at suitable times and judgements made on quality
- Data storage, reuse and comparison to determine current quality levels, compliance, trends and future predictions
- Data needs to be suitably protected, including data relating to people, financials, and sensitive requirements and/or measurements.

A wide range of models have been developed to specify and capture software quality metrics. We briefly review several here, with a view to newer metrics for cloud-based platforms, agile methods and large-scale software-intensive systems.

The Software Assurance Technology Center (SATC) at NASA introduced a wide range of software quality metrics applicable to most software processes, architectures, programming languages, and testing strategies. These are grouped into several areas. Requirements-level metrics are used to assess the quality of software requirements. This is fundamental as it doesn't really matter how well a team "does the thing right" (i.e., use best practice design, coding, testing, etc.), if they are not "doing the right thing" (i.e., building the right systems to meet stakeholders needs). Requirements-level quality metrics include completeness, correctness, and consistency of the requirements, commonly called the 3Cs (Pohl, 2010). Additional metrics include traceability—the ability to link requirements to design, code, test artefacts, and volatility—how changeable the requirements are and hence impact on system architecture, design, code, deployment, etc.

A great many code-level metrics have been developed. Classic ones include lines of code (often a poor productivity measure), cyclometric complexity, function point analysis, cohesion, coupling, and various kinds of complexity and size analysis. While historically applied to source code, many can also be applied to design-level models, especially when used for model-driven engineering activities, and even potentially to configuration models. A variety of metrics for user interface of systems have also been developed, many derived from HCI and usability research and practice. These have been applied to web interfaces, more recently to mobile interfaces, and are increasingly being applied to ubiquitous, haptic, virtual reality, touch, gesture, speech and other more human-centric interfaces (Albert and Tullis, 2013). Such metrics include simple completion rates (can or can't complete task), task time, user satisfaction, error rates, various interaction measures, and marketing-style metrics like return rates and conversion rates.

Software testing has historically been used as a major quality assurance achievement mechanism in software development. Many metrics have been developed to support quality assurance via testing. These include defects/bugs per lines of code, code coverage of testing (predominantly for unit testing approaches), fault localization, and identification of criticality of located defects (Kan, 2002).

Process-level metrics are used to qualify and quantify quality aspects associated with the software development process employed by a team. Examples include burn-down charts commonly used in agile methods to track progress, task completion rates, critical paths, and hours (and other resources) spent on development and assurance activities (Kitchenham, 1996).

Service-oriented and cloud-based systems have brought new demands to the evaluation of run-time performance of software systems with a view to meeting quality attributes in this area. Such metrics include traditional ones such as service availability, outage duration, mean-time between failures, completion time, and response time for requests (Papazoglou and van den Heuvel, 2003). More recent measures are needed to assess the quality of service and cloud application delivery, including network and storage device capacity, server capacity (in terms of compute power), web server capacity (number of concurrent requests, users supportable, etc.), instance start up/shut down for cloud elasticity measurement, mean-time to switch-over, and mean-time to system recovery after failure (Li et al., 2012).

1.6 CURRENT CHALLENGES AND FUTURE DIRECTIONS OF SOFTWARE QUALITY

A number of major challenges face software teams—and organizations and individual developers and operators—in maintaining software quality for today's, and tomorrow's, software-intensive systems.

Systems seem to grow ever more interdependent, meaning there are few systems that don't depend heavily on other, usually third-party systems, for major aspects of their components and operation and therefore quality. A failure or simply lower-than-acceptable level of quality in any one of these components or connected services may lead to unacceptable quality degradation in the system as a whole. This quality attribute problem may be to do with incorporating unmaintainable or unportable code; insufficient testing of a used service or the service integration; lower than required run-time performance, reliability, or excessive resource utilization; poor usability of integrated interfaces especially on mobile devices; inefficient or ineffective software process used for all or part of the system's development; or a failure in deployment environment or the user community, for example, comprising security of a component and thus the system as a whole. A number of trends increase these problems, some dramatically. The trend to DevOps, or Development-Operations, where the division between developing vs. maintaining a system disappears. The trend to service-oriented architectures and cloud computing platforms where there is huge dependence on others for necessary system infrastructure and indeed critical software components. The use of agile and global software engineering practices puts greater delivery demands and expectations on teams while greatly increasing challenges around team coordination and software management. The adoption of the "internet of things" (IoT) where many system components are software-intensive but rely on very heterogeneous hardware and networking components, themselves prone to various quality challenges.

Future SQA approaches and supporting techniques, tools, and processes will need to address these challenges. Quality processes, measurements, and management must be applied to diverse non-software components of systems, software components, and the system as whole. Run-time evolution of systems including deployment environment, networking, hardware, and integrated services will mean more run-time quality management is necessary. This will need to be paired with software quality meta-practices, that is, software being engineered with greater range of quality attributes measured and managed at run-time as well as development-time. High turn-around of changes in the DevOps paradigm, contracted platform provisioning in the cloud computing paradigm, and diverse integrated data sources in the IoT paradigm, will all need higher degrees and frequency of quality attention than traditional enterprise systems development. Distributed, agile teams and incorporation of large numbers of third-party services all require more precise definition of quality attributes and thresholds, agreement on quality maintaining processes, and more accurate predictive analytics associated with SQA practices.

Finally, big data applications have their own quality challenges, not just around their software systems but data quality, privacy, provenance, and scaling. It is highly likely that future quality assurance techniques and tools themselves need to make use of large-scale data analytics approaches to improve our ability to manage very diverse ranges of quality metrics, size of quality measurements and predictive analysis to proactively tackle emergent software quality problems.

1.7 CONCLUSION

In this chapter we have provided a general overview of software quality concerns and SQM. SQM is the collection of all processes that ensure that software products, services, and life cycle process implementations meet organizational software quality objectives and achieve stakeholder satisfaction. We have briefly described the basic SQM approaches including SQP, SQA, SQC, and SPI. Considering the topic of the book we have focused on SQM and in this context discussed the short history and evolution of software quality models. In addition the current state-of-the-art approaches on assessing system quality approaches have been discussed. Although a large body of knowledge on SQA exists, there are still many great challenges which require attention. The subsequent chapters in this book address some of the identified relevant issues.

REFERENCES

Albert, W., Tullis, T., 2013. Measuring the User Experience: Collecting, Analyzing, and Presenting Usability Metrics. Morgan Kaufmann.

Ali, N., Solis, C., 2014. Exploring how the attribute driven design method is perceived, In: Mistrik, I., Bahsoon, R., Eeles, P., Roshandel, R., Stal, M. (Eds.), Relating System Quality and Software Architecture. Morgan Kaufman Elsevier, United States, pp. 23−40. ISBN 9780124170094.

Ali, N., Rosik, J., Buckley, J. Characterizing real-time reflexion-based architecture recovery: an in-vivo multi-case study. In: Proceedings of the 8th International ACM SIGSOFT Conference on Quality of Software Architectures (QoSA'12). ACM, New York, NY, pp. 23−32.

Babar, M.A., Zhu, L., Jeffery, R., 2004. A framework for classifying and comparing software architecture evaluation methods. In: ASWEC, p. 309.

Bachmann, F., Bass, L., Klein, M., 2003. Deriving Architectural. Tactics: A Step Toward. Methodical Architectural. Design. CMU/SEI-2003-TR-004. ESC-TR-2003-004.

Bachmann, F., Bass, L., Klein, M., Shelton, C., 2005. Designing software architectures to achieve quality attribute requirements. In: Software, IEE Proceedings, vol. 152, issue 4, pp. 153−165.

Bardram, J.E., Christensen, H.B., Corry, A.V., Hansen, K.M., Ingstrup, M., 2005. Exploring quality attributes using architectural prototyping. In: Proceedings of First International Conference on the Quality of Software Architectures, LNCS, vol. 3712, pp. 155−170.

Bass, L., Clements, P., Kazman, R., 2010. Software Architecture in Practice, third ed. Addison-Wesley Professional.

Boehm, B., 1978. Characteristics of Software Quality, Vol 1 of TRW Series on Software Technology. North-Holland, Amsterdam, Holland.

Chrissis, M.B., Konrad, M., Shrum, S., 2003. CMMI Guidlines for Process Integration and Product Improvement. Addison-Wesley Longman Publishing Co., Inc.

Christensen, H.B., Hansen, K.M., 2010. An empirical investigation of architectural prototyping. J. Syst. Softw. 83 (1), 133−142.

Diaz-Pace, A., Kim, H., Bass, L., Bianco, P., Bachmann, F., 2008. Integrating quality-attribute reasoning frameworks in the ArchE design assistant. In: Proceedings of the 4th International Conference on Quality of Software-Architectures: Models and Architectures, LNCS, vol. 5281, pp. 171–188.

Dybå, T., Dingsøyr, T., 2008. Empirical studies of agile software development: a systematic review. Inf. Softw. Technol. 50 (9), 833–859.

Eixelsberger, W., Ogris, M., Gall,H., Bellay, B., 1998. Software architecture recovery of a program family. In: ICSE, pp. 508–511.

Emeakaroha, V.C., et al. 2010. Low level metrics to high level SLAs-LoM2HiS framework: bridging the gap between monitored metrics and SLA parameters in cloud environments. In: 2010 International Conference on High Performance Computing and Simulation (HPCS), IEEE.

Fenton, N.E., Pfleger, S.L., 1998. Software Metrics—A Rigorous and Practical Approach, second ed. International Thomson Press, London.

Franke, D., Weise, C. 2011. Providing a software quality framework for testing of mobile applications. In: 2011 IEEE Fourth International Conference on Software Testing, Verification and Validation (ICST), IEEE.

Galin, D., 2004. Software Quality Assurance: From Theory to Implementation. Pearson Education.

Garlan, D., Schmerl, B., 2004. Using Architectural Models at Runtime: Research Challenges. In: First European Workshop on Software Architecture, LNCS 3047. Springer, pp. 200–205.

Gorton, I., 2006. Essential Software Architecture. Springer-Verlang.

Gross, D., Yu, E., 2001. From non-functional requirements to design through patterns. Requirements Eng. 6 (1), 18–36.

Guide to the Software Engineering Body of Knowledge, 2015. SWEBOK Guide <https://www.computer.org/web/swebok>.

Harrison, N.B., Avgeriou, P., 2007. Leveraging architecture patterns to satisfy quality attributes. In: European Conference on Software Architecture, LNCS, pp. 263–270.

Harrison, N.B., Avgeriou, P., 2010. How do architecture patterns and tactics interact? A model and annotation. J. Syst. Softw. 83 (10), 1735–1758.

Huang, G., Hong, M., Yang, F.Q., 2006. Runtime recovery and manipulation of software architecture of component-based systems. Autom. Softw. Eng. 13 (2), 257–281.

IEEE Std 610.12-1990—IEEE Standard Glossary of Software Engineering Terminology, Corrected Edition, February 1991. In: IEEE Software Engineering Standards Collection, The Institute of Electrical and Electronics Engineers, New York, 1991.

IEEE, 1061-1992—IEEE Standard for a Software Quality Metrics Methodology, IEEE Computer Society, 1992, http://dx.doi.org/10.1109/IEEESTD.1993.115124.

ISO/IEC/IEEE 24765:2010(E)—IEEE Systems and Software Engineering Vocabulary, 2010.

ISO 9000-3:1997(E), Quality Management and Quality Assurance Standards—Part 3: Guidelines for the Application of ISO 9001:1994 to the Development, Supply, Installation and Maintenance of Computer Software, second ed. International Organization for Standardization (ISO), Geneva.

ISO 9000-3:2001 Software and System Engineering—Guidelines for the Application of ISO 9001:2000 to Software, Final draft. International Organization for Standardization (ISO), Geneva, unpublished draft, December 2001.

ISO/IEC Systems and Software Engineering—Systems and Software Quality Requirements and Evaluation (SquaRE)—System and Software Quality Models. ISO/IEC 25010:2011, 2011. Available from: <http://www.iso.org/iso/iso_catalogue/catalogue_tc/catalogue_detail.htm?csnumber=35733>.

Kan, S.H., 2002. Metrics and Models in Software Quality Engineering. Addison-Wesley Longman Publishing Co., Inc.

Kazman, R., Bass, L., Klein, M., 2006. The essential components of software architecture design and analysis. J. Syst. Softw. 79 (8), 1207−1216.

Kitchenham, B.A., 1996. Software Metrics: Measurement for Software Process Improvement. Blackwell Publishers, Inc.

Koschke, R., 2000. Atomic Architectural Component Recovery for Program Understanding and Evolution (Ph.D. thesis). Universität Stuttgart.

Koschke, R., Simon, D., 2003. Hierarchical reflexion models. In: Proceedings of the 10th Working Conference on Reverse Engineering, Victoria, Canada.

Li, Z. et al., 2012. On a catalogue of metrics for evaluating commercial cloud services. In: Proceedings of the 2012 ACM/IEEE 13th International Conference on Grid Computing. IEEE Computer Society.

McCall, J., Richards, P., Walters, G., 1977. Factors in Software Quality, vols. 1−3, NTIS AD-A049-014, 015, 055, November 1977.

Murphy, G., Notkin, D., Sullivan, K., 2001. Software reflexion models: bridging the gap between design and implementation. IEEE Trans. Softw. Eng. 27 (4), 364−380.

Patel, C., Ramachandran, M., 2009. Agile maturity model (AMM): a Software Process Improvement framework for agile software development practices. Int. J. Softw. Eng. 2 (1), 3−28.

Papazoglou, M.P., van den Heuvel, W.J., 2003. Service-oriented computing: state-of-the-art and open research issues. IEEE Comput. 40 (11).

Pohl, K., 2010. Requirements Engineering: Fundamentals, Principles, and Techniques. Springer Publishing.

Remco, C., Van Vliet, H., 2009. QuOnt: an ontology for the reuse of quality criteria. In: ICSE Workshop on Sharing and Reusing Architectural Knowledge, pp. 57−64.

Rozanski, N., Woods, E., 2011. Software Systems Architecture: Working with Stakeholders Using Viewpoints and Perspectives. Addison-Wesley.

Schulmeyer, G., 2007. Handbook of Software Quality Assurance. Artech House Publishers. fourth ed.

Software Engineering Institute, 2010. Software Architecture Glossary. <http://www.sei.cmu.edu/architecture/start/glossary/>.

Stoermer, C., Rowe, A., O'Brien, L., Verhoef, C., 2006. Model-centric software architecture reconstruction. Softw. Pract. Exper. 36 (4), 333−363, ISSN 0038-0644. http://dx.doi.org/10.1002/spe.v36:4.

Tvedt, R.T., Costa, P., Lindvall, M., 2004. Evaluating software architectures. Adv. Comput. 61, 1−43, <http://dblp.uni-trier.de/db/journals/ac/ac61.html#TvedtCL04>.

Tian, J., 2005. Software Quality Engineering: Testing, Quality Assurance, and Quantifiable Improvement. John Wiley & Sons.

Wojcik, R., Bachmann, F., Bass, L., Clements, P., Merson, P., Nord, R., et al., 2006. Attribute-Driven Design (ADD), Version 2.0. Technical Report CMU/SEI-2006-TR-023, SEI.

An introduction to modern software quality assurance

2

Bruce R. Maxim and Marouane Kessentini

Department of Computer and Information Science, University of Michigan-Dearborn,
Dearborn, MI, USA

2.1 INTRODUCTION

Software quality assurance (SQA) is something everyone talks about, but few seem to want to any spend time on. Many developers have the perception that it is more important to deliver software on time than to try to fix problems before deployment. This perception continues despite the fact that most software failures or disasters could have been avoided using software engineering techniques already known. In many cases, these quality problems could have been predicted because no independent audits of the product were allowed and company management ignored problems widely reported by software users (Hatton, 2007).

There are several major challenges to quality management in the new generation of software systems. Modern systems often make use of decentralized services (e.g., mobile services, cloud services, sensor services). Future computing systems are likely to be more evolutionary and adaptive than those in the past. Software development is often conducted by geographically distributed multinational teams with the additional quality challenges that come from this type of collaboration. Some software professionals believe that software engineering needs to take an end-to-end approach to quality management. Quality management is needed to help developers cope with both technical and trust issues. Quality management requires effective steering of quality processes, powerful version management of all types of artifacts, effective traceability support, and automation of tasks when possible. There is a need to improve goal-oriented orchestration of quality management activities. People must be motivated to want to collaborate and to expend effort on documentation and other quality management activities. Failing to involve all stakeholders throughout the development process further adds to quality management challenges when building software products (Breu et al., 2014).

2.2 REQUIREMENT CONFORMANCE VERSUS CUSTOMER SATISFACTION

Modern software engineers prefer to base definitions of quality on product attributes that can be measured so progress against quality goals can be tracked. The practice of adding features for their own sake to a software product does not seem to guarantee its quality will improve. Software engineering is a labor intensive task; it is hard to reduce costs without reducing quality. Much of the early efforts in SQA were focused on demonstrating that a program matched its specification without considering whether the specification itself was correct. Conformance to a specification does not by itself guarantee that a software product will meet its users' needs or goals. Some software engineers suggest that early assessment of user goals can help developers create products that satisfy customer needs (Lago et al., 2010).

Effective quality management (EQM) is one method proposed to help software quality managers to negotiate acceptable quality targets with input from a minimum set of stakeholders. This allows quality targets to be adjusted over the product life cycle if needed. EQM is an iterative process that that begins with an *identification* phase in which the product functions are identified and analyzes them to identify their value, the risks, and the quality risks. The *plan* phase produces a set of measures suitable for function validation and to help mitigate the function quality risks. A *do* phase executes the validation measures and a *check* phase involves comparing validation measures against product quality indicators. The *act* phase sets up corrective actions to improve product quality as needed. EQM has been successfully applied to several software process models as a means of resource allocation and adjustments to quality assurance activities during development (Poth and Suyaev, 2014).

2.3 MEASUREMENT

Sometimes it is hard to get stakeholders to agree on whether a system exhibits high quality or not, if their judgments rely entirely on personal opinion. Computer science often operates as a measurement free discipline and prefers the use of silver bullet tools and processes. Some of this is caused because defect tracking data collected in the name of software quality is often not used by developers. This defect data is often incomplete, incorrect, or imprecise with respect to the causes of specific defects. Yet, many software engineers believe that effective SQA or software process improvement (SPI) should be measurement based (Li et al., 2012).

Developers are only likely to be motivated to focus on SPI if they are convinced of its long term benefits. Otherwise developers are not likely to follow the quality protocols. The use of goal-oriented data collection has been suggested as one way to ensure that only meaningful data is collected. The goal/question/ metric (GQM) approach to SQA/SPI is one such technique. When using a GQM approach the first step is to start with a goal (specifying the purpose of measurement, object to be measured, issue to be measured, and viewpoint from which the measure is taken). The next step is to refine the goal into its major components by creating several questions that may be answered using quantifiable data. The third step is to specify measures or metrics needed to answer the questions and track conformance of the process and product to the goals. Several questions can make use of the same metrics. Several GQM models can have the same questions and metrics in common, if different viewpoints are taken into account (Basili et al., 1994). Goal related data collection has the best return on investment (ROI) (Li et al., 2012).

2.4 QUALITY PERSPECTIVES

Engineers have long considered quality as an important dimension of any manufacturing process. Software cannot be manufactured in the same sense as a physical artifact like an automobile. Even simple software applications are often customized when being developed for more than one type of customer or more than one application domain. Yet software quality finds its roots in many quality definitions that originated in manufacturing engineering. Garvin (1984) suggests that quality might be described from five different viewpoints. Perhaps the least compelling is the *transcendental view* that argues that quality is immediately recognizable and cannot be easily defined. The *user view* looks at quality in terms of whether it satisfies the users' goals or not. The *manufacturer's view* which focuses on how well a product conforms to its specification. The *product view* that attempts to link quality to the number of delivered functions and features in the product. The *value-based view* measures quality in terms of the how much a customer will pay for the product.

2.5 QUALITY MODELS

Several quality models and standards have been proposed in the software engineering literature. Each of these models consists of a number of factors or characteristics that should be present in high quality software. While it may be hard to measure some of these factors directly, most software developers would agree that monitoring these factors in a systematic manner can help produce high quality software.

McCall et al. (1977) proposed a useful list of factors that affect software quality. McCall's factors were developed from the perspective of system development and the system development process. McCall's intent was to create a set of quality factors that reflected both end-user needs and the developer priorities. These quality factors are usually organized into three groups as follows:

- Product operation factors
  - Correctness—the extent to which a program satisfies its specification
  - Reliability—the extent to which software completes its intended task without failure in a specified environment
  - Efficiency—the hardware, software, and programming resources required by a program to perform its function
  - Integrity—the extent to which access to data and software by unauthorized persons is controlled
  - Usability—the effort required to learn, use, enter data, and interpret program output.
- Product revision factors
  - Maintainability—the effort required to locate and fix program defects
  - Flexibility—effort required to modify an existing software system
  - Testability—effort required to create the test cases and procedures necessary to ensure software performs its required functions.
- Product adaptability factors
  - Portability—effort required to transfer a program from one computing platform or operating environment to another
  - Reusability—extent to which software components can be used in new applications
  - Interoperability—effort required to use software on more than one system.

Boehm proposed a model which attempted to quantitatively model software quality using a predefined set of attributes and metrics. He used three high-level characteristics to organize seven quality factors (Boehm et al., 1978). His definitions of these factors are similar to McCall's.

- Utility
  - Reliability
  - Efficiency
  - Usability
- Maintainability
  - Testability
  - Understandability
  - Flexibility
- Portability

The FURPS model proposed by Grady (1992) organizes the many of McCall's quality factors into the five categories shown below.

- Functionality—capability, compatibility, interoperability, portability, security
- Usability—human factors, documentation, responsiveness
- Reliability—availability, recoverability, predictability, accuracy

- Performance—speed, efficiency, capacity, scalability
- Supportability—maintainability, testability, adaptability, flexibility.

McCall's quality factors provide a basis for engineering software that provides high levels of user satisfaction by focusing on the overall user experience (UX) delivered by the software product. This cannot be done without also taking steps to ensure that the specification is correct and that software defects are identified early in the software development process. This philosophy is the basis of the evolutionary and agile processes favored by many developers today.

There is an ISO standard which defines a model for software quality (ISO 25010). This standard defines *a quality in use* model with five characteristics that are appropriate when considering a product use in a particular context (e.g., considering the use of a particular software product on a specific hardware platform by a human). This standard also defines *a product quality* model with eight characteristics that consider the static nature software products and the dynamic nature of computer systems.

- Quality in use
  - Effectiveness—accuracy and completeness user to achieve goals
  - Efficiency—resources expended to achieve user goals completely with desired accuracy
  - Satisfaction—usefulness, trust, pleasure, comfort
  - Freedom from risk—mitigation of economic, health, safety, and environmental risks
  - Context coverage—completeness, flexibility.
- Product quality
  - Functional suitability—complete, correct, appropriate
  - Performance efficiency—timing, resource utilization, capacity
  - Compatibility—coexistence, interoperability
  - Usability—appropriateness, learnability, operability, error protection, aesthetics, accessibility
  - Reliability—maturity, availability, fault tolerance, recoverability
  - Security—confidentiality, integrity, accountability, authenticity
  - Maintainability—modularity, reusability, modifiability, testability
  - Portability—adaptability, installability, replacability.

The ISO 25010 quality model is the newest (published in 2011), so it is not surprising that it has the most elements. The addition of the quality in use model to this standard highlights the importance of customer satisfaction in the overall assessment of software quality, more so than in some of the earlier models. The role of context in the assessment of quality will be discussed later in this chapter. The product quality factor model shows the importance of considering more than functional requirements assessing the overall quality of a software product. This was evident in all the quality models discussed in this section.

2.6 NON-FUNCTIONAL REQUIREMENTS

Non-functional requirements (NFRs) can be defined as quality attributes (e.g., usability, reliability, security) or general system constraints. They are not easy for stakeholders to articulate but they know that the software will not be usable without some of these non-functional characteristics (Chung and Leite, 2009).

A technique known as quality function deployment (QFD) can assist developers in identifying and prioritizing customer expectations quickly and effectively. Using QFD software engineers attempt to categorize requirements as normal (musts), expected (wants), or exciting (wows). Normal requirements are the requirements gathered from stakeholder meetings and must be present for the customer to be satisfied. Expected requirements are implicit to the product and are so basic that customers feel they do not need to state them. However, if they are not present customers will not be at all satisfied. Exciting requirements cause the delivered product to be highly satisfying to the stakeholders. QFD techniques are especially useful during the requirements elicitation activity (Revelle, 2004).

QFD uses the customer interviews, observation, surveys, and historic data as raw data in requirements gathering and produces a customer voice table. A customer voice table organizes the derived requirements according to stakeholder needs. Stakeholders are asked to rank each requirement according to their relative importance. The requirements with the highest ranks based on a stakeholder consensus become the core requirements for the system. The lowest ranked requirements become the exciting requirements, unless they are fundamental to the success of the system. This technique requires both early and frequent communication with the stakeholder to be successful. QFD is one technique to reduce the impact of requirements creep. Requirements creep is a situation in which the customer is constantly requesting new features as each software product increment is delivered for acceptance.

2.7 COST OF QUALITY

Large-scale software systems exhibit high complexity and become difficult to maintain. In fact, it has been reported that cost dedicated to maintenance and evolution activities is more than 80% of the total software costs. In addition, it has been shown that software maintainers spend around 60% of their time in understanding the code (Boehm and Basili, 2001).

In particular, object-oriented software systems need to follow some traditional set of design principles such as data abstraction, encapsulation, and modularity. However, some of these NFRs can be violated by developers for many reasons such as inexperience with object-oriented design principles, deadline stress, and much focus on only implementing main functionality. This high cost of maintenance activities could potentially be greatly reduced by providing automatic or semi-automatic solutions to increase system's comprehensibility, adaptability and extensibility to avoid bad-practices.

There is no question that software quality takes time and money. Lack of quality also costs money both to the users and the developers. It has been estimated that a defect costs ten times as much to repair when found during testing as compared to the costs of repairing the same defect if found during a review (Boehm and Basili, 2001). What costs should be considered as part of SQA?

The cost of quality includes the costs incurred by all quality-related activities pursued by the development team plus any support and maintenance costs that can be demonstrably related to lack of quality. These costs can be classified as having been generated by prevention activities, appraisal activities, and correcting failure.

Prevention costs include activities specifically designed to prevent poor quality in products or services (e.g., quality planning, new product reviews, quality improvement projects). Prevention costs should also consider those incurred by training for all quality activities.

Appraisal costs include associated with measuring, evaluating or auditing products or services to assure conformance to quality standards and performance requirements. These activities are used to gain insight into the product quality.

Failure costs include the costs resulting from products or services not conforming to requirements or customer/user needs. Failure costs can include those that are incurred in supporting, correcting, or replacing a product already shipped to a customer. These may also include costs associated with loss of confidence or diminished reputation (Wood, 2012).

2.8 VERIFICATION AND VALIDATION

Verification and validation (V&V) processes are central to SQA. The goal of software verification is to determine whether the product under construction is being built to match its specification. Verification attempts to answer the question "are the developers building the product correctly?" The goal of validation is to determine whether the proposed software product will meet its customer's expectations and needs. Validation attempts to answer the question "are developers building the right product?" V&V processes include analysis, evaluation, review, inspection, assessment, and testing (IEEE 1012-2012).

There are many types of testing that may be used during the V&V activities. One purpose of testing is to uncover defects in an existing software product. Since the test cases used should be based on the requirements, they will not be much good in determining the usefulness of a software product if the requirements do not describe the customer's needs. It is often the case that software requirements may need to evolve if the customer's needs change during product development. Many NFRs (e.g., reliability, security, safety) for a system cannot be assessed by executing a series of test cases and are often handled using reviews or inspections. The use of early review type activities involving the customer or end-users is a crucial part of the V&V process.

2.9 ROLE OF FORMAL METHODS

Most software engineers agree that it is difficult to create fault-free programs following a design, code, and test paradigm. There are some systems that cannot be completely tested before deployment (e.g., the Mars Rover). Formal software engineering methods purport to help a software team to "do it right the first time" by providing a mathematically based approach to program modeling and the ability to verify that the model is correct using mathematical proof. This is one means of verifying that a critical system will operate according to its specification independent of any subsequent testing processes (Pressman and Maxim, 2014).

There are a number of potential benefits to using formal methods in an effort to create defect free programs. Requirements written using natural language are often incomplete or ambiguous. Formal methods often model a program as a series of state transitions. This allows developers to focus on dynamic system behavior as it is tested. The simple act of modeling a system may uncover program defects by showing clearly how the implemented system is to avoid reaching an invalid state. However, there is no guarantee that the system being modeled meets its NFRs (Abrial, 2009).

Some opponents of formal methods argue that many of these practices are contrary to the tenets of agile process models. Some people argue that it is possible to combine elements of formal and agile processes to create better software products. Light-weight formal methods can add value to agile development by forcing developers to ensure that system safety requirements are being met by the evolving system (Black et al., 2009).

Formal methods can be used to assist in the process of automatically generating test cases from the system models by helping in the placement of assertions in program source code. Assertions written using formal notation can be machine checked for inconsistencies. Formal methods can provide the basis for defining correctness preserving code transformations.

The use of formal methods can slow the delivery of the first software increment, but they may also reduce the amount of rework during product lifetime if the requirements do not change. Supplementing agile methods with formal methods can help ensure that all requirements have been met (Sterling, 2010).

Formal methods are controversial. Their advocates claim that they can revolutionize software development. Their detractors think they are impossibly difficult to use. Meanwhile, for most people, formal methods are so unfamiliar that it is difficult to judge the competing claims (Hall, 1990). This might explain the lack of their widespread commercial use except in some safety critical system development projects.

2.10 ROLE OF TESTING AND AUTOMATED TESTING

Testing is an important part of the SQA process. Testing should be used throughout the software development process, not just at the end. Software engineers can use testing to demonstrate a system can deliver incremental functionality during development. Testing can be used to uncover system defects prior to delivery. Testing sometimes can uncover errors in system specifications. Testing can be used to improve system quality by seeking to minimize defects in the delivered product. It is difficult to prove any non-trivial program is correct (or defect free) by exhaustively processing every combination of valid and invalid test values, simply due to the sheer number of test cases required (Tutelage and Dubai, 2012).

The generation of test case input values may be distinguished into two general approaches: black-box based approaches and white-box based approaches (Rokosz, 2003; Yacoub, 2003). When using black-box techniques, the test values are generated using only the information contained in the software specification and without looking at the code used to implement a particular software component. When using white-box testing techniques software engineers generate test values that will exercise each line of code used to implement a software component. White-box test cases can only be created when testers have full knowledge of the code used to implement a piece of software.

In addition to black-box and white-box techniques, another widely-used technique for test generation is mutation analysis. Mutation analysis is a testing technique that was designed to evaluate the efficiency of a test set. Mutation analysis consists of creating a set of faulty versions or mutants of a program with the ultimate goal of designing a test set that distinguishes the program from all its mutants.

Mottu et al. (2008) have adapted this technique to evaluate the quality of test cases. They introduce some modifications in the transformation rules (program-mutant). Then using the same test cases as input an oracle function compares between the results (target models). If all results are the same, we can assume that the input cases were not sufficient to cover all the execution possibilities.

One motivation for using automated testing is to make it easier for the developers to have access to testing resources as soon as code is developed. There are two key benefits to this. The tests encode the expected behavior of a product feature and if the test succeeds the feature has been validated. It is still important to make sure the system changes introduced by the new feature have not introduced new defects. If testing can be automated, developers can perform regression testing immediately after implementing each new feature. The trick, of course, is to make it easy to generate the needed test cases and to make sure that all test cases are traceable to the groups of related features that are included in the software system (Kuehlemann, 2014).

Test automation is not an all-or-nothing proposition. It is relatively easy to process existing test cases automatically, if the necessary test cases can be identified. This requires some method to select the relevant test cases form a repository based on the product requirements. However, not every test case can be encoded using character or numeric data. When networks and distributed processes are involved it may not be possible to duplicate all combinations of system events without the use network simulation tools. Highly interactive active GUI (graphical user interfaces) are very difficult to write test cases for.

In some cases it would be helpful to generate test cases directly from the program source code or requirements models. This is a very difficult task and there is always the risk that either the source code or requirement model is incorrect. Automated testing tools often require quite a bit of editing of the source code before it can be used by a test case generation program. Alternatively, the program specifications may need to be written using formal notation prior to submitting them to a test case generation program. There is always the risk that the test case coverage will not be complete even with the use of a test case generator. Despite these limitations, organizations that automate the use of test case execution often experience considerable reductions in the effort required for testing during the product life cycle (Kuehlemann, 2014).

2.11 RELIABILITY

Software controlled devices seem to be everywhere. There is no doubt that reliability is an important part of the overall software quality picture. Reliability is one dimension of software quality that can be measured directly using historical system performance data. In software engineering reliability is defined as the probability of failure free operation in a specified environment over a defined period of time (Musa et al., 1987).

Reliability also has a psychological dimension. Regardless of the stated reliability values, if a user loses important resources at a critical time when the software fails, the system will not be deemed reliable by that user. Likewise, if the losses are minor and the timing is not inconvenient, a piece of software with relatively frequent failures may be perceived by a user as acceptably reliable (for a free or inexpensive software product).

It is important to use a consistent definition for what a failure is and to select an appropriate measure for time in any reliability calculation. In a strict sense, any evidence that software does not conform to its specification should be considered a failure. It may also be true that software which fails to satisfy user expectations can also be considered to have failed. The timing of failures in user satisfaction may be hard to determine, without sophisticated analytical work. Time may be measured using non-stop execution time, calendar time, number of error free transactions, or number of successful requests for service answered. The suitability of a selected time unit is tightly coupled to the type of system being measured.

Hardware reliability models used in mechanical or electrical engineering do not really apply to software. Hardware defects are based on the notion of wear. Software defects are often caused by design defects or changes in the software's operating environment. These are hard to anticipate or quantify.

One measure of reliability that seems to apply to both hardware and software is mean-time-between-failure (MTBF). MTBF is defined as the sum of the mean-time-to-failures (MTTF) and mean-time-to-repair (MTTR). It is important to consider how long it takes to repair a failure when considering writing a reliability specification. It may not always be wise to use a system with frequent failures and short repair times, but that may be preferable to a system that is down for months at a time when it does fail. There is the possibility that fixing one cause of failure may introduce other software defects (Lazaroni et al., 2011).

2.12 SECURITY

Reliability is an important prerequisite to software security. It is hard to conceive of a secure system that is unreliable, but easy to think of a reliable system that may be unsecure. Computing security breaches seem to appear frequently in the popular news media. Security must be a quality concern for software engineers building any software system that manages stakeholder resources, including intellectual property and identity information.

The focus of software security is proactively protecting assets (data, bandwidth, processor use) of value from attacks that will result in their loss. Developers cannot do a good job of securing a vulnerable system by making software changes in response to reports of vulnerabilities uncovered after assets have been lost or compromised. Like most quality concerns, security must be addressed at the beginning of the software process, built into the design, implemented in the coding, and verified during testing (Firesmith, 2012).

While it may not be possible to secure all assets from every possible attack, it is important to protect the most valuable assets. Valuable assets are determined by comparing the costs associated with their loss (damage repair or replacement) with the cost of protecting them (software development, hardware acquisition, business policies). Threat analysis is used to anticipate the conditions or threats that may be used to damage system resources or render them in accessible to authorized users. Once system assets, vulnerabilities, and threats have been identified controls to avoid attacks or mitigate their damage can be put into place. In some cases these controls may involve actions like backing up critical data, creating redundant system components, or ensuring that privacy controls are in place. Some assets (personal reputation or corporate branding) may be hard to protect as well as difficult to quantify when loss occurs.

The security assurance process is used to demonstrate to all stakeholders that you have built a secure product and inspire confidence that it can be used without unnecessary worry. A security case may be used to verify the contention that software satisfies the security claims made in its requirements. A security case has three elements: the security claims, the arguments used to link the claims to one another, and the body of evidence and assumptions that support the arguments. Several types of evidence may be used to support the case. Formal proofs of correctness, formal technical reviews focuses on security claims, checklist inspections by experts, and security test case execution results can be useful evidence (Sinn, 2008).

To be valid, a security case must satisfy three objectives. It must specify claims that are appropriate for the system under consideration (with stakeholder buy-in). It must document that suitable software engineering processes have been applied to achieve the claims. It must show that achievement of the claims is within the required level of risk. In many ways security engineering is a specialization of the risk management process (Redwine, 2010).

Trust indicates the level of confidence that one entity (system, organization, person) can rely on another. This means that one entity can expect another entity to behave exactly as excepted. One way of demonstrating this behavior is to focus on ensuring that a system conforms to its mitigation practices created along with its threat model. The evidence used to prove the security case must be acceptable to all system stakeholders if it is to be considered a trusted entity. Some quantifiable metrics based on testing, inspection, and analysis techniques may provide useful evidence. Making sure security test cases are traceable to the system security cases is helpful. Users of trustworthy systems should be convinced that the system has no exploitable vulnerabilities or malicious logic (Sinn, 2008).

Software quality metrics do not address trust assurance or security. In part, because most metrics do not take into account the deliberate and repeated attempts to make the system fail that are part of the security mitigation process. Effective security metrics need to be developed using historical data based on an entity's past behavior involving trust. These metrics might be similar to the seller rating on some e-commerce sites (Mead and Jarzombek, 2010).

2.13 SAFETY

People often bet their income and their personal safety on computer software results. They hope the software is working correctly. The implication is that low-quality software increases risks for both the developer and the end-user. Software is often a pivotal component of safety-rated systems involving humans (e.g., automotive, aircraft, or bioengineering applications). The impact of hidden defects in these systems can be catastrophic. In terms of software safety a catastrophic result is one that causes severe economic hardship or physical harm to its stakeholders. The SQA team may be responsible for assessing the impact of software failure and for initiating those steps required to reduce the risk of hazards becoming accidents (Gage and McCormick, 2004).

Software safety is the part of the SQA process that focuses on the identification and assessment of potential hazards that may affect software negatively and cause an entire system to fail. If hazards can be identified early in the software process, software design features can be specified that will either eliminate or control potential hazards.

Safety analysis is fundamental to safety critical system verification and validation. Ideally the safety analysis team should be independent from the software development team. As part of the analysis formal software inspections may be used detect and eliminate defects in the artifacts (e.g., code, specification, design) development process. One tool for identifying failures during inspections is a checklist that covers general failure classes for the type of system being developed. This type of checklist helps the inspectors focus on the fault types and their symptoms as they view the artifacts. It is important to note that this type of checklist covers only the main safety aspects for verification and needs to be augmented with other techniques (De Almeida et al., 2003).

A modeling and analysis process is conducted as part of the software safety effort. Initially, hazards are identified and categorized by criticality and risk. Once these system-level hazards are identified, analysis techniques are used to assign severity and probability of occurrence. To be effective, software must be analyzed in the context of the entire system. For example, a subtle user input error (people are system components) may be magnified by a software fault to produce control data that improperly positions a mechanical device. If and only if a set of external environmental conditions is met, the improper positioning of the mechanical device will cause a disastrous failure. Analysis techniques such as fault tree analysis, real-time logic, and Petri net models can be used to predict the chain of events that can cause hazards and the probability that each of the events will occur to create the chain (Ericson, 2005).

Once hazards are identified and analyzed, safety-related requirements can be specified for the software. That is, the specification can contain a list of undesirable events and the desired system responses to these events. Formal software engineering methods can add value to the safety assurance process by forcing developers to make sure the system safety property axioms are valid. The role of software in managing undesirable events is then indicated. As part of the safety assurance process safety cases are created to support the contention that the software supports the safety claims being asserted.

It is important for stakeholders to come to an agreement about the evidence necessary to demonstrate compliance of a system to the applicable safety requirements. Failing to come to an agreement as to how the safety standards are interpreted can prevent stakeholders from collecting or recording the right data. Recovering this information after the fact may lead to cost overruns and deployment delays. One tool for safety evidence planning involves the use of a questionnaire by all stakeholders to define details about what evidence to collect for each safety requirement and alternative ways of recording and structuring it. This approach is similar to that used in acceptance testing (Falessi et al., 2012).

Software reliability and software safety are closely related to one another, there are subtle differences between them. Software reliability uses statistical analysis to determine the likelihood that a software failure will occur. It is important to notes that note every failure result in a hazard or accident. Software safety examines the ways in which failures result in conditions that can lead to serious accidents. Failures should not be considered in isolation, they must be evaluated in the context of the entire computer-based system and its environment (Hardy, 2012).

2.14 REVIEWS AND USABILITY

The over-arching purpose of software engineering reviews is to improve the quality of selected products during a development project. Reviews differ in their levels of formality. A review might be a simple group evaluation of a product or a thorough examination of the work product using detailed quality checklist. Reviews are relatively inexpensive to conduct and they provide a huge return on the investment. Some software developers believe that reviews can help to identify 80% of the defects in a work product (Wiegers, 2002).

Conventional testing techniques can be used to help uncover defects present in the code used to implement user interface. However the task of assessing the quality of the UX often better accomplished by conducting usability reviews. Usability reviews are sometimes called heuristic evaluations. Like many software reviews, heuristic evaluations may include subjective assessment of software quality factors.

2.15 REVIEWS AND POSTMORTEMS

In traditional software development process models, reviews may be conducted after the completion of any project milestone. A project milestone may be the completion of a document or defined project iteration. It is important that there is some written artifact to review. The focus of this type of review is on early defect detection and ensuring that the work product meets its requirements. In reviews, team members often just work on identifying errors, not fixing them or determining their root causes. Repairing defects types is usually handled after the review summary is written (Wiegers, 2002).

Postmortems are a type of review that is usually conducted after a project is completed. Unlike a technical review that might focus on a single product, a postmortem evaluation focuses on the project as a whole. They are often conducted in a workshop format and the participants are made up of both software team members and other project stakeholders.

The purpose of a postmortem is to establish a consistent mechanism for extracting lessons learned in each project. Some postmortems may be very formal and involve reviewing metrics and measures as means of guiding quality (product metrics) and process (process metrics) improvement activities. It is important for the development team to compare the planned and actual schedules, collect and analyze software project metrics, get feedback from team members and customers, and record their findings in written form (Baaz et al., 2010).

In less formal process models, postmortems may involve simply listing the things that went right and the things that went wrong during the current build cycle. Some agile process models rely on the use of a type of review known as a retrospective to assist in process improvement. Retrospectives allow the development team the time to step back and reflect on the recently completed product iteration. Unlike postmortems that occur at the end of a project when it is too late to fix the problems, retrospectives may occur on daily basis with extremely short build cycles or sprints. This allows for small process and quality improvements on a regular basis.

Proponents argue that the use of agile retrospectives help teams to improve and increase their business value for their customers and their company. Teams are empowered since one benefit of retrospectives is that action items are defined and resolved by the team. Retrospectives often focus on root cause analysis to find the causes (not symptoms) of a problem and define actions to prevent it from recurring. When people understand the problems and their causes they are often more motivated to work on them. If retrospectives are done frequently they can lead to continuous improvement with considerable business value in the long run (Gonclaves and Linderss, 2014).

2.16 **USER EXPERIENCE**

The rapid growth in the number of mobile devices in the marketplace has brought renewed interest in usability as a dimension of quality. End-user satisfaction with a mobile app is determined by six important quality factors: functionality, reliability, usability, efficiency, maintainability, and portability (Andreou et al., 2005). Context-aware apps provide additional challenges for developers seeking to provide users with quality UXs.

The goal of mobile app testing is to uncover defects or issues that may lead to system failures. UX testing focuses on quality elements such as content, function, usability, use of context, navigability, performance, compatibility, interoperability, and security. The quality process incorporates reviews and usability assessments that are carried out throughout the development process. Test cases are derived from use cases viewed from the end user's perspective. These test cases emphasize real-time, end-to-end testing of the app on all supported device configurations (Pressman and Maxim, 2014).

Legal and ethical pressures suggest that mobile device interfaces need to account for device differences, cultural differences, computing inexperience, age, and user disabilities in order to provide a quality UX. The effects of poor usability may mean that users cannot complete their tasks or will not be satisfied with the results. This suggests that user-centered design activities may be beneficial in creating quality UXs (Shull, 2012).

Context allows the creation of apps that allow a device to be aware of its location, environment, user, and nearby devices. To achieve context awareness, mobile devices must produce reliable information in the presence of uncertain and rapidly changing data produced by several different devices (Korpipaa et al., 2003). These types of interaction are extremely hard to duplicate in the testing laboratory and hard to control in the field.

There are times when mobile users want to work with more than one device on the same content object (e.g., editing a document containing both images and text). Each device may have different interaction devices (key board or touch screen) as well as different physical screen display sizes and resolutions. The app may be expected to work on devices with or without access to the same network. This can make it extremely hard for developers to provide a consistent UX across multiple devices (Pressman and Maxim, 2014).

2.17 SOCIAL MEDIA, CLOUD COMPUTING, AND CROWDSOURCING

Social media has the potential to impact software engineering practice in many ways. The social processes around software development are highly dependent on engineers' abilities to find and connect with individuals who share similar goals and complementary skills, to harmonize each team member's communication and teaming preferences, to collaborate and coordinate during the entire software life cycle, and advocate for their product's success in the marketplace (Begel et al., 2010). The value of social media grows as the team gets larger and becomes more widely dispersed geographically.

When a social network is created for a software project the development team can draw from the collective experiences of all project stakeholders invited to participate in the network. The network can be used to speed up and improve communication among all stakeholders any time an issue, problem, or question comes up. This has the potential to improve quality.

These benefits do not come without risk to both privacy and security. Much of the work done by software engineers is viewed as proprietary to the company they work for. Allowing large numbers of outside stakeholders to have access to product and process information may help improve software quality. However, it is also possible that developers may not be open to sharing defect information within the social network, which may result in a decline in quality as defects and their repairs are hidden.

Anything having to do with the social or collaboration aspects of software development can lend itself well to the cloud. Project management, scheduling, task lists, requirements, and defect management all suit themselves well as these are at core group functions where communications is essential to keeping projects in sync and all members of the team—wherever they are located—on literally the same page (Gardner, 2009).

Cloud computing provides a mechanism for allowing access to all software engineering work products and process data. This allows team members the ability to conduct low risk trials of new software products and to provide feedback on them from any place in the world. The cloud provides new mechanisms to distribute and test beta software. Developers can share software engineering information with any group of stakeholders instantly.

Making use of cloud computing in a software engineering is not without risk and may have a negative impact on software quality in some cases. The cloud is dispersed over many servers and the architecture and services are often outside the control of a software team. As a consequence, there are multiple points of failure, presenting reliability and security risks. As the number of services provided by the cloud grows, the relative complexity of the software development environment also grows; this can also result in decline in software quality if developers are not attentive to the warning signs. Finally, if the cloud becomes the development environment, services must stress usability and performance. These attributes sometimes conflict with security, privacy, and reliability which bring up quality tradeoff considerations (Pressman and Maxim, 2014).

Many mobile app developers promote the importance of testing-in-the-wild as opposed to testing in the development lab. Some of the characteristics of in-the-wild testing include adverse and unpredictable environments, outdated browsers and plug-ins, unique hardware, and imperfect connectivity (both Wi-Fi and mobile carrier). In order to mirror real-world conditions, the demographic characteristics of testers should match those of targeted users, as well as those of their devices. Testing-in-the-wild is always somewhat unpredictable, and test plans must be adapted as testing progresses (Rooksby et al., 2009).

Creating test environments in-house is an expensive and error-prone process. Cloud-based testing can offer a standardized infrastructure and preconfigured software images, freeing the mobile app team from the need to worry about finding servers or purchasing their own licenses for software and testing tools.

The creation of global markets for software products has introduced new quality concerns in internationalization and localization. Internationalization is a product strategy that attempts to release a product to be used in several countries without any significant engineering changes. Localization is the process of adapting a global product to the needs of a specific region. It would be foolish to develop a software product in one country and release it in another without testing it. One strategy would be to outsource the testing, but there is an inherent loss of control in this type of testing.

Crowdsourcing has become popular in many online communities. Crowdsourcing could be used to engage localization testers dispersed around the globe outside of the development environment. To accomplish this, it is important to find a community that prides itself on its reputation and has a track record of successes. An easy-to-use real-time platform allowing community members to communicate with the project decision makers is also needed to maintain quality. To protect intellectual property, developers might only engage trustworthy community members who are willing to sign nondisclosure agreements (Reuveni, 2012).

2.18 MAINTENANCE AND CHANGE MANAGEMENT

Systems often need to change to remain viable. Maintenance is the software engineering activity charged with modifying software to meet its new functional and non-functional requirements or to repair defects. It is estimated that for many software products more that 50% of the development costs are dedicated to maintenance activities. Maintenance often begins before the product is completed and it is important to have some means of monitoring the effects of the system changes on the quality factors assigned to the product (Mallikarunja et al., 2014).

Maintainability was listed in many of the quality models we discussed earlier in this chapter. Maintainability can be defined as the ease with which developers can modify a software system. This is aided by quality attributes possessed by the system code and documentation that make them easy to understand and easy to see how changes in one system module can impact other modules. Formal change management procedures should be in place to ensure the system changes do not have negative impacts on required system quality attributes. In some cases, uncovering defects during system operation or noticing changes in quality attribute measures can serve as triggers for risk mitigation or SPI activities.

2.19 DEFECT ANALYSIS AND PROCESS IMPROVEMENT

A design defect or a code-smell is defined as a bad design choice that can have a negative impact on the code quality such as maintainability, changeability, and comprehensibility which could introduce bugs (Fowler et al., 1999). Code-smells classify shortcomings in software that can decrease software maintainability. They are also defined as structural characteristics of software that may indicate a code or design problem that makes software hard to evolve and maintain, and trigger refactoring of code. Code-smells are not limited to design flaws since most of them occur in code and are not related to the original design. In fact, most code-smells can emerge during the evolution of a system and represent patterns or aspects of software design that may cause problems in the further development and maintenance of the system.

Code-smells are unlikely to cause failures directly. In general, code-smells make a system difficult to change and this may cause developers to introduce bugs. It is often easier to interpret and evaluate the quality of systems by identifying code-smells than through the use of traditional software quality metrics. In fact, most of the definitions of code-smells are based on situations that are faced daily by developers. Most of the code-smells identify locations in the code that violate object-oriented design heuristics. The 22 Code Smells identified and defined informally by Fowler aim to indicate software refactoring opportunities and "give you indications that there is trouble that can be solved by a refactoring" (Fowler et al., 1999).

Defect counting techniques can sometimes give deceptive readings of software quality. The definition of what is or what is not a defect is not universally agreed upon. Defects are not equally difficult to identify or repair. It is the case that latent defects may linger in program code that has not been thoroughly tested. It is also the case that repairing one software defect may introduce new product defects or uncover serious design defects as they are repaired as suggested previously.

2.20 ROLE OF PRODUCT AND PROCESS METRICS

Several maintainability issues can be detected using quality metrics. The process consists of finding code fragments that violate structural or semantic properties such as the ones related to coupling and complexity. In this setting, internal attributes used to define these properties, are captured through software metrics, and properties are expressed in terms of valid values for these metrics. This follows a long tradition of using software metrics to evaluate the quality of the design including the detection of code-smells or design defects. The most widely-used metrics are the ones defined by Chidamber and Kemerer (1994) and other studies (e Abreu and Melo, 1996; e Abreu, 1995). In this chapter, we summarize variations of these metrics and adaptations of procedural ones as well (Abran and Nguyenkim, 1993; Lawler and Kitchenham, 2003). The list of metrics is described in Table 2.1.

2.21 STATISTICAL SQA

Statistical quality assurance techniques have helped some software organizations achieve a 50% defect reduction annually (Arthur, 1997). Statistical quality assurance reflects a growing trend throughout the industry to become more quantitative about quality. For software engineering, statistical quality assurance implies the following steps:

1. Information about software errors and defects is collected and categorized.
2. An attempt is made to trace each error and defect to its underlying cause.
3. Using the Pareto principle (80% of the defects can be traced to 20% of all possible causes), isolate the 20% (the vital few).
4. Once the vital few causes have been identified, move to correct the problems that have caused the errors and defects.

This relatively simple concept represents an important step toward the creation of an adaptive software process in which changes are made to improve those elements of the process that introduce error (Schulmeyer, 2007).

Six Sigma is one approach to product and process improvement that has gained acceptance in many industries globally, including those focused on software development. The Six Sigma methodology makes use of statistical techniques to improve process capability and reduce product defects. Defects are defined as any product attributes that are outside customer expectations. Removing these defects has the potential to increase the level of customer satisfaction. The metrics chosen are selected because they are aligned with the customer's goals for the product. The product is scored using these metrics. When metric values are not acceptably close to their predetermined values, the software developers suspect a defect may be present. Many of the metrics

Table 2.1 List of Some Quality Metrics

Metrics	Description
Weighted Methods per Class (WMC)	WMC represents the sum of the complexities of its methods
Response for a Class (RFC)	RFC is the number of different methods that can be executed when an object of that class receives a message
Lack of Cohesion of Methods (LCOM)	Chidamber and Kemerer define Lack of Cohesion in Methods as the number of pairs of methods in a class that do not have at least one field in common minus the number of pairs of methods in the class that share at least one field. When this value is negative, the metric value is set to 0
Number of Attributes (NA)	
Attribute Hiding Factor (AH)	AH measures the invisibilities of attributes in classes. The invisibility of an attribute is the percentage of the total classes from which the attribute is not visible
Method Hiding Factor (MH)	MH measures the invisibilities of methods in classes. The invisibility of a method is the percentage of the total classes from which the method is not visible
Number of Lines of Code (NLC)	NLC counts the lines but excludes empty lines and comments
Coupling Between Object classes (CBO)	CBO measures the number of classes coupled to a given class. This coupling can occur through method calls, field accesses, inheritance, arguments, return types, and exceptions
Number of Association (NAS)	
Number of Classes (NC)	
Depth of Inheritance Tree (DIT)	DIT is defined as the maximum length from the class node to the root/parent of the class hierarchy tree and is measured by the number of ancestor classes. In cases involving multiple inheritances, the DIT is the maximum length from the node to the root of the tree
Polymorphism Factor (PF)	PF measures the degree of method overriding in the class inheritance tree. It equals the number of actual method overrides divided by the maximum number of possible method overrides
Attribute Inheritance Factor (AIF)	AIF is the fraction of class attributes that are inherited
Number of Children (NOC)	NOC measures the number of immediate descendants of the class

discusses in the previous section can be tracked and monitored for value changes that might indicate a decline in quality. Root cause analysis is undertaken to determine the process weakness that caused the product defect. The goal is to produce product with zero defects (Siakas et al., 2006).

There is a software engineering specialization of the Six Sigma approach known as Software Six Sigma. Software Six Sigma is based on three principles: focus on customers, process orientation, and leadership based on metrics. It is a management strategy which relies on defect metrics as its main tool to reduce costs and improve customer satisfaction. Before using Software Six Sigma developers must know their customers' needs. The cost savings largely result from avoiding rework caused by delivering defective products and reduced customer satisfaction. The metrics used to monitor defects need to include quality factors that affect the UX (e.g., usability or reliability) as well as counting things like code smells. QFD is often used to keep the development team focused on customer quality goals (Fehlmann, 2003).

The steps for using Six Sigma for process improvement (DMAIC) are listed below.

- Set the goal—*Define*
- Define the metrics—*Measure*
- Measure where you go—*Analyze*
- Improve processes while you go—*Improve*
- Act immediately if going on the wrong path—*Control*

Six Sigma helps to speed up the test and integration parts of product development. It can be used to continuously improve processes and product quality, based on attributes of software products under development. It is an effective project management tool that can provide software engineers with tools to make data-based decisions (Redzic and Biak, 2006). In some cases this process may allow engineers to predict the occurrence of defects before they occur based on their prevalence.

There some reasons why statistical techniques for SQA have not been accepted by software developers. Some developers believe Six Sigma techniques are too complicated or too costly to use on routine projects. Some developers believe that software development does not follow standard processes like those present I manufacturing engineering. Some developers do not grasp the connection between process improvement and product improvement by reducing the points where defects are injected into the product (Siakas et al., 2006).

2.22 CHANGE MANAGEMENT

The easiest way to capture changes applied to program code is to track their execution in the development environment directly. Refactoring tracking can be realized (Ekman and Asklund 2004; Robes, 2007; Koegel et al., 2010) in programming environments. This approach is highly dependent on the environment used since it has to track the refactorings applied. Furthermore, manually performed refactorings may not be detectable since it is possible that changes which have been made obsolete by successive changes might be wrongly indicated. However, one major advantage automatic tracking is that the problem of hidden changes cannot occur, because every change is tracked.

In contrast to change tracking approaches, state-based refactoring detection approaches aim to reveal refactorings a posteriori on the base of the two successively modified versions of a software artifact. The detection of atomic changes on program code has a long history in computer science, but is still an ongoing research topic. Beside these, several approaches are tailored to detect refactorings in program code. For instance, Dig et al. (2008) proposed an approach to detect applied refactorings in Java code. They first perform a fast syntactic analysis, and subsequently, a semantic analysis in which also operational aspects like method call graphs are considered. After preprocessing and syntactical analysis have been conducted, conditions indicating the application of refactoring are evaluated. In Kim et al. (2012), a very recent approach for detecting refactorings improving several open issues of previous approaches has been proposed. In particular, the REF-FINDER tool is capable of detecting complex refactorings, which comprise a set of atomic refactorings using logic-based rules executed by a logic programming engine. However, refactorings which may overlap with atomic changes, referred to as floss refactorings, are only mentioned as future work.

2.23 AGILE DEVELOPMENT PROCESSES

Agile processes are on every software engineer's radar these days. The question of course is how to build software that meets customers' needs today and exhibits the quality characteristics that will enable it to be extended and scaled to meet customers' needs over the long term. Having working software is important. However many software products must also exhibit a variety of quality attributes (e.g., reliability, usability, and maintainability). Many agile concepts are simply adaptations of good software engineering principles. Some agile practices involve departures from traditional software engineering practices. Much that can be gained by considering the best of both approaches when thinking about software quality (Sterling, 2010).

Successful software engineering is sometimes viewed as a discipline dominated by human creativity, market forecasting, value judgments, and uncertainty levels similar to those found in the entertainment industry. In many software projects almost everything can be negotiable (people, funding, requirements, designs, tests, etc.). Quality metrics, while potentially useful, have few accepted benchmarks. With the exception of some quality aspects such as reliability, most aspects of quality (e.g., maintainability or usability) are often measured very subjectively. While quality can be measured very easily late in the development process, the costs of repairing defects is much higher than if they were uncovered before any code was written. Some agile proponents argue that given the uncertain nature of many software estimates that practitioners need more freedom to innovate through automation of measurement, traceability, progress reports, documentation, and change propagation. Practitioners also need to develop control measures and real-time development analytics that have been validated as quality measures (Cantor and Royce, 2014).

Agile process models properly applied do not call for abandoning the documentation and testing of the project artifacts. A key tenet of agile software engineering is its ability to manage changes. Part of this is based on early and frequent customer/stakeholder involvement of the software development team. This makes it easier to keep abreast of changes needed to satisfy the customers. Another part of this is reducing the documentation to the essential minimum, which means only maintaining the artifacts that are actually referred to by developers as the project moves forward. Some agile process models call for daily builds and refactoring after reviewing the latest build results with all stakeholders. Most agile process models also call for early creation of test cases based on the user stories created early in the development process. User stories describe how the software product will be used by a typical end-user to accomplish a specific task.

In agile processes similar to extreme programming (XP) project velocity is determined by keeping track of the number of user stories completed successfully. This makes it easier for developers to recognize when the project schedule is at risk of falling behind. This can be important to help project teams avoid over-commitment of resources, which often contributes to reduction in product quality. Pair programming is another dimension of some agile process models. Not only does this provide the benefits of synergistic problem-solving as the pairs tackle each user story, but it also can provide an opportunity for real-time software quality reviews as the developers review each other's work as it is created. Continuous integration of the pair-developed code into the larger project with the resulting integration and regression testing is another feature of agile processes that can support improved software quality (Beck, 2004).

Agile modeling attempts to add some of the benefits of software modeling to agile process. One claim of modeling is that it can often help to assess the quality of product as it is being engineered and built. Agile modeling is a collection of values, principles, and practices for modeling software that can be applied on a software development project in an effective and light-weight manner. Agile modeling adopts all of the values that are consistent with the agile manifesto. The most important point is that developers must have a purpose for creating a model. In part this means that content contained in a model is more important than its representation, as long as it communicates its meaning to its audience. Agile teams need to feel empowered to adapt the models to meet their needs and the needs of the stakeholders. The agile modeling philosophy recognizes that an agile team must have the courage to make decisions that may cause developers to reject a design and refactor. The team must also have the humility to recognize that technologists do not have all the answers and that the needs of all stakeholders should be respected and embraced by the development team (Ambler, 2002).

2.24 CONCLUSIONS/BEST PRACTICES

SQA is demanding and time consuming work. But it is essential work if developers are to produce software that conforms to its specifications and meets customer expectations. Some of the best practices for testing and SQA are summarized by Vargs and Cordoba (2001).

- Process—It is critical to define and document a process that is robust and endorsed by industry experts when trying to create a quality culture in any organization.
- Management commitment—The organization must be willing to commit the necessary resources (time, people, tools, equipment) needed to meet the quality targets for products under development and for SPI.
- Personal experience—The skills of the project personnel often determine the success of a project and software quality work is no exception to this.
- Deliverables—Requirements, test plans, and test cases must the defined early in the development process so developers create software products from a quality perspective.
- Tool usage—Use of tools to track and manage defects as well as create and execute test cases is requisite to increasing process maturity.
- Metrics—Developing quality metrics to track quality by allowing comparison to quality targets will increase the value and maturity of the V&V processes.
- Testing environment—Must allow developers to reproduce conditions in production environments when processing test cases.
- Test data—Data must be available to developers when the process schedule calls for the execution of the test cases for a component.
- Change management—Testing and development processes must track configuration changes and ensure that products will run in production environments.
- Developer awareness—Every business professional and every developer must be aware of the software quality process and believe that it adds value to their daily work.

This chapter described the importance of making SQA an umbrella activity that impacts all phases of software product development. SQA should begin during requirements gathering and continue during engineering, testing, and deployment regardless of the process used by the developers. Software quality goals should guide the developers as products are maintained and ultimately retired.

Quality is enhanced when requirements are documented and end-users are involved during their creation. Getting the requirements right makes it more likely the customer will be satisfied with the delivered software products. Tracking changes in requirements is important to ensure that the final software products will meet both their functional and quality requirements. The use cases created for a software product early in the software life cycle can provide a good basis for designing the product testing strategy. The test cases created as part of the testing procedures should be traceable to the requirements generated from the use case descriptions.

Continuous improvement should be the goal of every member of the software development organization. It is not enough to claim the use of a documented software quality methodology, compliance to the quality objectives for a product must begin long before testing. Reviews and inspections have been demonstrated as being both cost effective and invaluable in detecting product defects early in the software development cycles. Some agile processes make use of daily reviews for just this reason. Inspections are likely to be more effective when work product standards are defined early. Reviews often uncover defects which may have serious consequences if left uncorrected. For critical systems it is important to perform root cause analysis of these defects to determine any process weaknesses that allowed them to be introduced prior to testing.

The product's functional and non-functional requirements should form the basis of the software validation and verification efforts. Test cases and testing procedures should be formally designed and reviewed. Ad hoc testing is likely to miss potential defects in the software. Test cases should be used to demonstrate both the existence of software functionality and to attempt to uncover new defects. Procedures need to be created to ensure that conformance to the quality requirements is verified. Regression testing must be part of the system change and evolution procedures. Automated testing tools can make regression testing easier.

Presenting a complete exposition of all elements software quality is beyond the scope of this chapter. The remaining chapters in this book cover research on a number of emerging software quality practices.

REFERENCES

Abran, A, Nguyenkim, H, 1993. Measurement of the maintenance process from a demand-based perspective. J. Softw. Maintenance Res. Pract. 5 (2), 63−90.

Abrial, J, 2009. Faultless systems: yes we can!. IEEE Comput. 42 (9), 30−36.

Ambler, S., 2002. What is agile modeling (AM)? <http://www.agilemodeling.com/> (accessed 3.02.15.).

Andreou, A, et al., 2005. Key issues for the design and development of mobile commerce services and applications. Int. J. Mobile Commun. 3 (3), 303−323.

Arthur, L, 1997. Quantum improvements in software system quality. CACM 40 (6), 47−52.

Baaz, A, et al., 2010. Appreciating lessons learned. IEEE Softw. 27 (4), 72−79.

Basili, V. et al., 1994. Using measurement to build core competencies in software. <http://www.cs.umd.edu/∼mvz/handouts/gqm.pdf> (accessed 3.02.15.).

Beck, K., 2004. Extreme Programming Explained: Embrace Change. Addison-Wesley, Massachusetts, USA.

Begel A, DeLine R, Zimmerman T, 2010. Social media for software engineering. In: Proceedings on the Future of Software Engineering Research. ACM, November.

Black, S, et al., 2009. Formal versus agile: survival of the fittest? IEEE Comput. 42 (9), 37−45.

Boehm, B, Basili, V, 2001. Software defect reduction top ten list. IEEE Comput. 34 (1), 135−138.

Boehm, B, et al., 1978. Characteristics of Software Quality. North Holland Publishing, New York, USA.

Breu, R, Kuntzmann-Combelles, A, Felderer, M, 2014. New perspectives on software quality. IEEE Softw. 31 (1), 32−38.

Cantor, M, Royce, W, 2014. Economic governance of software delivery. IEEE Softw. 31 (1), 54−61.

Chidamber, S, Kemerer, C, 1994. A metrics suite for object oriented design. IEEE Trans. Softw. Eng. 20 (6), 476−493.

Chung, L, Leite, J, 2009. On Non-Functional Requirements in Software Engineering Conceptual Modeling: Foundations and Applications. Springer-Verlag, Heidelberg, Germany.

De Almeida, J, Camargo, J, Basseto, B, Paz, S, 2003. Best practices in code inspection for safety-critical software. IEEE Softw. 20 (3), 56−63.

Dig, D, Manzoor, K, Johnson, R, Nguyen, T, 2008. Effective software merging in the presence of object-oriented refactorings. IEEE Trans. Softw. Eng. 34 (3), 321−335.

e Abreu, F., 1995. The MOOD metrics set. In: European Conference on Object-Oriented Programming (ECOOP'95) Workshop on Metrics, Aarhus, Denmark.

e Abreu, F., Melo, W., 1996. Evaluating the impact of object-oriented design on software quality. In: Proceedings of the 3rd International Symposium on Software Metrics: From Measurement to Empirical Results (METRICS'96). IEEE Computer Society, Washington, DC, USA, pp. 90−99.

Ekman, T, Asklund, U, 2004. Refactoring-aware versioning in eclipse. Electron. Notes Theor. Comput. Sci. 107, 57−69.

Ericson, C, 2005. Hazard Analysis Techniques for System Safety. Wiley-Interscience, New Jersey, USA.

Falessi, D, Sabetzadeh, M, Briand, L, Turella, E, Coq, T, Panesar-Walawege, R, 2012. Planning for safety standards compliance: a model-based tool-supported approach. IEEE Softw. 29 (3), 64−70.

Fehlmann, T., 2003. Six sigma for software. <http://citeseerx.ist.psu.edu/viewdoc/download?doi=10.1.1.91.6736&rep=rep1&type=pdf> (accessed 15.01.15.).

Firesmith, D, 2012. Security and Safety Requirements for Software-intensive Systems. Auerbach, Massachusetts, USA.

Fowler, M, Beck, K, Brant, J, Opdyke, W, Roberts, D, 1999. Refactoring—Improving the Design of Existing Code. Addison-Wesley, Massachusetts, USA.

Gage, D., McCormick, J., 2004. We did nothing wrong. Baseline Magazine, March 4, 2004 <http://www.baselinemag.com/c/a/Projects-Processes/We-Did-Nothing-Wrong> (accessed 16.12.14.).

Gardner, D., 2009. Can software development aspire to the cloud? ZDNet.com April 28, 2009 <http://www.zdnet.com/blog/gardner/can-software-development-aspire-to-the-cloud/2915> (accessed 25.10.14.).

Garvin, D, 1984. What does product quality really mean? Sloan Manage. Rev. 1984 (Fall), 25−45.

Gonclaves, L., Linderss, B., 2014. Getting value out of agile retrospectives. Leanpub.

Grady, R, 1992. Practical Software Metrics for Project Management and Process Improvement. Prentice-Hall, New Jersey, USA.

Hall, A, 1990. Seven myths of formal methods. IEEE Softw. 1990 (September), 11−20.

Hardy, T., 2012. Software and System Safety. Authorhouse, Indiana, USA.

Hatton, L, 2007. The chimera of software quality. IEEE Comput. 40 (8), 102−103, 104.

IEEE 1012-2012, 2012. IEEE Standard for System and Software Verification and Validation. <http://standards.ieee.org/findstds/standard/1012-2012.html> (accessed 12.02.15.).

ISO 25010:2011, 2011. System and Software Quality Models. <https://www.iso.org/obp/ui/#iso:std:iso-iec:25010:ed-1:v1:en> (accessed 12.02.15.).

Kim, M, Notkin, D, Grossman, D, Wilson, G, 2012. Identifying and summarizing systematic code changes via rule inference. IEEE Trans. Softw. Eng. 39 (1), 45−62.

Koegel, M, Herrmannsdoerfer, M, Li, Y, Helming, J, Joern, D, 2010. Comparing state and operation-based change tracking on models. In: Proceedings of the IEEE International EDOC Conference.

Korpipaa, P, et al., 2003. Managing context Information in mobile devices. IEEE Pervasive Comput. 2 (3), 42−51.

Kuehlemann, A, 2014. Transforming Test Through Automation. <http://www.it-daily.net/downloads/WP-Coverity-Transforming-Testing-0613.pdf> (accessed 12.02.15.).

Lago, P, et al., 2010. Software architecture: framing stakeholders' concerns. IEEE Software 27 (6), 20−24.

Lawler, J, Kitchenham, B, 2003. Measurement modeling technology. IEEE Softw. 20 (3), 68−75.

Lazaroni, M, et al., 2011. Reliability Engineering. Springer, New York, USA.

Li, J, Stålhane, T, Conradi, R, Kristiansen, J, 2012. Enhancing defect tracking systems to facilitate software quality improvement. IEEE Softw. 29 (2), 59−66.

Mallikarunja, C, et al., 2014. A report on the analysis of software maintenance and impact on quality factors. Int. J. Eng. Sci. Res. 05 (1), 1485−1489.

McCall, J, Richards, P, Walters, G, 1977. Factors in Software Quality (Three volumes, NTIS AD-A) 49-014, 015, 055.

Mead, N, Jarzombek, J, 2010. Advancing software assurance with public−private sector collaboration. IEEE Comput. 43 (9), 21−30.

Mottu, J, Baudry, B, LeBron, Y, 2008. Model transformation testing: oracle issue. In: Proceedings of the 2008 IEEE International Conference on Software Testing Verification and Validation Workshop (ICSTW'08). IEEE Computer Society, Washington, DC, USA, pp. 105−112.

Musa, J, et al., 1987. Engineering and Managing Software with Reliability Measures. McGraw-Hill, New York, USA.

Poth, A, Suyaev, A, 2014. Effective quality management: value and risk-based software quality management. IEEE Softw. 31 (6), 79−85.

Pressman, R S, Maxim, B R, 2014. Software Engineering: A Practitioner's Approach. McGraw-Hill, New York, USA.

Redwine, S, 2010. Fitting software assurance into higher education. IEEE Comput. 43 (9), 41−66.

Redzic, C., Biak, J., 2006. Six sigma approach in quality improvement. In: Proceedings of Fourth International Conference on Software Engineering Research, Management, and Applications (SERA'06), August 2006, pp. 396−406.

Reuveni, D., 2012. Crowdsourcing provides answer to app testing dilemma. <http://www.wirelessweek.com/Articles/2010/02/Mobile-Content-CrowdsourcingAnswer-App-Testing-Dilemma-Mobile-Applications/> (accessed 9.09.15.).

Revelle, J, 2004. Quality Essentials: A Reference Guide from A to Z. ASQ Quality Press, Wisconsin, USA.

Robes, R., 2007. Mining a change-based software repository. In: Proceedings of the Workshop on Mining Software Repositories (MSR'07). IEEE Computer Society, pp. 15−23.

Rokosz, V, 2003. Long-term testing in a short-term world. IEEE Softw. 20 (3), 64−67.

Rooksby, J, et al., 2009. Testing in the wild: the social and organizational dimensions of real world practice. J. Comput. Support. Work 18 (9), 559−580.

Schulmeyer, G, 2007. Handbook of Software Quality Assurance. Artech House, Massachusetts, USA.

Shull, F, 2012. Designing a world at your finger tips: a look at mobile user interfaces. IEEE Softw. 29 (4), 4−7.

Siakas, K. et al., Integrating six sigma with CMMI for high quality software. In: Proceedings of the 14th Software Quality Management Conference (SQM'06), April 2006. British Computer Society, pp. 85−96.

Sinn, R, 2008. Software Security Technologies. Thomson Course Technology, Massachusetts, USA.

Sterling, C, 2010. Managing Software Debt: Building for Inevitable Change. Addison-Wesley, Massachusetts, USA.

Tutelage, M, Dubai, G, 2012. A research study on importance of testing and quality assurance in software development life cycle (SDLC) model. Int. J. Soft Comput. Eng. 2 (3), 251−257.

Vargs, J., Cordoba, J., 2001. 10 best practices for effective testing and QA implementation. Softek Trends & Vision Newsletter 4 (July).

Wiegers, K, 2002. Peer Reviews in Software. Addison-Wesley, Massachusetts, USA.

Wood, D (Ed.), 2012. Principles of Quality Costs. ASQ Quality Press, Wisconsin, USA.

Yacoub, S, 2003. Automated QA for document understanding systems. IEEE Softw. 20 (3), 76−82.

CHAPTER

Defining software quality characteristics to facilitate software quality control and software process improvement

3

I. Fleming
SQA.net, USA; SugarCRM Inc., Cupertino, CA, USA

3.1 OVERVIEW

Philip B. Crosby (Crosby, 1979) defined Quality as *conformance to requirements*, requirements meaning both the product and the customer's requirements. In order to produce a quality product, under this definition, the high-level product requirements are systematically broken down into detailed engineering specifications that will satisfy those requirements. Defining and then breaking down product requirements into measureable specifications facilitates both quality control, throughout the production life cycle, and process improvement initiatives such as CMMI® for development (CMMI®, 2010) and Six Sigma (Tennant, 2001).

In general, the mapping of high-level requirements to measurable engineering specifications can be done via traceability matrices. One popular requirements traceability method is Quality Function Deployment (QFD, Akao, 1994):

> *A method to transform qualitative user demands into quantitative parameters, to deploy the functions forming quality, and to deploy methods for achieving the design quality into subsystems and component parts, and ultimately to specific elements of the manufacturing process.*

The concept of QFD is to cross-reference the high-level qualitative requirements to measureable quantitative specifications (Glib, 1997) that will implement the given requirements. By way of a QFD example, consider the customer requirements for a *chocolate cookie*, one of which could be *good texture*.

The "good texture" customer requirement is qualitative but could be specified in quantitative terms of tensile strength, which is a measure of stress that a material can withstand while being stretched or pulled before failing or breaking. Experiments combined with market research would need to be performed to determine a tensile strength that customers preferred. Once known, the measure of tensile strength, in pounds per square inch (PSI), would be documented against the good texture requirement. Given a specified target PSI the QFD matrix could be further broken down in order to relate ingredients and cooking methods including temperature, time in oven, etc. that would satisfy the PSI specification that in turn satisfies the customer requirement of good texture.

The above example QFD characterization can be used for quality control to ensure the product is being built correctly and to deal with issues at the production step where they occur, rather than wait for the final product to fail. In addition, process improvement initiatives can reference documented repeatable steps and work products with known outcomes (measurements) from which to base any comparisons with outcomes from suggested procedural or ingredient changes.

In software engineering there have been a number of attempts to model and define qualitative requirements as well as quantitative engineering specifications in order to utilize requirements definition and traceability methods such as QFD, for software production. However, given the intangible nature of the software product (Brooks, 1975), the physical quality attributes typically used in manufacturing specifications (dimensions, weight, material, tensile strength, etc.) need to be replaced by more abstract attributes that specify, model, and measure software behavior. These software attribute specifications reference specialized models (complexity models, data flow diagrams, user interaction models, etc.) that are appropriate for the related qualitative software requirement characterizations of functionality, usability, supportability, reliability, and performance, etc.

The problem faced by software quality control professionals is which qualitative model of software requirement quality characteristics to use and how to break down those requirements into quantitative attributes that can be specified and measured, via testing and inspection, during software production. Equally problematic, for software process improvement (SPI) professionals, is establishing causal relationships from software issues to the ways and means of production.

3.2 PROCESS BASED APPROACHES TO SOFTWARE QUALITY

Prior to reviewing software quality characterization models it is worth noting process based approaches to software quality and the relationship these approaches have with software quality characterization. Total Quality Management (TQM, Martínez-Lorente et al., 1998) is a process-centered approach to quality management that has been embodied in SPI frameworks such as the Capability Maturity Model (CMM) for Software (Paulk et al., 1991). Under process-centered approaches to quality management, process performance measures are continually monitored in order to detect (and resolve) unexpected variation. Whilst performance metrics within TQM (or CMM) include *quality of the product* other key process elements are also monitored, including:

- Alignment with organizational mission
- Timely delivery
- Cost reduction
- Cycle time reduction

The software quality characterization model discussion that follows addresses the issues and opportunities for the quality of product measures within TQM (CMM) but does not directly address measurement of the other key elements of those process-centered quality management frameworks. That said the presence of a desired software quality characteristic, such as maintainability, would have an impact on nonproduct performance metrics such as the cost of the maintenance processes.

3.3 REVIEW OF THE STRUCTURE AND UTILITY OF SOFTWARE QUALITY CHARACTERIZATION MODELS

The following is a review of the overall structure and utility of three software quality characterization models: McCall (McCall et al., 1977), Boehm (Boehm et al., 1978) and ISO-9126 (ISO. ISO/IEC IS 9126, 1991). The intention of this review is to articulate and present the common structures of these models that facilitate software quality control during production and enable a continuous process improvement framework. More detailed descriptions of these models, including their comparative merits, can be found in prior studies (Jamwal, 2010; Wagner, 2013).

The three quality models presented in this chapter have been chosen on the basis of explaining a generalized approach to the design and utilization of the software quality characterization paradigm, as the examples given typify the structure and utility of such models. That said there are other notable models (Dromey, 1995; Grady and Caswell, 1987). The ISO-9126 standard has itself been replaced by ISO 25010 (SO/IEC 25010, 2011) although its overall structure and utilization is similar to the ISO-9126, for the purposes of this study.

3.3.1 QUALITY FACTOR PERSPECTIVES AND DEFINITIONS

Each of the models has a broad qualitative definition of the higher-level quality factors that would be desired in a software product. These sets of quality factor definitions are listed for each model, subdivided by *perspectives* for the McCall model and *general utility* categories for the Boehm model, (Tables 3.1, 3.2 and 3.3).

Table 3.1 McCall's 11 High-Level Quality Factors Subdivided by *Perspective*

The product revision perspective

Maintainability	Effort required to locate and fix an error in an operational program
Flexibility	Effort required to modify an operational program
Testability	Effort required to test a program to ensure it performs its intended function

The product transition perspective

Portability	Effort required transferring a program from one hardware configuration and/or software system environment to another
Reusability	Extent to which a program can be used in other applications—related to the packaging and scope of the functions that the various programs perform
Interoperability	Effort required to couple one system with another

The product operations perspective

Correctness	Extent to which a program satisfies its specification and fulfills the user's mission objectives
Reliability	Extent to which a program can be expected to perform its intended function with required precision
Efficiency	The amount of computing resources and code required by a program to perform a function
Integrity	Extent to which access to software or data by unauthorized persons can be controlled
Usability	Effort required to learn, operate, prepare input, and interpret output of a program

The ISO-9126 model, Table 3.3, defines functionality as a separate quality factor. In this sense functionality refers to the essential purpose of the software. Use cases, data flow diagrams, business rules and statements that define the essential operation of a system define functionality. Functionality is either present or absent in a software product whereas the nonfunctional requirements (usability, maintainability, performance, etc.) are present to a degree.

3.3.2 DEFINING CRITERIA FOR QUALITY FACTORS

Regardless of the groupings or definitions of quality factors, each of the models follows a common approach under which the quality factors are decomposed into further defining qualitative criteria.

By way of example McCall's model breaks down the reliability quality factor into the criteria listed in Table 3.4.

This decomposition of the qualitative quality factors occurs on all of the models and continues until the lowest level, which has one or more associated *metrics* that define(s) a quantitative measure that determines the presence or absence of the given defining qualitative criteria.

Table 3.2 Boehm's Seven Quality Factors Subdivided by *General Utility* Categories

As-is utility	
Reliability	Code possesses the characteristic reliability to the extent that it can be expected to perform its intended functions satisfactorily
Efficiency	Code possesses the characteristic efficiency to the extent that it fulfills its purpose without waste of resources
Usability	Code possesses the characteristic usability to the extent that it is reliable, efficient, and human-engineered
Maintainability	
Testability	Code possesses the characteristic testability to the extent that it facilitates the establishment of verification criteria and supports evaluation of its performance
Understandability	Code possesses the characteristic understandability to the extent that its purpose is clear to the inspector
Flexibility	Code possesses the characteristic modifiability to the extent that it facilitates the incorporation of changes, once the nature of the desired change has been determined
Portability	
Portability	Code possesses the characteristic portability to the extent that it can be operated easily and well on computer configurations other than its current one

Table 3.3 ISO-9126 Six High-Level Quality Factors

Functionality	The capability of the software product to provide functions, which meet stated and implied needs when the software is used under specified conditions
Reliability	The capability of the software product to maintain a specified level of performance when used under specified conditions
Usability	The capability of the software product to be understood, learned, used, and attractive to the user, when used under specified conditions
Efficiency	The capability of the software product to provide appropriate performance, relative to the amount of resources used, under stated conditions
Maintainability	The capability of the software product to be modified. Modifications may include corrections improvements or adaptation of the software to changes in environment, and in requirements and functional specifications
Portability	The capability of the software product to be transferred from one environment to another

Table 3.4 McCall's Breakdown of Reliability into Defining Criteria

Error Tolerance	Those attributes of the software that provide continuity of operation under nominal conditions
Consistency	Those attributes of the software that provide uniform design and implementation techniques and notation
Accuracy	Those attributes of the software that provide the required precision in calculations and outputs
Simplicity	Those attributes of the software that provide implementation of functions in the most understandable manner (usually avoidance of practices which increase complexity)

3.3.3 METRICS FOR DEFINING THE PRESENCE OF QUALITY FACTORS

3.3.3.1 Metric versus measurement

The terms metric and measurement in this chapter refer to the (ISO/IEC 14598-1, 1997):

Metric: A quantitative scale and method, which can be used for measurement.

Measurement: The process of assigning a number or category to an entity to describe an attribute of that entity.

Under these definitions a usability metric could be:

The amount of time it takes for a given user type to complete a task.

With an example related usability measurement being:

It should take no longer than 45 s for a novice user (just out of training) to book a sales order.

The metrics referenced within a software quality characterization model can be either internal metrics or external metrics.

Internal metrics: Used to assess or predict the quality, in terms of fitness for purpose, of the completed software product during its production by measuring the intermediate deliverables. Internal metrics relate to measures that are taken via reviews and inspections, which are software quality control verification activities that occur without the software being executed; such verification activities are also referred to as static testing (Kaner et al., 1988).

The following are examples of McCall's internal metrics for the "simplicity" defining criteria, related to the reliability quality factor, as decomposed in Table 3.4:

- Design organized in a top down fashion, the measure is yes or no.
- No duplicate functions, the measure is yes or no.
- Module independence, the processing within a module is not dependent on the source of input or destination of the output. The measure for this metric element is based on the number of modules, which do not comply with this rule.

Table 3.5 Example Quality Factor External Metrics

Usability	A *given user with defined experience* should be able to complete a *task* in less than two minutes
Maintainability	Mean Time To Repair (MTTR). The average time required repairing a failed component
Reliability	Mean Time Between Failure (MTBF). The average elapsed time between failures of a system during operation
Performance	The system response time of a transaction when the system is under a given (specified) load

Other examples of internal metrics include:

- Code complexity (McCabe, 1976)
- Functional cohesion: the degree to which elements in a module belong together (Yourdon and Constantine, 1979)
- Coupling or Dependency: degree to which each program module relies on each one of the other modules (Yourdon and Constantine, 1979).

Compliance with an industry standard, for example (Google Java Style, 2014) could also be used as an internal metric, to predict the presence of a given quality factor, maintainability, in the software under construction.

External metrics: Also referred to as customer, or end-user, metrics. Used to measure the presence of a given quality factor in a completed software product or component. The external metrics can only be determined by executing software during either the dynamic testing (Kaner et al., 1988) phases of the development life cycle or when it is operational in the production environment.

Functionality can in theory be verified via a code walkthrough but in practice the presence or absence of the required functionality, defined as an external metric, is more usefully determined by executing code. External metrics, unlike internal metrics, can be directly related to the higher-level quality factors such as usability or to the lower defining criteria such as accuracy.

Table 3.5 shows example external metrics that could be used to determine the presence or absence of the related quality factor requirement.

3.4 DEFINING AN ORGANIZATION'S SOFTWARE QUALITY CHARACTERIZATION MODEL

The following is a strategy to assist organizations to select, define, and tailor a quality characterization model for software quality control and software process improvement initiatives. The steps presented align with the essential construction (quality factor hierarchy) and components (internal and external metrics) of the three quality models previously described.

3.4.1 STEP 1: DOCUMENT THE QUALITY FACTORS AND MODEL HIERARCHY

For a given organization: the format, hierarchy, and selection of quality factors within the quality characterization model could be based on one of the existing models or could be one that is custom designed.

The decision as to which characterization model to use is a pragmatic one in that it is the consequences of using a given model that determine its value to an organization. For example, if an organization is producing software that has severe consequences for failure (e.g., hospital equipment, etc.) then availability will become an important factor along with emphasized reliability.

Having designed, or selected, a suitable quality characterization model the components of the model and its utilization need to be documented in the organization's centralized standards library.

3.4.2 STEP 2: DOCUMENT THE QUALITY CHARACTERIZATION MODEL'S INTERNAL METRICS

The internal metrics become the verification criteria, used by software quality control, for the presence of a given quality factor's defining criteria during software production. These metrics are also documented in the central standards library together with any relevant supporting document templates, standards, or rules that are related to the internal metric. The metrics and corresponding measurements can take many forms, for example, a yes/no checklist for the presence of desired criteria or reference to a documented set of standards that must be complied with. All of the referenced documentation for the internal metrics must also be documented in a centralized standards library.

3.4.3 STEP 3: DOCUMENT THE QUALITY CHARACTERIZATION MODEL'S EXTERNAL METRICS

The external metrics become the evaluation criteria of a given quality factor during the software testing phase of a project or during the operational life of the software. The external metric's measurement can be documented in the product requirements or related test plans to verify the presence of the given quality factor.

The requirements (functional and nonfunctional) themselves are broken down by quality factors so that the quality model defined in a standards library becomes a template for the software products requirement's structure. There should be standard descriptions for metrics that are related to a given quality factor but the actual measurements to be used are unique to the product (project) and as such need to be documented in relation to the individual product requirements.

3.4.3.1 Which external metrics should be documented as requirements?

External metrics are always used to gather measurements in order to assess the presence of a given quality factor. This gathering and monitoring is performed wherever the system is being used, either during testing pre-release software or during its operational usage. That said a decision as to which external metrics are documented as product requirements needs to be taken and this is a pragmatic one, which is dependent on the consequences of failure or lack of a specified requirement being present in the product.

Functionality will have a series of external metrics (documented as measureable test cases) to verify its presence in the product and these tests will be related to the product requirements. Inclusion of the nonfunctional quality factor measurements as requirements, that have to be satisfied, can be done when pertinent and material to the systems operation. For example if certain availability or performance levels are considered critical to operations, then those measures should be specified as product requirements.

3.4.3.2 Which external metrics should be subjected to dynamic testing?

The previous section examined which external quality metrics should be included in the product requirements, whether or not the measurements are taken from dynamic software testing pre-production or during the operational life of the software. The question of which quality factor external metrics should be tested prior to operational use is a separate issue from whether or not the external metric is included as a requirement to be *tested or observed.*

All functional external metric measurements, defined as test cases, should be tested prior to release. The following quality factors, however, are examples of external metric measurements that can only be taken by observing running software (which could be pre- or postproduction):

- Reliability
- Maintainability
- Flexibility.

There are other quality factors that can be tested as the software is being built, examples of these include:

- Usability
- Performance.

For the above external metric measurements, separate test plans can be produced to cross-reference the quality factors documented in the requirements. Where there is a specific requirement for a testable quality factor, expressed as an external metric measurement, then that test should be executed prior to production release.

The following is an example of a testable usability external metric measurement:

- Usability: a *novice* (the term *novice* to be defined) entry clerk should be able to book a sales order in less than 45 s, after reading the online documentation.

3.5 SOFTWARE QUALITY CONTROL'S UTILIZATION OF THE QUALITY CHARACTERIZATION MODEL

The following lists the software quality control activities, broken down by a generic development life cycle, that utilizes a given organization's software quality characterization model. The generic development life cycle presented does not imply a waterfall approach (Royce, 1970) and is also applicable to a development life cycle based on agile best practices (Beck et al., 2001).

3.5.1 SYSTEMS ANALYSIS

The product requirements document is subjected to review by software quality control. The review procedure itself, together with the requirements templates and internal metrics used in the review, should all be documented in the organizations standards library. The following are examples of aspects to be reviewed, which would have supporting internal metrics and measurements:

- Conformance to the documented standard format
- Completeness, in terms of containing all required quality factor sections (Functionality, usability, reliability etc.)
- Lack of ambiguity
- Each requirement is separately labeled (for later traceability)
- Each requirement, functional and nonfunctional, is measureable (based on an external metric).

3.5.2 SYSTEMS DESIGN

The systems design document(s) contain the basic architecture, modules, to be implemented and are also subjected to review by software quality control. The review procedure is similar to the products requirement review and the procedure itself with supporting documentation should be documented in the organization's standards library. The following are examples of system design aspects to be reviewed, which would have supporting internal metrics.

- Conformance to standard format
- Traceability, cross-reference, of requirement to design feature
- Modules are loosely coupled
- Modules are functionally cohesive.

3.5.3 DEVELOPMENT

The code itself is also subjected to software quality control in the form of static testing consisting of inspections and reviews. The review of the source code includes the following, which relate to format of the code as well as the presence of applicable internal metrics and measurements for the related quality factors:

- Code complexity
- Is the code structured as per guidelines?
- Use of go to statements
- Is the code documented as per standards?

3.5.4 TESTING THE PRESENCE OF EXTERNAL METRICS FOR A GIVEN QUALITY FACTOR

Code execution, dynamic testing, to determine the presence of the required quality factors takes place at various stages of the software life cycle and can be performed by quality control personnel and developers.

The following are types of testing that reflect the systems architecture and follow the overall construction and assembly of the software components into the final product:

- Unit testing
- Interface testing
- System testing.

Although the majority of dynamic testing, especially for commercial data processing systems, will be focused on functionality the following quality factors can also be tested for each of the types of architectural testing noted.

- Usability testing (needs to be a GUI component)
- Performance testing
- Security (intrusion) testing.

3.6 SPI UTILIZATION OF THE QUALITY CHARACTERIZATION MODEL

SPI's usage of software quality characterization models centers around the effectiveness of the procedures and standards used during software production at achieving their related quality factor requirements which are defined and measured using external metrics.

3.6.1 MEASURING AND MONITORING QUALITY FACTORS AND RELATED METRICS

During testing or operations, measurements based on external metrics can be evaluated to determine the presence of a given quality factor. As noted each quality factor can have one or more external metrics that measure the presence of the required quality factor in operational software. Whilst some of the quality factors (functionality, usability, and performance) can be measured by the presence or absence of defects, others are measured by the cost or effort involved in performing a given activity. The quality factors that are measured by the cost of performing some action include:

- Testability
- Flexibility
- Maintainability.

Whether the quality factor is measured by the presence of defects or resources being used, Key Performance Indicators (KPIs) (Parmenter, 2007) can be established to monitor the frequency or average cost of these measured events. In this way defect rate or resources consumed to complete a given task can be monitored and used as a potential indication that issues exist with software production.

Care should be taken, due to the essential difficulties of software (Brooks, 1975), in drawing conclusions from causal relationships between the means of production, measured by internal metrics, and KPIs monitoring the quality factor measurements based on external metrics taken during the software's operation. Although the internal metrics represent the measure for best practices of achieving the presence of the given quality factor, there are many other causal variables to changes in KPI. These other causal variables include:

- Volume of code being changed or implemented
- Complexity of code being changed or implemented
- Inter dependencies between other systems and changed code
- Programmer and testers expertise
- Variations in system usage.

Whilst it is possible to incorporate qualifying variables as common denominators when defining a KPI, the complexity of the code changed together with the other potential causal factors is so variable that KPIs can only be used as a basic indication that issues might be present with the related means of software production.

Whenever a software production process issue is suspected, by monitoring the KPIs, or a change to the production procedures and standards is being considered, then a formal process improvement initiative should be undertaken in order to analyze, understand, and make any appropriate changes.

3.6.2 PROCESS IMPROVEMENTS RELATED TO SOFTWARE QUALITY CHARACTERIZATION MODELS

When a potential area for process improvement has been identified then a project should be formed to manage the improvement. Six Sigma (Tennant, 2001) has a project methodology specifically for improving an existing process. The Six Sigma project methodology, DMAIC, for process improvement consists of the following stages:

Define the system, the voice of the customer and their requirements, and the project goals, specifically.

Measure key aspects of the current process and collect relevant data.

Analyze the data to investigate and verify cause-and-effect relationships. Determine what the relationships are, and attempt to ensure that all factors have been considered. Seek out root cause of the defect under investigation.

Improve or optimize the current process based upon data analysis using techniques such as design of experiments to create a new, future state process. Set up pilot runs to establish the process capability.

Control the future state process to ensure that any deviations from the target are corrected before they result in defects.

The terms *process capability* and *deviations from target* are significant within formal Statistical Process Control (Shewart, 1931) techniques, which were originally targeted at the process of manufacturing a physical product. For the purposes of defining process capability and process control of the procedures related to software product quality, a less formal approach can be taken. Within software production and monitoring, capability refers to the KPIs for external metrics being within certain ranges whilst process control refers to monitoring the internal metrics results for inconsistencies, which might lead to an issue in the software product.

Having set a goal for the process improvement project, in the form of a problem definition, root cause analysis of a given defect should be performed. As previously noted, in issues with the highly variable and volatile software environment, it is more useful to focus on individual cases (defects or resource consumption) and analyze a particular event rather than to draw conclusions from the overall defect and resource usage KPI trends.

For analysis and potential improvement the defect, or resource consumption, should be categorized as:

- Quality factor impacted: Functionality, Usability, Testability and Reliability, etc.
- Originating production stage: Requirements, Specification and Coding
- Likely cause(s): Misunderstood requirements, coding error, cross-contamination, i.e., regression, lack of modularity, etc.

The goal of the process improvement project for software quality characterization is to identify procedures and standards that are subjected to verification by software quality control, using internal metrics during the software's production, and increase their *effectiveness* in producing the associated quality factor in the finished product.

Care should be taken, by using such techniques as design of experiments (Baily, 2008), that any change to the procedures and standards is really an improvement that can be measured. By way of example, if a new coding standard is being proposed as a potential improvement to maintainability then a number of programs could be written to the new standard and evaluated for readability by a representative team of programmers. Other causal variables that are outside of the software quality characterization model context, such as programmer experience, could be documented and utilized elsewhere in training or minimum job requirements, etc.

3.7 CONCLUDING REMARKS

Application of manufacturing based quality control techniques that rely on the predictability of the quality of the final product, by measuring intermediate work components, is problematic for software production. The abstract, invisible nature of software, together with its dynamic and highly variable development and operational environments, create issues for software product characterization as well as issues with establishing causal relationships between the means of production and the quality of the finished product.

Selection of a suitable software quality characteristic model, together with understanding, documenting, and measuring the casual relationships between production procedures and the desired quality factors in the final product, is essential for any organization wanting to implement a proactive software quality control capability that can be subjected to process improvement.

REFERENCES

Akao, Y., 1994. Development history of quality function deployment. The Customer Driven Approach to Quality Planning and Deployment. Asian Productivity Organization, Minato, Tokyo, ISBN 92-833-1121-3.

Baily, R.A., 2008. Design of Comparative Experiments. Cambridge University Press, Cambridge, UK, ISBN 978-0521-68357-9.

Beck, K. et al., 2001. Available from <http://agilemanifesto.org> (retrieved October 2014).

Boehm, B.W., Brown, J.R., Kaspar, H., Lipow, M., McLeod, G., Merritt, M., 1978. Characteristics of Software Quality. North Holland Publishing, Amsterdam, the Netherlands.

Brooks, 1975. The Mythical Man Month. Addison-Wesley, Reading, MA, Chapter 14.

CMMI®, 2010. CMMI Product Team: CMMI for Development, Version 1.3 (CMU/SEI-2010-TR-033). Carnegie Mellon University, Software Engineering Institute, Pittsburgh, PA.

Crosby, 1979. Quality is Free. McGraw-Hill, New York, NY, ISBN 0-07-014512-1.

Dromey, R.G., 1995. A model for software product quality. IEEE Trans Softw Eng 21 (2), 146−162.

Glib, T., 1997. Quantifying the qualitative: how to avoid vague requirements by clear specification language. Requirenautics Quarterly, British Computer Society, UK, 12, 9−13.

Google Java Style, 2014. Available from: <https://google-styleguide.googlecode.com/svn/trunk/javaguide.html> (retrieved October 2014).

Grady, R.B., Caswell, D.L, 1987. Software Metrics: Establishing a Company-wide Program. Prentice-Hall, Inc, Upper Saddle River, NJ.

ISO/IEC 14598-1, 1459. Information Technology—Evaluation of Software Products—Part 1 General Guide. International Organization for Standardization, Geneva, Switzerland.

ISO/IEC 25010, 2011. Systems and Software Engineering—Systems and Software Quality Requirements and Evaluation (SQuaRE)—System and Software Quality Models. International Organization for Standardization, Geneva, Switzerland.

ISO. ISO/IEC IS 9126, 1991. Software Product Evaluation—Quality Characteristics and Guidelines for their Use. International Organization for Standardization, Geneva, Switzerland.

Jamwal Dr, D., 2010. Analysis of software quality models for organizations. Int J Latest Trends Comput 1 (2), (E-ISSN: 2045-5364) 19.

Kaner, C., Nguyen, H.Q., Falk, J., 1988. Testing Computer Software, second ed. Thomson Computer Press, Boston, MA, ISBN 0-47135-846-0.

Martínez-Lorente, A.R., Dewhurst, F., Dale, B.G., 1998. Total quality management: origins and evolution of the term. The TQM Magazine. MCB University Publishers Ltd, Bingley, UK.

McCabe, 1976. A complexity measure. IEEE Trans Softw Eng, 308−320.

McCall, J.A., Richards, P.K., Walters, G.F., 1977. Factors in Software Quality, Volumes I, II, and III. US Rome Air Development Center Reports, US Department of Commerce, USA.

Parmenter, D., 2007. Key Performance Indicators. John Wiley & Sons NJ, ISBN 0-470-09588-1.

Paulk, M.C., Curtis, B., Chrissis, M.B., Averill, E.L., Bamberger, J., Kasse, T.C., et al., 1991. Capability Maturity Model for Software. CMU/SEI-91-TR-24. Carnegie Mellon University, Software Engineering Institute, Pittsburgh, PA.

Royce, W., 1970. Managing the development of large software systems. Proceedings of IEEE WESCON 26 (August), 1−9.

Shewhart, W.A., 1931. Economic Control of Quality of Manufactured Product. D. Van Nostrand Company, New York, NY, ISBN 0-87389-076-0.

Tennant, G., 2001. Six Sigma: SPC and TQM in Manufacturing and Services. Gower Publishing Ltd, Farnham, UK, ISBN 0-566-08374-4.

Wagner, S., 2013. Software Product Quality Control: Chapter 2 Quality Models. Springer, Berlin, Germany, ISBN 978-3-642-38570-4.

Yourdon & Constantine, 1979. Structured Design: Fundamentals of a Discipline of Computer Program and Systems Design. Yourdon Press, Upper Saddle River, NJ, ISBN 0-13-854471-9.

Quality management and software process engineering

4

Nikhil R. Zope[1], Kesav V. Nori[2], Anand Kumar[3], Doji Samson Lokku[4], Swaminathan Natarajan[3] and Padmalata V. Nistala[4]

[1]*Tata Consultancy Services, Andheri (E), Mumbai, Maharashtra, India* [2]*International Institute of Information Technology, Hyderabad, Telangana, India* [3]*Tata Consultancy Services, TCS Innovation Labs—Tata Research Development and Design Centre, Pune, Maharashtra, India* [4]*Tata Consultancy Services, Hyderabad, Telangana, India*

4.1 MOTIVATION

A large Software Service Provider can have thousands of ongoing software projects. Each project has customer specific deliverables. For a Software Service Provider, this means that every project must have a custom process to produce custom deliverables that have acceptable quality.

- For a Software Service Provider to make and manage commitments to its customers, its software processes must be under statistical control. This is axiomatic in CMU SEI (Software Engineering Institute)'s CMMI (Capability Maturity Model Integration) framework (Watts, 1989) and is one of the basic needs in the study of processes as advocated by Deming. This is necessary for asserting *process qualities*.
- Deming's second principle in design of industrial processes—"*Process Step−Product Quality*": each product quality is built through the process, not tested for after-the-fact; this is made possible when *every* process step correlates with some product quality. A process step that does not correlate with anything that leads to a desirable (acceptable) product quality can be eliminated from the process with no observable impact. Japan's quality revolution can be attributed to *systemic* absorption of these ideas in all their industrial processes.
- A Computer Science manifestation of the above second principle emerged in the *Structured Programming* movement in the late 60s and the 70s: the Proof (of Correctness) is the Process (of Design and Development of Programs) (Floyd, 1967; Hoare, 1969; Dahl et al., 1972; Wirth, 1972,1974). This was

echoed later in the use of temporal logic to prove temporal properties of reactive programs during their development in Esterel (Gérard & Georges, 1992) leading to their slogan *WYPIWYE* (*What You Prove Is What You Execute*).

CMMI models are collections of best practices that help organizations to improve their processes. It is based on the erstwhile proposed Capability Maturity Model defining maturity levels of process management. The five levels of maturity in increasing level of maturity are: Initial, Managed, Defined, Quantitatively managed, and Optimizing. CMMI models are developed by product teams with members from industry, government, and the SEI from Carnegie Mellon University. SEI has taken the process management premise, "the quality of a system or product is highly influenced by the quality of the process used to develop and maintain it," and defined CMMs that embody this premise (CMMI-DEV, 2010). CMMI for Development (the CMMI relevant from the software development perspective) consists of best practices that address development activities applied to products and services (CMMI-DEV, 2010). It addresses practices that cover the product's life cycle from conception through delivery and maintenance. The emphasis is on the work necessary to build and maintain the total product (CMMI-DEV, 2010).

However, CMU SEI's CMMI framework (Watts, 1989) does not adequately address the "Process Step–Product quality" principle. The only commitments discussed in the CMMI framework are in relation to process qualities, for which a maturity framework is devised. The problem is further compounded by the fact that correctness is not the only product property of interest to Software Engineering; performance, availability, reliability, usability, maintainability, etc., are all equally important to practice, so much so that correctness is taken for granted by users in the problem domain. In terms of the Kano model (Kano et al., 1984) of classification of product qualities, functionality (correctness) is a property whose absence is unacceptable, but whose presence does not get any brownie points from the customer; the engineering (nonfunctional) properties of software are the differentiators and delighters.

In this book chapter we focus on assuring both product and process qualities through engineering of the process. We assume software is designed correctly; the software design part is discussed in other chapters. With the correct software design, post facto testing for software quality complements our approach in removing residual errors. Our approach has been developed in a large IT organization executing thousands of projects with a variety of clients. In such context detailed planning and discipline is necessary.

The chapter is organized as follows. We first present our notion of processes in Section 2 in order to set the context and specific meaning we have attached to ideas, followed by approaches used for quality management in Section 3. From thereon we get into software specific discussions. In Section 4, we briefly discuss software process and popular life cycle models, followed by software quality characteristics in Section 5. In Section 6 we further elaborate our approach towards engineering the software process for software quality assurance. We have divided Section 6 into four subsections. In first subsection we explain various phases and the rationale behind these phases and responsibilities within phases. In the second subsection we discuss how progress in software process can be managed within various software life cycle models followed by specific quality related approach and responsibility management. In the third subsection we discuss how process qualities in software development are addressed. In the last subsection we discuss constraints. Finally we present the conclusion in Section 7.

4.2 OUR NOTION OF PROCESS

A process has *outcomes*, the *destination* of the process. On the other side of the coin, a process is a *journey*. Both the *destination* and the *journey* have associated notions of quality. These qualities can be referred to as qualities of the outcome of the process and process qualities (performance parameters like time, cost, robustness, etc.), respectively. The outcome of a process must be at least of Acceptable quality. The realizations of these qualities make the process acceptable. Acceptable quality is the minimum expected quality (combination of different quality parameters with expected values) of the product/service for which customer of the product/service is willing to use the product/service. The principal qualities of the software development process are time and cost. Acceptability of these qualities means a fit of these values as acceptable to the vendor who executes these development phases and to the customer who outsources the work. The product design process that closely interleaves with the development process is our way of discussing software quality (ISO, 2011). These have to be correlated with the contract agreed upon by the customer and vendor. Clearly separating out the concern for software design from the development of the software and how this development process utilizes software design through fine interleave is a key contribution from our proposed approach.

A performed process manifests at least a sequence of activities. There could be multiple streams of sequential activities, indicating that these streams of activities are largely independent of each other. Processes can be identified at multiple levels of abstractions and granularity. A process can be represented in a hierarchical manner where it is comprised of multiple steps and each step can be decomposed into multiple comprising steps. An understanding of a process defined in this way requires an understanding of each of the different levels of hierarchy and abstraction and such a hierarchical representation of process can be considered as the Process/Work-Breakdown-Structure (WBS).

Process steps signify progress towards a final state of the outcome of the process. Each process step is a unit of work. The *progress* of a process is manifest through the *Goods and/or Services (Outcome of the Process)* with perceivable aspects of acceptable quality that every activity has as its outcome. This perception is inline with Deming's notion that every process step is meaningful only if it has a planned effect on outcome quality (Deming, 2000). Progress can therefore be conceived with configuration items of the outcome becoming manifest with requisite quality. Configuration items are recognized outcomes from the process like code, documents, software components, etc. Also, aligned with this idea of outcome quality, every process step contributes to process quality, such as *speed* of progress, *cost* of step, *availability and utilization of resources*, and *risk* of things going wrong. Process, therefore, has with it a *strategy* that dictates its manner of progress. Cost, time (speed of progress), planning for availability of resources, risk, agreed upon notions of acceptability, are all input parameters to such strategic analysis.

Activities in a process have enabling conditions resulting in ordering of activities in the process. Ordering of activities in a process is thus determined by these information flows characterized by the flow of configuration items designed as part of the outcome of the process. Another mechanism that affects the ordering of process steps in a process is dependencies. Dependencies exist within and across processes. They arise due to constraints put by resource sharing, resource availability at execution time, time and money constraints, and other management constraints. One example of dependencies can be seen as scheduling constraints.

A Process has a *lifetime*—from the start of the first activity of the process to the termination of the last activity of the Process. A Process is a set of related activities: we choose each activity being internally coherent and having professional responsibilities, as a principle for Process Design. Professional responsibilities are the responsibilities towards achieving the desired functional and nonfunctional properties from the activities for the software. Such an activity, called a *phase*, has internal professional responsibility. A Process produces Goods and/or Services as its outcomes. The outcomes have their own respective Qualities and Configurations. This separation of concerns in processes, this delineation, is essential for Quality Management, as it focuses on the professional competence and/or experience needed to undertake the said activity. Also, this separation of concerns is essential because it highlights a two-way relationship, a two-way dependency of information needed to effect completion of the activity of a phase, one for enabling the phase, and the other concerns for knowledge of the information used in the succeeding phase.

Figure 4.1 pictorially represents the different elements in a process and relationships between them.

We can understand the metamodel shown in Figure 4.1 in the context of the software process. A Software Process (SP) consists of various process steps. As we have discussed earlier, a collection of such steps denoting an area of professional responsibilities, is called a phase. The process step in this diagram denotes such phases with each phase consisting of process steps hierarchically which contain more process steps. The SP when performed results in software with desired qualities (process outcome qualities) and properties of the software process (process qualities) like time, cost, etc. Performing each activity in software process

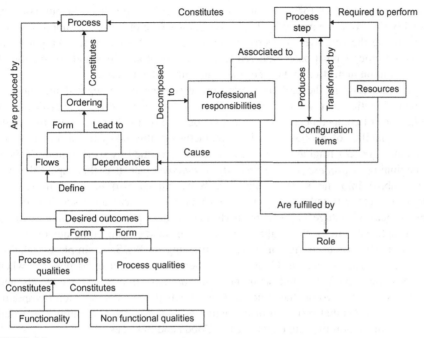

FIGURE 4.1

Process and its elements.

Adapted from Zope & Nori, 2008.

may require resources like machine, software, etc. and results in configuration items like documents, code files, or components, etc. Each process step signifies some professional responsibility like coding or testing or architecting which is fulfilled by a person playing the respective role. Ordering of the process steps, phases within the software process, is dependent on the flow of configuration items defined (i.e., the completeness of documents or programs required in each iteration) and dependencies generated due to resources management. Flow in specific context of software development is represented through progress model, discussed in detail in Section 4 and Section 6.2 of this chapter.

4.3 QUALITY MANAGEMENT

We discuss Quality Management here from the process perspective. We consider Quality Management as consisting of Quality Control and Quality Assurance. The American Society of Quality defines Quality Control as observation techniques and activities used to fulfill requirements for quality and defines Quality Assurance as the planned and systematic activities implemented in a quality system so that quality requirements for a product or service will be fulfilled. In our context, Quality Control is supported by Tools and Competence of people in supporting and performing the activities correctly while for Quality Assurance to take place the software process must be engineered to elicit the right activities and association of configuration items that makes the final outcome of the process.

As remarked in the earlier section, processes can be segregated into professional activities that we call phases. Such segregation indicates a professional coherence of competence. Next, a process could be focused on the work that leads to acceptability of an outcome. In manufacturing, this takes the form of work-systems—process fragments centered on tasks performed by workstations. This is a beginning of *process focus on quality of outcome*, and it is this aspect that we can imbibe into the software process. Workstations also have an impact on organized orchestrated use of tools, which provide a clear understanding of the mechanical advantage enjoyed by performance of a process task, and jointly a clear understanding of the quality induced, even standardized in the outcome.

A process has a configuration too, expressing its WBS. A simple correlation between a process and the Goods and/or Services it produces is possible when WBS is strongly correlated with the configuration structure of its Goods and Services. In other words, the structure that reflects process composition (temporal) of the fragments that reflected in the activities of the WBS, is strongly correlated to the composition of components of the Goods and Services.

Process Quality Management of the process is based on association of appropriate quality parameters to activities within WBS, the simplest being Speed and Cost to the owner of the process and derivations thereof. *Outcome Quality Management* of Goods and Services is reflected by association of appropriate quality parameters to the configuration items in their configuration structure. Consider configuration items to be components of Goods and Services. The tags associated with components usually depict the nonfunctional requirements (NFRs) to be satisfied by acceptable outcomes of the process. A classical *divide-and-conquer* strategy indicates that the segmentation of a component into sub-components is a result of the *divide* part of the strategy, and the *conquer* is a reflection of the composition part of the strategy, that asserts the quality tags. This divide-and-conquer strategy in outcome design leads to the WBS in process design. Outcome design translates into Quality Management for the purposes of delivering benefits to the recipient of the outcomes, whereas Quality Management first creates benefits to the vendor who carries out the process, which may pass on to the recipient of the outcome.

Processes are engineered with respect to tangible or measurable outcomes. Maturity in understanding the nature of value and satisfaction arising from outcomes, arise from *hazarding* measures for them, based on subjective experience and interviewing beneficiaries.

Complementing the above approach to bring out focus on quality through the divide-and-conquer strategy there are some common abstractions in processes that can be utilized for quality management. *Standards* are enforceable patterns of processes. We comply with standards. They usually arise from analysis of past experience. Compliance can be tested, inspected, and audited. This is a part of Quality Management. *Practices* are locally discerned patterns of activities. Here, locality is with respect to project, or scope of professional work. If *standards* and *practices* are amenable to formal analysis, then Quality Management can move from Quality Control to Quality Assurance. *Best Practices* are deemed by local experts as patterns of activities that are standards for the organization, or even the industry as a whole. Hence, they come into the realm of standards for the purposes of Quality Management. Internal to an organization, or to an industry, there could be several alternate patterns of activity to achieve an objective. These, we term as *Guidelines*. Guidelines are, like practices, specific to an organization or industry that should be complied to if applicable. If they are ignored in any specific circumstance, then there should be an accompanying explanation to the audit team.

Constraints in process performance arise from enabling information flows, strategies that direct its progress, and negotiation of acceptability of its outcomes. Further constraints arise when there is failure of any kind, be it with information flows, resources, their appropriateness and availability, improper process tasks, and their aggregations thereof, not resulting in acceptable process or outcome quality. Such risks of failure need to be appropriately mitigated in the engineering of the process.

4.4 SOFTWARE PROCESS (SP)

Section 2 has discussed essential information about processes, their constraints, their lifetimes, their strategies, their progress, and the resources needed to perform them. We now turn our attention to a specific class of processes, so that we can specialize these ideas to the SP. At the outset, we call abstractions for higher level activities as *phases*, and activities that cannot be broken down further as *tasks*. A group of related tasks that accomplish a meaningful subgoal, makes use of tools to contain effort and standardize quality form a *work-system*. Goal decomposition in a process is seen in terms of succession of activities performable by defined work-systems. That is, phases and work-systems are process abstractions, and tasks are *primitives* of a process. Phases can be identified with *professional responsibilities*, and work-systems can be identified with *technical goals* in partial fulfillment of professional responsibilities. Tasks can be identified with professional responsibilities of role-playing professionals.

In SP, all we know before engaging in software design are requirements to be met, and how they will be met emerges as we go along performing the tasks in SP. We can therefore conceive SP to be fine interleave between Software Design (SD), Software Design Process (SDP), and Software Construction Process (SCP). A related concern is the relative ordering of process execution, or more generally, the *progress model* for processes. In general, a process is *ready* to make progress when the input information needed for its execution is available. Process execution can select among ready processes based on the available resources.

The primary processes involved in software engineering—requirements, design, implementation, etc.—are connected by information flow dependencies: the results from requirements are an input to design; the results from design are an input to implementation, and so on. If the progress model is dictated primarily by these information flow dependencies, so that there is an attempt to fully establish the requirements before proceeding to design and so on, the result is the classic *waterfall* model (Sommerville, 2011) of progress.

As it happens, there are also some other information flow dependencies among processes besides the primary data flow referred to above. For example, design analysis information about achievable performance, reliability, etc. may influence requirements. Implementation convenience and technological aspects may influence design, as well as the need to support particular verification interfaces. In general, particular process decisions often do depend on decisions in other processes. Even cyclic dependencies are possible, where there may be mutual dependencies, for example, among collections of requirements and design decisions. A related consideration is information availability from the context, and the possibility of changes, for example, stakeholder needs, preferred tradeoffs, external interfaces and dependencies; relevant available technologies may all become clearer or evolve as the project proceeds.

Dealing with change and cyclic dependencies is easier with the *iterative* or *evolutionary* model of progress. The processes are viewed as a network of activities connected by information flows. Processes are allowed to make progress even if they have partial or uncertain information available to them, so that the outputs they generate may provide inputs to other processes. This requires additional iterations of process activities when refined inputs become available to them. Process execution proceeds until the network reaches quiescence, that is, the outputs of each process are consistent with its inputs, leading to an end-to-end network of consistent outcomes from stakeholder needs and requirements to the operational system. In iterative and evolutionary models, the outcomes from each process become successively more *mature* as the quality and certainty of the input information available to it increases.

A related consideration is that of project risks. These include technical feasibility risk, market risk, requirements risk, change risk (obsolescence due to changes in context during the development process), etc. The progress model can be adapted to mitigate risks or retire them early in the life cycle (to minimize wasted investments). In the *spiral* model (Boehm, 1988), progress is governed primarily by risk considerations: the activities performed early are precisely those required to address the major sources of project risk. *Agile* life cycle models (Beck et al., 2001) are designed primarily to mitigate requirements and change risk by shortening the development life cycle and creating direct and immediate contact between development teams and users.

Thus we can consider that the choices of life cycle/progress models are being driven primarily by risk considerations. There are different information risks (cyclic dependencies, unavailability of input information, uncertainty, change risk), and the progress model is determined by the dominant source of perceived risks.

- If all needed input information is available and change is limited (low overall information risk), then the waterfall model minimizes rework and delivers the best efficiency.
- If there are complex information dependencies and more change risk, then iterative or evolutionary models are more appropriate.
- If requirements risk and change risk is high, then the agile model is the strongest at mitigating these.
- If other project risks are dominant, then the spiral approach is better suited.

Under the cover of this strategic choice emanating from risk management, we now proceed in unraveling the phases of the software process. We do so by first choosing to look at these phases as seen in the Waterfall Model, as it is the most efficient one, when information flow conditions are met perfectly, and the progress model is clearly perceivable. The Waterfall Model is a simple sequence of professional Forward Engineering phases:

- Requirements Engineering and Management;
- Engineering Technical Specifications;
- System Architectural Design;
- Software Architectural Design;
- System Engineering Design;
- Software Engineering Design;
- Software Construction Engineering;
- Software Installation Engineering;
- Software Commissioning Engineering;
- Software Operations Engineering;
- Software Maintenance Engineering;
- Software Re(verse) Engineering.

4.5 SOFTWARE QUALITY

The quality of a software system is the degree to which the system satisfies the stated and implied needs of its various stakeholders, and thus provides value. It is a characterization of the software behavior and is a function of (i) outcomes of the software system, (ii) impact of the software system on its stakeholders, (iii) measure of the degree of satisfaction of customer needs, and (iv) measure of the capabilities of the software system to allow users accomplish tasks in real world. All the things that exist in the software system that contribute to the creation of value to stakeholders and are the carriers of value are considered as the various qualities of the system. It measures the excellence of the software system in a chosen dimension and is the basis for satisfying its stated purpose.

Traditionally, software quality is the degree to which the system satisfies the stated and implied needs of its various stakeholders; we extend it to state that software quality is the degree to which the system is able to deliver value to its stakeholders. In this case, it is the responsibility of software architects to identify those qualities that are of value and infuse them into the software system by design. When quality software systems are deployed and used by customers, they would then "appropriate" value. Therefore, architects need to establish quality characteristics that the system should have in order to be acceptable to all its stakeholders and also establish correlation between values desired by the various stakeholders and the proposed quality characteristics of the software system. There may be many-to-many relationships between qualities and value and satisfaction of these relationships during realization asserts that the solution delivers desired value.

As stated earlier, stakeholders' value arises from a set of qualities of the solution, such as functionality, integration, performance, security, usability, business continuity, response time, regulatory compliance, reusability, etc. There may be multiple instances of the quality in the system, for example, response time for different transactions, different aspects of security, etc. and each of the instances need to be identified separately. In essence, all the quality characteristics that are critical for the solution need to be identified and their interrelationships worked out. For each of these qualities, there must be a way of asserting their design. However, not all of the qualities might be of value from the customers point of view, some of them might be trivial, some of them noninteresting and some of them delightful. Therefore, it is necessary to find appropriate qualities which when present in the software system will deliver the desired value to stakeholders when the software system is put to use. As reference quality characteristics, either the ISO 9126 (ISO, 1991) or the subsequent ISO 25010 (ISO, 2011) product quality characteristics can be considered. A consortium for IT Software Quality has also created quality specification standards utilizing earlier standards like ISO 25010 (ISO, 2011) for automated quality characteristic measures for four characteristics: reliability, performance efficiency, security, and maintainability (CISQ, 2012). Figure 4.2 shows a list of quality attributes and subattributes from ISO 25010 (ISO, 2011).

4.6 QUALITY MANAGEMENT THROUGH SP ENGINEERING

In Section 3 we have discussed various ways Quality Management can be done through process engineering. In this section, we will discuss how these strategies take form in SP.

4.6.1 LOCALIZING FOCUS ON QUALITY

Software process engineering involves a collection of process fragments for phases (Requirements, Design, etc.) with information flows among them. Each

Attribute	Sub attribute	Attribute	Sub attribute
Functional suitability	Functional completeness	Reliability	Maturity
	Functional correctness		Availability
	Functional appropriateness		Fault-tolerance
Performance efficiency	Time behavior		Recoverability
	Resource utilization	Security	Confidentiality
	Capacity		Integrity
Compatibility	Co-existence		Non repudiation
	Interoperability		Accountability
Usability	Appropriateness recognizability		Authenticity
	Learnability	Maintainability	Modularity
	Operability		Reusability
	User error protection		Analyzability
	User interface aesthetics		Modifiability
	Accessibility		Testability

FIGURE 4.2

Software quality characteristics as per ISO 25010 (ISO, 2011).

process involves the performance of various activities and tasks, required to ensure that the outcomes of the process have acceptable quality.

Our artifice is to localize technical abilities into work-systems (that is the ability of how to organize the process, distribute responsibilities, and support them through appropriate infrastructure), and localize professional abilities into coordinated-and-synchronized collaborative phases. Professional responsibilities aid in seeing the big picture, whereas technical responsibilities piece together coherent localities, work-systems. Work-systems are supported by coordinated use of tools: tools provide service in the performance of tasks. From phases to work-systems the segmentation could be recursive, further introducing localities of technical responsibilities within professional or technical responsibilities.

With this background information, and the proviso that the concerns of Software Design will be discussed in a separate chapter, we now turn our attention to Software Construction Process. In our reckoning, Software Design is responsible for all the nonfunctional properties of the software. This is a prerequisite satisfied before the corresponding consequent phase of Software Construction Process starts. Software Construction Process is then responsible for the software technology chosen to implement the design, and to ensure that the designed properties in Software Design are not transgressed upon during construction, and the way in which the chosen technology is used. *Preserving designed properties* by noninterfering process steps amounts to Software Quality Assurance (SQA). Inspection, Testing and Process Audit all contribute to Software Quality Control (SQC). Process Engineering is responsible for all process properties that accrue from the work of software construction, such as speed of progress of software construction, cost of software construction, risk mitigation concerns addressed by software construction, in-process training, and resource allocation and utilization by software construction.

Traceability across process activities/phases is an age old requirement. But how do we constructively address it? The basic problem in human processes is that people do work in their heads, and we have no way of finding out what they have considered as inputs and the processes they followed to produce the outcome. Therefore, we are constrained to examine the output and the documents that they produce to substantiate their claims. This does not give any structure to the documents for the purposes of systematic analysis of their claims, either in terms of due diligence or in terms of being able to analyze how the work done adds up to the claims about the outcome. To get toward such a position, before the work is allocated to a role-playing person in the process, the responsibilities of the person undertaking the step have to be explicitly stated up-front, so that the person knows how the outcome has been assessed. In all this, the role-playing person is expected to have competence to perform the task, and professionally (answerable for actions for which he is remunerated) equipped to perform it. That is, the responsibility is a professional one for which the person is known to be educated and trained to accomplish the task on hand. The documents to make the claim of work done take a professional character and can therefore be architected (structured) up-front in order for the claim to be analyzed in its justification. This is why we have divided the process into phases that internally have professional responsibilities and the hand off between phases is well defined. The assumption is that the next phase is a refinement, in terms of responsibilities, over the previous one. That it has more details that do not interfere, are orthogonal to the responsibilities already met, and therefore the responsibilities are professional disjoint, and constructively additive, till the outcome is seen to be implementable, or is grounded in, in terms of target technology, and therefore needs no further refinement.

We will now get into specifics of how each phase contributes to quality management and quality related activities in each of the phases. We use the phases that we have mentioned in Section 4. This is the crux of our approach where quality is assured through designing process ensuring quality responsibilities are localized and then met by role-playing people with the right competence with the aid of tools. We discuss each phase below.

4.6.1.1 Requirements engineering and management

The very first phase of any process is to understand the needs to be met by its outcome. There is a need for this aspect to be *sound* (in relation to the *domain* of discourse), to be *complete,* and *consistent* so that a source of inefficiency in Process Management can be avoided by eschewing possibility of feedback in the process.

Soundness and *completeness* can be systemically tracked and foreclosed by methodological means like: (i) Zachman's Enterprise Architecture (Zachman, 1987) and Viable Systems Model (Beer, 1966) that support system understanding, and (ii) Policy Objective Matrix (Fukuda, 1997), and SEDAC (Fukuda, 1997) that address managerial concerns. *Consistency* has to be demonstrated for every instance of application of the methodology and this is the crux of overall *Quality Management*: *tests*, *inspections* and *audit* to assert that the known cases are handled effectively, contributing to overall Quality Control, and analysis and proof of structures of solutions devised to assert Quality Assurance.

The first step in *seeing into the system*, is in its first segmentation, which starts here in Requirements Engineering and Management. Such segmentation can be achieved by various methods of systems approach.[1] The nature of the segmentation is dictated by the approach taken. This segmentation gives rise to a configuration structure, the configuration items being annotated by attributes that signify qualities. The composition of these components lead to an understanding of how the resultant qualities of the system are aggregated and derived. Such composition is a means of asserting the properties of outcome of the process.

4.6.1.2 Engineering technical specifications

We note that having a technical specification means having a complete picture of the notion of acceptable outcome in technical terms. Basically this entails a configuration structure inherited from the previous phase, and a complete list of quality tags associated with these configuration items. We use the phrase Engineering Technical Specifications to indicate that there is foreknowledge that these specifications are concretely realizable by phases that come into play down the line. Documenting the completeness and soundness of the technical specification is a part of Quality Control, and documenting the consistency of the specification is a part of Quality Assurance to be effected by the close of this phase.

4.6.1.3 System architectural design

There are two architectural forms that are early composite structures which are perspicuous with respect to partial satisfaction of the outcomes. A *Functional architecture* is an early indication of the fact that the system realizes its functional objective that is easily discernible by the customer. This builds confidence in the customer that the system will be sound in relation to its specifications and requirements. A *Structural architecture* is an early indication of the resources needed to achieve the systems objective. Structures are place holders for all capacity planning exercises in architectural design. Structures provide a handle on

---

[1]We suggest use of Diksuchi problem solving methodology with appropriate systems methods segmenting systems towards understanding it. Cybernetic Influence Diagram (Murthy, 1994) can be used to arrive at systems description. This can be aided further by using SNAC methodology (Murthy & Sudhir, 1999) and Interpretive Structural Modeling (Warfield, 1976) to understand goals of the system and prioritize the goals.

the resources needed to satisfy quantitative understanding of how nonfunctional requirements (NFRs) can be met. Structures also provide a basis for the engineering of the function. An architectural design must make it evident that the system will indeed satisfy its functional needs. This is easy to assert through functional decomposition resulting from design. Tests, inspections and audit will provide hooks into Quality Control. They need to be devised at this stage. On the other hand, Quality Assurance exercises must document design rationale and how functional decomposition meets the system function. If the architectural design takes the structural route, then a minimal algorithmic weaving through the structures is necessary to depict how the function of the system is realized.

4.6.1.4 System engineering design

Information flows at this stage of System Architectural Design would assert the realizability of system function, and would have planned adequate capacities for the satisfaction of functional requirements. The System Engineering Design phase refines this system design to address *how* the NFRs will be realized. As we have discussed in earlier subsection, System Architectural Design addresses functional requirements. To aid the refinement of the functional solution discerned so far, we would find patterns of solutions that are known to exhibit the satisfaction of each of the NFRs.

Once the prioritization concerns regarding the order in which NFRs are to be satisfied are resolved, then quantitative levels of measures suitable for each NFR in the list are determined based on discussion with customers. At this point, design patterns of the solution to each NFR are successively applied to the solution so that quality tags associated with the configuration items in the solution have acceptable values. The application of the patterns will cause the configuration to be refined in localities of the solution, and appropriate quality tags to appear on the newly discerned configuration items.

4.6.1.5 Software architectural design

This is the first phase where ideas about software start appearing in the process. At this stage, software is still an idea, not a formal technological artifact. The more we formalize this idea, the better it will be for the succeeding phases in terms of formal traceability of properties enjoyed by the software by design. Equally, the more we will rely on Quality Assurance in Quality Management. In this sense, it will be good if we can define each succeeding stage of software emergence during development in as carefully formalized a manner as is possible.

4.6.1.6 Software engineering design

Software (Product) Engineering is concerned with the design of software so that all the NFRs expected of the software are met by conscious design. This is done extensively through application of Design Patterns, and is the subject matter of the next chapter.

4.6.1.7 Software construction engineering

The first activity to undertake in software construction is to choose relevant software technologies to implement the architected and engineered software solution. This done, we enter an activity to refine the engineered solution till the use of features of chosen technologies are evident. At this stage we devise coding patterns so that the refined solution is fully manifest in terms of the chosen technologies. Manual repeated application of these Coding Patterns will convert the refined engineered solution into code to be ready to execute on the chosen technologies.

4.6.1.8 Software installation engineering

A. Installation Design

Industrial Software Systems are huge ranging from a million lines of code to several tens of millions of line of code. They are never monolithic, and often are distributed systems. Installing such vast quantities of code systematically over a distributed IT infrastructure also needs detailed attention. An infrastructure describing data structure has to be created. A map of what code, what software goes into which part of infrastructure has to be created. A script has to be devised to distribute the software according to this map.

B. Installation

The above script has to be proactively executed to perform the distribution. Another possibility is that each system in the infrastructure checks the current version, globally set, with its local version. If these are different, then the system reactively identifies the software to be loaded.

4.6.1.9 Software commissioning engineering

Before the system can commence its execution, all the data must be in readiness. A data migration plan to move data from the old system to the new system must be created. In this plan, there needs to be defaults or computational procedures have to be defined to fill in data not available in the old system.

4.6.1.10 Software operations engineering

During the construction phase, all the software platforms to be used have to be identified. Should there be occasion to use System Management Tools, such as IBM's Tivoli, or HP OpenView or CA's UniCentre, then the coding should attend to the patterns to report usage of system resources by the applications. This will lead to an operational view of resource loading and make it possible to know why and by how much the system resources need to be increased (by hot standby if possible).

4.6.1.11 Software maintenance engineering

This phase is not strictly a part of the Forward Engineering Cycle represented by the Waterfall Model. All complex systems are Living Systems. Evolutionary change is the one constant in their working. This results in corrective maintenance or perfective maintenance activities to attend to the forces of change. In principle every change request requires one to reverse the forward engineering cycle. One needs to do this to go back far enough to discern the affected part. Then, we again engage in a forward engineering cycle by attending to the new requirement. In practice, change requests are bunched together when their localities of change lie within an acceptable neighborhood.

4.6.1.12 Software re(verse) engineering

If the full forward engineering cycle is documented, then reverse engineering is easy. Otherwise we are in a one-to-many possible reversals.

4.6.2 CONTROLS BASED ON "PROGRESS" AND LIFE CYCLE MODELS OF SP

Whilst enabling a process activity or step is a primary means of enabling the execution of a process, we may need other means of establishing such enabling conditions and perhaps even pursue activities conditionally. One such means is based on the notion of process "progress." The purpose or goal of a process is to produce an acceptable "outcome."

The general nature of an outcome could be the production of Goods or Services. At any stage of the process, we can attempt to portray the extent of Goods or Services produced thus far. We call this portrayal a measure of the progress of a process. By trying to understand what needs to be next produced, we can check whether the enabling information flow constraints for producing that part of the outcome are available. Based on such availability, we can schedule appropriate process fragments to produce such pertinent parts of the outcome. That is information flow constraints are the only enabling aspects for performing a process step or process phase. But the performance need not follow according to the linear sequence suggested by the *Waterfall model* (Sommerville, 2011). Prior attempts to configure the goods and the effect that has on the work-breakdown-structure help in identifying potential Waterfall process fragments to produce these configuration items. And it is amongst these process fragments that we need to search for information flow constraint enabled ones.

The process fragments so enabled proceed up to a point when the enabling information flow constraints are not satisfied. Then, this whole scheduling process is initiated again. At any given point in time, there is a list of configuration items describing the yet-to-be-built parts of the outcome. Each of the configuration items in the list has associated process fragments with its corresponding

Waterfall model:
1. Moves outwards from requirements to acceptable qualities through lifecycle phases
2. Ripples
3. In the end whole of acceptable qualities is realized.

Agile model:
1. Initial roadmap created by choosing which requirements and what acceptable properties are to be implemented
2. Follows waterfall for the chosen software to be developed
3. Roadmap incrementally extended until whole product is covered
4. For each chosen element of the roadmap 2 is repeated.

FIGURE 4.3

Progress towards software qualities in Waterfall and Agile models.

work-breakdown-structure. A crucial concern is: is the configuration item fully enabled for construction by a Waterfall Model Process?

Suppose it is possible to incrementally evolve a road map of Goods to be acceptably produced. Such a road map would lead to agile process cycles until the full acceptable Goods are produced by successive Waterfall Processes, the whole being a version of the *Agile Process* (Beck et al., 2001). On the other hand, if such a road map cannot be envisioned, then the enabled process elaboration takes the shape of an evolutionary *Spiral Process Model* (Boehm, 1988). Figures 4.3 and 4.4 represent these models with respect to progress in software realization.

4.6.3 PROCESS QUALITY AND QUALITY MANAGEMENT

Generally speaking Quality Management takes on hues of either Quality Control or Quality Assurance. Furthermore, as so much depends on human experience and its subjectivity, attempts towards Excellence towards Quality take on further subjective criteria. Process (Quality) Maturity, benchmarks, tracking with respect to benchmarks vis-a-vis continuous improvement efforts, etc. Furthermore, there is Product or Outcome Quality and there is Process Quality. We are concerned with Process Qualities here, the chief ones being time and cost, a process being engineered for defect prevention, and the ability of the process to faithfully build

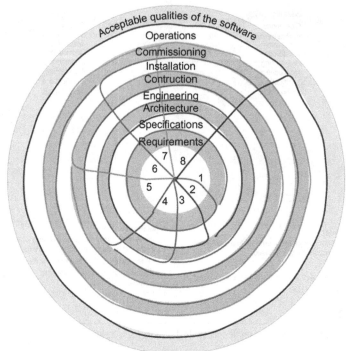

Spiral model:
1. Successive spirals (1–8) reach out from requirements to acceptable qualities
2. Each spiral follows the waterfall method until information flow constraints disallow further progress

FIGURE 4.4

Progress towards software qualities in Spiral model.

designed product qualities. Time and cost management are typical management concerns, similar to such concerns in *any* process, and we will not delve into them here. Suffice it to say that resource allocation and utilization, and scheduling amongst enabled process activities, steps are the principal concerns here. They provide little inputs from software per se except in demarcating the boundaries of the problem and identifying the scope of process fragments. We have stressed several times that when design is based on empirical experience, Quality Control kicks in through a testing regimen, and when Design is based on theory, Quality Assurance kicks in and is based on checklists post process steps, activities and fragments, claiming faithful process veracity vis-a-vis design. This latter point is tricky and is dependent on tools, where quality assurance is implicit and automatic, or dependent on competence of role-playing personnel acting in the process. We note that in both cases, Quality Assurance is dependent on program analysis techniques: in the case of tools, its action is dependent on an internal algorithmic analysis of software (program) property, which conditionally enables the action to transform its input work-products into quality assured output work-products; in the case of role-playing people performing manual intellectual activity in the process, post facto the process the person has to claim due diligence. This is based on the person's understanding of relevant program analysis, in the light of which an action is taken to induce required design quality in the output work-products. This action requires the role-playing associate to be competent in order to claim output work-product quality, implying training with respect to quality, either in general terms or in terms of specific project requirements. Qualifying competence of role-playing associates in a process is therefore critical to quality assurance and should be rightfully taken as a part of Process Engineering.

Designing a process also entails detailed attention to corrective action in case of process failures with regard to meeting constraints.

- Is it a failure of governance, where adherence to values espoused by the organization are not met? This is a contextual condition, and we are lucky if it is discovered at the time of failure, otherwise serious backtracking of the process is needed right up to the point of failure. The need for undo and redo primitives for process step performance is indicated by this condition.
- Is the failure a management failure? That is, is it a failure of meeting outcome objectives? Again, this implies that some constraints were not checked early enough, needing backtracking capabilities in process performance as described in acting on governance failures.
- Is it an administrative failure? This implies that appropriate resources were not provisioned at the right time and place in the process. The resources could be properly licensed computing resources, or similarly licensed software tools.
- Is it the failure of knowledge-work, manually effected by associates in the process? This situation points to inadequate training of associates allocated to process steps or process fragments. Which means that they do not understand the intricacies of program analysis that enables a process step, or they do not have a grip on the action that induces required quality in the output work-product.
- All of the above indicate different levels of management failures in a project, each needing a properly scoped corrective action for the project or for the organization as a whole. It is our presumption that the way governance failures are handled would be at the organizational level, and the rest would be at a project level.

In passing, we remark that similar analysis is necessary for coping with failures in the *design* process.

4.6.4 CONTEXTUAL CONSTRAINTS

There may be situational or contextual constraints not determinable by the Process, such as the time by which the process should complete, the total cost incurred by process performance, etc. These are external constraints imposed by the environment. Some of the other factors outside the control of the process are: the risk of not producing an acceptable outcome, the risk of failure of an activity or step, the risk of unavailability of resources for engaging in process performance, the risk of inadequacy or incapability or incompetence of a resource to effect acceptable work towards an acceptable outcome. Process Management action is required, in terms of planning, to ensure that these risks remain as potential risks and do not precipitate into actual failures of the process. Process Management action is required to plan adequate and appropriate corrective action in case of process failure.

4.7 CONCLUSION

It is possible to engineer software process in such a way that the contribution from each phase of the process and activities in each phase toward resultant software quality is apparent. We have presented one such approach. The phases start with requirements for the software and go beyond realization of software towards its maintenance. Software lifecycles models which are chosen based on required process qualities dictate how phases are carried out and progress with respect to software realization. Each phase preserves qualities that are designed in the previous phase. Contextual constraints also affect the achievement of software quality and hence handling them by engineering the process is essential. Localization of focus on software quality can also be achieved through standards, practices, and guidelines; abstractions we have discussed in this chapter. Without software designed to meet intended qualities no amount of process engineering can assure qualities of the software. We have discussed software design in another chapter. Fine interleave between software design and software construction is one of the primary characteristics of software process. Configuration structure of both process (WBS) and software (PBS) can be expressed and related with each other to engineer software process at further detailed level. We are working on notation to express such a relationship as part of further work.

REFERENCES

Beck, K., Beedle, M., Van Bennekum, A., Cockburn, A., Cunningham, W., Fowler, M., et al., 2001. Manifesto for Agile Software Development.
Beer, S., 1966. Diagnosing the System for Organisations. John Wiley, London and New York.
Boehm, B.W., 1988. A spiral model of software development and enhancement. Computer 21 (5), 61−72.
(CISQ) Consortium for IT Software Quality, 2012. CISQ Specifications for Automated Quality Characteristic Measures. Available from: <http://it-cisq.org/wp-content/uploads/2012/09/CISQ-Specification-for-Automated-Quality-Characteristic-Measures.pdf>.
CMMI-DEV, C.M.M.I., 2010. for Development, Version 1.3. Software Engineering Institute.

Dahl, O.J., Dijkstra, E.W., Hoare, C.A.R., 1972. Structured Programming. Academic Press, London, UK.

Deming, W.E., 2000. Out of the Crisis, First MIT Press Ed. MIT Press, Cambridge, MA.

Floyd, R.W., 1967. Assigning meanings to programs, mathematical aspects of computer science. In: Schwartz, J.T. (Ed.) volume 19 of Proceedings of Symposium on Applied Mathematics, A.M.S.

Fukuda, R., 1997. Building Organizational Fitness: Management Methodology for Transformation and Strategic Advantage. Productivity Press, Portland, OR.

Gérard, B., Georges, G., 1992. The esterel synchronous programming language: design, semantics, implementation. Sci. Comput. Programming 19 (2), 87−152.

Hoare, C.A.R., 1969. An Axiomatic Basis for Computer Program. Communications of the ACM 12 (10), 576−580.

International Organization for Standardisation. (ISO), 1991. ISO/IEC: 9126 Information technology-Software Product Evaluation-Quality characteristics and guidelines for their use -1991.

International Organization for Standardization. (ISO), 2011. IEC 25010: 2011: Systems and Software Engineering−Systems and Software Quality Requirements and Evaluation (SQuaRE)−System and Software Quality Models.

Kano, N., Searku, N., Takahashi, F., Tsuji, S., 1984. Attractive quality and must be quality. Himshitsu (The Journal of Quality, Japanese Society for Quality Control) 14, 39−48.

Murthy, P.N., 1994. Systems practice in consulting. Syst. Pract. Action Res. 7 (4), 419−438.

Murthy, P.N., Sudhir, V., 1999. Multi Modeling Approach to Enterprise Analysis and Modeling. TCS Internal, QMS Guidelines.

Sommerville, I., 2011. Software Engineering, ninth Ed. Addison-Wesley, Boston, MA, p. 29.

Warfield, J.N., 1976. Societal Systems, Planning, Policy and Complexity. Wiley, New York.

Watts, S.H., 1989. Managing the Software Process. Addison Wesley Professional, MA.

Wirth, N., 1972. Systematic Programming: An Introduction. Prentice Hall, NJ, USA.

Wirth, N., 1974. Algorithms + Data Structures = Programs. Prentice Hall, NJ, USA.

Zachman, J.A., 1987. A framework for information systems architecture. IBM Syst. J. 26 (3), 276−292.

Zope, N., Nori, K., 2008. Process meta-modeling: a design perspective. TCS Internal Technical Report.

Architecture viewpoints for documenting architectural technical debt

5

Zengyang Li[1,4], Peng Liang[2,3] and Paris Avgeriou[1]

[1]*Department of Mathematics and Computing Science, University of Groningen, Groningen, The Netherlands* [2]*State Key Lab of Software Engineering, School of Computer, Wuhan University, Wuhan, People's Republic of China* [3]*Department of Computer Science, VU University Amsterdam, Amsterdam, The Netherlands* [4]*International School of Software, Wuhan University, Wuhan, People's Republic of China*

5.1 INTRODUCTION

In recent years, there has been an increasing interest in technical debt (TD) in the software engineering community by both practitioners and researchers (Li et al., 2015). TD is a metaphor, coined by Ward Cunningham in 1992 "for the tradeoff between writing clean code at higher cost and delayed delivery, and writing messy code cheap and fast at the cost of higher maintenance effort once it is shipped" (Buschmann, 2011; Cunningham, 1992). This metaphor was initially concerned with source code development. Currently, the concept of TD has been extended to the whole software lifecycle, such as software architecture (SA), detailed design, and testing (Brown et al., 2010; Ozkaya et al., 2011).

As Allman pointed out, "TD is inevitable since the team almost never has a full grasp of the totality of the problem when a project starts" (Allman, 2012). Thus, it is more realistic to manage TD rather than try to eliminate it completely. Furthermore, in some cases, TD is intentionally incurred to achieve some business advantages by sacrificing certain technical aspects such as sound modularity and encapsulation. This way, TD is not necessarily a "bad thing" if we have full knowledge of the consequences of the TD.

At the architectural level, architectural technical debt (ATD) is caused by architecture decisions that consciously or unconsciously compromise system quality attributes (QAs), particularly maintainability and evolvability (Li et al., 2014a, b. Like all other types of TD, managing ATD is of great essence. Especially, given the fundamental influence of SA in software development, it is of paramount importance to manage ATD, in order to achieve a high-quality SA especially in terms of its maintainability and evolvability.

To facilitate ATD management (ATDM), ATD needs to be documented, so that it becomes explicit and visible to involved stakeholders. If ATD is not documented, architecture decision-making is very likely to ignore it and its impact on candidate decisions. Consequently, undocumented ATD items will keep collecting interest (i.e., effort required to fix the corresponding design issues), leading to a prohibitive cost in system maintenance and evolution. To the best of our knowledge, there are no approaches for systematically documenting ATD.

To facilitate the documentation of ATD, we propose to adopt the architecture documentation approach mandated by ISO/IEC/IEEE 42010 (ISO/IEC/IEEE, 2011), which is based on architecture viewpoints. ISO/IEC/IEEE 42010 is an international standard, which defines requirements on the description of system, software and enterprise architectures. ISO/IEC/IEEE 42010 suggests identifying the stakeholders of a system and subsequently eliciting their concerns, so that appropriate viewpoints can be found or constructed to frame those concerns.

To define architecture viewpoints related to ATD (ATD viewpoints in short), we identified a number of stakeholders that are involved in ATDM and the typical concerns of those stakeholders. The identified stakeholders and their concerns were collected during our previous mapping study on TD (Li et al., 2015). Since the concerns are related to different aspects of ATD and cannot be framed by a single ATD viewpoint, we propose six ATD viewpoints, each of which frames a number of concerns related to ATD. This is in line with the guidelines of ISO/IEC/IEEE 42010 (ISO/IEC/IEEE, 2011). Note that, the verb *frame* used in this chapter has the same meaning as in ISO/IEC/IEEE 42010 standard, where "*frame* is used in its ordinary language sense: to formulate or construct in a particular style or language; to enclose in or as if in a frame; to surround so as to create a sharp or attractive image" (ISO/IEC/IEEE, 2011).

We briefly outline the six viewpoints. First, the ATD Detail viewpoint provides detailed information of ATD items that are incurred by architecture decisions that compromise system evolvability or maintainability (Li et al., 2014a). Second, the ATD Decision viewpoint deals with the relationship between architecture decisions and ATD items, showing which ATD items were incurred or repaid by which architecture decisions. Third, the ATD Stakeholder Involvement viewpoint addresses the responsibilities of stakeholders in ATDM during the architecting process, showing who took what actions on the ATD items during the current architecture iteration. Fourth, the ATD Distribution viewpoint deals with the distribution of the amount of the ATD over ATD items of a software system and the change of the ATD amount between milestones. Fifth, the ATD-related Component viewpoint deals with the relationship between system components and ATD items. Last, the ATD Chronological viewpoint addresses the evolution of ATD items across time.

To validate the effectiveness of the proposed ATD viewpoints in a real-life environment, we carried out a case study in which the ATD viewpoints are used to document ATD in an industrial project. The case is an information system in a large telecommunications company. The system mainly analyzes test data in various formats of telecommunications equipment and generates test reports about the quality of the tested equipment. The results of this case study show that the documented ATD views can effectively facilitate the documentation of ATD. Specifically, the ATD viewpoints are relatively easy to understand; it takes an acceptable amount of effort to document ATD using the ATD viewpoints; and the documented ATD views are useful for stakeholders to understand the ATD in the software project.

The main contributions of this chapter are threefold. First, we identified a set of stakeholders and their concerns on ATD, building on the results of our recent systematic mapping study. Second, six architecture viewpoints were proposed to address stakeholders' concerns on ATD. Third, we provide evidence from an industrial case study regarding the effectiveness of the proposed ATD viewpoints in documenting TD.

The rest of this chapter is organized as follows: Section 5.2 introduces the background and related work on ATD and its management as well as TD documentation; Section 5.3 presents the typical stakeholders involved in the ATDM process and their concerns regarding ATD; Section 5.4 describes the proposed ATD viewpoints including an example view for each of the viewpoints; Section 5.5 presents a case study which evaluates the effectiveness of the proposed ATD viewpoints in an industrial software project; and Section 5.6 concludes this chapter with future research directions.

5.2 BACKGROUND AND RELATED WORK

In this section, we elaborate the concept of ATD, and then examine the related work on TD documentation.

5.2.1 ARCHITECTURAL TECHNICAL DEBT

TD is essentially invisible to end users: they are not aware of the existence of TD when they are using a software system that delivers on its features. Conceptually, TD concerns the technical gaps between the current solutions and the ideal solutions, which may have negative influence on the system quality, especially maintainability and evolvability (Kruchten et al., 2012). ATD is a type of TD at the architecture level (Li et al., 2015). It is mainly incurred by architecture decisions that result in immature architectural artifacts that compromise maintainability and evolvability of a software system. In contrast, code-level TD is concerned with the quality of the code and is usually incurred by the poor structure of the code and noncompliance with coding rules as well as violations of coding best practices (i.e., bad code smells).

Maintainability and evolvability are the two main system QAs that are compromised when ATD is incurred. Maintainability is defined in the ISO/IEC 25010 standard (ISO/IEC, 2011), in which quality models for systems and software are defined. According to ISO/IEC 25010, maintainability includes the following subcharacteristics (i.e., QAs): modularity, reusability, analyzability, modifiability, and testability. Evolvability is not defined in either ISO 9126 or ISO/IEC 25010. We define software evolvability as the ease of adding new functional and nonfunctional requirements. Typical ATD includes violations of best practices, or the consistency and integrity of SAs, or the adoption of immature architecture techniques (e.g., architecture frameworks). A concrete example is the creation of architecture dependencies that violate the strict layered architectural pattern, that is, a higher layer having direct dependencies to layers other than the one directly below it; this compromises modularity, a subcharacteristic of maintainability. Another example of ATD is the adoption of Microsoft .NET 2.0 as running environment for a software system, which would hinder the implementation of new features that are well supported by an updated .NET version (e.g., .NET 4.5); thus, this compromises evolvability. In summary, ATD essentially results from the compromise of modularity, reusability, analyzability, modifiability, testability, or evolvability during architecting.

As Steve McConnell pointed out, TD is classified in two basic types: the TD that is incurred unintentionally and the TD that is incurred intentionally (McConnell, 2008). Accordingly, ATD can be classified into intentional and unintentional ATD. The former ATD is incurred by strategic compromises of maintainability and evolvability in architecture decision-making. The latter can be incurred by poor architecture decisions during architecting or violations of architecture rules and conformance during detailed design and coding. Both types of ATD need to be managed in the software lifecycle (Li et al., 2014a).

ATD can be seen as an important type of risk for a software system in the long term, but ATD is often ignored by the architecture and management teams. The main reason is that ATD is concerned with the cost of the long-term maintenance and evolution of a software system instead of the short-term business value that can be easily observed. However, ATD cannot be ignored forever; as the ATD in a software system accumulates incrementally, sooner or later problems will arise: maintenance tasks become hard to conduct, new features become difficult to introduce, system QAs are challenging to meet, etc.

5.2.2 TECHNICAL DEBT DOCUMENTATION

Not every type of TD needs to be documented. For instance, the code-level TD that can be automatically detected and measured by tools, does not necessarily have to be documented, since we can monitor the change of this type of TD by running the supporting tools. In contrast, the TD that cannot be automatically identified by tools needs to be systematically documented by other means; if not documented, this type of TD tends to be ignored by related stakeholders and, thus, it becomes invisible and cannot be managed. Most ATD is very difficult to identify and measure, as this cannot be automated. Therefore, once identified, this kind of ATD should be documented for further management.

There is little work on TD documentation. In our recent mapping study on TD (Li et al., 2015), we only found four studies (Guo and Seaman, 2011; Holvitie and Leppänen, 2013; Seaman and Guo, 2011; Zazworka et al., 2013) that proposed to use TD items to represent and document TD. A TD item is a unit of TD in a software system. An example TD item is a "God" class with information about its location, estimated cost and benefit, responsible developer, intentionality, and TD type (design TD in this case). The TD in a software system is comprised of multiple TD items. The four aforementioned studies provided their own templates to document single TD items. All four TD item templates contain the following common fields: ID, location, responsible developer, TD type, and description (Li et al., 2015). Furthermore, each template also contains part of the following fields: principal, interest, interest probability, interest standard deviation, name, context, intentionality, correlation with other TD items, and propagation rules (Li et al., 2015). The last two fields (correlations and propagation rules) deserve further attention as they are helpful in analyzing the impact of TD items. Guo and Seaman proposed to record the correlations between TD items, but they did not specify the kinds of correlations between two TD items (of the same type or different types) (Guo and Seaman, 2011). Holvitie and Leppänen proposed to document so-called "propagation rules," which refer to implementation parts (e.g., packages, classes, and methods) that propagate TD (Holvitie and Leppänen, 2013). We consider that the propagation rules are important for managing TD since this information can be helpful in measuring TD and coming up with solutions to resolve TD.

The approaches proposed in the four aforementioned studies fall short in a number of ways compared with the approach proposed in this chapter. First, none of those four studies systematically extracted stakeholders' concerns on TD; therefore, there is no evidence that the documented TD items using those approaches (i.e., TD item templates) cover all necessary information interesting to related stakeholders. Second, all those approaches document individual TD items without showing the relationships between TD items, the holistic view of all TD items, and the evolution of the TD. Third, none of those TD item templates is dedicated to documenting TD at the architecture level (ATD). To the best of our knowledge, the only dedicated work on documenting ATD is the template for recording ATD items proposed in our previous work (Li et al., 2014a). This ATD item template was adapted in the ATD Detail viewpoint in this chapter (Table 5.4).

5.3 TYPICAL STAKEHOLDERS AND CONCERNS

We provide definitions of four core concepts used in this chapter before going into the details of stakeholders and concerns for the ATD viewpoints. These definitions are adopted as is from ISO/IEC/IEEE 42010 (ISO/IEC/IEEE, 2011):

- *Stakeholder*: "individual, team, organization, or classes thereof, having an interest in a system" (ISO/IEC/IEEE, 2011).

- *Concern*: "interest in a system relevant to one or more of its stakeholders" (ISO/IEC/IEEE, 2011).
- *Architecture view*: "work product expressing the architecture of a system from the perspective of specific system concerns" (ISO/IEC/IEEE, 2011).
- *Architecture viewpoint*: "work product establishing the conventions for the construction, interpretation, and use of architecture views to frame specific system concerns" (ISO/IEC/IEEE, 2011).

We identified a number of stakeholders that have interests in ATD and the typical concerns of those stakeholders. The identified stakeholders and their concerns were collected during our recent mapping study on TD (Li et al., 2015) (see Section 5.3.2), in which we analyzed all available peer-reviewed scientific papers on TD. These stakeholders and their concerns are described in Sections 5.3.1 and 5.3.2, respectively. The ATD viewpoints are presented in Section 5.4.

5.3.1 ATD STAKEHOLDERS

ATD stakeholders are those who perform ATDM activities, and who are directly affected by the consequences of ATD. The ATDM process includes five main activities: ATD identification, measurement, prioritization, monitoring, and repayment (Li et al., 2014a). Architects, the development team, and architecture evaluators perform ATDM activities, such as ATD identification and ATD repayment. Project managers, customers, the development team, and architects are directly influenced by the consequences of ATD. The ATD stakeholders are described in detail as follows:

- *Architects* are concerned with all aspects of ATD incurred by architecture decisions. They are responsible for managing ATD explicitly and effectively to keep the architecture healthy enough. They perform all the five aforementioned ATDM activities in the ATDM process (Li et al., 2014a).
- *Architecture evaluators* take the ATD incurred by architecture decisions into account to assess the impact of the ATD on the quality of architecture. They can consider the known ATD as input and identify the existing but yet-unknown ATD as part of output during architecture evaluation. They conduct the ATD identification, measurement, and prioritization in the ATDM process (Li et al., 2014a).
- *Project managers* are mainly concerned with the consequences of the ATD which may cause a delayed release, changed release plan, or decreased quality of the product in the end. They are also concerned with assigning appropriate development team members to addressing different pieces of ATD. They are involved in ATD prioritization in the ATDM process (Li et al., 2014a).
- *Development team* is concerned with the cost of ATD in terms of the maintenance and evolution effort to a project. Development team members mainly include requirements engineers, designers, developers,

maintainers, and testers. They are involved in ATD identification, measurement, and repayment (Li et al., 2014a).

- *Customers* are concerned with the impact on software product quality, the total cost of repaying ATD, and the time to market of new releases.

5.3.2 CONCERNS ON ATD

We came up with the concerns on ATD in the following two ways: (i) concerns derived or adapted from generic concerns on TD that were identified during our mapping study on TD (Li et al., 2015); (ii) the concerns derived from the ATDM activities in the ATDM process proposed in our previous work (Li et al., 2014a). The ATD concerns are listed in Table 5.1. The details on how we came up with the ATD concerns are described in Appendix A.

Most of the ATD concerns are self-explanatory and, thus, we only describe two concerns in more detail: The concerns C16 and C17 are about the change rates of ATD benefit and cost, which are defined as the increased or decreased ATD benefit and cost in current iteration compared with the previous iteration. The proposed ATD viewpoints frame all the identified concerns. One concern can be framed by multiple ATD viewpoints, for example, concerns C12 and C13 are framed by both the ATD Detail viewpoint and the ATD Decision viewpoint. The ATD viewpoints addressing each ATD concern are presented in Table 5.1. An "X" denotes that the viewpoint in the corresponding column addresses the concern in the corresponding row.

We assign the ATD concerns to different types of stakeholders according to their roles. Table 5.2 shows the stakeholders of the ATD viewpoints and their concerns. Architects are concerned with all aspects of the ATD in a software system because architects need to have full knowledge of an architecture. Architecture evaluators are concerned with the aspects that are related to the architecture rationale, how the architecture satisfies the requirements of a project, and what the risks on the architecture quality are. Project managers are concerned with the aspects that are related to project management, such as cost of software maintenance and evolution, risks on software quality, and human resources management within the project. The development team pays more attention to the effort and cost of maintenance and evolution activities. The customers hold the concerns related to the cost, quality, and delivery time of products.

5.4 ATD VIEWPOINTS

We developed a set of ATD viewpoints, each framing part of the concerns listed in Table 5.1. Each ATD viewpoint frames one or more concerns and a concern can be framed by more than one ATD viewpoints. These ATD viewpoints were constructed in an iterative process driven by the stakeholder concerns on ATD.

Table 5.1 Concerns Related to ATD and their Corresponding Viewpoints

ID	Concern Description	ATD Detail Viewpoint	ATD Decision Viewpoint	ATD-Related Component Viewpoint	ATD Distribution viewpoint	ATD Stakeholder Involvement Viewpoint	ATD Chronological Viewpoint
C1	What ATD items have been incurred?	X			X		
C2	How much ATD does a software system have?	X			X		
C3	How much is the benefit of ATD item A?	X			X		
C4	How much is the cost of ATD item A?	X					
C5	How much is the interest of ATD item A?	X					
C6	What is the priority of ATD item A to be repaid?	X					
C7	What is the impact of ATD item A on software quality?	X					
C8	Which stakeholders were involved in ATD item A?	X				X	
C9	What ATD items affect stakeholder SH?	X				X	
C10	Which elements in the architecture design does ATD item A relate to?	X		X			
C11	What is the rationale for incurring ATD item A?	X					
C12	What is the architecture decision that incurs ATD item A?	X	X				
C13	What architecture decision(s) are made to repay ATD item A?	X	X				
C14	When does ATD item A change?	X					
C15	When should ATD item A be repaid?	X					
C16	How fast is the total ATD benefit and cost of a software system changing?				X		X
C17	How fast are the benefit and cost of ATD item A changing?				X		X
C18	What ATD items have changed since Iteration I?				X		
C19	What change scenarios are impacted by ATD item A?	X					
C20	How does an ATD item A propagate and accumulate in development?	X			X		
C21	Is ATD in a software system under acceptable level?				X		

Table 5.2 Stakeholders of ATD Viewpoints and their Concerns

Stakeholders	Concerns
Architects	C1, C2, C3, C4, C5, C6, C7, C8, C9, C10, C11, C12, C13, C14, C15, C16, C17, C18, C19, C20, C21
Architecture evaluators	C1, C2, C3, C4, C5, C6, C7, C10, C11, C12, C13, C16, C17, C18, C20, C21
Project managers	C2, C6, C8, C9, C15, C16, C17, C18, C20, C21
Development team	C4, C5, C8, C9, C10
Customers	C2, C16

Table 5.3 Typical Stakeholders of the ATD Detail Viewpoint and their Concerns

Stakeholders	Concerns
Architects	C1, C3, C4, C5, C6, C7, C8, C9, C10, C11, C12, C13, C14, C15, C19, C20
Architecture evaluators	C1, C3, C4, C5, C6, C7, C10, C11, C12, C13
Project managers	C6, C15
Development team	C4, C5, C9, C10

The construction of these viewpoints was also inspired by our previous work (van Heesch et al., 2012), where we provide a set of architecture viewpoints for documenting architecture decisions. We describe the ATD viewpoints following the template for documenting architecture viewpoints provided by ISO/IEC/IEEE 42010 (ISO/IEC/IEEE, 2011). The template suggests to document an architecture viewpoint in multiple parts. We present the following parts for each ATD viewpoint in each subsection: the name, an overview, the typical stakeholders and their concerns, as well as an example view conforming to the ATD viewpoint. The model kinds and correspondence rules for the ATD viewpoints will be detailed in Appendix B to ensure the readability of the current section. In Appendix B, the definition of each ATD viewpoint is presented in a subsection; these definitions can act as guidelines to create views conforming to the viewpoint.

5.4.1 ATD DETAIL VIEWPOINT

ATD Detail viewpoint presents the detailed information of individual ATD items in a software system. The stakeholders and concerns of this viewpoint are shown in Table 5.3. These concerns center mainly around the properties of ATD items, including the cost, benefit, rationale, related change scenarios, and so forth.

We codify the details of an ATD item using a template (Table 5.4), which is an adaptation based on the ATD item template proposed in (Li et al., 2014a). A view conforming to the ATD Detail viewpoint is comprised of multiple ATD items, and each is described using the template. Each element of an ATD item has an associated description as listed in Table 5.4. Compared with the ATD template used in Li et al. (2014a), we add new elements "Priority," "Intentionality,"

Table 5.4 Template for Documenting an ATD Item

ID	A unique identification number of the ATD item that serves as a key in other views
Name	A short name of this ATD item that indicates the essence of this ATD item
Version	The current version number of the ATD item (e.g., 5)
Date	The date when this ATD item was identified or updated
Status	The current status of the ATD item. The types of status are described in detail in Appendix B.5
Priority	The priority of this ATD item to be repaid if this ATD item is unresolved. The priority is a positive natural number between 1 and 10. A larger number indicates a higher priority
Intentionality	The ATD item can be incurred intentionally or unintentionally
Incurred by	The architecture decision that incurs this ATD item. ATD can be incurred by architecture decisions made by architects, or by designers and developers not conforming to those architecture decisions
Repaid by	The architecture decisions that repays this ATD item
Responsible	The person or team who is responsible for managing this ATD item
Compromised QA	The QA(s) that are compromised (modularity, reusability, analyzability, modifiability, testability, or evolvability)
Rationale	The reason why the ATD item was incurred
Benefit	The value gained if the ATD item remains unresolved. The benefit is comprised of two parts: 1. *Measureable benefit* that can be measured in development effort (e.g., person-days) 2. *QA benefit* that cannot be transferred into effort. We can estimate the benefit level of each beneficiary QA
Cost	The cost suffered by incurring this ATD item, which is the sum of principal and interest described below
Principal	The cost if this ATD item is resolved at the time when the ATD item is identified
Interest	The interest that this ATD item accumulates (the interest is calculated based on the predicted change scenarios described below)

Table 5.4 Template for Documenting an ATD Item *Continued*

Change scenarios					
	#	**Scenario Description**	**Consequence**	**Scenario Interest**	**Probability**
	1	Scenario 1	Consequence of scenario 1	I1	P_1
	2	Scenario 2	Consequence of scenario 2	I2	P_2
	...	...	...	...	...
	n	Scenario n	Consequence of scenario n	I_n	P_n

Calculation of the interest of this ATD item (total interest) = $\sum_{k=1}^{n} I_k \times P_k$

Architecture diagram	A diagram or model that illustrates the concerned part in the architecture design
History	Change history of this ATD item

Stakeholder	Action	Status	Iteration	Date
Name <Stakeholder role>	Action that the stakeholder performed on the ATD item	Status when the action was completed	Iteration endpoint name	When the action was performed

Adapted from Li et al. (2014a).

as well as "Repaid by," refine the candidate status set of the "Status" element, and revise the element "History." The status "unresolved" in the "Status" element in Li et al. (2014a) is further refined to "identified," "measured," "remeasured," and prioritized. The "History" element of an ATD item includes five subelements: a *Stakeholder* who performs an *Action* on this ATD item, causing it to have a specific *Status*, on a specific *Date* that is in the period of a certain development *Iteration*. The aforementioned "action" can be *identify, measure, re-measure, prioritize,* and *repay*, and accordingly a "status" can be *identified, measured, remeasured, prioritized,* and *resolved*. An example documented ATD item following the ATD Detail viewpoint is shown in Table 5.5.

5.4.2 ATD DECISION VIEWPOINT

Architecture decisions are treated as first-class entities of architectures and play an essential role in architecture design (ISO/IEC/IEEE, 2011; Jansen and Bosch, 2005). ATD can be incurred by architects, designers, and developers, while all of them can do this intentionally or unintentionally. Architecture decisions made

Table 5.5 Example ATD Detail Model of an ATD Item

ID	ATD1
Name	Poor support for report format and style customization
Version	4
Date	September 30, 2013
Status	Resolved
Priority	9 (out of 10)
Intentionality	Intentional
Incurred by	Architecture decision 10 (AD10): using pre-defined Excel templates for product quality reports
Repaid by	Architecture decision 25 (AD25): replacing pre-defined Excel templates with Excel automation
Responsible	Hui
Compromised QA	Evolvability
Rationale	To speed up the implementation of the feature of product quality reports, we decided to use the pre-defined Excel templates instead of Excel automation to set the formats and styles of the report files, since we did not have experience in Excel automation development. We saved 15 person-days
Benefit	15 person-days
Cost	32.8 person-days
Principal	25 person-days
Interest	7.8 person-days

Change scenarios

#	Scenario Description	Consequence	Scenario Interest	Probability
S10	Add a new report type for product line A	Manually add a new type of report template and test it for product line A	3 person-days	0.8
S11	Add a new product model for product line B	Manually update and test all the existing report templates	1 person-day	0.9
S13	Add a new product line	Manually add and test all types of report templates for the new product line	5 person-days	0.9

Architecture diagram

Customized Report → Excel Handler → Fixed Report

Legend: Component — Provide service to

History

Stakeholder	Action	Status	Iteration	Date
Architect1 << Architect >> Developer5 << Developer >>	Identify	Identified	Release 16.0	August 5, 2014
Architect1 << Architect >> Developer5 << Developer >>	Measure	Measured	Release 16.1	August 22, 2014
Architect1 << Architect >>	Prioritize	Prioritized	Release 16.1	August 22, 2014
Developer5 << Developer >>	Repay	Resolved	Release 16.2	September 16, 2014

Table 5.6 Typical Stakeholders of the ATD Decision Viewpoint and their Concerns

Stakeholders	Concerns
Architects	C12, C13
Architecture evaluators	C12, C13

during architecting entail compromises and trade-offs made by architects, potentially together with involved stakeholders during architecture design. Architects usually have to make compromises on technical solutions to meet the business needs such as release deadline or saving short-term cost. ATD is part of the result of such compromises. In addition, new architecture decisions are continuously made to repay existing ATD. Therefore, ATD can be managed based on architecture decisions (Li et al., 2014a).

The ATD Decision viewpoint describes which architecture decisions have incurred ATD items and which architecture decisions are made to repay ATD items. The typical stakeholders of ATD Decision viewpoint and their addressed concerns related to ATD are listed in Table 5.6. The details of the ATD Decision viewpoint are described in Appendix B.2. Figure 5.1 shows a fragment of an example ATD Decision view.

5.4.3 ATD-RELATED COMPONENT VIEWPOINT

This viewpoint illustrates bidirectional relations between architecture components and unresolved ATD items. By "ATD item *A* relates to component *Comp*," we mean that component *Comp* needs to be modified to repay ATD item *A*. Typical stakeholders of the ATD-related Component viewpoint and their concerns are depicted in Table 5.7. A fragment of an example ATD-related Component view is shown in Table 5.8, in which an "X" references that the ATD item in the corresponding row relates to the component in the corresponding column. Note that, due to the limited space, we do not show the names of the ATD items, which practitioners should provide in real cases. The names of the ATD items can be found in the ATD Decision view shown in Figure 5.1.

5.4.4 ATD DISTRIBUTION VIEWPOINT

The ATD Distribution viewpoint shows how the amount of ATD cost and benefit (see Section 5.4.1) distributes over each ATD item and how the amount of total ATD cost and benefit changes in a software system during development. With this viewpoint, we can easily understand the change of the accumulated ATD of a software system and the cost variation of each ATD item during two iterations. The typical stakeholders of this viewpoint and their concerns framed by this

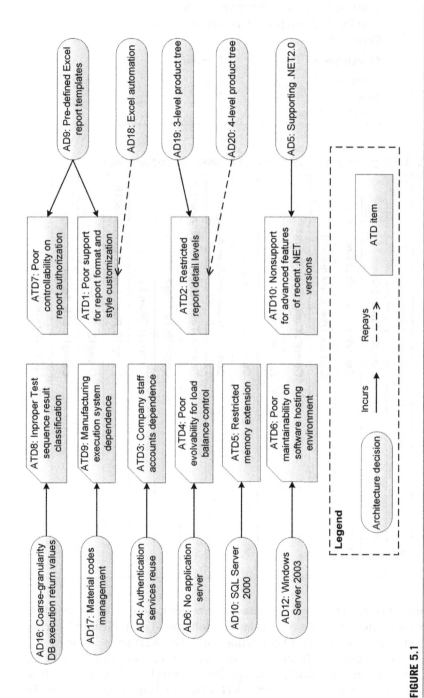

FIGURE 5.1

Fragment of an example ATD Decision view.

Table 5.7 Typical Stakeholders of the ATD-Related Component Viewpoint and their Concerns

Stakeholders	Concerns
Architects	C10
Evaluators	C10
Development team	C10

Table 5.8 Fragment of an Example ATD-Related Component View

ATD Item	Comp1: DB Handler	Comp2: General Query	Comp3: Product Test Controller	Comp4: User Management	Comp5: Customized Report	Comp6: Fixed Report	Comp7: Excel Handler	Comp8: Quality Analysis Algorithm	Comp9: Test Result File Management	Comp10: FTP Tool	Comp11: Client UI	Comp12: Fixed Report Generator UI	Comp13: SQL Server	Comp14: FTP Server	#(Components)
ATD1					X	X	X								3
ATD2	X	X			X	X		X							5
ATD3				X									X		2
ATD4	X	X			X										3
ATD5	X	X			X	X									4
ATD6	X	X													2
ATD7		X			X	X	X								4
ATD8	X	X	X			X	X	X							6
ATD9			X												1
ATD10		X	X		X			X				X	X		6
#(ATD items)	5	7	3	1	7	5	3	3	0	0	1	1	1	0	

viewpoint are shown in Table 5.9. These concerns are mainly about the benefits, costs, and their changes of the ATD items in a software system. Figure 5.2 shows a fragment of an example ATD Distribution view. The ATD items in Figure 5.2 are those from Figure 5.1. In this example view, we can see that: ATD items ATD1 and ATD2 are completely repaid at *Release V16.1*; ATD item ATD10 is identified at *Release V16.2*; ATD item ATD4 has the highest amount of ATD

Table 5.9 Typical Stakeholders of the ATD Distribution Viewpoint and their Concerns

Stakeholders	Concerns
Architects	C2, C3, C4, C16, C17, C18, C20, C21
Evaluators	C2, C3, C4, C16, C17, C18, C20, C21
Project managers	C2, C16, C17, C18, C20, C21
Customers	C2, C16

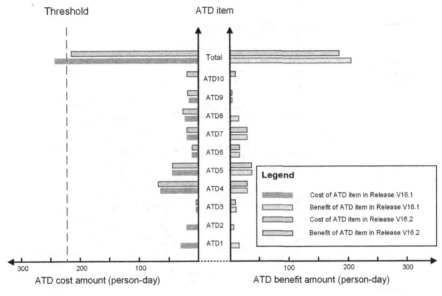

FIGURE 5.2

Fragment of an example ATD Distribution view.

cost in *Release V16.1* and *Release V16.2*; and the amount of accumulated ATD of this project has decreased since *Release V16.1*. In an ATD Distribution view, only the measurable benefit of each ATD item is shown, while the QA benefit is not. The threshold line in Figure 5.2 denotes how much ATD can be tolerated in a software system. The threshold is defined by the project manager and the customer, taking into account the project budget, release planning, labor, project size, and other related factors.

5.4.5 ATD STAKEHOLDER INVOLVEMENT VIEWPOINT

The ATD Stakeholder Involvement viewpoint describes the responsibilities of the involved stakeholders regarding the managed ATD items. Views governed by this

Table 5.10 Typical Stakeholders of the ATD Stakeholder Involvement Viewpoint and their Concerns

Stakeholders	Concerns
Architects	C8, C9
Project manager	C8, C9
Development team	C8, C9

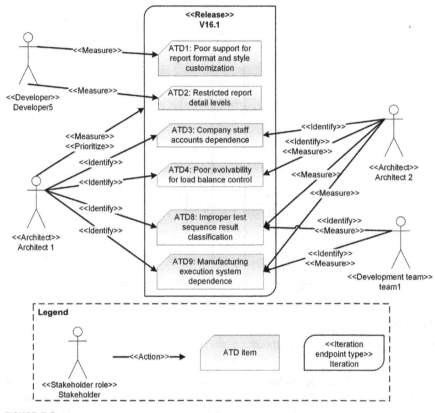

FIGURE 5.3

Fragment of an example ATD Stakeholder Involvement view.

viewpoint show ATD items, actions, and stakeholders involved in the ATDM process within one specific iteration. Table 5.10 shows the typical stakeholders of the ATD Stakeholder Involvement viewpoint and their concerns framed by it. The stakeholders of this viewpoint include technical ones (e.g., architects) that participate in the management of ATD, and project managers who are concerned with the human resources assigned to ATD items. Figure 5.3 depicts an example ATD Stakeholder Involvement view.

Table 5.11 Typical Stakeholders of the ATD Chronological Viewpoint and their Concerns

Stakeholders	Concerns
Architects	C14, C17
Project managers	C17

5.4.6 ATD CHRONOLOGICAL VIEWPOINT

This viewpoint focuses on the change of the ATD items in a software system over time. From this viewpoint, we can see how ATD is managed along the time-line, that is, what ATD items are dealt with in each iteration and how each ATD item is handled over time. This viewpoint also shows the benefit and cost of the measured ATD item, and the benefit delta and cost delta of the remeasured ATD item. Typical stakeholders of the ATD Chronological viewpoint and their concerns are shown in Table 5.11. A fragment of example ATD Chronological view is depicted in Figure 5.4.

5.5 CASE STUDY

To validate the effectiveness of the proposed ATD viewpoints in a real-life environment, we carried out a case study in which the ATD viewpoints were used to document ATD in an industrial project. We designed and reported the case study following the guidelines proposed by Runeson and Höst (Runeson and Höst, 2009). However, we have not included the section on data analysis suggested by the guidelines, since only descriptive statistics were used to analyze the data collected in the case study.

5.5.1 STUDY OBJECTIVE AND RESEARCH QUESTIONS

The goal of this case study, described using the Goal-Question-Metric approach (Basili, 1992), is: *to analyze* ATD viewpoints *for the purpose of* evaluation *with respect to* their effectiveness in documenting ATD, *from the point of view of* ATD stakeholders *in the context of* industrial software development.

We define effectiveness in documenting ATD as being comprised of the following aspects:

- *Understandability of the ATD viewpoints.* The understandability of the ATD viewpoints themselves (e.g., typical stakeholders and framed concerns, model kinds, and correspondence rules) reflects to what extent the stakeholders can generate the corresponding ATD views efficiently and correctly. If the ATD viewpoints cannot be easily understood, they are not likely to be adopted for ATDM.

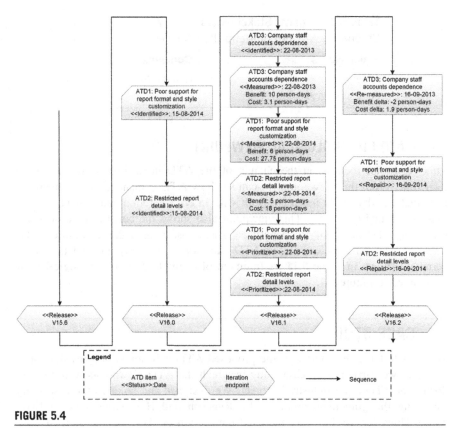

FIGURE 5.4

Fragment of an example ATD Chronological view.

- *Effort for collecting necessary data and further producing ATD views.* How easy data collection is, affects the feasibility of using the ATD viewpoints in practice. If the data collection is too complicated and time-consuming, stakeholders would be reluctant to use the viewpoints. In addition, the effort it takes to document the ATD views with available information plays a major role in their adoption.
- *Usefulness in helping stakeholders to understand the ATD in software systems.* This aspect is concerned with whether the views conforming to the ATD viewpoints can enhance stakeholders' understanding on the current state of the ATD and is comprised of three parts: (i) whether stakeholders perceive the actual health level of the SA compared to their pre-conception; (ii) which ATD views are useful to understand ATD; and (iii) which ATD views are promising to be adopted by the stakeholders both to produce and consume the views.

Accordingly, we ask three research questions (RQs), each corresponding to one aspect of effectiveness of the ATD viewpoints, respectively:

*RQ*1: How easy is it to understand the ATD viewpoints?

*RQ*2: How easy is it to collect the required information for generating ATD views governed by the ATD viewpoints and to document ATD views with the gathered information?

*RQ*3: Do ATD views effectively support stakeholders to understand the ATD?

5.5.2 STUDY EXECUTION

This case study was conducted to empirically evaluate how the proposed ATD viewpoints can effectively support stakeholders to document and understand ATD. This case study is evaluatory in nature since the case study aims at evaluating the effectiveness of the ATD viewpoints in an industrial environment.

5.5.2.1 Case description

The case is an information system in a large telecommunications company in China. The system analyzes the test data in various formats of telecommunications equipment and generates various types of reports about the quality of the tested telecommunications equipment. This system also provides the functionality of managing and controlling whether a piece of telecommunications equipment is allowed to proceed in tests.

The software project team includes a project manager, two architects, and nine development team members. The project manager, two architects, and six development team members participated in this case study; the remaining three developers were not available. The software system has a history of around seven years. Its size is about 760,000 lines of source code, and around 290 person-months (approximately 50,000 person-hours) has been invested in this project.

5.5.2.2 Data collection

5.5.2.2.1 Data to be collected

To answer the RQs defined in Section 5.1, we collected the data items listed in Table 5.12, where the target RQ for each data item is listed. We also collected the participants' information on their experience in software industry (Table 5.13) and the related information on the selected software project in this case study (Table 5.14).

5.5.2.2.2 Data collection method

Interviews were the main method to collect data in this case study. As suggested in Runeson and Höst (2009), interviews allow us to get in-depth knowledge about the topics of interest in the case study, by asking a series of questions about the interview topic to the participants of the case study. We used semi-structured interviews in this case study, which allowed us to adjust the order of the planned questions according to the development of the conversation between the

Table 5.12 Data Items to be Collected

#	Data Item	Range	RQ
D1	How easy it is for the participants to understand the ATD viewpoints	Ten-point Likert scale. One for extremely hard, ten for extremely easy	RQ1
D2	How easy it is for the participants to collect the required information for generating the ATD views	Ten-point Likert scale. One for extremely hard, ten for extremely easy	RQ2
D3	How much effort it needs to document the ATD views with gathered information	Four-point Likert scale: little, not too much, a little bit too much but acceptable, unacceptably too much	RQ2
D4	How different it is between the actual health level of the architecture and the health level that the participants considered it to be	Five-point Likert scale: much higher than, higher than, roughly equal to, lower than, and much lower than	RQ3
D5	How useful each ATD viewpoint is in facilitating the understanding of ATD	Five-point Likert scale: not useful, somewhat useful, moderately useful, very useful, not sure	RQ3
D6	Which ATD views the participants are willing to use to document ATD (produce information), and which views to use to maintain their knowledge about ATD (consume information) and subsequently manage ATD	n.a.	RQ3

Table 5.13 Information Related to the Study Participants

#	Participant Data Item	Scale Type	Unit	Range
PD1	Time the participants have worked in software industry	Ratio	Years	Positive natural numbers
PD2	Time the participants have worked as developers	Ratio	Years	Positive natural numbers
PD3	Time the participants have worked in the company	Ratio	Years	Positive natural numbers
PD4	Time the participants have worked in the domain that the case belongs to	Ratio	Years	Positive natural numbers
PD5	Time the participants have worked in the current company	Ratio	Years	Positive natural numbers
PD6	Time the participants have been involved in the current project	Ratio	Years	Positive natural numbers
PD7	Received dedicated training in SA	Nominal	n.a.	Yes or No
PD8	Experience level of the participants in SA	Ordinal	n.a.	Five-point Likert scale[a]

[a]The five-point Likert scale: (a) No knowledge on SA, (b) some knowledge on SA but never involved in architecting, (c) experience in architecting small software systems ($\geq$50,000 lines of code), (d) Experience in architecting big software systems (>50,000 lines of code), and (e) Chief architect of big software systems.

Table 5.14 Information Related to the Selected Case

#	Case Data Item	Scale Type	Unit	Range
CD1	The number of the architecture decisions for analysis	Ratio	Decisions	Positive natural numbers
CD2	The number of ATD items documented in the software project	Ratio	ATD items	Positive natural numbers
CD3	The number of change scenarios used to calculate the cost and benefit of ATD items	Ratio	Change scenarios	Positive natural numbers
CD4	Duration of the selected project in this case study	Ratio	Months	Positive natural numbers
CD5	Project effort	Ratio	Person-months	Positive natural numbers
CD6	Project size in lines of code	Ratio	Lines of code	Positive natural numbers

researcher and the participants. In addition, semi-structured interviews allowed us to explore in more depth the interview topics by asking follow-up questions based on the participants' answers. We interviewed all the nine participants with different sets of questions depending on each participant's role in the selected software project.

5.5.2.2.3 Data collection process

In order to answer the RQs presented in Section 5.1, we divide the case study into three parts (preparation, workshop, and interview) which include seven tasks (Task1–Task7), as described in Figure 5.5.

Part 1—Preparation.

Task1: Recall architecture decisions. The architects recalled the architecture decisions of the software system following the guidelines provided by the authors, and documented the architecture decisions using a template provided by the authors.

Part 2—Workshop.

Task2: Present ATD viewpoints. The first author presented the schedule of the workshop, the ATD viewpoints, and the change scenario template to the participants (i.e., the architect, manager, and development team).

Task3: Collect change scenarios. The project manager provided a list of change scenarios that may happen in the coming 3 months[1]. A change scenario describes a possible major change in a software system. Typical change scenarios

---

[1]There are three builds every month, but whether a build will be released depends on the severity of the resolved bugs and the urgency of the new requirements.

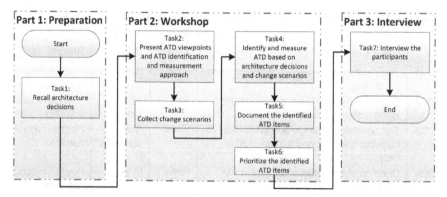

FIGURE 5.5

Procedure of the case study.

include: (i) the unimplemented features that are planned in the roadmap of the software system, (ii) the known but unresolved bugs, and (iii) the maintenance tasks that improve certain QAs of the implemented architecture.

Task4: *Identify and measure ATD based on architecture decisions and change scenarios.* We provided guidelines on how to perform the identification and measurement of the ATD. All participants worked together on this task following the guidelines. The chief architect documented the identified ATD items using the ATD item template (i.e., the ATD Detail viewpoint).

Task5: *Document ATD items.* The chief architect documented the identified ATD items using the ATD Decision, ATD-related Component, and ATD Stakeholder Involvement viewpoints. He also improved the ATD Detail view created in Task4.

Task6: *Prioritize the identified ATD items.* The participants read the ATD views generated in Task4 and Task5, and then prioritized the ATD items based on their understanding and the results of their discussions on the documented ATD views.

Part 3—Interview.

Task7: *Interview the participants.* We first asked the participants to fill in a questionnaire regarding their experience in software industry (Table 5.13). After that, one author interviewed the participants one by one using semi-structured questions.

This workshop in Part 2 took around 4 h. The schedule of the workshop is described in Table 5.15. Each interview in Part 3 lasted between 45 and 65 min.

5.5.3 RESULTS

We first present the collected information about the participants and the selected case (i.e., the software project) in this case study, then answer each of the RQs defined in Section 5.1, in the following subsections.

Table 5.15 Schedule of the Workshop

#	Step	Participants	Time	%
1	Task2	All	40 min	18
2	Task3	All	10 min	4
3	Break	All	10 min	4
4	Task4	All	80 min	36
5	Task5	The chief architect	40 min	18
6	Task6	All	45 min	20
Total time			225 min	100

Table 5.16 shows the information on the participants' experience in software industry. All the participants have worked in IT industry for 7 or more years except Developer5 who has 3.5-year experience in IT industry. Four participants have experience in architecting big software systems (which size is more than 50,000 lines of code); two have experience in architecting small software systems (which size is less than 50,000 lines of code); while the remaining three have no experience in architecting, but they have knowledge of SA.

The selected software project in this case study is a relatively big project (see CD4, 5 and 6 below). The information about the case is described below:

- CD1, No. of the architecture decisions for analysis: 20.
- CD2, No. of documented ATD items: 10.
- CD3, No. of change scenarios used to calculate the cost and benefit of ATD items: 26.
- CD4, Duration of the software project: seven years.
- CD5, Project effort: around 290 person-months (about 50,000 person-hours).
- CD6, Project size in lines of code: around 760,000 lines of code.

5.5.3.1 Understandability of ATD viewpoints (RQ1)

The results of the understandability of the ATD viewpoints are described in Table 5.17. All ATD viewpoints received an average score above eight, except for the ATD Detail viewpoint. This indicates that the ATD viewpoints are relatively easy to understand. The ATD Detail viewpoint received an average score of 6.8, which indicates some issues in understanding it.

5.5.3.2 Ease of collecting the required information and documenting ATD views (RQ2)

The collection of required information was performed by all the participants in the workshop, while the documentation of ATD views was only performed by the chief architect. Table 5.18 shows the ease of collecting the needed information for creating the ATD views. A higher score (in the range between 1 and 10) means that the corresponding piece of information is easier to collect. The

Table 5.16 Participants' Experience Information

Participant	PD1: Years in Software Industry	PD2: Years as a Developer	PD3: Years in the Company	PD4: Years in the Domain	PD5: Years in the Current Role	PD6: Years in the Project	PD7: Dedicated SA Training	PD8: Experience Level in SA
Architect1	8	8	8	6	6	6	Y	Chief architect of big software systems
Architect2	9	6	9	2	5	2	Y	Experience in architecting big software systems
Manager1	10	5	13	7	7	7	Y	Experience in architecting big software systems
Developer1	7	7	7	5	5	5	N	Some SA knowledge but never involved in architecting
Developer2	8	8	5	3	7	3	N	Experience in architecting small software systems
Developer3	9	9	4	2	1	1	Y	Experience in architecting small software systems
Developer4	9	6	6	3	3	3	N	Some SA knowledge but never involved in architecting
Developer5	3.5	3.5	3.5	1.5	3.5	1.5	Y	Experience in architecting big software systems
Tester1	7	7	6	0.1	0.1	0.1	N	Some SA knowledge but never involved in architecting

Table 5.17 Understandability of ATD Viewpoints

ATD Viewpoint	Architect1	Architect2	Manager1	Developer1	Developer2	Developer3	Developer4	Developer5	Tester1	Mean score	Median Score
ATD Detail viewpoint	8	6	6	5	6	5	7	9	9	6.8	6
ATD Decision viewpoint	7	10	7	8	8	5	10	10	9	8.2	8
ATD-related Component viewpoint	8	10	6	9	10	9	10	9	10	9.0	9
ATD Distribution viewpoint	8	9	9	7	8	8	6	10	8	8.1	8
ATD Stakeholder Involvement viewpoint	8	10	5	9	8	8	9	9	10	8.4	9
ATD Chronological viewpoint	9	10	5	7	10	7	7	9	9	8.1	9

Table 5.18 Ease of Collecting Required Information for ATD Views

Required Information	Architect1	Architect2	Manager1	Developer1	Developer2	Developer3	Developer4	Developer5	Tester1	Mean Score	Median Score
Architecture decision that incurs an ATD item	5	9	5	5	6	5	9	8	8	6.7	6
Architecture decision that repays an ATD item	7	8	7	7	6	5	9	8	6	7.0	7
Compromised QA	8	9	6	8	6	7	9	9	9	7.9	8
Rationale	7	8	7	7	5	5	9	9	9	7.3	7
Benefit	5	10	3	7	4	2	9	8	6	6.0	6
Principal	5	7	4	3	4	3	8	7	6	5.2	5
Change scenarios	6	9	7	3	8	4	9	8	9	7.0	8
Consequence of a change scenario	5	9	7	3	7	6	9	8	9	7.0	7
Potential interest incurred in a change scenario	6	9	4	4	4	2	3	7	8	5.2	4
Probability of the potential interest incurred in a change scenario	6	5	4	8	4	8	5	9	8	6.3	6
Affected components	6	9	5	8	8	6	10	9	9	7.8	8

benefit, principal, interest, and interest probability received scores lower than 7. The compromised QA and affected components received the highest scores.

The ATD views were documented by the chief architect. The chief architect documented the ATD items using the ATD Detail viewpoint along the ATD identification and measurement (i.e., Task4) which took 80 min. In addition, there were 40 min (in Task5) dedicated to ATD documentation. Considering that the chief architect only spent around one fourth of the 80 min in documenting ten ATD items in Task4, the total time for ATD documentation was around one hour ($80*1/4 + 40 = 60$ min) in this case study. During the interview with him, he argued that documenting the ATD views needs an acceptable amount of effort, but this amount of effort was a little bit more than expected (i.e., a little bit too much but acceptable). Specifically, documenting the ATD Detail view requires increased effort, while generating other ATD views was comparatively much easier. He suggested that a dedicated tool supporting them to generate ATD views would make ATD documentation much easier, since the information in the ATD Detail view can be used to automatically generate the rest of the views.

5.5.3.3 Usefulness in understanding ATD (RQ3)

We investigated the usefulness in understanding ATD in the following three aspects: (i) the difference of the architecture health level of the current architecture compared with what they initially thought, (ii) how useful the participants thought the ATD viewpoints to be in facilitating their understanding of ATD in the software system, and (iii) ATD viewpoints that the participants are willing to use for managing ATD.

- *Architecture health level.* In the interviews, we asked the participants to compare the architecture health level based on the documented ATD views, with their initial assessment of the health level. As shown in Table 5.19, six participants argued that the architecture health level is lower than that they thought it to be; one considered that the former is much lower than the latter; and two believed that the former is roughly equal to the latter.
- *Understanding ATD.* In our interviews with the participants, we asked them about how useful they perceived the ATD views to be in understanding ATD in the system. Table 5.20 shows the answers to this question. There are five candidate answers: *not useful, somewhat useful, moderately useful, very useful,* and *not sure.* Most of the participants considered that the ATD Detail view, ATD Decision view, ATD-related Component view, and ATD distribution view are *very useful* in understanding ATD in this case study.
- *Preferred ATD views.* During the interviews, we asked the architects about which ATD views they are willing to use to document ATD in their future projects (produce ATD views). As shown in the "Willing to use" columns of Table 5.21, both architects are willing to use the ATD Detail view, ATD Decision view, ATD-related Component view, and ATD Distribution view to

Table 5.19 Architecture Health Level Compared with the Previously Estimated

Participant	Architecture Health Level
Architect1	Lower than
Architect2	Much lower than
Manager1	Lower than
Developer1	Roughly equal to
Developer2	Lower than
Developer3	Lower than
Developer4	Lower than
Developer5	Lower than
Tester1	Roughly equal to

document ATD. We asked the other seven participants (i.e., the manager, developers, and tester) about which ATD views they are willing to get informed regarding the ATD in their projects (consume ATD views). As shown in the "Willing to get informed by" columns of Table 5.21, most of the seven participants preferred the ATD Detail view, ATD-related Component view, and ATD Distribution view to keep up to date with ATD in the system and further manage it. In addition, three out of the seven participants preferred the ATD Decision view. The ATD Stakeholder Involvement view and ATD Chronological view were considered as the least useful ATD views.

5.5.4 INTERPRETATION

We discuss our interpretation of the case study results for the RQs as follows.

5.5.4.1 Interpretation of the results regarding RQ1

RQ1 is about the understandability of the ATD viewpoints. As shown in Table 5.17, the ATD Detail viewpoint received an average score of 6.8, while each of the other viewpoints received an average score above eight. These scores indicate good understandability of the ATD viewpoints, considering that the case study participants spent only 40 min (as described in Table 5.15) on learning the viewpoints. Among the six ATD viewpoints, the ATD-related Component viewpoint received the highest score, since (i) this viewpoint does not introduce new concepts, and (ii) they are more interested in this viewpoint as components are more related to the daily work of most of the case study participants. The ATD Detail viewpoint received the lowest score, because some of the participants suggested that (i) this viewpoint introduces several new concepts, such as principal and interest; and (ii) an ATD Detail view contains too much information and it takes time to understand and remember every element of the view (even though participants considered it to be rather comprehensive).

Table 5.20 Usefulness of the ATD Views in Understanding ATD

Participant	ATD Detail View	ATD Decision View	ATD-Related Component View	ATD Distribution View	ATD Stakeholder Involvement View	ATD Chronological View
Architect1	Moderately useful	Moderately useful	Very useful	Moderately useful	Moderately useful	Moderately useful
Architect2	Very useful	Very useful	Very useful	Very useful	Moderately useful	Very useful
Manager1	Moderately useful	Very useful	Moderately useful	Very useful	Somewhat useful	Moderately useful
Developer1	Very useful	Moderately useful	Very useful	Moderately useful	Somewhat useful	Moderately useful
Developer2	Very useful	Somewhat useful	Somewhat useful	Very useful	Somewhat useful	Somewhat useful
Developer3	Very useful	Very useful	Very useful	Very useful	Somewhat useful	Somewhat useful
Developer4	Very useful	Moderately useful	Moderately useful	Very useful	Moderately useful	Somewhat useful
Developer5	Very useful	Very useful	Very useful	Very useful	Somewhat useful	Moderately useful
Tester1	Moderately useful	Very useful	Very useful	Moderately useful	Very useful	Somewhat useful

Table 5.21 ATD Views that the Participant are Willing to Use or Get Informed by

ATD Viewpoint	Willing to Use		Willing to Get Informed by						
	Architect1	Architect2	Manager1	Developer1	Developer2	Developer3	Developer4	Developer5	Tester1
ATD Detail view	X	X	X	X	X	X	X	X	X
ATD Decision view	X	X		X		X		X	X
ATD-related component view	X	X		X		X	X	X	X
ATD Distribution view	X	X	X		X		X	X	X
ATD Stakeholder involvement view									
ATD Chronological view								X	

5.5.4.2 Interpretation of the results regarding RQ2

RQ2 is concerned with the ease of collecting the required information and subsequently creating the ATD views. As shown in Table 5.18, the case study participants gave relatively low scores to the elements that needed to be estimated, including benefit, principal, potential interest incurred in a change scenario, and probability of the potential interest incurred in a change scenario. When collecting these elements, participants were faced with the difficulties of measuring them for each ATD item. In practice, there lacks an effective approach to measure the elements aforementioned. We need such an ATD measurement approach that is efficient, easy to operate, and with acceptable accuracy. The architecture decisions that incur or repay ATD items also received relatively low scores. The ease of collecting these architecture decisions reflects the ease of ATD identification, which requires significant effort. In addition, collecting architecture decisions that incur and repay ATD items received similar scores (i.e., 6.7 and 7.0, respectively), which indicates that collecting these two types of architecture decisions needs similar amount of effort. This is mostly because one can identify a specific architecture decision that incurs an ATD item only when he or she already comes up with a better solution to repay the ATD item.

Creating the ATD views costs more effort than the chief architect expected. This was for two main reasons. First, creating the ATD Detail view manually is time-consuming since there are many elements that need to be filled in for each ATD item. Second, there was no dedicated supporting tool for generating ATD views during the case study. Instead, we provided Excel templates to help with the ATD views generation. When generating the ATD views, the chief architect needed to read the required information from different Excel files or sheets of the same file, and checked the information in one ATD view with the other ATD views to maintain the consistency between all ATD views.

Considering that the total time spent for ATD documentation in this case study was around one hour, we argue that the cost of ATD documentation was rather minimal. In practice, the effort needed in ATD documentation for a project, largely depends on the number of ATD items to be documented. Furthermore, the effort needed also depends on the number of ATD viewpoints chosen to document ATD. Practitioners do not necessarily have to choose all the viewpoints to document ATD in their projects. Instead, they can choose the ATD viewpoints that are most interesting and useful for their projects. In addition, practitioners may select part of the elements in the ATD Detail view that are most useful for their projects and that are required to create views conforming to other selected ATD viewpoints. In practice, the architect would be mainly responsible for ATD documentation. Developers may also be involved in ATD documentation, since their work may influence the ATD. For instance, when developers have resolved a specific ATD item, they can update the status and history of this ATD item in the ATD Detail view.

5.5.4.3 Interpretation of the results regarding RQ3

RQ3 focuses on the usefulness in facilitating stakeholders' understanding on the ATD in the selected software project in the case study. As shown in Table 5.19, all participants considered that the health level of the SA is lower or roughly equal to what they thought before this case study. This indicates that the documented ATD views can help the participants to reach a consensus on the understanding of the architecture's health. Especially, seven out of nine participants (including the two architects and the project manager) considered the architecture to be less healthy than what they expected before the case study. In the interviews with the architects and project manager, they suggested that they had never systematically collected and documented the data on the negative consequences caused by the compromises on the system's maintainability and evolvability.

Although documenting the ATD Detail view is time-consuming, all the participants were willing to use this view in managing ATD in the future. This is mainly because this view contains rich information about ATD items and this information provides the basis to generate other ATD views. The ATD Decision view, ATD-related Component view, and ATD Distribution view were considered more useful than the ATD Stakeholder Involvement view and ATD Chronological view, and most participants were willing to use these three ATD views to manage ATD. This is mostly because these ATD views provide holistic views on all the documented ATD items. Stakeholders can find interesting and valuable information in these views without examining the detailed individual ATD items. The ATD Stakeholder Involvement view was regarded as the lease useful view, since this view is not relevant to the key properties (e.g., cost, benefit, related architecture decisions) of ATD items.

5.5.5 IMPLICATIONS FOR RESEARCH AND PRACTICE

The results of this case study have implications for both research and practice, as follows:

Implications for research

- Industry welcomes the introduction of the concept of ATD and considers that ATDM is important to keep the long-term health of the architecture. Thus, there is momentum to perform ATD research involving the participation of industry.
- ATD documentation approaches should consider reusing existing artifacts (e.g., documented architecture decisions and change scenarios), so that the effort needed to apply ATD documentation approaches can be reduced. Thus, researchers are encouraged to devise approaches that make as much reuse as possible; this would increase their adoption rate in industry.
- Tool support for ATD documentation approaches is essential for practical use of the approaches in industry. Researchers are encouraged to develop prototype tools that provide such support, and further improve the tools with industrial evaluation.

Implications for practice

- Critical ATD analysis and systematic ATD documentation can help the project team to get an in-depth understanding of the health level of the current architecture.
- Practitioners can choose to document ATD using those ATD viewpoints that are most interesting and useful for their projects and can be afforded in terms of required effort. They do not necessarily have to use all the ATD viewpoint in their projects.

5.5.6 THREATS TO VALIDITY

We discuss the threats to validity according to different types of validity suggested in the guidelines of reporting case study research (Runeson and Höst, 2009). Internal validity is not discussed since we do not investigate causal relationships but only evaluate the ATD viewpoints that we proposed.

Construct validity reflects "to what extent the studied operational measures really represent what the researcher have in mind and what is investigated according to the research questions" (Runeson and Höst, 2009). A potential threat in case studies is that operational measures are not clearly defined so that the collected data cannot be used to effectively answer RQs. To mitigate this threat, before this case study was performed, we clearly defined the RQs, and the data items that need to be collected for answering each RQ. All these data items were collected during the interviews with the participants. Another potential threat is that the participants may have different understandings on the interview questions from the researchers, so that the collected data are not what the researchers expect. In order to alleviate this threat, before the case study, we invited an architect from another company to do a pilot case study. We revised and improved the interview questions according to the feedback from the invited architect. We believe that the threats to construct validity were significantly reduced by the two measures taken above.

External validity is concerned with the generalizability of the case study results (Runeson and Höst, 2009). In case studies, there is always a threat to external validity, since only one or several cases are studied, which makes statistical generalization impossible. Seddon and Scheepers (2012) suggest to generalize the results of a single study using *analytic generalization:* "arguing, based on similarities between relevant attributes of things in a sample and things in other settings, that knowledge claims based on the sample are also likely to hold true in those other settings." According to the theory of analytic generalization, we believe that the study results are valid for those software projects with similar project and team sizes as well as application domains. In addition, although the case study only took place in a company in China and the cultural context may have played a role in the results, we believe that the study results hold true in similar culture backgrounds. To confirm the aforementioned generalization claims, replication of the study with different project and team sizes in other countries would be desirable.

Reliability is concerned with to what extent the data and the analysis are dependent on the specific researchers (Runeson and Höst, 2009). To make the case study replicable, before we performed the case study, we defined a protocol for this case study in which we clearly defined the RQs, data items to be collected for each RQ, interview questions to collect the needed data items, concrete operation steps, and required resources for each step. However, different people may have different understandings on the protocol. To validate the protocol, we invited an architect from another company to carry out a pilot study following the protocol, as already mentioned in "construct validity." We revised the protocol according to the feedback received as follows: (i) we improved the Excel templates for producing ATD views; (ii) we fine-tuned the timeline of the workshop; (iii) we reordered a few interview questions; (iv) we provided candidate answers for those interview questions that the participants felt difficult to answer; (v) we reformulated several interview questions that partially overlapped with other questions; and (vi) we also reformulated those interview questions containing new concepts that were not introduced in our tutorial. This pilot study effectively improved the data collection procedure and the understandability of the interview questions. Note that we did not include the data collected in the pilot study in the data analysis.

5.6 CONCLUSIONS AND FUTURE WORK

ATD has important influence on the long-term health of SAs, especially on maintainability and evolvability. When left unmanaged, ATD may accumulate significantly, making maintenance and evolution tasks hard to complete. To facilitate ATDM, ATD needs to be recorded in a systematic manner to make it visible to stakeholders and thus facilitate ATD communication and understanding.

To systematically document ATD, in this chapter, we proposed six architecture viewpoints for documenting ATD in software systems. Each ATD viewpoint addresses one or more stakeholders' concerns on ATD, which were collected from literature on TD and derived from ATDM activities. The viewpoints are as follows: (i) The ATD Detail viewpoint is concerned with the detailed information of ATD items in a software system. (ii) The ATD Decision viewpoint is concerned with the relationship between architecture decisions and ATD items. (iii) The ATD Stakeholder Involvement viewpoint is concerned with the responsibilities of stakeholders in the process of ATDM. (iv) The ATD Distribution viewpoint is concerned with the distribution of the amount of the ATD over ATD items and the change of the ATD amount between milestones. (v) The ATD-related Component viewpoint is concerned with the relationship between system components and ATD items. (vi) The ATD Chronological viewpoint is concerned with the evolution of ATD items.

To evaluate the effectiveness of the proposed ATD viewpoints in documenting ATD, we conducted a case study in an industrial project in a large telecommunications company. The results of the case study show that: (i) the ATD viewpoints are relatively easy to understand; (ii) some of the data (including benefit, principal, interest, and interest probability) that need to be estimated require more effort to collect, compared with other data, such as the compromised QA and affected components; creating an ATD Detail view also requires relatively more effort while generating the other ATD views are much easier; acceptable effort is needed to generate views using the proposed ATD viewpoints; and (iii) the ATD viewpoints are useful in understanding ATD. To summarize, this empirical evaluation shows that the ATD viewpoints can effectively help the documentation of ATD.

The impact of this work is twofold: it contributes (i) to the domain of SA with a set of ATD viewpoints for architecture description, and (ii) to empirical software engineering and the body of evidence regarding ATDM.

As regards future work, first, we plan to replicate the case study in more industrial cases with different project and company sizes as well as culture contexts, and continuously revise the ATD viewpoints according to the feedback collected during the case studies. Second, since we received positive feedback from the empirical evaluation on the proposed ATD viewpoints, the next step is to design and develop a dedicated tool to assist with the generation of architecture views conforming to the ATD viewpoints. The tool support can reduce the needed effort by reusing ATD description elements, keep the consistency between ATD views, and improve the traceability between different ATD views.

ACKNOWLEDGMENT

This work is partially supported by AFR-Luxembourg under the contract No. 895528 and the NSFC under the grants No. 61170025 and No. 61472286. We are thankful to all the participants in the case study and the architect in the pilot study for their help.

APPENDIX A. ATD CONCERNS

We came up with the concerns on ATD according to two sources: (i) concerns adapted or derived from the concerns on TD in general (TD concerns) collected during our mapping study on TD (Li et al., 2015); (ii) concerns derived from ATDM activities in the ATDM process proposed in our previous work (ATDM activities) (Li et al., 2014a). From the first source (mapping study), we extracted TD concerns from the primary studies through: (i) the problems addressed by the primary studies; and (ii) the problems expected to be solved in future work of the primary studies. We subsequently derived ATD concerns from the identified TD concerns, based on the following criteria: (i) if a TD concern is directly related to the architecture (i.e., not the system details), then the concern is considered as an ATD concern; OR (ii) if a TD concern is not about architecture but makes sense to ATD stakeholders, then this concern is regarded as an ATD concern.

From the second source (ATDM activities presented in Li et al., 2014a), we derived ATD concerns based on the concrete tasks performed in each ATDM activity and the intents of the tasks. For instance, in the ATDM activity *ATD measurement*, the involved tasks are to estimate the benefit, interest, and cost of each ATD item, thus, we got the ATD concerns on the quantities of these properties of ATD items. As a result, we derived the ATD concerns C2, C3, C4, and C5. All the resulting ATD concerns and their detailed sources are shown in Table 5.22.

APPENDIX B. VIEWPOINT DEFINITIONS AND CORRESPONDENCE RULES

In this section, we first propose a shared metamodel of the six ATD viewpoints, then give each ATD viewpoint a detailed definition that can act as guidelines to generate ATD views governed by the ATD viewpoint, and finally define the correspondence rules for the ATD viewpoints.

B.1 METAMODEL OF ATD VIEWPOINTS

To facilitate the generation of ATD views that are governed by the proposed ATD viewpoints, we constructed a common metamodel that integrates all the elements of the ATD viewpoints. The metamodel also serves to maintain traceability

Table 5.22 ATD Concerns and their Sources

Description of Source	Derived Concerns	Concern Source
How can I efficiently measure how much debt I already have? (Eisenberg, 2012)	C2	TD concern
How large is my technical debt? (Nugroho et al., 2011)		
How much interest am I paying on the debt? (Nugroho et al., 2011)	C5	TD concern
What is the consequence of holding onto a debt for future maintenance? (Nugroho et al., 2011)	C19, C20	TD concern
Is the debt growing, and how fast? (Nugroho et al., 2011)	C16, C17	TD concern
Technical debt can be considered as a particular type of risk in software maintenance and the problem of managing technical debt boils down to managing risk and making informed decisions on what tasks can be delayed and when they need to be paid back (Guo and Seaman, 2011)	C6, C15	TD concern
The analysis and measurement of TD-Principal can guide critical management decisions about how to allocate resources for reducing business risk and IT cost (Curtis et al., 2012)	C4, C6	TD concern
A technical debt "SWAT" team, led by one of the company's most senior architects, tasked with learning how to reduce the technical debt and then rolling that knowledge out to the rest of the development staff, should be established (Gat and Heintz, 2011)	C13	TD concern
Which delayed (maintenance) tasks [a type of TD] need to be accomplished, and when (Seaman and Guo, 2011)	C6, C15	TD concern
The proposed approach to technical debt management centers around a "technical debt list." The list contains technical debt "items," each of which represents a task that was left undone, but that runs a risk of causing future problems if not completed (Seaman and Guo, 2011)	C1	TD concern
Overall, it is important for a project team to understand (i) where TD exists in a system so that it can be tagged for eventual removal, (ii) the cost of removing TD (i.e., Principal), and (iii) the consequences of not removing TD (i.e., Interest) (Falessi et al., 2013)	C4, C5, C10	TD concern

(Continued)

Table 5.22 ATD Concerns and their Sources *Continued*

Description of Source	Derived Concerns	Concern Source
The person who takes on technical debt is not necessarily the one who has to pay it off (Allman, 2012)	C8	
Is technical debt increasing or decreasing for a system or for a component? (Seaman and Guo, 2011)	C18	TD concern
How much debt is "too much" (i.e., high interest) versus manageable (i.e., low interest)? (Eisenberg, 2012)	C21	TD concern
Developers tend to vote for investments into internal quality but managers often tend to question these investments' values and, therefore, tend to decline to approve them (Bohnet and Döllner, 2011)	C7	TD concern
Our questions focus on how technical debt is propagated along those dependencies and how technical debt accumulates at various points in the chain (McGregor et al., 2012)	C20	TD concern
It enables taking into account not only the sunk cost of development but also the cost yet to be paid to reduce the amount of technical debt (Gat, 2012)	C4	TD concern
Practices related to identification provide the developer ways to identify Technical Debt in the code whereas classification helps to categorize them in order to understand the reason (Krishna and Basu, 2012)	C11	TD concern
After acquiring the source implementation components for technical debt, the *DebtFlag* mechanism completes the projection by propagating technical debt through dependencies while following a possible rule set (Holvitie and Leppänen, 2013)	C10, C20	TD concern
ATD identification detects ATD items during or after the architecting process. An ATD item is incurred by an architecture decision; thus, one can investigate an architecture decision and its rationale to identify an ATD item by considering whether the maintainability or evolvability of the SA is compromised (Li et al., 2014a)	C1, C7, C11, C12	ATDM activity
ATD measurement analyzes the cost and benefit associated with an ATD item and estimates them, including the prediction of change scenarios influencing this ATD item for interest measurement (Li et al., 2014a)	C2, C3, C4, C5	ATDM activity

Table 5.22 ATD Concerns and their Sources *Continued*

Description of Source	Derived Concerns	Concern Source
ATD prioritization sorts all the identified ATD items in a software system using a number of criteria. The aim of this activity is to identify which ATD items should be resolved first and which can be resolved later depending on the system's business goals and preferences (Li et al., 2014a)	C6	ATDM activity
ATD monitoring watches the changes of the costs and benefits of unresolved ATD items over time (Li et al., 2014a)	C9, C14, C16, C17, C18, C19, 21, C21	ATDM activity
ATD repayment concerns making new or changing existing architecture decisions in order to eliminate or mitigate the negative influences of an ATD item (Li et al., 2014a)	C13, C15,	ATDM activity

and consistency between different ATD views. Figure 5.6 shows the metamodel of the ATD viewpoints. The elements in the dark part of Figure 5.6 are concepts adopted from ISO/IEC/IEEE 42010 (ISO/IEC/IEEE, 2011). An *architecture decision* can incur *ATD item*(s), which is adopted from our previous work (Li et al., 2014a) and shown in details in Table 5.4. An *ATD item* relates to one or more *components*, which are influenced by one or more architecture decisions. One or more architecture decisions can be made to repay ATD item(s). An *ATD item* has a specific *status*. An *ATD item* has some *cost* to the future maintenance and evolution of a software system, which is the reason why the ATD item should be managed. The cost of an ATD item has a *principal* and *interest*. The interest of an ATD item is comprised of one or more *scenario interests*, each corresponding to a *change scenario* impacted by the ATD item. A change scenario has an associated *probability*, indicating the possibility that the change scenario will happen. An *ATD item* has some *benefit*(s) which is the reason why the ATD item is incurred. An *ATD item* has a *compromised quality attribute*, i.e., one of the six QAs mentioned in Table 5.4. An ATD item can raise new *system concern*(s) when the ATD item has significant impact on the system under consideration. For instance, if the ATD item is possible to negatively influence over certain functionality of the system, a new system concern is raised to eliminate or mitigate the negative influence. An *ATD rationale*, which considers the *benefit* and *cost* of the corresponding ATD item, tells why the ATD item is incurred. A *stakeholder* performs an *action* on an *ATD item*, for which the *status* of the ATD item is changed. An ATD item corresponds to an *intentionality*, indicating that it was incurred intentionally or unintentionally. An ATD item may be changed in an *iteration* that has one *iteration endpoint*.

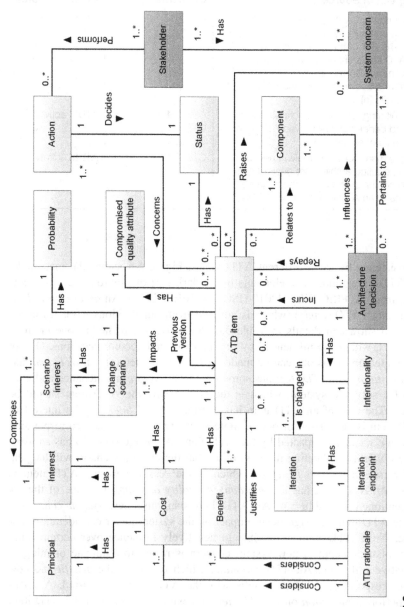

FIGURE 5.6

Metamodel of the ATD viewpoints.

FIGURE 5.7

Metamodel of ATD Decision viewpoint.

B.2 ATD DECISION VIEWPOINT

The ATD Decision viewpoint shows the relationships between ATD items and architecture decisions of a software system. A view conforming to the ATD Decision viewpoint shows all ATD items, which were incurred from the beginning of the ATDM process till the current iteration in a software system, and their relationships with related architecture decisions.

B.2.1 Model kind

The metamodel of the ATD Decision viewpoint is shown in Figure 5.7. This metamodel documents the model kind, which describes the conceptual elements for architectural models that conform to the ATD Decision viewpoint. The notation of UML class diagrams is used to describe this metamodel.

The constraints listed below apply to the elements within this model kind:

- Every ATD item has a unique ID and name.
- Every architecture decision has a unique ID and name.
- An ATD item is incurred by one architecture decision.
- An ATD item is repaid by one or more architecture decisions.
- An architecture decision can incur or repay zero or more ATD items.

B.3 ATD-RELATED COMPONENT VIEWPOINT

The ATD-related Component viewpoint shows the components that are related to ATD items. The number of the related components to a specific ATD item may vary in different versions over time, but, in a view conforming to the ATD-related Component viewpoint, it only shows the ATD items and their related components in the latest versions.

B.3.1 Model kind

The metamodel of the ATD-related Component viewpoint is shown in Figure 5.8. This metamodel documents the model kind, which describes the conceptual elements for architectural models that conform to the ATD-related Component viewpoint. The notation of UML class diagrams is used to describe this metamodel.

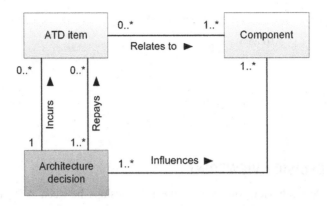

FIGURE 5.8

Metamodel of ATD-related Component viewpoint.

The constraints listed below apply to the elements within this model kind:

- Every ATD item has a unique ID and name.
- Every component has a unique ID and name.
- An ATD item relates to one or more components.
- A component is related to zero or more ATD items.

B.4 ATD DISTRIBUTION VIEWPOINT

The ATD Distribution viewpoint shows the costs and benefits of all ATD items in two neighboring iterations.

B.4.1 Model kind

The metamodel of the ATD Distribution viewpoint is shown in Figure 5.9. This metamodel documents the model kind, which presents the conceptual elements for architectural models that conform to the ATD Distribution viewpoint. The notation of UML class diagrams is used to describe this metamodel. An iteration endpoint has a date and a type that can be chosen from the following:

- *Milestone*: "A version of the architecture that has reached a stable state (or an intermediate stable state)" (van Heesch et al., 2012).
- *Release*: "A version of the architecture that is delivered to a customer of made available to the public for use" (van Heesch et al., 2012).

The constraints listed below apply to the elements within this model kind:

- Every ATD item has a unique ID and name.
- Every iteration has exactly one endpoint with a unique name.

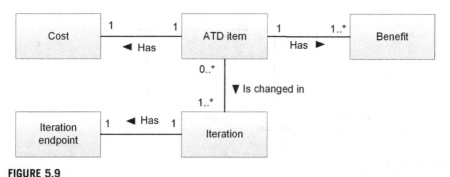

FIGURE 5.9

Metamodel of ATD Distribution viewpoint.

- An ATD item has one or more benefits. A benefit can be technical benefit (e.g., QA benefit) or nontechnical benefit (e.g., business benefit). Only the measurable benefit is shown in the ATD Distribution viewpoint.
- An ATD item has one cost. The cost is the sum of principal and interest of the ATD item.
- An ATD item (its benefit and cost) can change in one or more iterations.
- In each iteration, zero or more ATD items (their costs and benefits) change.

B.5 ATD STAKEHOLDER INVOLVEMENT VIEWPOINT

The ATD Stakeholder Involvement viewpoint shows the responsibilities of relevant stakeholders in the ATDM process. A view conforming to the ATD Stakeholder Involvement viewpoint presents the activities performed by the involved stakeholders on ATD items in the current iteration and their statuses.

B.5.1 Model kind

The metamodel of the ATD Stakeholder Involvement viewpoint is shown in Figure 5.10. This metamodel documents the model kind, which describes the conceptual elements for architectural models that conform to the ATD Stakeholder Involvement viewpoint. The notation of UML class diagrams is used to describe this metamodel.

A *Stakeholder* conducts an *Action* on an *ATD item* in a specific development *iteration*, the *Status* of this ATD item changes accordingly. A stakeholder can be any of the defined stakeholders in Section 5.3.1. We defined the following types of actions in the ATDM process according to the key ATDM activities (Li et al., 2014a):

- Identify: stakeholders find out the location of the ATD item.
- Measure: stakeholders estimate the benefit and cost of the ATD item.
- Re-measure: stakeholders estimate the benefit and cost of an ATD item that was measured in previous iterations.

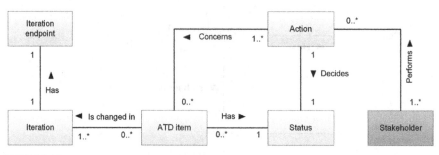

FIGURE 5.10

Metamodel of ATD Stakeholder Involvement viewpoint.

- Prioritize: stakeholders assign a priority to be resolved to the ATD item based on available information related to this ATD item, such as interest.
- Repay: stakeholders resolve the ATD item by making new or modifying existing architecture decisions.

Accordingly, the status of an ATD item can be *Identified, Measured, Remeasured, Prioritized*, and *Resolved*.

The constraints listed below apply to the elements within this model kind:

- Every ATD item has a unique ID and name.
- Every iteration has an iteration endpoint with a unique name.
- All ATD items that changed in one iteration are shown.
- Every stakeholder shown performed at least one action.
- Every stakeholder has a unique name and at least one role.
- Every action points to an ATD item or an iteration endpoint. If the target is an iteration endpoint, the corresponding action is performed for all ATD items changed in that iteration.

B.6 ATD CHRONOLOGICAL VIEWPOINT

The ATD Chronological viewpoint shows how the ATD items in a software system evolved over time and how they were managed in the ATDM process.

B.6.1 Model kind

The metamodel of the ATD Chronological viewpoint is shown in Figure 5.11. This metamodel documents the model kind, which describes the conceptual elements for architectural models that conform to the ATD Chronological viewpoint. Again, the notation of UML class diagrams is used to describe this metamodel.

The constraints listed below apply to the elements within this mode kind:

- Every ATD item has a unique ID and name.
- Every ATD item has exactly one status at a time.
- Every iteration has exactly one endpoint with a unique name.

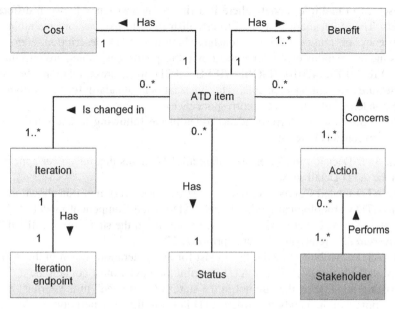

FIGURE 5.11

Metamodel of ATD Chronological viewpoint.

- Every ATD item shown is changed in one or more iterations.
- Only an ATD item with the status "measured" shows its benefit and cost.
- Only an ATD item with the status "remeasured" shows its benefit delta and cost delta compared with the previously measured benefit and cost, respectively.

B.7 ATD DETAIL VIEWPOINT

The ATD Detail viewpoint provides a comprehensive textual description of each ATD item documented in a software project. A view conforming to the ATD Detail viewpoint is comprised of multiple models, each used to describe a single ATD item.

B.7.1 Model kind

The metamodel for the ATD Detail viewpoint is identical to the common metamodel for all the ATD viewpoint as shown in Figure 5.6.

B.8 CORRESPONDENCES BETWEEN VIEWPOINTS

We have proposed six ATD viewpoints to document ATD. We use multiple views governed by these ATD viewpoints to document the ATD of a software system. Each ATD view is comprised of one or more models. Because the same subject is represented in multiple models, there is a risk of inconsistency between different models. Therefore, there is a need to establish rules to express and maintain the consistency of cross-model relationships between ATD description elements. Cross-model relations can be expressed by correspondences, which are introduced in ISO/IEC/IEEE 42010 (ISO/IEC/IEEE, 2011) to express relations between architecture description elements. This international standard further introduces correspondence rules to govern correspondences.

We define a set of correspondence rules in the following to keep the consistency between ATD views:

- An ATD Decision model must contain all ATD items that have ever appeared in the ATD Detail views.
- An ATD-related Component model must exist for every iteration shown in the ATD Chronological model. Every ATD-related Component model contain the ATD items which latest versions are in the status of "identified," "measured," "remeasured," and "prioritized."
- An ATD Distribution model must exist for every iteration shown in the ATD Chronological model. Every ATD Distribution model must contain the existing ATD items that are not in the status of "resolved" in the earlier iteration, and the newly identified ATD items in the later iteration.
- An ATD Stakeholder Involvement model must exist for every iteration shown in the ATD Chronological model. Every stakeholder involvement model must contain the involved stakeholders and their actions in the versions of ATD items belonging to the respective iteration.
- An ATD Chronological model must contains all ATD items that have ever appeared in the ATD Detail views.
- The status of an ATD item in the ATD Detail model must correspond to the status of the latest occurrence of the ATD item in the ATD Chronological model.
- The history of an ATD item represented in the ATD Detail model must contain all actions that are performed by the related stakeholders on that ATD item shown in all ATD Stakeholder Involvement models.

REFERENCES

Allman, E., 2012. Managing technical debt—shortcuts that save money and time today can cost you down the road. Commun. ACM 55 (5), 50—55.

Basili, V.R., 1992. Software Modeling and Measurement: The Goal/Question/Metric Paradigm. University of Maryland at College Park, pp. 1—24. <http://drum.lib.umd.edu/bitstream/1903/7538/1/Goal_Question_Metric.pdf> (accessed on 10.01.15.).

Bohnet, J., Döllner, J. 2011. Monitoring code quality and development activity by software maps. In: Paper Presented at the Proceedings of the 2nd International Workshop on Managing Technical Debt (MTD'11), Waikiki, Honolulu, HI, USA.

Brown, N., Cai, Y., Guo, Y., Kazman, R., Kim, M., Kruchten, P., et al. 2010. Managing technical debt in software-reliant systems. In: Paper Presented at the Proceedings of the FSE/SDP Workshop on Future of Software Engineering Research (FoSER'10), Santa Fe, New Mexico, USA.

Buschmann, F., 2011. To pay or not to pay technical debt. IEEE Softw. 28 (6), 29–31.

Cunningham, W., 1992. The WyCash portfolio management system. In: Paper Presented at the Proceedings of the 7th Object-Oriented Programming Systems, Languages, and Applications (OOPSLA'92), Vancouver, BC, Canada.

Curtis, B., Sappidi, J., Szynkarski, A., 2012. Estimating the size, cost, and types of technical debt. In: Paper Presented at the Proceedings of the 3rd International Workshop on Managing Technical Debt (MTD'12), Zurich, Switzerland.

Eisenberg, R.J., 2012. A threshold based approach to technical debt. SIGSOFT Softw. Eng. Notes 37 (2), 1–6.

Falessi, D., Shaw, M.A., Shull, F., Mullen, K., Keymind, M.S., 2013. Practical considerations, challenges, and requirements of tool-support for managing technical debt. In: Paper Presented at the Proceedings of the 4th International Workshop on Managing Technical Debt (MTD'13), San Francisco, CA, USA.

Gat, I., 2012. Technical debt as a meaningful metaphor for code quality. IEEE Softw. 29 (6), 52–54.

Gat, I., Heintz, J.D., 2011. From assessment to reduction: how Cutter Consortium helps rein in millions of dollars in technical debt. In: Paper Presented at the Proceedings of the 2nd International Workshop on Managing Technical Debt (MTD'11), Waikiki, Honolulu, HI, USA.

Guo, Y., Seaman, C., 2011. A portfolio approach to technical debt management. In: Paper Presented at the Proceedings of the 2nd International Workshop on Managing Technical Debt (MTD'11), Waikiki, Honolulu, HI, USA.

Holvitie, J., Leppänen, V., 2013. DebtFlag: technical debt management with a development environment integrated tool. In: Paper Presented at the Proceedings of the 4th International Workshop on Managing Technical Debt (MTD'13), San Francisco, CA, USA.

ISO/IEC, 2011. Systems and Software Engineering—Systems and Software Quality Requirements and Evaluation (SQuaRE)—System and Software Quality Models ISO/IEC 25010:2011, pp. 1–34.

ISO/IEC/IEEE, 2011. Systems and Software Engineering—Architecture Description. ISO/IEC/IEEE 42010:2011(E) (Revision of ISO/IEC 42010:2007 and IEEE Std 1471-2000), pp. 1–46.

Jansen, A., Bosch, J., 2005. Software architecture as a set of architectural design decisions. In: Paper Presented at the Proceedings of the 5th Working IEEE/IFIP Conference on Software Architecture (WICSA'05), Pittsburgh, PA, USA.

Krishna, V., Basu, A., 2012. Minimizing technical debt: developer's viewpoint. In: Paper Presented at the Proceedings of the International Conference on Software Engineering and Mobile Application Modelling and Development (ICSEMA'12), Chennai, India.

Kruchten, P., Nord, R.L., Ozkaya, I., 2012. Technical debt: from metaphor to theory and practice. IEEE Softw. 29 (6), 18–21.

Li, Z., Liang, P., Avgeriou, P., 2014a. Architectural debt management in value-oriented architecting. In: Mistrik, I., Bahsoon, R., Kazman, R., Zhang, Y. (Eds.), Economics-Driven Software Architecture. Elsevier, Waltham, MA, USA, pp. 183–204.

Li, Z., Liang, P., Avgeriou, P., Guelfi, N., Ampatzoglou, A., 2014b. An empirical investigation of modularity metrics for indicating architectural technical debt. In: Paper Presented at the Proceedings of the 10th International Conference on the Quality of Software Architectures (QoSA'14), Marcq-en-Bareul, France.

Li, Z., Avgeriou, P., Liang, P., 2015. A systematic mapping study on technical debt and its management. J. Syst. Softw. 101 (3), 193−220.

McConnell, S., 2008. Managing Technical Debt. Construx, pp. 1−14. <http://www.construx.com/uploadedFiles/Construx/Construx_Content/Resources/Documents/Managing%20Technical%20Debt.pdf> (accessed on: 10.01.15.).

McGregor, J.D., Monteith, J.Y., Jie, Z., 2012. Technical debt aggregation in ecosystems. In: Paper Presented at the Proceedings of the 3rd International Workshop on Managing Technical Debt (MTD'12), Zurich, Switzerland.

Nugroho, A., Visser, J., Kuipers, T., 2011. An empirical model of technical debt and interest. In: Paper Presented at the Proceedings of the 2nd International Workshop on Managing Technical Debt (MTD'11), Waikiki, Honolulu, HI, USA.

Ozkaya, I., Kruchten, P., Nord, R.L., Brown, N., 2011. Managing technical debt in software development: report on the 2nd International Workshop on Managing Technical Debt, held at ICSE 2011. SIGSOFT Softw. Eng. Notes 36 (5), 33−35.

Runeson, P., Höst, M., 2009. Guidelines for conducting and reporting case study research in software engineering. Empir. Softw. Eng. 14 (2), 131−164.

Seaman, C., Guo, Y., 2011. Measuring and monitoring technical debt. In: Zelkowitz, M. (Ed.), Advances in Computers, vol. 82. Elsevier, London, UK, pp. 25−45.

Seddon, P.B., Scheepers, R., 2012. Towards the improved treatment of generalization of knowledge claims in IS research: drawing general conclusions from samples. Eur. J. Inf. Syst. 21 (1), 6−21.

van Heesch, U., Avgeriou, P., Hilliard, R., 2012. A documentation framework for architecture decisions. J. Syst. Softw. 85 (4), 795−820.

Zazworka, N., Spinola, R.O., Vetro', A., Shull, F., Seaman, C. 2013. A case study on effectively identifying technical debt. In: Paper Presented at the Proceedings of the 17th International Conference on Evaluation and Assessment in Software Engineering (EASE'13), Porto de Galinhas, Brazil.

Quality management and Software Product Quality Engineering

Padmalata V. Nistala[1], Kesav V. Nori[2], Swaminathan Natarajan[3], Nikhil R. Zope[4] and Anand Kumar[3]

[1]*Tata Consultancy Services, Hyderabad, Telangana, India* [2]*International Institute of Information Technology, Hyderabad, Telangana, India* [3]*Tata Consultancy Services, TCS Innovation Labs—Tata Research Development and Design Centre, Pune, Maharashtra, India* [4]*Tata Consultancy Services, Andheri (E), Mumbai, Maharashtra, India*

6.1 LIMITATIONS OF THE CURRENT SOFTWARE PRACTICES

The current software engineering practice involves creation of generic organizational processes (ISO/IEC 12207, 2008; CMMi, 2010) applicable for any project within the organization. Processes and software quality assurance (SQA) practices are defined generically independent of the specific product being developed. These organizational processes provide guidance on concerns to be addressed in software, life cycle models, phases, activities, tasks, artifacts to be created, and so on. This approach has proved very effective over the past couple of decades in establishing basic maturity of SQA practices in organizations. Practices such as planning, reviews, verification and validation (V&V), metrics, and tracking are currently the norm in any mature software development organization. However, this approach is intrinsically limited in the support that it can provide for ensuring that the quality goals of specific products, such as performance, reliability, and security are met. While the general guidance on requirements definition, design and V&V activities such as reviews and testing is sufficient to ensure that there is a systematic approach to quality activities, it is entirely up to people to ensure that they conceptualize the right set of quality requirements, deploy the right kind of tools and techniques, and identify the right activities needed to produce right decisions and outcomes. This limits the contribution that the generic processes and SQA practices can make toward consistent achievement of product quality across projects in an organization.

The context of software product quality is set up with definitions of key terms as per accepted industry standards.

- *Software product:* Set of computer programs, procedures, and possibly associated documentation and data (ISO 12207, 2008). Product includes intermediate products, and intermediate products intended for users such as developers and maintainers.
- *Software quality:* The degree to which a software product satisfies stated and implied needs when used under specified conditions (ISO 25010, 2011).

Here, the software quality is defined from the perspective of the product being built, so in this chapter, software quality is referred to as software product quality. Understanding both the stated and implied needs play a critical role in determining the quality of the software product. In the following sections, some of the challenges faced in quality management in projects are analyzed and issues with current quality practices are discussed.

6.1.1 QUALITY MANAGEMENT DURING THE LIFECYCLE

The process of software engineering converts and transforms high level stated needs into an end product through various intermediate software artifacts such as requirements, use cases, design diagrams, code, test cases, and so on. Any medium to large software system will have hundreds of requirements to satisfy and it is a challenge to ensure that each requirement is allocated to a product module/part, is analyzed correctly, designed sufficiently and built as per the design, and is tested completely. Organizational processes recommend various quality assurance activities to be performed at each phase, but there are quality challenges (Jones, 2012; Kan, 2002) resulting from the way the software processes and quality are currently managed in software projects.

a. In projects, the quality of deliverables is primarily assured through reviews, walkthroughs and testing activities. There is substantial focus on independent testing but as a discipline testing is a quality control activity and cannot provide assurance on the building of quality. Generic reviews and walkthroughs of phase wise deliverables largely depend on the capability of the subject matter expert doing the review. There is no consistent method or technique to detect problems induced at a specific phase as part of quality assurance activity in that phase.

b. A quality assurance tool used to identify gaps in the composition of software elements across various lifecycle phases is the Traceability Matrix. Often, the traceability maintained in projects is a document level linkage of artifacts without the necessary details of elements breakdown in an artefact and relationships among elements. Hence, it does not fulfill the purpose of finding missing or incorrect mapping of elements from one phase to another.

The quality management questions to be addressed with respect to lifecycle process are:

- How to strengthen quality assurance activities in lifecycle processes and detect problems induced at a life cycle phase as part of SQA process at the same phase and prevent slippage to the next phase?
- How to ensure traceability of software products at an element level?

6.1.2 MANAGING SOFTWARE QUALITY REQUIREMENTS

It has been observed that systems are frequently redesigned not because they are functionally deficient, but because they are difficult to maintain, port, or scale, or are too slow. These qualities are over and above the functionality, which is the basic statement of system capabilities and also referred to as Software Quality Requirements or Nonfunctional Requirements. Several times, these software quality requirements may or may not be explicitly stated as requirements and are implicit. Statistics (Jones, 2012) show that a high percent of the defects are due to nonfunctional (also referred to as structural defects) related problems such as security, performance, reliability, and usability. The quality management questions to be addressed with respect to addressing quality requirements are:

- How to know the various quality requirements to be considered in a product?
- How to uncover these quality requirements even when the user or customer has not specified these requirements?
- How to assert design of these qualities into the system through a systematic process?

6.1.3 SUPPORT FOR UTILIZING INSTITUTIONAL KNOWLEDGE

Quality achievement depends on the engineering decisions. These engineering decisions should not require reinvention of the wheel each time, but should ride on engineering techniques from institutional knowledge gained over time and experience from previous projects. Organizations spend considerable effort to capture relevant project knowledge and specialized knowledge for particular application domains and place it in knowledge databases (Nonaka, 1995). Researchers have discussed the phenomenon of organizational knowledge creation, recognition of knowledge types and conversion of knowledge from one type. However in practice, there are huge challenges in exploiting this organization knowledge for engineering quality during the software development life cycle. The problem is multifold:

a. Knowledge organization which is artifact based in the form of assets, code, and templates that directly outline solution approach and may not always contain contextual information, the relevant problem, and scenarios of application.

b. Current approach of quality engineering in software process which does not facilitate linking quality engineering techniques in knowledge databases to corresponding process steps.

c. Gaps in knowledge uptake—looking up knowledge sources, using the right keywords, assessing applicability, and identifying the most relevant knowledge.

Overall, it is difficult for a person unfamiliar with the asset to correlate the knowledge asset to the problem in hand and implement the solution. Hence, the quality management questions to be addressed with respect to knowledge reuse are:

- How to structure, represent, and organize these knowledge assets such that context information is tied and correlated to the reusable solution?
- How to make organization and searching for engineering techniques more meaningful and how to link the most appropriate knowledge asset to the problem in hand and the corresponding software process activities?

6.2 PRINCIPLES OF SOFTWARE PRODUCT QUALITY ENGINEERING

To address the quality challenges discussed in Section 6.2 and for systematic achievement of software product quality, a product quality engineering approach is proposed in the form of key principles for quality management to be adhered to by software processes.

This approach outlines generic quality assurance principles to be built into the quality management systems and leverages earlier work (Nori, 2006) and some of the existing standards appropriately (ISO 25010, 2011; ISO TS 30103, 2014) at the implementation level. Each principle focuses on an engineering attitude to be adopted to resolve specific software product quality concerns.

Figure 6.1 depicts these principles in a pictorial manner.

6.2.1 HOLISTIC VIEW OF PRODUCT QUALITY

Quality is a holistic concept. All qualities including those that are not explicitly articulated for a system, act as a whole. Based on systems principles of holism and multidimensionality (Gharajedaghi, 2005), this principle has been formulated to understand product quality in a holistic manner from a perspective of both stated and unstated needs. This principle ensures that from the product conception stage, critical software quality characteristics (QCs) and quality requirements are not missed in the product design.

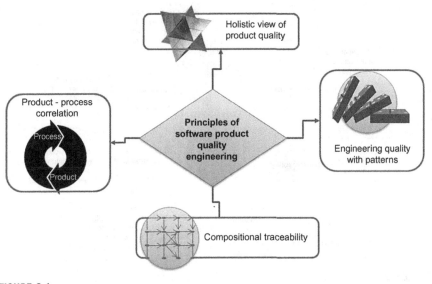

FIGURE 6.1

Principles of Software Product Quality Engineering.

> The first principle, *Holistic View of Product Quality* states that "A software product shall adopt a holistic view of quality and must consider critical QCs along with functionality from its conception stage."

Figure 6.2 depicts a holistic view of product quality. It has the functionality at the center symbolizing the core of the system with other major software QCs surrounding the functionality. These qualities are considered as the key quality pillars for any IT system and the proposed approach adopts a holistic view with equal focus on functionality and other QCs. Absence of any of these qualities during system conception and/or requirements stage, will lead to serious issues during the later stages. ISO 25010 (2011) standard for software product quality requirements defines QCs and recommends classification into QCs and sub-QCs. For a comprehensive view on quality, we adopt ISO 25010 standard classification scheme of QCs, which are defined in Table 6.1.

It is proposed that the QC/sub-QCs are customized and extended and a custom product quality taxonomy tree specific to the organization business unit is defined considering a holistic perspective of the domain and technology constraints. Having this kind of taxonomy for product QCs helps to identify software quality requirements against each QC/sub-QC and to evaluate its relevance from the perspective of the product being built. It aids to understand software quality requirements in a holistic manner from all the above quality dimensions and discover quality requirements not elicited by the user or customer but critical for functioning of overall system.

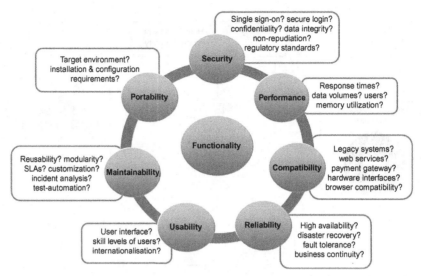

FIGURE 6.2

Holistic View of Product Quality.

Table 6.1 Definitions—Quality Characteristics

Functionality	Degree to which a product or system provides functions that meet stated and implied needs when used under specified conditions
Security	Capability of software product to protect information and data so that unauthorized persons or systems cannot read or modify them and authorized persons or systems are not denied access to them
Performance	Capability of software product to provide appropriate performance, relative to the amount of resources used, under stated conditions
Compatibility	Capability of software product to have two or more of its systems or components exchange information and/or perform their required functions while sharing the same hardware or software environment
Reliability	Capability of software product to maintain a specified level of performance when used under specified conditions for a specified period of time
Usability	Extent to which a product can be used by specific users to achieve specific goals with effectiveness, efficiency and satisfaction in a specific context of use
Maintainability	Capability of software product to be modified. Modifications may include corrections, improvements or adaptations of the software to changes in environment and in requirements or functional specifications
Portability	Capability of the software product to be effectively and efficiently transferred from one hardware, software, or other operational or usage environment to another

6.2.2 ENGINEERING QUALITY WITH PATTERNS

As per Alexander et al. (1977) "Each pattern describes a problem which occurs over and over again in our environment, and then describes the core of the solution to that problem, in such a way that you can use this solution a million times over, without ever doing it the same way twice." These patterns provide a common vocabulary for designers to use, communicate, document, and explore design alternatives. Gamma et al. (1995) recommend recording experience in designing object-oriented software as design patterns and documenting some of the most important design patterns and presenting them as a catalog. Even though they were talking about patterns in object-oriented software, what they say is true about capturing design experience relevant to quality techniques as well as knowledge related to requirements, implementation, testing, deployment, and operations support. This concept of patterns has been leveraged to engineer software QCs understood through the previous principle, *Holistic View of Product Quality*. Patterns connect the quality problem to the proven engineering techniques to achieve quality.

> The second principle, *Engineering Quality with Patterns* states that "A software product shall establish a specific product QC during each phase through the application of suitable quality patterns from organizational knowledge."

A *Quality pattern* is a proven solution to a product quality problem and is defined as "Description of the quality problem and the essence of its solution to enable the solution to be reused in different settings." Two aspects to quality assurance using the concept of patterns are a uniform structure for quality patterns and a searchable catalog of patterns.

6.2.2.1 Structure of a quality pattern

Table 6.2 outlines the structure of a pattern that includes key attributes for structuring and organization of pattern. In addition to the attributes generally identified (Alexander, 1979), specific attributes are defined for quality patterns in the context of software product quality. This uniform structure for quality patterns helps to formulate and represent organization knowledge in a consistent manner.

6.2.2.2 Catalog of quality patterns

It is possible to formulate and express the existing knowledge assets in the organization in the form of quality patterns as per the structure outlined. These quality patterns can be created for each QC and sub-QC and are made available as a searchable repository so that the application of patterns in a project is by engineering design, not by chance. Consistent uptake of knowledge across organizations is facilitated by formulating these assets as quality patterns with a structure. Each pattern is associated with a tagging scheme: specific QC which needs to be

Table 6.2 Structure of Quality Pattern

Software process	Software life cycle phase where the quality problem is relevant, links the pattern to the corresponding software process
Pattern name	A handle used to describe a design problem, its solution, and consequences
Quality characteristic	Quality property that needs to be established. Maps the quality problem and solution to the relevant quality dimension
Problem and its context	Specific software quality problem and its context. It describes specific design problems
Pattern solution	Solution elements that make up design, their relationships, responsibilities, and collaborations
Consequences	Results and trade-offs of applying the pattern
Index	Tagging scheme
Solution pattern diagram	Diagrammatic representation of the solution pattern, if available

established, software process area, and where applicable, additionally tagged with the domain/subdomain and applicable context (e.g., technology, type of project). This tagging scheme can be used to systematically identify and deliver the relevant knowledge assets to the projects to which they are applicable. The focused reuse of quality patterns brings in engineering validation and asserts establishment of quality property.

6.2.2.3 Functional Correctness Patterns

Functionality of software is engineered from the first principles. The semantic definition of programming languages provides us a complete *pattern language* for reasoning about programs. Thus, an algorithmic build-up of the function desired, in terms of the primitive operations made available by hardware, and control structures thereof, is an engineering design of the function desired (Dijkstra, 1972; Niklaus 1973). Some of these proof techniques are shown in Table 6.3. These proof structures provide classical patterns for programs, which aid in analysis and validation for correctness of programs.

This pattern oriented approach helps to organize knowledge assets in a structured manner and tagging schemes assists searching for appropriate patterns and filtering based on the context and consequences. They support Quality Assurance exercises.

6.2.3 COMPOSITIONAL TRACEABILITY

Management of software quality is facilitated by the identification of the software configuration structure, derived by successive decomposition of the product and associated compositional logic. Product Breakdown Structure (Svensson & Malmqvist, 2002) is widely used in manufacturing industry for breakdown of

Table 6.3 Patterns for Functional Correctness

1. Mathematical induction

$$\{I: = 0; \; F: = G(I);$$
$$\text{while } I < \; = \max \text{do}\{I: = I + 1; \; F: = H(I)\};$$

Notes: Initial value of *I* is 0; *F*, a Cartesian product of iterated variables in the state of the program is initialized by *G(I)*; *I* sweeps through natural numbers in the interval [0,max]; let *P* be a property/quality of the program; if *P(0)* is true; and *P(I* + 1) is true when *P(I)* is true then by mathematical induction *P* is true of the interval [0,max].

2. The Sequencing Rule of Inference

$$\frac{P\{s1\}Q, \; Q\{s2\}R}{P\{s1; s2\}R}$$

If Property *P* is *true* of the variables in the State of a program, and is an antecedent of program step s1, and property *Q* is the consequent after the execution of program step s1, with *Q* as the antecedent of program step s2, and if the execution of s2 leads to the establishment of *R*, then *P{s1;s2}R* can be inferred. This is the Rule of inference for sequential composition of steps in programs.

---

a product into its required components and to understand the relationships between them. Software configuration structure leverages the concept of product breakdown structure to analyze and establish compositional traceability among the elements of software products.

> The third principle, *Compositional Traceability* states that "A software product must exhibit compositional traceability through decomposition and composition of elements in its configuration structure."

Compositional traceability extends the definition of traceability to include compositional equivalence between specification and the collection of elements that address the specification, that is, it includes validation of the compositional logic. While traceability identifies the relationship between specification and elements that address them, compositional traceability includes analysis that the elements collectively meet the specification. A configuration item is a product part or component. Figure 6.3 illustrates a typical view of the software configuration structure with multiple layers and configuration items based on decomposition and composition principles. Within each layer, relevant configuration items are decomposed and identified. These configuration items are composed across layers. In Figure 6.3 Req. stands for a requirement, spec for specification and BO for business object.

This structure provides a base platform to conceive and manage the software product, provides visibility into the composition of product parts and configuration items throughout the lifecycle and helps to identify significant inconsistencies in the composition of configuration items, which if undetected, could potentially manifest as defects in later phases.

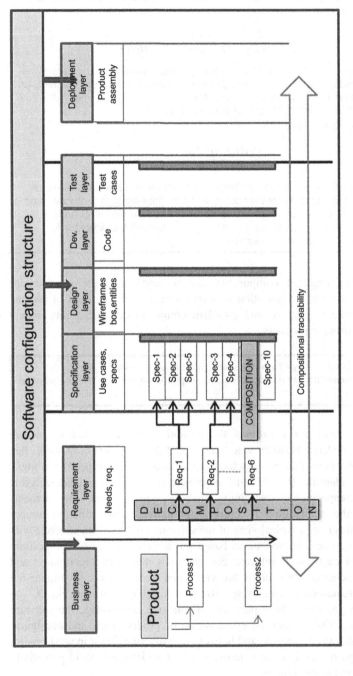

FIGURE 6.3

Software Product Configuration Structure - Overview.

© 2013 IEEE. Adapted, with permission, from "Establishing content traceability for software applications: An approach based on structuring and tracking of configuration elements," by Nistala, P.; Kumari, P., Traceability in Emerging Forms of Software Engineering (TEFSE), 2013 International Workshop, pp. 68–71, 19 May 2013

6.2.4 PROCESS—PRODUCT CORRELATION

Organizational processes (ISO 12207, 2008) are defined in terms of a set of outcomes, the generic activities and tasks needed to achieve the outcomes. To address the limitations of generic abstracted organizational processes in terms of providing specific quality assurance guidance with respect to a product being built, it has been proposed to add a product-specific layer of process definition that identifies the set of process instances needed to deliver each system element, and the outcomes, activities, tasks, and deliverables associated with that instance. This captures what needs to be done to deliver the product within the process.

> The fourth principle, *Process—Product Correlation* states that "A software product, in addition to generic project processes, shall have a layer of product-design processes that correlate to achievement of quality goals of the particular product in terms of outcomes, activities, tasks and deliverables."

It is proposed that the software process is instantiated with respect to the product designed in terms of product quality engineering principles, with the provision that product design always precedes software construction, even if it is just-in-time. It is product design that sets the agenda for the correspondingly succeeding part of the software development process.

For example, Entry—Task—Verification & Validation—Exit (ETVX) (Radice et al., 1985) is a simple process framework describing the required activities for an operational process that can be used to develop system or application software. For each configuration item, this ETVX process model can be applied and work breakdown structure is created. The result satisfies the Deming principle (Deming, 2000) of establishing correlation between process and product and builds quality assurance though increased process support interweaved with product design. The configuration items of software components that emerge from software configuration structure correspond to work breakdown structure.

This helps to bring accountability and the required resources and plan for assuring the quality of each software configuration item. "Product—Process Correlation" is a key primitive principle to operationalize all other product quality principles.

6.3 CASE STUDY

The implementation of product quality engineering approach and principles is presented in this section with illustrative fragments from a large solution development project "Quote Platform" for an international client. The project followed the modified waterfall process model. Given the complexity of business systems, stringent quality demands and multiple teams involved, ensuring quality of the deliverables was a challenge. The quality challenges were addressed and quality assurance was strengthened by implementing the key product quality engineering principles discussed in this section. The implementation methodology and case results for some of these principles are discussed in earlier works (Nistala and Priyanka, 2013a, b; Nistala et al., 2013). While each principle implementation needs a detailed discussion, this section provides a brief insight on case implementation.

6.3.1 PROCESS INSTANTIATION AND CONFIGURATION STRUCTURE

The first key augmentation to quality assurance process is instantiating the process for the project through "Process–Product Correlation." The generic process of "Outcomes," "Tasks," and "Process Constraints" is instantiated and elaborated specific to the software product "Quote–Portal." Each process step is created specific to the product to be built and explicit correlation between process step and product is ensured. As the process is instantiated specific to the product, augmentation is done through principle "Compositional Traceability." Here the software configuration structure is created through decomposition of functionality to realize business outcomes and objectives. Table 6.4 illustrates partial views of the software process instantiated specific to the product and the software configuration structure. The purpose of this table is to provide illustration of implementation and process and configuration structure are partially shown here (...indicates more records).

On applying software quality engineering principles, instantiated process and software configuration structure are created specific to the product and compositional traceability analysis can now be performed on the configuration structure. Key gaps in the product composition are identified through this analysis and are captured in Table 6.6.

6.3.2 SOFTWARE QUALITY REQUIREMENTS

Next key augmentation to quality assurance process were elicitation of a comprehensive set of software quality requirements by adopting a "Holistic View of Product Quality" and engineering the qualities understood in a holistic manner through "Engineering Quality with Patterns." The product quality requirements were identified for Functionality and major product QCs such as Security, Performance, Reliability, Usability, Compatibility, and so on. Each of these qualities have sub-qualities defined in the form of a "Quality Map" with QCs and sub-QCs. In order to achieve consistency in requirements elicitation, this quality map has been formulated as a requirement quality pattern and linked as an SQA constraint to the requirements elicitation activity. Table 6.5 outlines the Requirement pattern–Product Quality Map.

Table 6.4 Process Instantiation and Software Configuration Structure

Process Instantiation	Software Configuration Structure

Outcomes
• Identify high level business outcomes for the system in focus—"Quote Portal"
   – The portal to have the ability to provide indicative quotes for clients
   – ....
Tasks
• Formulate business objectives to be met by the software system from all quality dimensions to realize the outcomes
   – To register new customers and to retrieve existing customer information
   – To compute price for the Quote by comparing with competitor information
   – ...
• Elicit requirements to realize each objective by identifying configuration elements of the product and eliciting requirements
   – Elicit requirements for "Portal – Quote platform: Customer registration"
   – Elicit requirements for "Portal – Quote platform: Maintain Quote Basis"
   – ....
• Establish a relationship between elements in the configuration structure and analyze for compositional traceability
   – ...
	Portal—Quote Platform
	• Customer Registration
	   – ....
	• Quote Request.
	   – ....
	• Maintain Quote Basis
	   – Maintain Requestor
	   – Maintain Intermediary Details
	   – Maintain Lives
	   – Maintain Quote Basis
	   – Maintain Benefit Basis
	   – Maintain Funds
	   – Maintain Competitor Info
	• Request Underwriting Decision
	   – ....
	• Request Quote Calculation
	   – ...
	• Request Output
	• Work Management
	• Underwrite Quote
	• Price Quote
	• Quote Output
	• Apply for Annuity
	• Internal Book.
	   – ....

A representative set of quality requirements corresponding to major quality dimensions mapped using the *requirement quality pattern* and gap analysis are as follows:

- Security quality dimension, user registration, authentication, role privilege management, protection of data and code, audit logging and data corruption prevention. Security requirements analysis using the *requirement quality pattern* above resulted in gaps in quality requirements related to session time out, control of access to code, cryptography and key management, input, output data validation, and so on.
- Performance dimension, response times for single quote platform business services, channels, and interfaces were identified as requirements. Also, the

Table 6.5 Requirement Pattern—Product Quality Map [ISO 25010]

Software process	Requirement Elicitation
Pattern name	Product Quality Map Pattern
Quality characteristic	All
Problem and its context	How do we know the various quality requirements or NFRs to be considered in a product?How to uncover these quality requirements when the user or customer has not specified these requirements?
Solution pattern	Product Quality Requirement Classification Scheme consisting of QCs and sub-QCs (Quality characteristics and sub-Quality Characteristics)—based on ISO 25010 software product quality requirements and evaluation. (Refer to the diagram below)
Consequences	Understanding the quality dimensions of the systems and identifying software quality requirements as explicit requirements.
Index	Technical requirements, Software quality requirements, NFRs, QCs and Sub-QCs

Solution pattern diagram

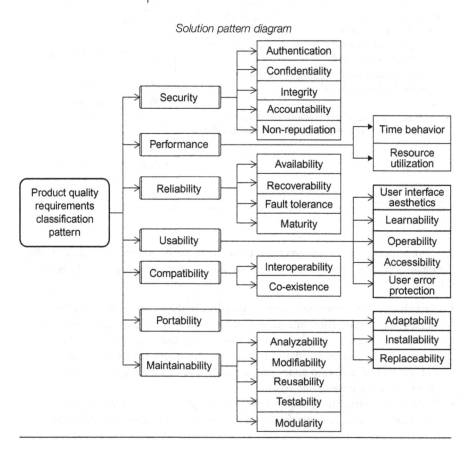

projected data volumes were captured. Performance requirements analysis using the *requirement quality pattern* resulted in gaps in quality requirements related to resource utilization and capacity planning from a future growth perspective.

- The system had a number of external and internal interfaces with which data is exchanged and used. All those interface processing requirements are identified under compatibility dimension. Also compatibility with various channels such as web, email, and call center are identified. Compatibility requirements analysis using the *requirement quality pattern* resulted in gaps in quality requirements related to browser compatibility.
- Reliability requirements include high availability requirements for business services, interfaces and channels; fault tolerance and recoverability requirements in the form of Recovery Point Objective and Recovery Time Objective values. Analysis resulted in detection of gaps related to availability requirements for email and call center channels.
- Usability dimension includes requirements on esthetics of the application, ease of use, navigation intuitiveness, and consistency of interactions, and so on. Analysis resulted in detection of gaps related to user error protection and accessibility requirements.
- Portability included requirements related to adaptability requirements of business services for specific operation contexts. Analysis using the *requirement quality pattern* resulted in detection of gaps related to installability and replicability requirements.
- No Maintainability requirements were initially identified. Analysis pointed to gaps related testability and modifiability requirements.

Use of requirement quality pattern from the organizational knowledge base has helped to elicit a comprehensive set of requirements corresponding to various QC/sub-QCs and to identify key gaps in software quality requirements. These gaps are populated into Table 6.6, a consistency tracker.

Table 6.6 Consistency Tracker

Phase	Quality Characteristic	Inconsistency
Requirements	Functionality	Quote Request Functionality: Requirements missing regarding requesting quote through telephone, post, fax
Requirements	Functionality	Quote Request Functionality: Requirements missing to handle quote request for existing customers
Requirements	Functionality	Quote Request Functionality: The registration of new customer for quote request is missing
Requirements	Performance	Resource utilization and capacity planning from a future growth perspective
Requirements	Reliability	Availability requirements for channels—email and call center

6.3.3 CONSISTENCY TRACKER

Augmentation of SQA with quality engineering principles helps in performing an analysis which results in detection of gaps or inconsistencies corresponding to QCs at a specific phase. Table 6.6 shows a partial listing of inconsistencies entered into the "Consistency Tracker" from the SQA activities of the previous sections. These inconsistencies, if undetected, could potentially manifest as defects in the later phases.

6.4 CONCLUSION

The wide variety of projects in IT organizations makes it undesirable to depend solely on the accumulated domain knowledge of people to make the right product and process choices to achieve product quality. Several quality challenges that commonly occur in the realization of stated and implicit needs of software systems have been identified. It is necessary to strengthen the overall quality processes with respect to product quality and provide as much systemic support as possible so that quality can be achieved in a consistent manner across people and projects. In this chapter, a product quality engineering approach has been proposed to assert software quality by connecting the generic software processes defined at the organization level to specific product quality concerns through quality engineering techniques. These principles address and assert quality concerns from the problem space to the solution space for the complete software life cycle.

The first principle "Holistic view of product quality" sets up the problem and identifies the quality requirements in a comprehensive manner supported by the ISO standard; the second principle "Engineering quality with patterns" maps a specific quality problem to the solution space with patterns and validates the resulting solution structure through proofs, patterns and algorithms; the third principle "Compositional traceability" distributes quality responsibility over the configuration structure; the fourth principle "Process–product correlation" correlates the product design to implementable process steps. Overall, these principles when applied to software systems provide significant support for product quality achievement, when compared to the current SQA practices of defining generic processes and ensuring conformance. The Case study section shows that by applying this approach, many quality challenges can be addressed and product quality can be systematically engineered and achieved. The complementary benefit is that engineers perceive the value of these principles embedded in SQA processes, because now the process gives them clear guidance on what needs to be done to successfully deliver their product, so that they can do it right the first time. Further research is toward building patterns for engineering quality, further validation of approach through case studies, and working out mechanisms to integrate these principles into quality management systems.

REFERENCES

Alexander, C., 1979. The Timeless Way of Building. Oxford University Press, New York, NY.

Alexander, C., Ishikawa, S, Silverstein, M, Jacobson, M, et al., 1977. A Pattern Language. Oxford University Press, New York, NY.

CMMI for Development, November 2010. Version 1.3 - SEI Digital Library, Publisher: Software Engineering Institute, Carnegie Mellon University. < http://www.sei.cmu.edu/reports/10tr033.pdf > .

Deming, W.E., 2000. Out of the Crisis, First MIT Press ed. MIT Press, Cambridge, MA.

Design Patterns: Elements of Reusable Object-Oriented Software, Pearson Education, USA, 1995.

Gamma, E., Helm, R., Johnson, R., Vlissides, J., 1995. Design Patterns: Elements of Reusable Object-Oriented Software. Addison Wesley.

Gharajedaghi, J., 2011. Systems Thinking: Managing Chaos and Complexity, third ed. Elsevier, USA.

ISO/IEC 12207, 2008. Systems and Software Engineering—Software Life Cycle Processes.

ISO/IEC 25010, 2011. Systems and Software Engineering—Systems and Software Quality Requirements and Evaluation (SQuaRE)—System and Software Quality Models.

ISO/IEC/IEEE 24765, 2010. Systems and Software Engineering—Vocabulary.

ISO/IEC TS 30103, 2014. Software and Systems Engineering—Lifecycle Processes—Framework for Product Quality Achievement.

Jones, C., 2012. Software Quality in 2012: A Survey of the State of the Art. <http://sqgne.org/presentations/2012-13/Jones-Sep-2012.pdf>.

Kan, S.H., 2002. Metrics and Models in Software Quality Engineering.

Kan, S.H., 2003. Metrics and Models in Software Quality Engineering. Pearson Education, USA.

Niklaus W., 1973. Systematic Programming: An Introduction, Prentice-Hall Series in Automatic Computation, USA.

Nistala, P., Kumari, P., 2013. Establishing content traceability for software applications: An approach based on structuring and tracking of configuration elements,"Traceability in Emerging Forms of Software Engineering (TEFSE)", International Workshop, pp.68–71.

Nistala, P., Priyanka, K., 2013a. An approach to carry out consistency analysis on requirements validating and tracking requirements through a configuration structure. In: Proc. 21st IEEE RE '2013.

Nistala, P., Priyanka, K., 2013b. Establishing content traceability for software applications: an approach based on structuring and tracking of configuration elements. In: Proc. 7th International Workshop on Traceability in Emerging Forms of Software Engineering (TEFSE), Col-located with ICSE 2013.

Nistala, P., Bharadwaj, A., Priyanka, K., 2013. An approach to manage NFRs in agile methodology: expanding product roadmap to include NFR features based on holistic view of product quality. In: Improving Systems and Software Engineering Conference, ISSEC 2013.

Nonaka, I, Takeuchi, H, 1995. The Knowledge Creating Company. Oxford University Press.

Nori, K VSwaminathan, N, 2006. A framework for software product engineering. In: Asia-Pacific Software Engineering Conference.

Ole-Johan Dahl, E.W., Dijkstra, C.A.R., 1972. Hoare, Structured Programming. Academic Press.

Radice, R.A., Roth, N.K., O'Hara Jr, A.C., Ciarfella, W.A., 1985. A programming process architecture. IBM Syst. J. 24 (2), 79–90.

Svensson, D., Malmqvist, J., 2002. Strategies for product structure management at manufacturing firms. J. Comput. Inf. Sci. Eng. 2 (1), 50–58.

"Filling in the blanks": A way to improve requirements management for better estimates

7

Luigi Buglione[1,2], Alain Abran[2], Maya Daneva[3] and Andrea Herrmann[4]

[1]*Engineering Ingegneria Informatica SpA, Rome, Italy* [2]*Ecole de Technologie Supérieure (ETS), Montréal, Canada* [3]*University of Twente, Enschede, The Netherlands* [4]*Herrmann & Ehrlich, Stuttgart, Germany*

7.1 INTRODUCTION

Software and systems project estimation often takes place in the early project stages and depends on the completeness and quality of the available requirements documents. The quality of these requirements is, in turn, highly influenced by the requirements management practices of the project organization. Poor requirements management is detrimental to project estimation. Various problems in requirements elicitation and specification lead to underestimation or estimation errors larger than expected. Such problems include:

1. "implicit," ambiguous or missing requirements;
2. lack of homogeneous granularity in the way functional requirements (FRs) are documented;
3. nonfunctional requirements (NFRs) often not considered or quantified during estimation (Abran, 1995, Buglione, 2012, Chung et al., 1999).

To address the number and severity of such issues and improve overall management of a software project, we propose two approaches for improving requirements elicitation and specification:

1. Adoption of quality models (QMs) for NFRs (e.g., ISO 25010, ISO 21351:2005 (2005), ISO/IEC 25010:2011, 2011; FURPS, Grady and Caswell, 1987; PMBOK5, PMI, 2013)
2. An update of Quality Function Deployment (QFD) tailored to better "visualize" requirements between customers (VoC—Voice of Customer) and IT service providers (the "technical" view) (Hauser and Clausing, 1988).

This method is named QF^{2}D (Quality Factor through Quality Function Deployment) (Buglione and Abran, 2001) and utilizes the latest ISO standards and empirical evidence from industrial practices.

Each approach contributes to completeness, unambiguity, homogenous granularity, and quantification of FR and some NFR. In addition, both facilitate discussion between stakeholders for creating the right synthesis of features to put into system production.

Our objective is to achieve effective and improved estimations for any project within an organization through reinforcement of the Requirements Engineering (RE) discipline. Our revised QFD (which we call QF^{2}D) focuses on requirements based on measurable entities (e.g., organization, project, resources, process, product levels). This chapter illustrates the application of the solution to one of the ISO 25010 characteristics, namely portability. Included is a sample calculation illustrating application of the technique and how it provides added value. The chapter ends with a discussion of the proposed solution and its implications for research and practice.

The chapter makes three contributions. First, our approach is multidisciplinary in nature and provides a holistic view of three related subareas of software engineering: requirements engineering, software cost estimation, and quality assurance which, typically, are studied by different communities, from perspectives deemed important within each community. Empirical software engineering research usually treats these three subareas in isolation without explicitly investigating how achievements in one subarea may impact the others. Furthermore, little is known about the synergies that might result from leveraging each subarea's specific processes and practices. Our chapter contributes to this understanding.

Second, we contribute to the field of RE by providing a cost estimation perspective to the use of QFD in RE. Prior research has acknowledged the merits of QFD as an efficient RE technique; however, empirical RE studies on QFD have been carried out, chiefly from a technical engineering perspective. By including the cost estimation perspective, we revisit the QFD concepts in terms of implications for implementing best cost estimation practices. For example, we make explicit that the quality of RE deliverables in a project has a profound impact on the achievable quality of the project estimates.

Third, we contribute to the area of software effort estimation by increasing awareness of the need and value of including NFRs into the project estimation process. Currently, the well-known functional size measurement (FSM) techniques aid project estimation based on FRs; there is relatively little research on how to leverage knowledge available about NFRs in the early project stages. Our solution contributes directly to this issue. For illustrative purposes, we have selected the portability NFRs as a context for applying our proposed approach.

This chapter is structured as follows. Section 7.2 summarizes the state of the art on application of the QFD technique for translating customer requirements into technical requirements. Section 7.3 discusses how better RE practices, together with QMs for improving NFRs, can help achieve higher estimation capabilities. Section 7.4 introduces our proposed QF^{2}D method, with additional considerations for "filling in the blanks" with the "what-to-look-for" list concept. Section 7.5 provides an example of its application to the portability NFR. Section 7.6 presents our conclusions and next steps for this work.

7.2 MEETING THE "VOICE OF THE CUSTOMER": QFD

The QFD technique was developed in the late 1960s in Japan as a means of translating customer requirements (the "Voice of the Customer") into appropriate technical requirements throughout development and production of a product. Combining customer and technical requirements improves the initial product design, preventing "forgetting" or loss of some relevant requirements, while combining the various stakeholder viewpoints for validating, prioritizing, and managing requirements. The technique was introduced into North America in the 1980s and its initial focus on the product was extended to the whole production chain, the "4 phases of QFD": House of Quality (HoQ—or Design), Parts (or Details), Process, and Production (Figure 7.1; Crow; Dean, 1992; Herzwurm et al., 1998; Richardson, 1998; The Matrix of Change (MoC)).

QFD includes a series of matrices (VV.AA., 1994) to represent data; the most commonly used matrix is the "House of Quality" (HoQ) (Hauser and Clausing, 1988) presented in Figure 7.2.

Basically, HoQ presents the intersection of two dimensions: the horizontal (the "Whats" or customer requirements) and the vertical (the "Hows" or technical requirements). With respect to product development, the "Whats" identify the characteristics of the product and/or services desired by the customer while the "Hows" identify the way to achieve the "Whats." For a detailed explanation of HoQ and how to complete the matrix, refer to Herzwurm et al. (1998), The Matrix of Change (MoC) and Guinta and Praizler (1993). The relationship matrix, the central part of HoQ, is the heart of the system, presenting the prioritization of the "Whats" through attribution of importance ratings. This rating is calculated by multiplying each

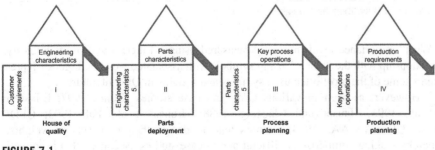

FIGURE 7.1

Four QFD phases (Hauser and Clausing, 1988).

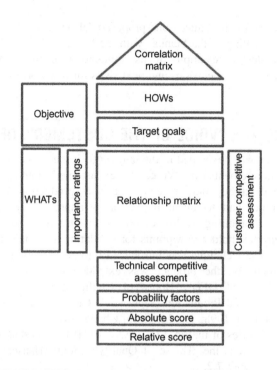

FIGURE 7.2

House of quality (HoQ) structure (Hauser and Clausing, 1988).

⊙	−9	5	9	●	−9	H	−5	✓ Strong positive
○	−3	2	4	○	−3	M	−3	✓ Medium positive
△	−1	−1	1	▽	−1	L	−1	✗ Medium negative
	(a)	(b)	(c)		(d)	(e)		✗ Strong negative
								(f)

FIGURE 7.3

Different QFD symbols and weights.

"What" importance level (normally measured using a Likert scale) by its intensity relationship with the "Hows," using symbols with associated weights. Figure 7.3 presents some of the most often used symbols and weights in QFD literature.

However, as seen in various QMs and case studies (Conti, 1997; Eriksson et al., 1996; Hauser and Clausing, 1988; Hrones et al.; Fall 1993; QFD/ CAPTURE; VV.AA., 1994), authors tend to design their own sets of weights, thereby making comparisons difficult across case studies. Because QFD is so well known, we thought it would be informative to illustrate a mapping to the QFD weights and symbols with ISO 14598-1 (ISO/IEC JTC1/SC7/WG6, IS 14598-1, 1997), as shown in Table 7.1.

Table 7.1 QF^{2}D Symbols and Weights

Weight	QF^{2}D Symbol	ISO Rating	Global Rating
3	●	Excellent	
2	◉	Good	Satisfactory
1	○	Fair	
0	Blank	Poor/absent	Unsatisfactory

This matrix approach to QFD is, in effect, a communication tool: it allows for a balanced consideration of requirements and provides a mechanism to communicate implicit knowledge throughout the organization. But it is a means and not an end: the real value is in communication of information and priorities, and more collaborative decision-making among individuals in the numerous functional departments involved in product development, from Marketing to Product Support. QFD helps development personnel to maintain the proper focus on the most relevant requirements and to minimize misunderstanding of customer needs. For these reasons, QFD represents an effective communication and quality-planning tool (Hauser and Clausing, 1988). For example, QFD has been used in the manufacturing industry with great success, leading to significant reduction in overall project costs (e.g., 50%), project cycle time (e.g., 33%), and major increases in productivity (e.g., 200%) (Guinta and Praizler, 1993). In the 1980s, Software Development environments, experimented with QFD where it was referred to as Software QFD (SQFD). SQFD (Haag et al., 1996, Nayar et al., 2013) is an adaptation of the HoQ scheme, which utilizes Technical Product Specifications as the "Hows" of the matrix. A peculiarity of SQFD is that it does not use the "roof" of the House (the "Correlation Matrix" in Figure 7.4) which shows positive and negative relationships among the "Hows." Figure 7.4 shows a basic SQFD model structure.

Some QFD adaptations to the software field:

- The Distributed QFD (DQFD) (Berga et al., 1997; Hrones et al., Fall 1993) by Digital Equipment Corporation is a tailored version for local and global groups involved in defining product requirements
- The Zultner QFD Project is an "essential minimum method to identify high-value needs, product characteristics and project tasks, quickly" (Zultner, 1995). Its main focus is on shortening project schedules by a more efficient management of risks using well-known quality tools through application of the Theory of Constraints by E.M. Goldratt
- Eriksson et al. (1996) studied the need to join process and product analysis to ascertain whether the user requirements of both product and project issues were correctly determined and thereby obtain customer acceptance
- Richardson (1997, 1998) QFD-based model was developed as a tool to aid implementation of a Software Process Improvement (SPI) action plan for small and medium-sized companies, using Bootstrap as the reference SPI model. This SPI/HoQ (Figure 7.5) gives the organization the full list of priorities to follow to reach the greatest improvement in software processes

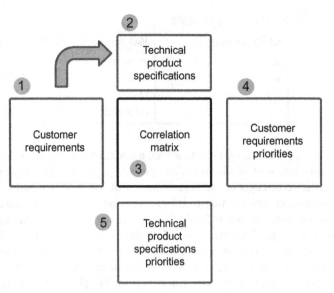

FIGURE 7.4

Basic SQFD model (Haag et al., 1996).

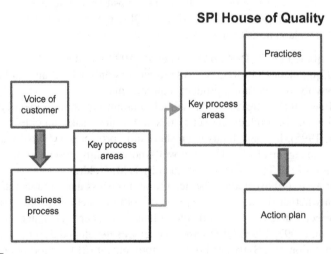

FIGURE 7.5

The SPI/HoQ matrix cascade.

- The "Matrix of Change" (MoC) project of the Massachusetts Institute of Technology (The Matrix of Change (MoC); Brynjolfosson et al., 1997) shares similarities with Richardson's model and helps managers identify critical interactions among processes, providing useful guidelines for Change Management.
- Herzwurm et al. (1998, 2003) rethought QFD for RE and developed the continuous QFD model as a way to manage requirements in highly volatile environments.

Since its aim is to compare two different viewpoints and make the invisible visible, QFD can help bring out implicit, ambiguous or not overly granular requirements between customer and providers, effectively reducing "scope creep" which many projects fail to estimate.

7.3 "FILLING IN THE BLANKS": HOW TO FURTHER IMPROVE ESTIMATION CAPABILITY?

The "scope creep" concept is used in the FSM community to refer to "*additional functionality that was not specified in the original requirements, but is identified as the scope is being clarified and the functions defined.*" A poor estimate due to improper management of requirements impacts not only on the (absolute) working effort and related costs, but also on the project duration and milestones for main project deliverables. Thus, "filling in the blanks" might be the solution for better requirements management throughout the whole project life cycle. In this section, we list the main issues and some suggestions for improving estimation capability.

7.3.1 WHAT COULD BE MISSING? COMING BACK TO EARLY PHASES...

Even though management techniques such as QFD have been known for years, the Software Project Management community still experiences a fairly high percentage of failed or not completely successful projects (Standish Group, 2011). Time and cost are the two most used perspectives to judge success, but these are traceable to and impacted by the way requirements are currently managed in these projects. A key contribution of the FSM community to the Project Management discipline was to properly define the "scope" of a project through better definition from early stages, thereby reducing the so-called "cone of uncertainty" (McConnell, 2006) (Figure 7.6). From an improvement viewpoint, three main drivers come into focus: (i) better management of stakeholders; (ii) better elicitation of requirements; and (iii) better use of historical data as a further source of information at estimate. These are discussed briefly.

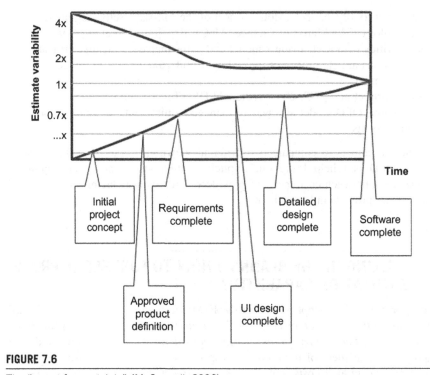

FIGURE 7.6

The "cone of uncertainty" (McConnell, 2006).

- The involvement of more (or different) stakeholders, to verify and ensure that all interested viewpoints are involved in the initial requirement elicitation phase. For example, there is a 20-year history of empirical RE studies on stakeholder analysis, all highlighting the importance of early involvement of end users in a more constructive way for achieving usability and operability objectives (Kassab et al., 2009). Empirical evidence also substantiates the claim that early project phases should involve more stakeholders who are not the "customer" per se (Lauesen, 2002). The customer is the "business," not necessarily the final user. Thus, a clearer differentiation of roles and contributions with different viewpoints is a way to insert more inputs (rows) into the QFD "Customer" (left) side.
- Analysis of the distribution of requirements by "status" over the software development life cycle, classifying them in at least three categories (green: properly elicited; yellow: not sufficiently granular or ambiguous; and red: implicit requirements) can help an organization become aware of its RE maturity level. The "iceberg metaphor" (Buglione and Abran, 2002) together with a "traffic light" color scheme depicts such a concept. The goal is to have mostly green requirements, at most a few yellow, and least of all reds. Following that metaphor, if the project is a ship, having a larger green light

(the tip of the iceberg) will increase visibility (i.e., the distance between the project and the level of information needed to properly manage it in time to avoid collision).

Typically, most project requirements are properly elicited (green light) but a significant number are not properly formulated (ambiguous) nor granular enough to be properly sized or estimated. An example is a request to "manage" a new dataset. From a functional viewpoint, a "manage" requirement may be translated into five elementary processes (Create, Read, Update, Delete, List). However, if there are no explicitly stated assumptions about the way a user interface (UI) is to be designed, this could reduce from the outset the number of potential elementary processes that need to be taken into account in a sizing technique. Another "yellow" element is insufficiently specified NFRs which users deem important to the system. Many analysts group NFRs into a single section within a requirement document instead of evaluating and estimating work and effort for single NFR. Such limited detail on NFR could lead to underestimation of the whole project effort and cost from the beginning (see the yellow light area in Figure 7.7). Last but not least, are red lights resulting from implicit requirements, typically coming from the customer side (e.g., normative or organizational constraints that a provider should remember to take into account, but that are not explicitly mentioned). Such uncertainty for evaluating, estimating and sizing requirements associated with yellow-red lights (respectively the "not granular/ambiguous" and "implicit" requirements) is the area to "tackle" to progressively transform red-and-yellow-flagged requirements into green-flagged ones (Daneva, 2010).

In software estimation, utilizing past experience and data from similar projects may facilitate the estimation of current and future projects (Erasmus and Daneva, 2015). Therefore a consolidated organizational shared repository with common data and information is an important knowledge management element for estimating future projects (Daneva, 2011).

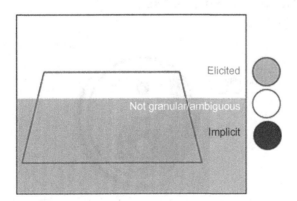

FIGURE 7.7

The ICEBERG metaphor.

Building on this discussion, we might ask: Do we need to rework requirements because of a lack of quality and quantity in their elicitation in earlier phases? What would be a useful improvement to QFD for increasing project estimation capability?

7.3.2 WORKING ON REQUIREMENTS

QFD can be further improved if the list of customer requirements to be analyzed on the left side of the matrix in Figure 7.2 would:

- Include more and different requirements from stakeholders not previously interviewed. By enlarging analysis of the initial scope a better understanding of eventual side effects between the customer and the technical viewpoints in the QFD matrix would result.
- Start from a "checklist" approach to capture areas of potential interest for being translated into useful requirements. In day to day life, a "what-to-buy" list is a particularly useful and simple solution at shopping time. Similarly, this "what-to-look-for" list concept is found in a number of apps for smartphones, for example, for not forgetting items in luggage when traveling.
- Use a common terminology at the same level of granularity. For instance, if the FSM community adopted the elementary/ functional process concept as the lowest granular level for sizing transactions, this would facilitate reuse of requirements and ensure comparability across projects. Moreover, comparability would allow benchmarks or identification of the most requested issues/topics against a certain type of project.

There are two fundamental types of requirements to take into account:

- functionality (the "What"; SEVOCAB; ISO/IEC/IEEE 24765:2010, 2010) which, in ISO language, is given by functional user requirements (FURs)
- quality (the "How") which is given by NFRs, the two sides or aspects of the "yin-yang" representation (Figure 7.8).

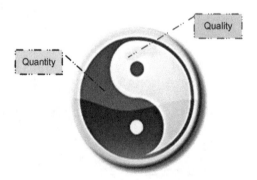

FIGURE 7.8

Quantity (FUR) and quality (NFR)—a "Yin-Yang" representation.

Since each aspect has its own properties (attributes) and measures, not taking into account both sides of the coin in the Requirements phase can lead to a suboptimal overall solution.

As a multifaceted term, "quality" is an aggregator for multiple attributes. For example, if you had to express why you appreciate a certain food, you would list a series of attributes such as: flavor, taste, presentation, freshness of ingredients, quality/price ratio, etc. A next step would be to quantify them by sharing a "counting" method. In software engineering both elicitation and quantification of NFR are supported in the QM.

A QM can be defined as a shared list of attributes/characteristics that an entity of interest can possess, expressing its nonfunctional aspects ("how") (Dromey, 1995). A QM is typically articulated in one or many tiers with a hierarchy of attributes (a number of high-level attributes, refined into a series of low-level ones). To complete a QM, another tier is typically added containing a number of measures to quantify the attributes.

The value of such a QM is to provide clear and unambiguous definitions which can be shared among project stakeholders. In addition, by serving as a checklist during elicitation, a QM improves NFR completeness leading to quantified NFR described on the same level of granularity. There are many RE methods for eliciting FRs, such as process analyses, and standardized notations, such as use cases, each aiming for FRs with the same level of granularity. It is less probable that a stakeholder will forget to mention important FRs, while NFRs are often overlooked and their refinement is left to the software engineers.

This section presents a list of QM highlighting their peculiarities. Figure 7.9 depicts a history of QM standards development over the last 40 years.

The Factors-Criteria-Model was proposed in the mid-1970s by the Air Force Systems Command (McCall et al., 1977). It contained 11 factors (first tier) and 23 criteria (second tier), each factor linked to two or more criteria. Of course, as in any QM, each element needs to have a clear definition with unambiguous statements. Factors were classified at three points along the software life cycle (SLC): product operation, product revision, and product transition. One year later, Boehm et al. (1978) proposed his own QM, with 7 high-level characteristics (1st level) and 12 primitive characteristics (2nd level). In this QM, a high-level characteristic was linked to two or more primitive characteristics. In 1986 ISO released the first

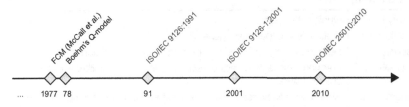

FIGURE 7.9

(Most known) QMs over recent years.

version of its own QM (ISO/IEC 9126, 1991), which included 6 characteristics and 18 sub-characteristics. Here each high-level characteristic was subdivided into a more refined list, but with no crosslinks. IEEE 1061-1992 (IEEE Std 1061-1992, 1992) was adopted using the QM model described in ISO 9126:1991 (ISO/IEC 9126, 1991), which included an Appendix list of attributes. In 1998, IEEE 1061-1998 deleted the list, considering instead an open list of values. Ten years later, ISO refined its view on quality and proposed a new version for ISO/IEC 9126 QM (ISO/IEC 9126-1, 2001). It introduced the concept of multiple stakeholder viewpoints: internal (providers), external (customers), and quality-in-use (users). The first two were defined with 6 characteristics and 26 sub-characteristics, each low-level characteristic being linked with one or more processes from the ISO 12207 process model to achieve additional process improvement. The "quality-in-use" view had four additional characteristics. Ten years later, ISO again revised its view on quality, developing the ISO 25000 series, in particular ISO 25010:2011 (ISO/IEC 25010:2011, 2011) which included 8 characteristics and 38 sub-characteristics for the main QM (i.e., the internal−external quality view in the old 9126 series) plus 5 more characteristics and 11 sub-characteristics for the quality-in-use part. QMs can be easily adopted also to a service (not only to a software deliverable) (Axelos Ltd., 2011). Reviewing the technical literature, other QMs include:

- *FURPS(+)*: The acronym FURPS (Functionality, Usability, Reliability, Performance, Supportability) refers to a software product quality taxonomy proposed by Grady and Caswell (1987). It explicitly includes more attributes: the "+" (addition sign) is a reminder to include other concerns related to Design, Implementation, Interface and Physical requirements (Table 7.2).
- *ECSS-E-10A* (ECSS, 2005): The European Cooperation for Space Standardization (ECSS) organization has developed a coherent, single set of standards for use in all European space activities. Among the several standards produced, "technical requirements" are also dealt with (Abran et al., 2013).
- *COSMIC NFR-Initiative*: COSMIC (the Common Software Measurement International Consortium) also proposed a classification structure for NFRs (COSMIC, 2014) subdivided into Systems Software product quality requirements, System Demographics and Technical Constraints, and Project constraints.

Table 7.2 The Quality Attributes Included in the FURPS + Model (Grady and Caswell, 1987)

Quality item	Quality attributes
Functionality	Feature set, capabilities, generality, security
Usability	Human factors, aesthetics, consistency, documentation
Reliability	Frequency/severity of failure, recoverability, predictability, accuracy, mean time to failure
Performance	Speed, efficiency, resource consumption, throughput, response time
Supportability	Testability, extensibility, adaptability, maintainability, compatibility, configurability, serviceability, installability, localizability, portability

7.3.3 WORKING WITH STAKEHOLDERS (WITH THE PROPER REQUIREMENTS)

Another contextual aspect related to requirements processes addresses stakeholders and their interactions. The fewer perspectives taken into account, the lower the potential (valid) requirements to be filtered, discussed, and then approved. Stakeholder Management and Requirements Elicitation are two areas in which many guides and frameworks have focused in recent years (PMI, 2013). For completeness and perspective from the various viewpoints, requirements should be grouped by stakeholders, as many RE text books indicate (Lauesen, 2002). In the original QFD the left side of the matrix represented the "Customer" viewpoint. However, more often than not, there is no single customer, but many involved in the Requirements Elicitation process (PMI, 2013; Herrmann and Daneva, 2008). To account for this, our proposal for improving the project estimation process begins by improving the requirements processes. We leverage a technique we created (Buglione and Abran, 1999) called QF (Quality Factor), which calculates and manages the overall quality value of a software product from several viewpoints. More specifically, we account for three perspectives, which we refer to as E/S/T, Economical, Social, and Technical. We defined them using the ISO 9126 QM (now ISO 25010, ISO/IEC 25010:2011, 2011), expressed as a normalized value (from 0 to 1) on a ratio scale:

- "E" viewpoint represents management
- "S" expresses the viewpoint of the final users
- "T" viewpoint, the technical team working on the project.

The QF technique assists matching a viewpoint against one or more QM subcharacteristics, which may lead an analyst to ask questions to elicit a requirement not previously noted. For example, "accessibility" is an attribute useful for both business users and developers, while "modularity" would typically be of interest to developers only. Moreover, functional requirements and functionality features are more likely selected by business managers and/or users.

Creating such associations between requirements and their sources facilitates the creation of "profiles" (or "patterns") that can be stored into an organizational project repository and made available for later use, for example, for comparing past and new project estimates (ISO15939 refers to this as MEB—Measurement Experience Base). For example, this could be used in situations where a project manager may need to check if the correct project scope has been defined starting from a proper requirement elicitation involving the right (primary and secondary) stakeholders.

The application of a QM standard taxonomy (using one of the QMs previously discussed) may provide support during the requirement elicitation step in "filling in the blanks." Therefore the QF contribution is to propose the grouping of customer requirements using at least two more criteria:

- by customer perspective
- by a "standard" QM taxonomy (at least for the nonfunctional side).

As previously discussed, this may reduce the uncertainty of the scope defined and applied at the estimation stage against a better defined scope (Kassab et al., 2007) at the end of the Requirements stage and, lastly, at the end of the project.

7.4 IMPROVING QFD: QF^2D

We proposed (Buglione and Abran, 2001) an extension of the original QFD technique, called QF^2D, which features:

- Inclusion of the QF technique: QF can help refine the initial customer requirements by adopting a QM as a template for capturing areas of potential interest for the requirement elicitation, associating them to interested stakeholders (adopting three perspectives, E/S/T, as a minimum hypothesis, or soliciting more, if needed)
- Reapplication of QF^2D at different SLC phases (early stages, design, deployment) to compare the alignment of requirements along the project life cycle, representing a sort of "quality gate" and avoiding project go-ahead before addressing a problem—as in the Total Quality Management (TQM) logic (e.g., Kanban, Kaizen).

Figure 7.10 shows the structure and interactions between two matrices: the D/M or Development/Maintenance matrix and the A or Assessment matrix, which assesses the implemented features within a software product. Applying the QF technique first to the D/M matrix, quantifies the target goal for the quality of the software product, defined from the three viewpoints (E/S/T) on the basis of the ISO software product QM (e.g., ISO 9126-1 or the newer 25010). Such quality goals and quality indications must be taken into account in the development of the software product.

Next, the software requirements are analyzed, designed, coded, tested, and evaluated. In the second or A-matrix, the list of the product features delivered are

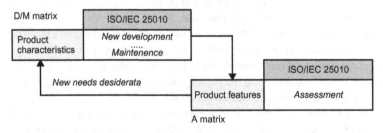

FIGURE 7.10

D/M and A matrices and QF^2D life cycle.

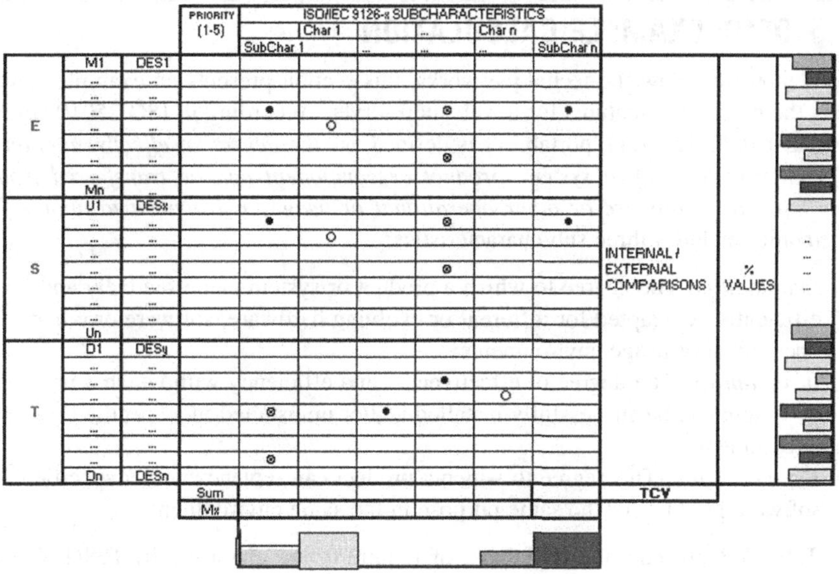

FIGURE 7.11

A sample D/M matrix.

matched against the ISO sub-characteristics list to assess the product. Comparing values between the two matrices provides feedback based on testing (from D/M to A-matrix) and new requirements (from A to D/M matrix). In this way, QF²D provides an organization the opportunity to monitor the quality of a software product in a dynamic way across the entire life cycle.

Figure 7.11 shows the structure of the two matrices with the three viewpoint dimensions (E/S/T) on the left (assuming n possible people per each group), together with their sets of quality requirements (Targets *DESi*). Then for each, a priority is assigned on a Likert scale (from 1 to 5), and then the ratings of the sub-characteristics are assigned.

Note that some variables (concepts and names) used in QF²D are the same as those in the initial version of the QFD technique. For example, the variable *TCV* stands for "Total Characteristic Value" and represents the total value for one of the quality characteristics listed in ISO 25010 in the consolidation of the opinions from the three interest groups (Economical, Technical and Social) after filling the QFD matrix. Here, TCVmax represents the maximum value assumed by TCV if all respondents were to rate every quality characteristic at the maximum value. The final quality value obtained from such a calculation is named QF²D and is equivalent to the QF value in the original QF technique (i.e., the two models share the same formula).

7.5 QF²D: EXAMPLE CALCULATION

To demonstrate how the technique works, this section presents an example using only the *portability* features for a web shop server. According to ISO 25010 (ISO/IEC 25010:2011, 2011), portability is defined as "*the degree of effectiveness and efficiency with which a system, product or component can be transferred from one hardware, software or other operational or usage environment to another.*" Portability includes three sub-characteristics:

- *Adaptability*: The degree to which a product or system can effectively and efficiently be adapted for different or evolving hardware, software or other operational or usage environments.
- *Installability*: The degree of effectiveness and efficiency with which a product or system can be successfully installed and/or uninstalled in a specified environment.
- *Replaceability*: The degree to which a product can replace another specified software product for the same purpose in the same environment.

Table 7.3 presents the initial list of requirements, classified by E/S/T viewpoints and associated to one of the three portability sub-characteristics previously mentioned.

The second step is to refine and group duplicated requirements about the same topic, for example, RQ-01 and RQ-05 express the same request. Here the grouped requirements, marked with grey/white background color, for example, RQ-01, RQ-05, RQ-07 are the first group (Table 7.4).

The list of grouped requirements is simplified and refined into a list of refined requirements (RRs) as follows (Table 7.5).

The next figure shows the results from the D/M matrix with an overall QF²D value of 22.44%.

For clarity, below we provide an explanation of our example in more detail:

1. *TCVmax is assigned a value of* 450. This value is calculated through a formula adapted from the original QF²D method (Buglione and Abran, 2001). For our simplified example only 3 out of the 31 sub-characteristics in the ISO 25010 QM are used. The TCVmax is calculated as the maximum value achievable if all requirements are at the highest priority and value. Thus *TCVmax* is given by
   - the number of RRs (not the entire number of RRs but the number considered by each stakeholder, from each of their perspectives, thus the summation of Managers + Users + Developers requirements) *multiplied by*
   - the number of sub-chars (three portability sub-chars) *multiplied by*
   - the max rating per RR (3) *multiplied by*
   - the max priority per RR (5).

   Thus TCVmax = 10*3*3*5 = 450.

Table 7.3 Portability Example: Initial List of Requirements (RQ)

RQ#	Requirements Statement	E/S/T Views	Sub-Characteristics
RQ-01	Future Windows and UNIX versions must be supported in future	E, S	Adaptability
RQ-02	The web shop server can be easily updated to a newer version	S	Adaptability Replaceability
RQ-03	The client needs to run on current versions of Internet Explorer, Firefox, and Opera	E, S	Adaptability
RQ-04	Future versions of Internet Explorer, Firefox, and Opera browsers must be supported in future	S	Adaptability
RQ-05	The web shop server software shall easily be adapted by the development team to future Windows and UNIX versions	E	Adaptability
RQ-06	The client software needs to run on Internet Explorer 11, 10, 8, and 7, Firefox 33, 31, 22, 17, 10, and 4, and Opera 11 to 25	E	Adaptability
RQ-07	The web shop client software needs to easily be adapted by the development team to future Windows and UNIX versions	E	Adaptability
RQ-08	The web shop server software can be installed on Windows Servers as well as UNIX servers	E	Installability
RQ-09	The web shop server needs to be easily installed	S	Installability
RQ-10	The web shop server software needs to be installed and run on Microsoft Windows Server 2003, 2008 and 2012, and on OpenSolaris	T	Installability
RQ-11	The web shop server software needs to be delivered with an installer program which includes preconfigured parameters	T	Installability
RQ-12	The installer program needs to update from older versions to the newer versions	T	Installability
RQ-13	The installer program needs to allow to uninstall the server software	T	Replaceability

2. *TCV is assigned the value of* 101, which is determined by the sum of the priority weights applied per each RR per group. Therefore, TCV = 69 (*Adaptability*) + 8 (*Installability*) + 24 (*Replaceability*) = 101, as in the "Sum" row of Figure 7.12.
3. *Distribution of (refined) requirements by stakeholders*: Re-grouping the initial list of requirements it is apparent that the Economic viewpoint (managers, the so-called "business") has more "voice" (impact) than the other stakeholders. This kind of analysis is useful for properly balancing the number of initial requests by stakeholders, by examining those requirements where one or more groups are completely missing or visibly less present. For example, it would

Table 7.4 Portability Example: Requirements Grouped by Issue/Topic

RQ#	Requirements Statement	E/S/T Views	Sub-Characteristics
RQ-01	Future Windows and UNIX versions must be supported in future	E, S	Adaptability
RQ-05	The web shop server software shall easily be adapted by the development team to future Windows and UNIX versions	E	Adaptability
RQ-07	The web shop client software need to easily be adapted by the development team to future Windows and UNIX versions	E	Adaptability
RQ-02	The web shop server can be easily updated to a newer version	S	Adaptability Replaceability
RQ-09	The web shop server needs to be easily installed	S	Installability
RQ-08	The web shop server software can be installed on Windows Servers as well as UNIX servers	E	Installability
RQ-10	The web shop server software needs to be installed and run on Microsoft Windows Server 2003, 2008, and 2012, and on OpenSolaris	T	Installability
RQ-11	The web shop server software needs to be delivered with an installer program which includes preconfigured parameters	T	Installability
RQ-03	The client needs to run on current versions of Internet Explorer, Firefox, and Opera	E	Adaptability
RQ-04	Future versions of Internet Explorer, Firefox, and Opera browsers must be supported in future	S	Adaptability
RQ-06	The client software needs to run on Internet Explorer 11, 10, 8, and 7, Firefox 33, 31, 22, 17, 10, and 4, and Opera 11 to 25	E	Adaptability
RQ-12	The installer program needs to update from older versions to the newer versions	T	Installability
RQ-13	The installer program needs to allow to uninstall the server software	T	Replaceability

be illogical to discuss UI design with only the technical development specialists and not include users.

4. *Priority*: Too many "high" priorities (most are 4-points ratings) makes for difficult planning in a short timeframe but reveals the opportunity to re-balance priorities to allow for better scheduling from an agile project management perspective (more iterations with less content each but on a regular, incremental basis, as for example using Scrum).

5. *Sub-characteristics coverage*: Our example indicates (Figure 7.12) that approximately 70% of attention has been paid to *Adaptability* and less than 8% to *Installability* (in the middle between yellow and red lights, using the Iceberg metaphor). While such a situation may be fine with stakeholders, it could indicate a lack of attention in developing requirements that address

Table 7.5 Portability Example: List of RRs

RRQ#	RQ#	Requirements Statements	E/S/T Views	Sub-Characteristics
RRQ-01	RQ-01	Future Windows and UNIX versions must be supported in future	E, S	Adaptability
RRQ-02	RQ-05 RQ-07	The web shop server software shall easily be adapted by the development team to future Windows and UNIX versions	E	Adaptability
RRQ-03	RQ-02 RQ-11	The web shop server can be easily updated to a newer version, delivered with an installer program which includes preconfigured parameters	S, T	Adaptability Replaceability
RRQ-04	RQ-08 RQ-09 RQ-10	The web shop server software needs to be installed on Windows Servers (Microsoft Windows Server 2003, 2008, and 2012) as well as UNIX servers (OpenSolaris)	E	Installability
RRQ-05	RQ-03 RQ-06	The client needs to run on current versions of Internet Explorer (11, 10, 8, and 7), Firefox (33, 31, 22, 17, 10, and 4) and Opera (11 to 25)	E	Adaptability
RRQ-06	RQ-04	Future versions of Internet Explorer, Firefox and Opera browsers must be supported in future	S	Adaptability
RRQ-07	RQ-12	The installer program needs to update from older versions to the newer versions (e.g., from v04 directly v06)	T	Installability
RRQ-08	RQ-13	The installer program needs to allow to uninstall the server software	T	Replaceability

those sub-characteristics. This is the benefit of using the checklist approach: Are we overlooking something? Again, crossing sub-characteristics by viewpoint, it appears that Adaptability is more important to managers and users than to technical development specialists, at least in terms of who is originating the request. This may lead to further refinement of the initial list of requirements (the yellow light in the iceberg metaphor), enlarging the project scope with more activities included in the first version of the project Gantt chart. The larger the scope, the greater the effort estimated at this stage. In light of the "cone of uncertainty" trend previously discussed, beginning with a scope that includes all FUR and NFRs that might possibly be included in the project, would reduce such uncertainty. This means applying more effort in the early stages of the project, however, this would result in savings of time and money at the release and deployment steps, ensuring better overall project quality.

			PRIORITY (1-5)	ISO.IEC 25010:2011 Sub-Chars		
				Portability		
				Adaptability	Installability	Replaceability
E	M1	RRO-01	4	3	0	0
	M2	RRO-02	4	3	0	0
	M3	RRO-04	4	3	0	0
	M4	RRO-05	4	1	0	0
S	U1	RRO-01	2	1	0	0
	U2	RRO-03	5	2	0	3
	U3	RRO-06	4	2	0	0
T	O1	RRO-03	3	3	0	1
	O2	RRO-07	4	0	2	0
	O3	RRO-08	3	0	0	2
	Sum			69	8	24
	Mx			6,900	0,800	2,400

TCV = 101
TCVmax = 450

QF²D = 0,2244

Symb ISO Rating

Symb	Rating
●	3
◎	2
○	1
	0

		Tot value	%		%	Tot %
CVI	Portability	101	100,00	1 Adaptability	68,32	100,00
				2 Installability	7,92	
				3 Replaceability	23,76	
	TCV	101	100,00			

FIGURE 7.12

Portability example: the D/M matrix.

6. *Overall QF²D value at the requirement stage*: As seen earlier, this value (22.44%) is apportioned solely to the "Portability" issues. It reveals a low value over the potential, maximum achievable. This could lead, in a further step, to refining the requirements list by (i) better definition of the existing requirements or (ii) adding new requirements. In either case, the project proposal would acquire a higher value by reducing uncertainty in the requirements, leading to a more reasonable estimate of quantity, time (in terms of effort and duration) and cost. Such an approach, applied over time within an organization gathering historical data into the MEB (referred to in Section 7.3.3), would reduce Mean Relative Errors. More than calculating an (absolute) value or number, QF²D makes the analysis visual, stressing more where to "fill in the blanks," allowing one to start there for any improvement.

After filling the D/M matrix, the product is produced and the variability between the Requirements phase and Construction is assessed. The "Assessment" A-matrix is filled out in the same way as proposed, considering any requirements added/changed/deleted during the project against the same schema. There are three possible situations:

• *Same QF²D values*: Confirmed values about the same set of requirements from the engaged stakeholders should reveal a low variability in terms of effort and cost.

- *QF^2D value higher in the initial "D/M" matrix*: In this situation, by comparing the two matrices in detail analysis might reveal the project scope was reduced during the project lifetime, due to project constraints (e.g., budget cuts) or a higher value expected than actually observed in the final product (same priorities, lower ratings per each requirement).
- *QF^2D value higher in the final "A" matrix*: Again, by comparing the two matrices in detail analysis might reveal a larger project scope with underestimates (more features produced than initially forecasted or same features but underestimating detailed sub-requirements).

Therefore, this would mean that if QF^2D values were different, room for potential improvements might exist which could be further understood by analyzing the overlap between the two matrices. Mapping the QM sub-characteristics against a process model (e.g., Maturity & Capability Model (Crosby, 1979) such as CMMI (CMMI Institute, 2010) or SPICE (ISO 15504, ISO/IEC 15504-5:2006 (2006)) or directly against the organization Quality Management System) would allow us to determine the action plan through the list of corrective/improvement actions ISO/IEC 14764:2006 (2006).

7.6 CONCLUSIONS AND NEXT STEPS

Despite five decades of research, software project estimation remains a challenge. Much has been learned over the years about the way a project lives and evolves, yet projects still fail. A root-cause analysis of poor estimates often leads to have achieved wrong or improper project scope definitions, thus an incomplete and insufficiently granular requirement analysis at the early project stages. QFD is a TQM tool that evolved in the 1960s for translating VoC into technical requirements. In this chapter we proposed an improvement to QFD, namely QF^2D, which includes a stronger focus on multiple customer groups and the application of QMs for reducing the likelihood of overlooking some requirements at the outset. We achieved this by using QM taxonomies as checklists, with the aim of reducing the "cone of uncertainty" for project estimates. An additional element was to establish a repository of data and qualitative information on projects, what ISO calls in 15939:2007 a MEB, which can used as input to refine estimates for next projects.

Thus, the larger the requirement scope from the beginning of a project, the more precise the number of tasks (and related efforts) introduced into the project's Gantt chart and the more accurate the estimates and actual values at project termination.

From our discussion of the calculation example, we list the advantages to using QF^2D:

- *Match & balance different viewpoints*: Be aware that there is no single truth but many. A refined stakeholder analysis which combines multiple perspectives is useful to complement the initial list of requirements allowing a better and more appropriate definition of project scope from early phases (Herzwurm et al., 2013; Li et al., 2012).

- *Do not overlook potential requirement areas of interest for the project*: The "template-list" approach using a QM taxonomy as the "columns" of a traditional QFD matrix may prevent overlooking potential issues useful for the analysis. In this way project scope would more likely be properly defined from the initial analysis, reducing the probability of not including something interesting/ important from the beginning that otherwise could be asked to be introduced later in the project life cycle as an implicit change request (Daneva et al., 2013).
- *Analyze historical data in order to determine possible "quick win" improvements*: A proper use of historical data from the MEB can help reveal patterns for creating clusters of projects (Grimm et al., 2011) sharing the same needs and quality profile. Historical data could also help to reduce the overall project effort by re-using some elements shareable among the similar projects, in particular during the early life cycle stages (Abran et al., 2007).
- *Adopt a standard glossary and taxonomy of NFR and NFR-characteristics* (IFPUG/COSMIC Glossary): Another benefit emerging from such an approach is for developers to share a glossary using a "standard" taxonomy. This could lead to a narrowing of the differences between definitions and applications of a concept by different teams, which, with a more consolidated way of working, would save the organization effort and money (Glinz, 2005).

In order to better refine the technique our immediate next step includes further empirical evaluations of the method with respect to effort to apply, ease of use and quality of requirements in controlled environments; and, by using data from our own MEB, to derive "quality profiles" typical of a cluster of projects in order to reduce the effort for doing the next estimate.

If you don't get the requirements right, it doesn't matter how well you do anything else.

Karl Wiegers

REFERENCES

Abran, A., August 21−25 1995. Quality—The intersection of product and process. In: 6th IEEE International Software Engineering Standard Symposium (ISESS'95). Montréal, Canada.

Abran, A., Garbajosa, J., Cheiki, L., November 2007. Estimating the test volume and effort for testing and verification & validation. In: IWSM-MENSURA 2007 Conference. Palma de Mallorca, Spain. <http://goo.gl/r90UUG>.

Abran, A., Al-Sarayreh, K.T., Cuadrado-Gallego, J.J., 2013. A standards-based reference framework for system portability requirements, computer standards and interfaces (CSI). Elsevier 35 (4), 380−395.

Abran, A., Moore, J.W., Bourque, P., Dupuis, R., Tripp, L.T., Guide to the Software Engineering Body of Knowledge (SWEBOK), 2014 Version, IEEE. <http://www.computer.org/web/swebok>.

Axelos Ltd. ITIL (IT Infrastructure Library) v3 Refresh 2011, Core Guides, 2011, UK.

Berga, E., Krogstieb, J., Sandvoldc, O., 1997. Enhancing user participation in system design using groupware tools. In: IRIS20 Conference. Hankø Fjordhotel, Norway, August 9–12.

Boehm, B.W., Brown, J.R., Lipow, H., MacLeod, G.J., Merrit, M.J., 1978. Characteristics of Software Quality. Elsevier, North-Holland.

Brynjolfosson, E., Austin Renshaw, A., van Alstyne, M., The Matrix of Change. Massachusetts Institute of Technology, Cambridge, USA, Working Paper # 189, January 1997. <http://goo.gl/Qh1b6Q>.

Buglione, L., 2012. The Next Frontier: Measuring and Evaluating the NonFunctional Productivity, MetricViews. IFPUG Newsletter 6(2), 11–14. <http://goo.gl/nVwdxr>.

Buglione, L., Abran, A., 1999. Multidimensional software performance measurement models: a tetrahedron-based design. In: Dumke, R., Abran, A. (Eds.), Software Measurement: Current Trends in Research and Practice. Deutscher Universitats Verlag GmbH, Wiesbaden, Germany, pp. 93–107.

Buglione, L., Abran, A., March 22–23, 2001. QF^{2}D: Quality Factor through QFD Application. In: Qualita'01 (4th International Congress on Quality and Reliability), Annecy, France, ISBN 2-9516453-0-0, pp. 34–39.

Buglione, L., Abran, A., ICEBERG: a different look at Software Project Management, IWSM2002 in "Software Measurement and Estimation". In: 12th International Workshop on Software Measurement (IWSM'02). October 7–9, 2002, Magdeburg (Germany). Shaker Verlag, ISBN 3-8322-0765-1, pp. 153–167.

Chung, L., Nixon, B.A., Yu, E., Myolopoulos, J., 1999. Nonfunctional Requirements in Software Engineering. Springer, ISBN 978-0792386667 <http://goo.gl/JCEyPg>.

CMMI Institute. CMMI-DEV (CMMI for Development) v1.3, Technical Report, CMU/SEI-2010-TR-033, Software Engineering Institute, USA, November 2010. <http://goo.gl/ZqDhy6>.

Conti, T., 1997. Organizational Self-Assessment. Chapman & Hall, London, UK.

COSMIC, Guideline on managing "Nonfunctional Requirements" for software, v0.23, July 2014. <http://cosmic-sizing.org/>.

Crosby, P.B., 1979. Quality is Free. McGraw-Hill, New York, USA, ISBN 0-451-62585-411.

Crow, K., 2002. Customer-Focused Development with QFD, DRM Associates, Palos Verdes, CA, USA. <http://goo.gl/ykYbeM>.

Daneva, M., 2010. Balancing uncertainty of context in ERP project estimation: an approach and a case study. J. Softw. Maintenance Evol. Res. Pract. 22 (5), 310–335.

Daneva, M., 2011. Uncertain context factors in ERP project estimation are an asset: insights from a semi-replication case study in a financial services firm. Int. J. Software Eng. Knowl. Eng. (IJSEKE) 21 (3), 389–411.

Daneva, M., Buglione, L., Herrmann, A., 2013. Software architects' experiences of quality requirements: what we know and what we do not know? In: 19th International Working Conference on Requirements Engineering—Foundation for Software Quality, REFSQ'13, April 8–11, 2013, Essen, Germany, pp. 1–17.

Dean, E.B., Quality function deployment for large systems. In: 1992 International Engineering Management Conference, Eatontown, NJ, October 25–28, 1992.

Dromey, R.G., 1995. A model for software product quality. IEEE Trans. Software Eng. 21 (2), 146−162.

ECSS, Space Engineering—System Engineering: Part 6. Functional and Technical Specifications, European Cooperation for Space Standardization, ECSS-E-10 Part 6A rev.1, October 31, 2005. <www.ecss.nl>.

Erasmus, P., Daneva, M., 2015. ERP services effort estimation strategies based on early requirements. In: 2nd International Workshop on Requirements Engineering for the Pre-contract Phase, REFSQ'15, March 23.

Eriksson I.V., McFadden F., Tiittanen A.M., Improving software development through quality function deployment. In: 5th International Conference on Information Systems Development. ISD'96, Golansk, Poland, September 24−26, 1996. <http://goo.gl/f5oQSC>.

Glinz, M., September 2005. Rethinking the notion of nonfunctional requirements, In: Proceedings of the 3rd World Congress on Software Quality (3WCSQ), Munich, Germany. <http://goo.gl/ncAxpQ>.

Grady, R., Caswell, D., 1987. Software Metrics: Establishing a Company-Wide Program. Prentice-Hall, Inco. Upper Saddle River, NJ, USA, ISBN 0138218447.

Grimm, J., Denavs, D., Mazur, G., Using QFD to design a multi-disciplinary clinic. In: 23rd Symposium on Quality Function Deployment, December 3, 2011, San Diego, CA. <http://goo.gl/g2Cy3e>.

Guinta, L.R., Praizler, N.C., 1993. The QFD Book: The Team Approach to Solving Problems and Satisfying Customers through Quality Function Deployment. Amacom Books, ASIN 081445139X.

Hauser, J.R., Clausing, D., 1988. The house of quality. Harv. Bus. Rev. 66 (3), 63−73, (May-June).

Haag, S., Raja, M.K., Schkade, L.L., 1996. Quality function deployment: usage in software development. Commun. ACM 39 (1), 41−49.

Herrmann, A., Daneva, M. 2008. Requirements prioritization based on benefit and cost prediction: an agenda for future research. In: 16th IEEE International Requirements Engineering Conference (RE'08), September 8−12, 2008, Barcelona, Spain, pp. 125−134.

Herzwurm, G., Helferich, A., 2004. Customer-focussed selection and prioritization of common and variable features with quality function deployment. In: 2nd Groningen Workshop on Software Variability Management.

Herzwurm, G., Ahlemeier, G., Schockert, S., Mellis, W., Success factors of QFD projects. In: World Innovation and Strategy Conference, August 3−5, 1998, Sydney, Australia, pp. 27−41.

Herzwurm, G. Schockert, S., Breidung, M., Dowie, U., Requirements engineering for application development in volatile environments using continuous quality function deployment. In: 2003 International Conference on Software Engineering Research and Practice, Las Vegas, pp. 440−447.

Herzwurm, G., Pelzl, N., Krams, B., QFD and cloud computing: a survey on the prioritization of security requirements for cloud computing. In: Proceedings of the 19th International Symposium on QFD 2013, Santa Fe, NM.

Hrones Jr., J.A., Jedrey Jr., B.C., Zaaf, D., 1993. Defining global requirements with distributed QFD. Digit. Tech. J. 5 (4).

IEEE Std 1061-1992: Standard for a Software Quality Metrics Methodology, 1992.

ISO/IEC 9126, 1991. Information Technology—Software Product Evaluation—Quality Characteristics and Guidelines for their Use. International Organization for Standardization, Geneva.

ISO/IEC JTC1/SC7/WG6, IS 14598-1, 1459. Information Technology—Software Product Evaluation—Part 1: General Overview. International Organization for Standardization, Geneva.

ISO/IEC 9126-1, 9126. Software Engineering Product Quality—Part 1: Quality Model. International Organization for Standardization, Geneva.

ISO 21351:2005. Space Systems—Functional and Technical Specifications. International Organization for Standardization, Geneva.

ISO/IEC 14764:2006, 2006. Maintenance Process. International Organization for Standardization, Geneva.

ISO/IEC 15504-5:2006. Information Technology—Process Assessment—Part 5: An Exemplar Process Assessment Model. International Organization for Standardization, Geneva.

ISO/IEC/IEEE 24765:2010, 2010. Systems and Software Engineering—Vocabulary. International Organization for Standardization, Geneva, <http://goo.gl/HDhO3H>.

ISO/IEC 25010:2011, 2011. Systems and Software Engineering—Systems and Software Quality Requirements and Evaluation (SQuaRE)—System and Software Quality Models. International Organization for Standardization, Geneva.

Kassab, M., Daneva, M., Ormandjieva, O., Scope Management of Nonfunctional Requirements. In: 33th EUROMICRO Conference on Software Engineering and Advanced Applications (EUROMICRO'33), August 29–31, 2007, Luebeck, Germany. IEEE Computer Society, pp. 409–417.

Kassab, M., Daneva,M., Ormandjieva, O., Towards an early software effort estimation based on functional and nonfunctional requirements. IWSM/Mensura 2009: 182–196.

Lauesen, S., 2002. Software Requirements: Styles and Techniques. Wiley, Addison-Wesley, USA.

Li, Y.-L., Chin, K.-S., Luo, X.-G., 2012. Determining the final priority ratings of customer requirements in product planning by MDBM and BSC. Expert Systems with Applications 39 (1), 1243–1255.

McCall, J.A., Richards, P.K., Walters, G.F., 1977. Factors in Software Quality, Vol. I, II, III: Final Tech. Report, RADC-TR-77-369, Rome Air Development Center, Air Force System Command, Griffiss Air Force Base, NY.

McConnell, S., 2006. Demystifying the Black Art. Microsoft Press, USA.

Nayar, N., Sharma, T., Bansal, S.K., Saxena, S., November 2013. Implementation of "XP-QFD" in a Small Scale Project. Int. J. Comp. Appl. (0975-8887) 82(10). <http://goo.gl/WT6RGL>.

PMI, Project Management Body of Knowledge (PMBOK), 5th ed., January 2013. <www.pmi.org>.

QFD/CAPTURE homepage. <http://www.qfdcapture.com>.

Richardson, I., October 1997. Quality function deployment: a software process tool? In: 3rd Annual International QFD Symposium, Linkoping, Sweden. <http://goo.gl/B5Cnm9>.

Richardson, I., Using QFD to develop action plans for software process improvement. In: SEPG'98 Conference, April 1998.

SEVOCAB, Software Engineering Vocabulary. <http://www.computer.org/sevocab>.

Standish Group, The CHAOS Manifesto: Think Big, Act Small, 2011. <http://goo.gl/0ncjrS>.

The Matrix of Change (MoC) Homepage. <http://ccs.mit.edu/moc/>.

VV.AA., QFD: The Customer-Driven Approach to Quality Planning and Deployment. In: Mizuno, S., & Akao, Y. (Eds.), APD, 1994.

Zultner, R.E., 1995. Blitz QFD: better, faster and cheaper forms of QFD. Am. Program. 8, 24–36.

Investigating software modularity using class and module level metrics

8

Michael English, Jim Buckley and J.J. Collins

Lero, University of Limerick, Ireland

8.1 INTRODUCTION

Quality can be considered the "totality of features and characteristics of a product that bear on its ability to satisfy given needs" (IEEE, 1983). This suggests that software quality is entirely driven by customers' expectations and its ability to meet those expectations. More recent definitions of software quality move past this perspective to encompass distinct characteristics of quality. For example, the ISO 25010 standard (ISO/IEC, 2010) defines quality in terms of eight characteristics: Functional Suitability, Performance, Compatibility, Usability, Reliability, Security, Portability, and Maintainability.

Many of these characteristics will evolve over the lifetime of successful software systems. Frequently the functionality required by users will change as the needs of companies evolve and they seek competitive advantage from their software systems. With respect to security, users may desire new levels of authentication associated with biometric data as opposed to passwords. Alternatively, based on a corporate merger, there may be new interoperability (compatibility) requirements placed on a company's existing software systems. All such evolutions involve software maintenance of the existing system and, as such, maintainability is considered an underpinning and prevalent quality concern (Slaughter et al., 1998). Software maintenance has been defined as the "modification of a software product after delivery to correct faults, to improve performance or other attributes, or to adapt the product to a changed working environment" (IEEE, 1983). By extension maintainability can be defined as that ease with which the system accommodates such modification.

Various authors have suggested that a large proportion of software effort is consumed during software maintenance (Lehman, 1980; Schneidewind, 1987; Kemerer, 1995) and evolution, with figures quoted ranging up to 80% of the total lifecycle software costs (Banker et al., 1991). While these studies are dated and need revisiting (Kemerer and Slaughter, 1997), the increasing scale and complexity of software systems suggest that the effort expended in maintenance will have increased in the interim. Hence increasing software maintainability is an important economic requirement for companies with large long-lived information systems, and it has been suggested that software systems' maintainability has become an important research concern within software engineering (Kemerer and Slaughter, 1997).

The ISO, software quality standard classifies maintainability into the sub-characteristics of Modularity, Reusability, Analyzability, Modifiability, and Testability. This work focuses on the software sub-characteristic of modularity, a characteristic that the ISO standard defines as the "degree to which a system or computer program is composed of discrete components such that a change to one component has minimal impact on other components" (ISO/IEC, 2010). This is based on the information hiding principle proposed by Parnas (Parnas, 1977). It states that design decisions should be decoupled into separate modules, so that these separate design decisions can be changed independently (without disrupting other modules).

Traditionally the modularity characteristic has been assessed through modularity metrics at the class level (Chidamber and Kemerer, 1994; Harrison et al., 1998; English et al., 2010). However, given the increased scale and complexity of software systems, this class level modularity information can be overwhelming (Abdeen et al., 2011). The volume of metrics-based data points for a large number of classes in complex systems challenges developers to identify those areas in the code that should be targeted when improving code quality, a phenomenon which we will refer to as information overload. Consequently, more recent research has focused on assessing modularity at higher levels of abstraction such as packages and "modules," where the term module is loosely defined, but is typically based on the package structure and/or some expert evaluation (Sant'Anna et al., 2007; Sarkar et al., 2007, 2008; Abdeen et al., 2011). This more abstract information provides a more manageable representation of the modularity of the system, but does so with lesser granularity, a phenomenon which we refer to as information loss.

A prerequisite to address these issues, is a satisfactory definition of a module and this has proven to be particularly challenging, particularly when distinguishing High Level Modules (HLMs) from other modular constructs such as packages (Sant'Anna et al., 2007; Sarkar et al., 2008). While at first glance, it appears self-evident that HLMs equate to collections of packages, an analysis of the target system used in this research reveals that specific collections of packages do not always seem to equate well to HLMs. So here, using guidance from the architectural views in (Bass et al., 2012), we define a HLM as a grouping of explicit programming structures—packages and/or directories, that cumulatively demonstrate high modularity.

Hence, we characterize high quality candidate HLMs through a number of software metrics that inform on the quality of candidate modules at high abstraction levels in software systems. These metrics focus on the proportion of internal connections in a candidate module and on its connections with other parts of the system. This is the main focus of this chapter.

However, an additional analysis is performed to evaluate the existence of relationships between metric information at different levels of abstraction. The motivation for this work is to address the tension between information loss at higher levels of abstraction and information overload at more detailed levels of abstraction, as discussed above. One could, for example, envisage the need for such mediation in a metrics workbench that supports developers' navigation from higher levels of modularity to more focused investigation at lower levels of granularity.

8.2 SOFTWARE QUALITY MEASUREMENT

Software is pervasive in all aspects of life, for example, in medical devices, cars, household appliances, smart phones, and nuclear power stations. The development and evolution of large software systems is a time and resource intensive activity. Even with the increasing automation of software development/evolution activities, resources are still scarce. Therefore, we need to be able to provide accurate information and guidelines to software architects and designers to help them improve the quality of their software. Thus, software measurement is necessary to assist these decision making processes before and during the software development lifecycle. As DeMarco famously stated: "You cannot control what you cannot measure" (DeMarco, 1986).

Software Maintainers often require high-level knowledge of a system prior to undertaking specific maintenance tasks (Sharif et al., 2015). Such knowledge can facilitate the more in-depth understanding of the specific parts of a system that need to be changed to address the maintenance task and to ensure that any potential ripple effects are anticipated and managed (Jordan et al., 2015). Then, maintainers can use their resources more efficiently to deliver higher quality products in a timely manner. The high-level knowledge of a system and the more focused knowledge required to support maintenance tasks can be supported by utilizing software measures at various levels of granularity, helping software maintainers to refine their focus to the parts of the software system that require their attention the most.

8.3 SOFTWARE MEASUREMENT

Fenton and Pfleeger (1998) define measurement as "the process by which numbers or symbols are assigned to attributes of entities in the real world in such a way as to define them according to clearly defined rules." Thus, a measure is a number or symbol which is assigned to an attribute in order to characterise that attribute. A software metric has been defined as "an objective mathematical measure of software that is sensitive to differences in software characteristics.

It provides a quantitative measure of an attribute which the body of software exhibits" (Gaffney, 1981).

Measurement in software engineering facilitates quantification of the products (e.g., specification, design, code), processes (e.g., testing, design process) and resources (e.g., people, teams, hardware) of software engineering activities, thus providing valuable insight to management and technical staff (Fenton & Neil, 2000). They state that the "future for software metrics lies in using relatively simple existing metrics to build management decision support tools that combine different aspects of software development and testing and enable managers to make many kinds of predictions, assessments and trade-offs during the software lifecycle."

However, Fenton and Neil also state that software measurement has not gained widespread acceptance within software organizations. As a result, this area of research needs to be expanded and its usefulness in the practice of software development needs to be established.

Ejiogu (1991) and Abreu and Carapuça (1994) have proposed criteria for effective software metrics. Like Fenton and Neil, they highlighted the need for metrics to be simple and easily computable, but also programming language independent and clearly defined and objective; a guideline increasingly being adopted by the community (Sarkar et al., 2008; English et al., 2012). In this chapter we adopt these criteria by using simple and clearly defined metrics which are (OO) programming language independent, to investigate the use of software metrics (for classes and modules) to provide insights on the modularity of large-scale software.

8.4 SOFTWARE MODULARITY

Modular software development is a design technique that emphasizes the separation of a software system's functionality into independent, interchangeable modules. It is based on Parnas' pioneering work on the information hiding principle, where design decisions that are most likely to change are compartmentalized within programming structures called modules (Parnas, 1972), and where these programming structures are of restricted accessibility to the rest of the system. The goal of information hiding is to protect the rest of the system from these design changes in that, if a design decision changes, the resulting code change is limited to the associated programming module.

The principle of information hiding is embodied in a technique called "encapsulation" and this technique has been realized through the concept of modules at various levels of abstraction in software systems:

- Functions allow software developers to encapsulate algorithmic and procedural aspects liable to change
- Classes allow the developers to encapsulate the procedures and their associated data-structures that are liable to change

- Java packages and components are larger-scale abstractions that have more recently been used in this fashion. Java packages organize java classes into namespaces, providing a modular decomposition. Likewise software components have been defined as macro-units "of composition with contractually specified interfaces and context dependencies only" (Szyperski et al., 2002)
- Interfaces provide structured access to these classes, packages, and components.

So, for example, if a module changes internally without changing interfaces that other modules rely on, the change will not propagate throughout the rest of the system. This gives rise to the design principle of "program(ming) to interfaces, not implementation" (Gamma et al., 1995). Adherence to this principle also results in software where modules are easier to replace, provided that their replacement's interface is consistent with the original. Overall, the system is easier to evolve because clients are less tightly coupled to the concrete implementations that realize the required interfaces, implying a greater separation of concerns and lower likelihood of widespread change.

Given the large effort expended on evolving successful software systems after deployment (Lehman, 1980; Schneidewind, 1987; Banker et al., 1991; Kemerer, 1995) and the tightly associated problem of delocalized change-propagation (Bennett and Rajlich, 2000; Black, 2001), modular decomposition must be considered an important indicator of a software system's quality. The question then arises as to how to assess software modularity in specific software systems. Two of the most popular measures amongst researchers are coupling and cohesion. Coupling is the degree of interdependence between the different modules in a system (Stevens et al., 1974), and cohesion is the extent to which a module's individual parts are needed to perform the same task (Yourdon and Constantine, 1979). While some authors of empirical work in this area have asked developers for their subjective opinion of coupling and cohesion with respect to accepted coupling/cohesion scales (Buckley et al., 2008), most work in this area has been focused on using coupling and cohesion metrics and some of the core work in this area is now presented.

8.5 COUPLING AND COHESION METRICS

Since modularity is a key concept of the object-oriented paradigm, many OO coupling and cohesion metrics are presented in the literature. Some of the most well-known OO coupling metrics are described here:

1. Coupling between object classes (CBO) (Chidamber and Kemerer, 1994): "CBO for a class is a count of the number of other classes to which it is coupled." Two objects are coupled if "one of them acts on the

other, i.e., methods of one use methods or instance variables of another." This measure of coupling includes coupling due to inheritance and couplings where a class acts as either a server or a client (or both). Chidamber and Kemerer state that "excessive coupling between object classes is detrimental to modular design."

2. Number of Associations (NAS) (Harrison et al., 1998): is a metric that "counts repeated invocations as a single occurrence of coupling." This metric includes the parents and derived classes of a class in its definition. A class can only contribute once to the value of the NAS metric. Coupling to classes in software libraries and basic types is excluded.

3. Response for a class (RFC) (Chidamber and Kemerer, 1994): RFC is a measure of the magnitude of the response set for a class. The response set is composed of all the methods in the class itself and all the methods which can be called from the methods in the class. This metric includes all methods that could be called indirectly in response to a message being received by a class.

4. Lack of Cohesion in Methods (LCOM) (Chidamber and Kemerer, 1994): LCOM is a count of the number of method pairs in a class which share no common instance variables in that class.

It is notable that all of these well-known coupling and cohesion metrics focus on the class level of abstraction. More recently, researchers have focused on larger levels of granularity, reflecting the increasing scale of current software systems. The next section describes this work in more detail.

8.6 COUPLING AND COHESION METRICS AT HIGHER LEVELS OF GRANULARITY

Sarkar et al. (2008) proposed a suite of metrics that could characterize modularity at the "module" level, a module being defined by the authors as a package, or groups of packages (as defined manually by author inspection and/or the opinions of a knowledgeable developer). This elaborate suite of metrics is composed of 12 formally-defined metrics that characterize the coupling and cohesion of these modules, their complexity, their interface as declared though actual interfaces and abstract classes, and the degree to which their declared interface is adhered to. For example, their "Non-API method Closedness" Index calculates the difference between the interface as used and the declared interface, with a range from zero to one. One typifies the best case where all inter-module calls are made through the defined interface and zero indicates the worst case where all inter-module traffic by-passes the defined interface.

Other work (Abdeen et al., 2011) argues for a metric characterization of legacy systems based on the assumption that most of these systems do not explicitly declare APIs. Instead they define a set of metrics based entirely on the package structure of the system (assuming a direct one-to-one relationship between modules and packages). In this work they consider the API of a package as the "package classes that interact with classes of other packages" rather than any explicitly declared sets of APIs. They propose an Index of Inter-Package Usage and an Index of Inter-Package Extending, defining a set of coupling and cohesion metrics between packages based on these premises.

Similarly, other researchers have looked at coupling and cohesion at the package level. With regard to cohesion, Martin (2000, 2005) looked at the internal cohesion of packages, based on the interdependencies between classes in that package. However, Sant'Anna et al. (2007) argue for a more nuanced application of modularity metrics in general. Specifically they note that module structure may be considered a dominant decomposition but that it does not reflect architectural concerns that are typically cross-cutting, like exception handling, or persistence. They propose a set of metrics that address this issue, including Concern Diffusion over Architectural Components (CDAC) and Lack of Concern-based Cohesion (LCC) in an architectural component. Their preliminary evaluations suggest that these metrics compliment the more traditional modularity metrics employed by researchers. In their metrics, the architectural units are components and connectors but the concerns referred to have to be manually annotated in the system by the system architect. This latter requirement substantially increases the workload required to apply these metrics, both initially and as the software system evolves over time. This is particularly true if this annotation happens at a detailed level of granularity like operations, as suggested by the authors.

This review of the literature suggests several issues:

1. Researchers tend to focus on one level of abstraction only. For Chidamber and Kemerer (1994), that level of abstraction was classes. For Martin (2005) and Abdeen et al. (2011) it was package level, and for Sarkar et al. (2008) it was HLMs which seemed to be packages or groups of related packages. While Bhattacharya et al. (2012) modeled the software structure at the granularity of functions (function-level interaction) and modules (module-level interaction), showing the value in metrics at both level, no effort was made to illustrate potential relationships between the metric-analyses they performed at different levels of abstraction. It might be interesting to assess such relationships. For example, if outliers at higher levels of abstraction, in terms of metric analysis, indicate outliers at lower levels of abstraction, it might provide a powerful mechanism that would allow analysts focus in on interesting classes within package hierarchies while limiting their initial information overload.

2. HLMs are difficult to define. While many researchers work exclusively at the package level (Misic, 2001; Martin, 2005; Ponisio and Nierstrasz, 2006; Sant'Anna et al., 2007; Abdeen et al., 2011), Sant'Anna et al. (2007) arguments suggest a requirement for a more nuanced definition of HLMs. Sarkar et al. (2008) tried to achieve this through a range of measures including obtaining expert input, but these efforts come at a substantial cost, a disadvantage also noted by Sant'Anna et al. (2007). It would be interesting to attempt to characterize HLMs using more automated approaches.

3. The metrics proposed by academic researchers have become increasingly diverse and fine-grained, in an attempt to more accurately and comprehensively embody the different aspects of modularity. While this is an admirable goal, it does suggests that practitioners will find it more difficult to perceive the subtleties of these individual metrics and more difficult to understand their relevance to the software at hand. Hence, in line with the observations of Fenton and Neil (2000), Ejiogu (1991), and Abreu and Carapuça (1994), we consider it important to employ simple metrics that are usable by practitioners but still inform on our core goals, as expressed in bullet points 1 and 2.

In summary, we argue for simpler metrics that can inform across all levels of granularity in software systems. Where these levels of granularity are not explicitly defined in the language's semantics (e.g., at larger-than-package levels of granularity) we argue for a metric-based characterization of modules, towards the goal of successfully identifying HLMs.

8.7 COUPLING AND COHESION METRICS UTILIZED IN THIS STUDY

The metrics utilized in this study are based on interactions between entities, where the entities are either classes (abstract or concrete) or java interfaces. An interaction exists between two classes if those classes are coupled in some way. The direction of each interaction is important. The flow of data between modules was considered by Yourdon and Constantine (1979) when they used the terms afferent flow and efferent flow to represent the flow of data towards and away from a module respectively. From this the concepts of afferent coupling (Ca, also called Fan-in coupling) and efferent coupling (Ce, also called Fan-out coupling) were coined. Fan-in coupling and Fan-out coupling can be calculated for modules at different levels of abstraction. The concepts of coupling and cohesion in a system with a modular structure can also be represented via the concepts of inter-module coupling and intra-module coupling respectively (Allen et al., 2001). These metrics, which are utilized in the empirical study in this chapter, are now defined in the context of Java software (e.g., java interface) but can easily be adapted for any object-oriented programming language.

- Intra-Module Coupling: This is a count of the number of directed edges in the Module Dependence Graph (MDG) between entities (classes/interfaces) inside the module.
- Inter-Module Coupling: This coupling is a count of the number of directed edges in the MDG that cross the module boundary, that is, go from an entity inside the module to an entity outside the module or vice versa.

- Cluster Factor (Mitchell & Mancoridis, 2006): This metric calculates the proportion of intra-module dependencies divided by the total number of the dependencies (intra-module coupling plus inter-module coupling) of a module.
- Fan-in Coupling (Ca) (Martin, 2005): The Fan-in coupling for a module is the number of java classes or interfaces outside the module that use classes or interfaces in the module (incoming dependencies).
- Fan-out Coupling (Ce) (Martin, 2005): The Fan-out coupling for a module is the number of java classes or interfaces outside the module that are used by classes or interfaces in the module (outgoing dependencies).
- FanIO: This is a combination of Fan-in coupling and Fan-out coupling. The FanIO for a module is the number of java classes or interfaces that use or are used by classes or interfaces in the module.
- Instability (Martin, 2000): This metric was proposed to assess the Stable Dependencies Principle (Martin, 2000). It is a measure of the potential impact of a change related to the module (Ducasse et al., 2011). It is calculated as $Ce/(Ca + Ce)$.
- Abstractness (Martin, 2000): This metric is a measure of the abstractness of a module. It is the proportion of abstract classes and interfaces in a module to the total number of classes and interfaces in the module.
- Distance (Martin, 2005): Martin proposes that a well formed module should have either high Abstractness and thus be a candidate for usage: that is, have high Fan-in and low Fan-out, or low Abstractness and thus is better characterized as a client, with high Fan-out. The Distance metric is the absolute distance of the sum of Abstractness (A) and Instability (I) from 1, i.e. $D = |A + I - 1|$.

8.8 EMPIRICAL STUDY

In this section we report on an empirical study undertaken to investigate the modularity of open source software systems. It is a case study, based as it is on observation (Zelkowitz and Wallace, 1998) and investigation of a contemporary phenomenon (Robson, 2002; Yin, 2013). In this instance the phenomenon is the modular composition in Open Source software. While the work is positivist in perspective (Klein & Myers, 1999) and approached in a quantitative fashion through established software metrics, the aim at this point is exploratory (Robson, 2002). Specifically it aims to explore the plausibility of the specified hypotheses on one suitable Open Source system in depth, as a precursor to a more elaborate study.

In terms of characterizing individual modules in the Open Source system, it is an embedded case study (Yin, 2013), where there are multiple data points within the one case but, in terms of identifying relationships between levels in the package hierarchy, the study can be considered holistic (Yin, 2013). Regardless, the units of analysis are modules within the case of interest: the Open Source system. The design of the study is now reported in line with the guidelines proposed by Runeson and Höst (2009).

8.9 OBJECTIVES AND RESEARCH QUESTIONS

The study examines the module-level structure of Weka, a large Open Source software system. Its objective is to characterize modularity at high levels of abstraction and, through that characterization, investigate if the macro-structure insights derived reflect trends at lower levels of modularity (and vice versa). This objective leads to the following research questions:

- Can we characterize through metrics, HLMs in Weka, and thus indicate good/bad candidate HLMs?
- Are coupling metrics at this high level of modularity reflective of coupling metrics at lower levels of granularity?

8.10 EMPIRICAL DESIGN

8.10.1 SYSTEM SELECTION

For this initial exploratory study, one system was chosen, based on several requirements. The system had to be successful and large. It had to have a modular decomposition, ideally composed of classes, and package or directory hierarchies. Weka is one such system (http://www.cs.waikato.ac.nz/ml/weka/index.html). It contains a hierarchical directory structuring of its code-base (often represented as packages), with 10 on level 1, 39 on level 2 and 87 in all (Figure 8.1).

It has 259,000 LOC and its continued success can be measured by its recent download (over 1197 in the week from 03/04/2015 to 09/04/2015, according to the Sourceforge download statistics at http://sourceforge.net/projects/weka/files/weka-3-6-windows-x64/stats/map). The unit of analysis within this case study is "module", where module refers to any structuring construct provided by an implementation language, including classes, packages, and directories. As the system is Open Source and our analysis relies on this Open Source material only, ethical approval was not considered necessary for this initial study.

8.10.2 DATA COLLECTION AND ANALYSIS

The target of our analysis is the modules in the Open Source Software system Weka. These are the classes, packages, and directories in the system, and we use third degree, or archival data (Benbasat et al., 1987; Lethbridge et al., 2005) in the form of software metrics to address our research questions.

In terms of characterizing modularity with respect to HLMs, we select directories as candidate HLMs, but any arbitrary grouping of java classes and interfaces could be employed. For these directories, we evaluate their candidature as HLMs using the Cluster Factor and Distance metrics as defined previously.

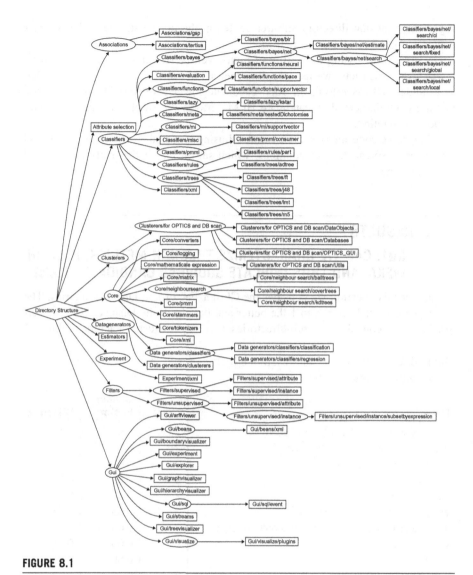

FIGURE 8.1

The directory structure of Weka.

We look at the top-ranked directories initially in terms of Cluster Factor. The Distance metric, which reports on the degree to which a module is well formed with respect to Abstractness and Instability, is employed to further triangulate the results towards candidate high-module identification (Stake and Savolainen, 1995), as per good case study practice (Runeson and Höst, 2009).

In addition, we traverse the directory structure to look for directories where the Cluster Factor increases substantially in moving from one level to another, suggesting that that directory sub-tree rooted at the node with the higher Cluster Factor is a good candidate as a HLM.

In terms of assessing the ability of high-level metric information to inform on lower level constructs, we use coupling metrics to see if those that are classified as candidate HLMs inform on good candidate lower level modules and if those that are contraindicated as candidate HLMs inform on lower level modules with respect to coupling.

The source code metrics were extracted using Understand (Scitools, 2015) and a number of spreadsheet calculations, which sat on top of the analyses provided by Understand.

8.11 RESULTS

8.11.1 RQ1: CAN WE CHARACTERIZE THROUGH METRICS, HLMs IN WEKA, AND THUS INDICATE GOOD/BAD CANDIDATE, HLMs?

To answer this question we consider the Cluster Factor and Distance metrics. The closer the Cluster Factor is to 1 the better and the closer the Distance to 0 the better. We first consider the sub-directories with high Cluster Factors. Table 8.1

Table 8.1 Cluster Factor and Distance Metrics for 20% of Sub-directories of Weka with Highest Cluster Factor

Name	Level	Cluster Factor	Distance
weka/clusterers/forOPTICSAndDBScan	2	0.59	0.13
weka/core/mathematicalexpression	2	0.60	0.75
weka/associations/tertius	2	0.62	0.04
weka/gui/boundaryvisualizer	2	0.62	0.08
weka/classifiers/pmml	2	0.65	0.15
weka/classifiers/pmml/consumer	3	0.65	0.15
weka/clusterers/forOPTICSAndDBScan/OPTICS_GUI	3	0.65	0.14
weka/classifiers/bayes	2	0.66	0.11
weka/gui/visualize	2	0.66	0.56
weka/gui/experiment	2	0.67	0.03
weka/classifiers/bayes/net	3	0.68	0.07
weka/core/pmml	2	0.71	0.37
weka/gui/hierarchyvisualizer	2	0.75	0.50
weka/gui/streams	2	0.79	0.23
weka/gui/beans	2	0.82	0.03
weka/gui/graphvisualizer	2	0.83	0.39
weka/gui	1	0.84	0.08
weka/gui/sql	2	0.86	0.28

shows the Cluster Factor and Distance values for the 20% of sub-directories with the biggest Cluster Factor values. The level of a sub-directory is its remoteness from the root directory of the source code of the system. It is noteworthy that 9 of the 17 packages here are weka/gui or sub-directories of the weka/gui package. This suggests that weka/gui or several sub-directories of weka/gui may constitute suitable HLMs. In fact, at different levels of granularity, both weka/gui *and* several of its subdirectories may be considered HLMs. In addition, four sub-directories of weka/classifiers also appear in Table 8.1, suggesting that these sub-directories may constitute HLMs.

The Distance metric for the sub-directories in Table 8.1 varies widely, with the sub-directories of weka/core/mathematicalexpression, weka/gui/visualize and weka/gui/hierarchyvisualizer being outliers, having Distance values of 0.75, 0.56, and 0.50, respectively. These high Distance outliers suggest that these sub-directories may not be suitable candidates for HLMs.

The bottom 20% of sub-directories in Weka according to the Cluster Factor metric is presented in Table 8.2. Of the 17 sub-directories in this table, 13 are very small with six or less classes or interfaces defined. This contributes to the very low Cluster Factor values as there are very few entities within the sub-directory, reducing the opportunity for intra-module coupling. These sub-directories are in various high-level directories: six are subdirectories of weka/classifiers and five are subdirectories of weka/filters. It should be noted that the

Table 8.2 Cluster Factor and Distance metrics for the 20% of Sub-directories in Weka with Lowest Cluster Factor

Name	Level	Cluster Factor	Distance
weka/classifiers/xml	2	0.00	0.33
weka/experiment/xml	2	0.00	0.17
weka/filters/supervised	2	0.00	0.38
weka/classifiers/mi/supportVector	3	0.00	0.11
weka/core/neighboursearch/covertrees	3	0.00	0.60
weka/filters/supervised/attribute	3	0.00	0.36
weka/filters/supervised/instance	3	0.00	0.11
weka/gui/visualize/plugins	3	0.00	0.75
weka/classifiers/bayes/net/search/fixed	5	0.00	0.00
weka/classifiers/meta/nestedDichotomies	3	0.03	0.05
weka/filters/unsupervised/instance	3	0.05	0.22
weka/gui/beans/xml	3	0.05	0.08
weka/filters/unsupervised	2	0.06	0.51
weka/filters/unsupervised/attribute	3	0.07	0.52
weka/classifiers/misc	2	0.09	0.00
weka/classifiers/trees/ft	3	0.10	0.20
weka/datagenerators/classifiers/regression	3	0.11	0.00

Table 8.3 Cluster Factor and Distance Metrics for Level 1 and Level 2 (averages) in Weka

Name	Num Classes and Interfaces	Level 1		Average Level 2	
		Cluster Factor	Distance	Cluster Factor	Distance
weka/filters	88	0.26	0.47	0.03	0.44
weka/core	285	0.33	0.82	0.44	0.43
weka/datagenerators	30	0.37	0.11	0.23	0.00
weka/clusterers	58	0.38	0.08	0.59	0.13
weka/attributeSelection	51	0.40	0.06		
weka/experiment	48	0.41	0.44	0.00	0.17
weka/classifiers	491	0.47	0.22	0.29	0.16
weka/estimators	21	0.48	0.40		
weka/associations	57	0.53	0.05	0.38	0.09
weka/gui	968	0.84	0.08	0.69	0.25

directories in Table 8.2 are in general further from the root directory than the directories in Table 8.1. This is to be expected as the Cluster Factor will increase in moving towards the root of the directory hierarchy.

Somewhat surprisingly the cumulative Distance reported in these 17 directories is not much more elevated than the cumulative Distance reported in Table 8.1.

Table 8.3 presents the Cluster Factor and Distance metrics for all directories which are direct sub-directories of the root directory and thus at level 1 in the directory hierarchy. It also presents the average Cluster Factor and the average Distance for the subdirectories of each of these directories.

Given that the average Cluster Factor for all 87 sub-directories in the Weka system is 0.35, and the average Distance metric is 0.21, many of the sub-directories in Table 8.3 have Cluster Factors which are above the average and Distance values below the average. Thus they could be considered as candidate HLMs. These level 1 sub-directories are weka/gui, weka/associations, weka/attributeSelection, weka/clusterers and weka/datagenerators, making them stronger candidates as HLMs. For the other packages mentioned in Table 8.3 (especially weka/filters and weka/core), their low value for Cluster Factor and their high value for the Distance metrics calls into question their candidacy as HLMs and suggests that further analysis is required.

Another stream of evidence can be garnered from a comparison of the Cluster Factor and Distance metrics at level 1 with the average values of these metrics at level 2 (also presented in Table 8.3). Large decreases in the Cluster Factor in moving from a directory on one level to its sub-directories on the next level suggest that the directory may be an appropriate candidate as a HLM. The inverse suggests that the subdirectories might make better candidates. The Cluster Factor metric decreases going from level 1 to level 2 for three of the candidates mentioned (weka/gui, weka/associations and weka/datagenerators) adding weight to

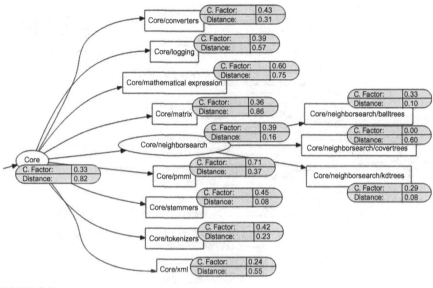

FIGURE 8.2

The Cluster Factor and Distance for weka/core and its sub-directories.

their candidacy. However for weka/core the Cluster Factor increases going from level 1 to level 2 suggesting that HLM candidates are better selected from the lower hierarchy level.

To investigate this phenomenon further we consider the sub-directories of weka/gui, weka/core and weka/filters. Using the data in Figure 8.2, the average Cluster Factor for sub-directories of weka/core is 0.44 which is greater than for core itself. While the Distance metric is relatively high for many of the sub-directories of weka/core, some of the sub-directories do exhibit characteristics that may support their candidature as HLMs, especially weka/core/pmml.

The picture is not quite so clear for weka/core/mathematicalexpression which has a high Cluster Factor but a high Distance also. Many of the subdirectories of weka/core have a small number of entities, with six of the nine sub-directories having 13 or less entities. It is likely that these sub-directories should be grouped (amongst themselves or with other sub-directories) to try to form other candidate HLMs.

Figure 8.3 which presents GUI and its sub-directories, suggests that GUI itself a good candidate for a high level and that several of its sub-directories could also be considered good modules (e.g., weka/gui/beans, weka/gui/graphvisualizer, weka/gui/sql and weka/gui/streams), as implied in Table 8.1.

A comparison of the Cluster Factor for weka/filters with its subdirectories weka/filters/supervised and weka/filters/unsupervised suggests that even though the Cluster Factor for weka/filters is low (Figure 8.4) compared to other level 1 sub-directories, this value is very high compared to the Cluster Factor of each of its sub-directories. This suggests that one of the best candidates within this directory is weka/filters itself.

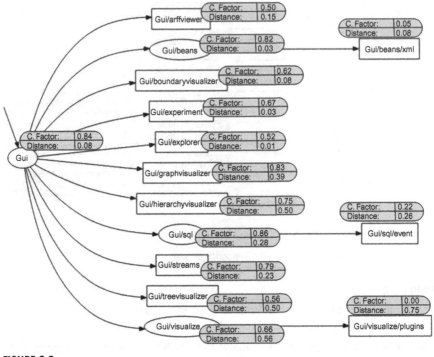

FIGURE 8.3

The Cluster Factor and Distance for weka/gui and its sub-directories.

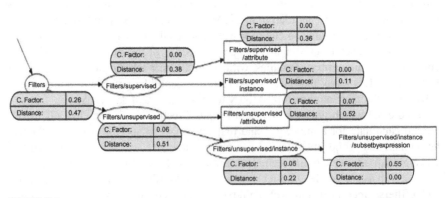

FIGURE 8.4

The Cluster Factor and Distance for weka/filters and its sub-directories.

8.11.2 RQ2: ARE COUPLING METRICS AT THIS HIGH LEVEL OF MODULARITY REFLECTIVE OF COUPLING METRICS AT LOWER LEVELS OF GRANULARITY?

To answer this research question, the module level and class level metrics need to be compared. Figures 8.5 and 8.6 present scatter plots of this comparison for all the sub-directories of the system, comparing classes and directories' Fan-in and Fan-out. Both scatter charts suggest correlations between the coupling metrics at different levels of granularity and so a more encompassing analysis was performed.

Table 8.4 shows the Spearman correlation coefficients for the module level coupling metrics (FanIO/FanIn/FanOut) with the average or maximum across each module of the corresponding class level coupling metric. The first row in the table considers each sub-directory of the source code as a potential module and each subsequent row in the table treats the sub-directories at that level beneath the root source directory as potential modules. All of these correlations are significant ($p < 0.01$). In general the correlations for Level 1, Level 2 and Level 3 are statistically significant at the 0.01 level (denoted by an *), except for two correlations at Level 2. The correlations are also quite high (most are >0.7). If modules are considered high-level sub-directories in the system then this suggests that in general the class level metrics reflect the module-level metrics in the Weka system.

However the individual scatter charts presented in Figures 8.5 and 8.6, do suggest large variability exists within these correlations and so care must be taken not to consider the relationship between these coupling metrics at different levels of abstraction as *de facto*.

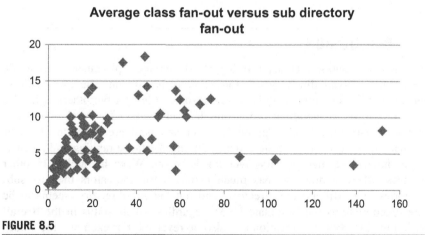

FIGURE 8.5

Comparison of sub-directory and class level Fan-out metrics.

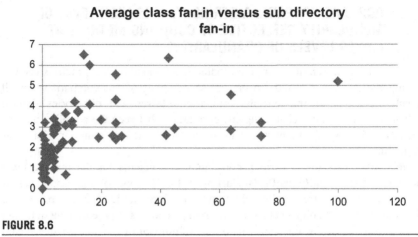

FIGURE 8.6

Comparison of sub-directory and class level Fan-out metrics.

Table 8.4 Spearman Correlations—Sub-directory and Class Level Coupling Metrics

Weka	FanIO/ AvgCl	FanIn/ AvgCl	FanOut/ AvgCl	FanIO/ MaxCl	FanIn/ MaxCl	FanOut/ MaxCl
All directories	0.6*	0.752*	0.602*	0.909*	0.775*	0.912*
Level 1	0.588	0.827*	0.48	0.903*	0.863*	0.751*
Level 2	0.601*	0.754*	0.652*	0.849*	0.734*	0.901*
Level 3	0.695*	0.591*	0.732*	0.928*	0.582*	0.943*

8.12 DISCUSSION

These results suggest that determining HLMs by their placement in specific levels in the software directory structure alone is insufficient. The approach presented here yields several candidate HLMs, some at level 1 but others at level 2 and 3 in the Weka hierarchy. For example, weka/gui *and* several of its subdirectories (/streams, /beans, /graphvisualizer and /sql) are supported in their candidacy by their overall Cluster Factor ranking, Distance ranking and an analysis of how these metrics vary over levels in the Weka hierarchy. In other instances, where a directory has much better metric indicators than its subdirectories (e.g., /filters) the directory, and not the sub-directory, seems to be more appropriate as the candidate HLM, regardless of its status in the overall metric rankings. But this situation can also be reversed. For example, the values presented in Figure 8.2 suggest that weka/core/pmml is a better candidate HLM than its parent directory weka/core.

Weka/classifiers is a more subtle candidate. Table 8.3 suggests that it is would make a better candidate HLM than its sub-directories. But the overall rankings (Table 8.1) suggest that several of its sub-directories (/bayes, /bayes/net, /pmml, and /pmml/consumer) and not weka/classifier itself, would make the best candidate HLMs. This apparent contradiction is because, while several of the sub-directories are good candidate HLMs, several other sub-directories are not and the average information for level 2 (presented in Table 8.3) hides this variety. This would suggest consideration of both weka/classifiers and the highly ranked sub-directories as candidate HLMs.

While most candidate HLMs were supported by the Distance metric, it should be noted that this metric gave similar levels of support to those directories which were lowly ranked with respect to the Cluster Factor metric. The top 20% overall-ranked candidate HLMs (as per Table 8.1) had an average Distance metric of 0.24, whereas the bottom 20% ranked candidate HLMs (as per Table 8.2) only had a marginally higher average Distance: 0.26. It seems that this metric was impacted upon by the level of the directories in the hierarchy, going from 0.44 at level 1 to 0.18 at level 2: It is likely that the further down a directory is in the hierarchy it will have lower Fan-out, lessening its Instability, while, across all the directories of Weka, there is a low proportion of abstract classes and interfaces, lowering the directory's Abstractness. Inspection of the Abstractness/Instability scatter plots reveals that this is the case where most low-level directories fall below Martin's Abstractness/Instability "optimum" score.

While acknowledging the requirement for a system expert's verification of candidate HLM's we see this analysis as a way of potentially filtering the material to be presented to experts and thus a means of limiting the effort that they must expend. In this example we have suggested 16 candidate HLMs out of a total of 87 directories within the Weka system. If corroborations from experts are forthcoming as the metric suite used to propose candidate HLMs is refined, the research may even move to a more automated solution.

In terms of finding relationships between metrics at different levels of abstraction, the results are also encouraging. Specifically, we found strong correlations between the coupling metrics of sub-directories at different levels and the classes they contain. This offers the prospect of more efficient navigation by analysts studying software systems whereby they can study lesser amounts of (large-grained) metric information in order to focus in on relevant metric information at lower levels.

8.13 **VALIDITY AND RELIABILITY**

Positivist studies are assessed with respect to external validity, internal validity, and construct validity (Runeson and Höst, 2009). Possibly the main limitation of this study is with respect to external validity: the degree to which the results can be applied to real systems in general. This study was exploratory in nature and thus only reports on one Open Source system. The findings would need to be replicated on many other systems, both open source and proprietary, before they could be considered valid. However, in its exploratory role, it does provide some initial evidence towards the postulate that metric information can identify candidate HLMs in software systems. It also suggests that high-level metric information can inform to some degree on lower level metric information, although the variability in the lower level information does suggest that the correlation cannot be totally trusted.

While triangulation was employed to heighten construct validity, we see it as imperative that the candidate modules, as derived from these metrics, are corroborated by knowledgeable architects or designers of such systems. Obtaining experts' opinion on HLMs within several Open Source or commercial software systems would provide a benchmark for this and for other modularity work that is sorely missing in the field. This is related to an internal validity issue which questions whether the metrics actually reflect modularity concepts. As noted by Sant'Anna et al. (2007), a more nuanced identification of modules may be required, especially as factors such as cross-cutting concerns are considered, and this is only possible through the insight of experts.

In terms of reliability the study scores highly, based on the automatic extraction and analysis of the metrics by Understand and Excel. However, it should be noted that while Understand is widely accepted and utilized by other researchers in the software metrics area (Olague et al., 2008; Rahman and Devanbu, 2013), it is not the only metric tool. Different interpretations of metrics in these different tools mean that the results presented here may be slightly unreliable when compared to those generated by a different suite of tools.

8.14 CONCLUSION

Software modularity evaluation research to date has tended to focus on a single level of abstraction and historically this has tended to focus at the class level in object-oriented systems. Some more recent research has focused on java packages and higher level modules. However, it is clear that defining such higher level modules is difficult. This paper leveraged software modularity metrics to semi-automate the process of identifying candidate HLMs in software systems and proved successful in proposing several groupings of directories that had elevated levels of modularity. However, the Distance metric was not as useful as expected in distinguishing candidate HLMs.

Given the size and complexity of software systems nowadays, software metrics extracted at a low-level of granularity could lead to information overload. Therefore, we also investigated if metrics extracted at higher levels of granularity reflect metrics extracted at lowers levels of granularity. We found strong correlations between metrics at the class level and metrics at higher levels of granularity which suggests that the more coarse-grained metrics can be used to help support software practioners search towards parts of the source code that may be of interest. We do acknowledge that findings identified in this work need to be supported with additional investigation including expert opinion.

However, there are a number of software design and development practices that are exceptions to this and need to be considered. These include:

- Factories and other creational patterns that induce concrete dependencies across sub-trees.
- Extension interfaces that use concrete classes to support callbacks across sub-tree boundaries.
- Cases where one is interfacing with hardware—e.g., robot control architectures—tend to introduce concrete implementations high up the tree.
- Design decisions to reduce indirection in order to address performance engineering concerns.
- Programming practices such as programming to implementation possibly induced through punishing release schedules or organizational structures.

These exceptions indicate that expert evaluation is required to confirm or negate the candidate HLMs identified by the proposed approach.

Our future work will expand the empirical analysis to incorporate a large cohort of software systems and will involve system experts to assess the candidate high-levels modules proposed by the approach outlined in this work. Our future work will also include the development of visualization tool support to facilitate the navigation of the source code directory hierarchy and the supplementation of the nodes in such a visualization with the appropriate modularity metrics. Such a visualization tool would facilitate tracing the metrics across levels and between levels in the hierarchy and would support the identification of candidate HLMs.

ACKNOWLEDGMENT

This work was supported, in part, by Science Foundation Ireland grants 10/CE/I1855 and 12/IP/1351 to Lero—the Irish Software Engineering Research Centre (www.lero.ie).

REFERENCES

Abdeen, H., Ducasse, S., Sahraoui, H., 2011. Modularization metrics: assessing package organization in legacy large object-oriented software. In: 2011 18th Working Conference on Reverse Engineering (WCRE).

Abreu, F. B. e., Carapuça, R., 1994. Object-oriented software engineering: measuring and controlling the development process. In Proceedings of the 4th International Conference on Software Quality, McLean, VA.

Allen, E.B., Khoshgoftaar, T.M., Chen, Y., 2001. Measuring coupling and cohesion of software modules: an information-theory approach. In: Software Metrics Symposium, 2001 (METRICS'01). Proceedings. Seventh International, IEEE.

Banker, R.D., Datar, S.M., Kemerer, C.F., 1991. A model to evaluate variables impacting the productivity of software maintenance projects. Manag. Sci. 37 (1), 1−18.

Bass, L., Clements, P., Kazman, R., 2012. Software Architecture in Practice. Addison-Wesley, Upper Saddle River, NJ, USA.

Benbasat, I., Goldstein, D.K., Mead, M., 1987. The case research strategy in studies of information systems. MIS Q. 11 (3), 369−386.

Bennett, K.H., Rajlich, V.T., 2000. Software maintenance and evolution: a roadmap. In: Proceedings of the Conference on The Future of Software Engineering. Limerick, Ireland, pp. 73−87.

Bhattacharya, P., Iliofotou, M., Neamtiu, I., Faloutsos, M., 2012. Graph-based analysis and prediction for software evolution. In: Proceedings of the 34th International Conference on Software Engineering. Zurich, Switzerland. IEEE Press, pp. 419−429.

Black, S., 2001. Computing ripple effect for software maintenance. J. Softw. Maintenance Evol. Res. Pract. 13 (4), 263−279.

Buckley, J., LeGear, A.P., Exton, C., Cadogan, R., Johnston, T., Looby, B., et al., 2008. Encapsulating targeted component abstractions using software Reflexion Modelling. J. Softw. Maintenance Evol. Res. Pract. 20 (2), 107−134.

Chidamber, S.R., Kemerer, C.F., 1994. A metrics suite for object oriented design. IEEE Trans. Softw. Eng. 20 (6), 476−493.

DeMarco, T., 1986. Controlling Software Projects: Management, Measurement, and Estimates. Prentice Hall PTR, Upper Saddle River, NJ, USA.

Ducasse, S., Anquetil, N., Bhatti, M.U., Cavalcante-Hora, A., 2011. Software Metrics for Package Remodularisation. [Research Report] 2011. < hal-00646878 >.

Ejiogu, L.O., 1991. Software Engineering with Formal Metrics. QED Information Sciences, Inc.

English, M., Buckley, J., Cahill, T., 2010. A replicated and refined empirical study of the use of friends in C++ software. J. Syst. Softw. 83 (11), 2275−2286.

English, M., Cahill, T., Buckley, J., 2012. Construct specific coupling measurement for C++ software. Comput. Lang. Syst. Struct. 38 (4), 300−319.

Fenton, N.E., Neil, M., 2000. Software metrics: roadmap. In: Proceedings of the Conference on The Future of Software Engineering. ACM, Limerick, Ireland, pp. 357−370.

Fenton, N.E., Pfleeger, S.L., 1998. Software Metrics: A Rigorous and Practical Approach. PWS Publishing Co, Boston, MA, USA.

Gaffney, J.E. Jr. 1981. Metrics in software quality assurance. In: Proceedings of the ACM'81 Conference. B. Levy, pp. 126−130.

Gamma, E., Helm, R., Johnson, R., Vlissides, J., 1995. Design Patterns: Elements of Reusable Object-Oriented Software. Addison-Wesley, Longman Publishing Co., Inc., Boston, MA, USA.

Harrison, R., Counsell, S.J., Nithi, R.V., 1998. An evaluation of the MOOD set of object-oriented software metrics. IEEE Trans. Softw. Eng. 24 (6), 491−496.

IEEE, 1983. IEEE Std. 729-1983 Standard Glossary of Software Engineering Terminology (ANSI).

ISO/IEC, 2010. ISO/IEC 25010—Systems and Software Engineering—Systems and Software Quality Requirements and Evaluation (SQuaRE)—System and Software Quality Models, ISO/IEC.

Jordan, H., Rosik, J., Herold, S., Botterweck, G., Buckley, J., 2015. Manually Locating Features in Industrial Source Code: The Search Actions of Software Nomads. In: Lucia, A.D., Bird, C., Oliveto, R. (Eds.), International Conference on Program Comprehension. IEEE, Florence, Italy.

Kemerer, C., 1995. Software complexity and software maintenance: a survey of empirical research. Ann. Softw. Eng. 1 (1), 1–22.

Kemerer, C., Slaughter, S., 1997. Methodologies for performing empirical studies: report from the international workshop on empirical studies of software maintenance. Empir. Softw. Eng. 2 (2), 109–118.

Klein, H.K., Myers, M.D., 1999. A set of principles for conducting and evaluating interpretive field studies in information systems. MIS Q. 23 (1), 67–93.

Lehman, M.M., 1980. Programs, life cycles, and laws of software evolution. Proc. IEEE 68 (9), 1060–1076.

Lethbridge, T., Sim, S., Singer, J., 2005. Studying software engineers: data collection techniques for software field studies. Empir. Softw. Eng. 10 (3), 311–341.

Martin, R., 2005. The Tipping Point: Stability and Instability in OO Design. Available from: <http://www.drdobbs.com/the-tipping-point-stability-and-instabil/184415285> (retrieved 10.03.15.).

Martin, R.C., 2000. Design Principles and Design Patterns. Available from: <http://www.objectmentor.com/resources/articles/Principles_and_Patterns.pdf> (retrieved 10.03.15).

Mitchell, B.S., Mancoridis, S., 2006. On the automatic modularization of software systems using the bunch tool. IEEE Trans. Softw. Eng. 32 (3), 193–208.

Olague, H.M., Etzkorn, L.H., Messimer, S.L., Delugach, H.S., 2008. An empirical validation of object-oriented class complexity metrics and their ability to predict error-prone classes in highly iterative, or agile, software: a case study. J. Softw. Maintenance Evol. Res. Pract. 20 (3), 171–197.

Parnas, D.L., 1972. On the criteria to be used in decomposing systems into modules. Commun. ACM 15 (12), 1053–1058.

Parnas, D.L., 1977. Use of Abstract Interfaces in the Development of Software for Embedded Computer Systems, p. 34.

Ponisio, L., Nierstrasz, O., 2006. Using Context Information to Re-architect a System. In: SMEF'06, Software Measurement European Forum, pp. 91–103.

Rahman, F., Devanbu, P., 2013. How, and why, process metrics are better. In: Proceedings of the 2013 International Conference on Software Engineering. San Francisco, CA. IEEE Press, pp. 432–441.

Robson, C., 2002. Real World Research. Blackwell.

Runeson, P., Höst, M., 2009. Guidelines for conducting and reporting case study research in software engineering. Empir. Softw. Eng. 14 (2), 131–164.

Sant'Anna, C., Figueiredo, E., Garcia, A., Lucena, C.P., 2007. On the modularity of software architectures: a concern-driven measurement framework. In: Software Architecture. F. Oquendo. Springer, Berlin Heidelberg, vol. 4758, pp. 207–224.

Sarkar, S., Kak, A.C., Rama, G.M., 2008. Metrics for measuring the quality of modularization of large-scaled object-oriented software. IEEE Trans. Softw. Eng. 34 (5), 700–720.

Sarkar, S., Rama, G.M., Kak, A.C., 2007. API-based and information-theoretic metrics for measuring the quality of software modularization. IEEE Trans. Softw. Eng. 33 (1), 14–32.

Schneidewind, N.F., 1987. The state of software maintenance. IEEE Trans. Softw. Eng. 13 (3), 303–310.

Scitools, 2015. Understand. Available from: <https://scitools.com/> (retrieved 10.03.15.).

Sharif, K.Y., English, M., Ali, N., Exton, C., Collins, J.J., Buckley, J., 2015. An empirically-based characterization and quantification of information seeking through mailing lists during Open Source developers' software evolution. Inf. Softw. Technol. 57 (0), 77–94.

Slaughter, S.A., Harter, D.E., Krishnan, M.S., 1998. Evaluating the cost of software quality. Commun. ACM 41, 67–73.

Stake, R.E., Savolainen, R., 1995. The Art of Case Study Research. Sage Publications, Thousand Oaks, CA.

Stevens, W.P., Myers, G.J., Constantine, L.L., 1974. Structured design. IBM Syst. J. 13 (2), 115–139.

Szyperski, C., Gruntz, D., Murer, S., 2002. Component Software: Beyond Object-Oriented Programming. Addison-Wesley, Longman Publishing Co., Inc., Boston, MA, USA.

Misic, V.B., 2001. Cohesion is structural, coherence is functional: different views, different measures. In: Software Metrics Symposium, 2001 (METRICS'01). Proceedings. Seventh International.

Yin, R.K., 2013. Case Study Research: Design and Methods. SAGE Publications, Thousand Oaks, CA.

Yourdon, E., Constantine, L.L., 1979. Structured Design. Prentice-Hall, Englewood Cliffs, NJ.

Zelkowitz, M.V., Wallace, D.R., 1998. Experimental models for validating technology. Computer 31 (5), 23–31.

Achieving quality on software design through test-driven development

9

Eduardo Guerra[1] and Maurício Aniche[2]

[1]*National Institute of Space Research (INPE), Associated Laboratory for Computing and Applied Mathematics, São José dos Campos / SP-Brazil* [2]*University of São Paulo (USP) Department of Computer Science, São Paulo / SP-Brazil*

9.1 INTRODUCTION

Test-driven development (TDD) has become popular among developers as it is one of the most important practices in any agile method, such as Extreme Programming (Beck, 2004). The practice suggests developers write a unit test before the production code in short cycles (Beck, 2002; Astels, 2003). In practice, a developer first introduces a new failing test, and then writes the smallest piece of code possible in the production code in order to make the test suite execute successfully. As a final step, the code is refactored, if necessary, to provide a better structure to the current solution.

There is some discussion in the software engineering community about whether TDD can be used to achieve software quality. Although the practice contains the word "test" on its name, a common speech among practitioners is that TDD drives developers toward a better code and class design. The idea is reinforced by many well-known book authors, such as Kent Beck (2002), Robert Martin (2002), e Nat Pryce (2009), and Dave Astels (2003).

Many different studies and controlled experiments were conducted in the last years evaluating the effects of TDD through many different point of views, such as internal and external quality, productivity, learning difficulties, etc. Just to mention a few, Janzen (2005) shows that TDD practitioners (from now on, called TDDers) developed code that contained 50% less bugs than the code developed by non-TDD practitioners. George and Williams (2003) showed that, although TDDers were less productive, their code had better external quality than non-TDDers. They also presented that those TDDers were believed to spend less time debugging their code. Janzen again (Janzen and Saiedian, 2006) shows that his students, when practicing TDD, used more object-oriented concepts than the ones that did not practice TDD. Li (2009) shows, by means of a qualitative study with professional developers, that TDD leads developers to a simpler class design, a consequence of the constant refactoring.

However, as with any scientific work, there are always some threats to their validity, so that it prevents researchers reaching a final answer about its effects. In practice, getting all these benefits is not as simple as it looks like. Some researchers have noticed that the effects of the practice (such as improving class design) are not natural or as clear as expected (Aniche et al., 2011; Siniaalto and Abrahamsson, 2008).

TDD is not a silver bullet. In this chapter, instead of trying to prove that TDD is more effective than traditional development, we will focus on discussing how developers can improve their code and design through the use of TDD. We will dive into the practice and present how it should be used in order to achieve quality in software design, such as high cohesion, low coupling, and less complexity. The end of each section presents an objective list of recommendations that summarize what is being said. We present other design techniques that can complement TDD in fields that are out of its scope. We expect that, after reading this chapter, a developer will be able to practice TDD and deliver high quality software, at a very productive pace.

9.2 EVIDENCES ON THE INFLUENCE OF TDD ON SOFTWARE QUALITY

Most studies that investigated the effects of unit testing and TDD on production code focused on external quality (e.g., bug-proneness). In this section, we present studies that focus on the quality of the design and other aspects of internal quality. It is worth to notice that many empirical studies that evaluated the effects of unit testing in class design relied on the TDD technique, as it highlights the writing of unit tests and their use to reflect upon the design.

Janzen (2005) showed that the code complexity was much smaller and the code coverage was higher in code written using TDD. Another study by Janzen (Janzen and Saiedian, 2006), with three different groups of students, showed that the code produced using TDD made better use of object-oriented concepts, and responsibilities were better distributed into different classes, while other teams produced a more procedural code. In addition, tested classes were 104% less coupled than non-tested classes, and methods were 43%, on average, less complex than the non-tested ones.

George and Williams (2003) showed that, although TDD can initially reduce the productivity of inexperienced developers, 92% of the developers in a qualitative analysis thought that TDD helped to improve code quality. 79% believed that the practice promotes a simpler class design.

A study by Erdogmus et al. (2005) with 24 undergraduate students showed that TDD increased productivity. However, no difference in code quality was found.

Langr (2001) showed that TDD increased code quality, facilitated maintenance, and helped to produce 33% more tests when compared to traditional approaches.

Dogsa and Batic (2011) also found an improvement in class design when using TDD. According to the authors, the improvement was a consequence of the simplicity that TDD adds to the process. They also affirmed that the test suites created during the practice favors constant code refactoring.

Li (2009) conducted a case study in which she collected the perceptions of TDD practitioners about the benefits of the practice. She interviewed five developers from software companies in New Zealand. The results of the interviews were analyzed and discussed in terms of code quality, software quality, and programmer productivity. Regarding code quality, Li concluded that TDD guides developers to simpler and better-designed classes. In addition, the main factors that contribute to these benefits are the confidence to refactor and modify the code, a higher code coverage, a deeper understanding of the requirements, a code easier to understand, and the elevated satisfaction of the developers.

TDD practitioners usually make use of other agile practices, such as pair programming. This makes the evaluation of the practice more difficult. Madeyski (2006) observed the results of groups that practiced TDD, groups that practiced pair programming, and the combination of them, and he was not able to show a significant difference between teams that used TDD and teams that used pair programming in terms of class package dependency management. However, when combining the results, he found that TDD helps to manage dependencies at class level.

Muller and Hagner (2002) showed that TDD does not result in better quality or productivity. Steinberg (2001) showed that code produced with TDD is more cohesive and less coupled. Participants also reported that defects were easier to fix.

9.3 TDD AS A DESIGN TECHNIQUE

The first references about TDD state that it is a technique that can be used for software design and development (Beck, 2002; Astels, 2003). Based on them, the software API is designed throughout the tests, defining how a client of that code, which can be any other module, should interact with it. The internal design is performed through refactorings, which should be considered in every cycle.

Of course, there are many other ways to use TDD. It also can be used only for the implementation. In this approach, the software is designed in a previous step, perhaps by using diagrams, and the classes APIs are already defined when the TDD is performed. The internal class design is the only one that is performed during TDD in this scenario. By having a previous design, the TDD is used only as an implementation technique that helps the development to move forward more safely and to achieve a good test coverage on the software classes. Another varion of the practice is what the industry calls *Acceptance TDD (ATDD)*. Practitioners develop acceptance tests using TDD mentality. By using this approach the tests consider the software as a whole and does not focus on the definition of its internal design.

It is important to state that this chapter considers TDD as a *design technique*, as a tool that can be used in the context of software development to achieve internal quality. By using TDD for design purposes, the test code is used to express the desired design that will be further implemented on production code. In this context, an analogy can be drawn between tests and UML diagrams, since they are different approaches to represent the software design. As in a diagram, the developer should know the design that s/he wants to express in order to represent it. The design does not "just happens" because of the tool that is being used to express it.

However, as a design tool, TDD tries to guide the developer in the direction of some good principles of object-oriented design. While it is wrong to say that by using only TDD all the design problems will be addressed, it is correct to say that it encourages the usage of some important design values. The next paragraphs highlight these values, explaining why TDD mechanics can drive the developer toward their application.

Some design techniques, specially the ones that use diagrams upfront, encourage the software designer to think further of the current need of the application. Following this approach, the designer tries to predict future extension points and classes, adding them early into the class structure. TDD states that the developed code should be the simplest possible to make the current test suit to pass. This practice ensures that the design focus is on the current functionality, and does not on assumptions or predictions that can lead to an overdesigned structure. So, *simplicity* and *focus on current functionality* are two design characteristics that are achieved by this mechanic.

There are different styles of TDD that use different kinds of test for the development. Although the tests can be functional or focused on the component, unit tests are the most common type of test on TDD, since the original books about this technique encourage its usage (Beck, 2002; Astels, 2003). To unit test a class, it should be decoupled from its dependencies, since the test should verify its behavior apart from them. The technique that is usually applied to achieve this kind of test is the usage of test doubles, such as stubs or mock objects. Since the tests are created before, driving the class design, the capacity to decouple the dependences to enable their substitution for test doubles is naturally included on the developed classes. So, *low coupling* is an important design value that can be achieved by performing TDD with unit testing.

Since all the design is driven by tests, it is expected that *testability* is an attribute that happens naturally by using TDD. Since the test code is written first, developers intuitively define an API that can be easily tested. This also happen with the functionality, which is divided in small portions that make viable the test of them separately. The usage of TDD encourages this characteristic because it is easier to test small pieces of functionalities than to create tests for logic that mix different application concerns. Looking from this point of view, TDD can help the classes to have a *higher cohesion*, since it is easier to group the small amount of functionality that makes sense together. Despite TDD not helping in the definition and division of modules, it can be stated that TDD helps to achieve *modularity* by encouraging the software division in smaller modules.

Another characteristic of TDD from the design point of view is that the software application design is considered a continuous task that is performed through the source code implementation. The presence of a refactoring phase on the small TDD cycles reinforces that developers should always look at the code and think if there is another solution or structure that can be implemented, better than the first one. Because of that, it can be affirmed that TDD considers the *design evolution* every time that a new functionality is added into the system. This is an important property for a design method to be used in agile methodologies, in which the requirements can change and the software is delivered in small iterations.

Based on that, it is possible to observe that TDD has several characteristics on its mechanics that reinforce the introduction of several design qualities on software. However, these qualities are not enough to guarantee that a suitable design is used in for the problems of the developed application. Some important points of an application design, such as the domain model and the architecture, are out of TDD scope. The following sections present why TDD does not help in such design domains and what other practices and techniques can be used to complement it.

Summary of Recommendations:

- Define in the beginning of the project if TDD will have the role of a software design technique.
- If TDD is going to be used for design, face tests as a tool to define the class design, making its code maintainable.
- Define the tests considering only current requirements, and develop the current application considering only those.
- Define the test approach that will be used to test each kind of component in the architecture.
- Create test suites for different components by grouping tests related with the same concern, to achieve cohesion and modularity.
- Do not try to find the definitive solution on the first version. Use the tests to support the code refactoring safely.

9.4 MODELING RELATIONS WITH TDD

On object oriented design, the dependence between classes and objects is an important point. The division of responsibilities among the system classes is important to achieve cohesion on a single class and decoupling between classes that collaborate. On classical upfront design methodologies, a diagram is usually applied to represent the relation between the classes and interfaces, such as composition, aggregation, dependence, inheritance and abstraction. In TDD all these relationships can be modeled, but in a different way.

The goal of this section is to present how modeling of class relations are done when TDD is used as the design technique. In order to do that, the first subsection presents the main concepts about mock object, followed by a subsection that explain how they are used to model dependencies. Further, the final subsection presents how hierarchy and abstractions rise in a software developed by TDD.

9.4.1 MOCK OBJECTS

An important tool to model dependencies in TDD, such as aggregation and composition, is *mock objects*. A mock object is a test double that can replace dependencies for test purposes (Mackinnon et al., 2001; Freeman et al., 2004). As the mock is able to replace the dependency without the class awareness, it should share an abstraction, such as a superclass or an interface, with the actual dependency. The mock object also can have other two responsibilities: to emulate the behavior needed for the test scenario and to allow verifications to be performed on the dependence invocations.

The behavior emulation is used to create different test scenarios for the class that is being developed. This should be used when the behavior of the tested class depends on the return of a dependency invocation. The effect is not necessarily a method return, but can also be an exception or a modification on a parameter variable.

The mock object should also be able to record the invocations that it receives in order to perform verifications. These verifications have the goal to check if the developed class is performing the expected invocations in its dependencies. The verifications can focus on which method is invoked, on the number of invocations, on the method parameter values, and on the method invocation order. Which one should be used will depend on the class requirements about how it should interact with its dependencies based on each ones responsibilities and collaborations.

Mock objects can be created as helper classes used for test. These classes should implement the dependency abstraction and provide internal logic to record the information needed from method calls and to allow the configuration of the expected behavior to simulate different test scenarios. Additionally, this class should also provide additional methods in order to allow the verifications to be invoked on the test method when needed.

However, the most common approach for creating mock objects is by using mock frameworks. By following this approach, the mock characteristics, such as its behavior and expectations, are defined on the test method itself and generated dynamically by the framework. For more complicated mocks, the usage of mock frameworks makes the creation of it less painful. Another advantage is that all the testing logic is defined in the test method, reducing the indirection.

Summary of Recommendations:

- Use mock objects to simulate a dependency of the tested class in a unit test.
- The mock object should be used to both verify the expected calls of the tested class and simulate the behavior of the dependency for the test scenario.
- Mock frameworks can help in the definition of complex mocks, and keep all the definitions in the test method.

9.4.2 DESIGNING DEPENDENCIES

The modeling of dependencies by using TDD happens by the definition of mock objects. When creating a unit test for a system class, the developer should be aware of the class responsibilities and its possible collaborations. This definition does not need to be formally defined in a diagram or in a document. However, it should be based on the design solution that the developer wants to apply. It can be based on the separation of concerns from reference architecture or on the participants of a design pattern that is being implemented.

When the test is being created, the definition of a mock can be used to model the dependency API and the division of responsibilities between the developed class and the dependency (Guerra et al., 2013). The first step is to create the mock and add it to the developed class. How this object is added to the developed class is an important design decision, because it defines how the dependency is bound to its lifecycle. For instance, if the dependency is added in the constructor, it is usually a mandatory dependency that will follow the class on its lifecycle. However, if it is added by using a setter method, it can be changed during the tested object existence. At last, the dependence can be a parameter in a method, which means that it is used only locally and it is not attached to the target class. In other words, how the dependence is inserted in the tested class reveals how both object's lifecycle relates.

The next step is to define which methods of the dependency, the tested class on a test scenario, should call. When a developer defines in a test that a mock method should be invoked, s/he is actually defining what kind of collaboration the developed class needs from its dependency in that scenario. This is the test driven approach to express test the role of each class in this collaboration. It clearly defines the contract between them to enable them to cooperate.

It is important to highlight that the mock is usually defined based on an abstraction, such as an abstract class or an interface. So, all the methods defined for the mock object, except the ones used for verification, are actually defined in this abstraction. So, following this approach, the contract between the class and the dependence is defined, and the actual dependence implementation can be performed later on a further TDD session.

Although the dependency modeling can be done by using mock objects, not all dependencies should be mocked. A bad consequence of mocking is that the dependency's contract becomes coupled to the test code, which makes it harder to be modified. Because of that, a mock should be used to design more stable contracts. The ones that are important for the application's internal API or to the division of roles according to the adopted architecture. Internal dependencies that do not have or should not have impact on the external class API, can be hidden from the test, making it easier to be refactored in the future.

In this sense, to create or not a mock object for dependency can be considered a design decision on TDD modeling. When a mock is created and defined on test, there must be a meaningful relation in the system context, and it should be more stable. When it is decided to not create a mock, there is a local collaboration which is not important for the system as a whole, but only to achieve the class responsibility. It allows the adopted approach to be refactored in the future without a huge impact on other parts of the system.

When the dependency of the developed class already exists and has a well-defined API, there is no need to design the dependency. When that happens, the TDD can be performed by using a mock object in order to isolate the behavior of the developed class. But it can also be done considering the whole component, including the target class and the dependency on the test (Fowler, 2007).

Summary of Recommendations:
- Define how the dependency is related to the tested class lifecycle by how the mock is introduced on the object for test.
- Create methods on the dependency interface based on the tested class needs for external class collaboration.
- Use mocks to design meaningful system dependencies and avoid creating mocks for internal dependencies that are encapsulated inside the tested class.
- Use mock creation as a way to express design decisions.

9.4.3 HIERARCHY AND ABSTRACTIONS

In order to create the mock object of a dependency, its abstraction should be defined. Based on this approach, TDD is a design technique that encourages the modeling of the interface apart from the behavior. This is how the initial abstractions emerge in the TDD development. The abstraction can be used to develop classes with different behaviors, and also to develop proxies and decorators that add functionality on different classes from the same abstraction.

By having an abstraction, several implementations that follow the abstraction can be developed to fulfill different behaviors for a given component. When a common behavior is detected on these different components, a refactoring toward the usage of inheritance can be performed. Following this approach, common methods and attributes can be pulled up in order to capture on the superclass the common behavior of that kind of class.

The inheritance can also emerge when a single class has several conditionals that reflect different behaviors that it can have based on an attribute value. The refactoring to replace conditionals by polymorphism can be used to transform that single class into a class hierarchy in which the subclass and not an attribute determines the behavior.

When practicing TDD, the abstraction emerges from the need to decouple dependencies for testing purposes. On the other hand, the inheritance usually appears through refactoring, both when classes of the same abstraction share some behavior or when a single class with several behaviors can be split in several subclasses. This approach helps to avoid the inheritance over engineering, which can be detected when you find a superclass with only one subclass. Following this, the inheritance will only arise when the superclass really represent an abstraction of different concepts in the application domain.

Summary of Recommendations:

- Define dependencies operations based on abstractions.
- Refactor toward inheritance when several implementations of an abstraction share the same behavior.
- Extract new hierarchies by refactoring conditionals with polymorphism where it is appropriate.
- Do not think of using inheritance before it is needed.

9.5 LARGE REFACTORINGS

The implementation of the simplest solution for a given test suite is a very important practice on TDD. The main goal of this practice, as stated before in this chapter, is to encourage the simplicity of the solutions and the focus on the current requirements. However, this approach has a drawback, which is that it can generate situations where the current solution is not suitable for the next requirements.

One can argument that an upfront design can prevent this situation by considering future and potential requirements on the design, based on a detailed requirements elicitation method. On the other hand, most of these predicted requirements may never happen, or, when they happen, they should be probably different from foreseen ones. TDD believes that the time to refactor the software when needed should demand less effort than the implementation of all foreseen requirements. Another impact from this approach is that keeping the code simple, makes it is easier to maintain and evolve.

A large refactoring is often seen as a consequence of a mistake or a wrong design. However, it is normal to happen when practicing TDD as a design technique. It is a direct consequence of the focus on the simplest solution. This refactoring may be not performed on the same TDD session. They may be necessary on future iterations, due to the evolution or change on the requirements. When the large refactoring is needed, it is not precise to say that the design was wrong, but that "it was suitable for the previous requirements" and "unsuitable for the current ones."

In a design created with TDD, classes are usually decoupled, which usually makes changes isolated inside specific classes. However, there are some situations in which the refactoring is large, usually involving things that affect several parts of the source code. Inside a class, the largest changes often involve modification on the data structure, since several parts of methods execution may depend on it. When more classes are involved, changes are usually on the classes API that are used by other classes.

In a recent paper (Guerra, 2014), the author reported a big refactoring that happened on the development of a framework by using TDD. In this refactoring, due to a change in requirements, a sequence of calls that are processed as soon as they were received, now needed to be stored and processed when the sequence is finished. In this situation, it was necessary to make a change in the data structure and on how it was processed by the class. However, it was restricted to that class.

As recommended in the literature (Fowler, 1999; Kerievsky, 2004), refactorings should be performed step by step, executing the tests after each one is performed. Finding a refactoring path where the behavior is preserved between the steps can be hard. In order to achieve that, sometimes it is necessary to keep both the old solution and new solution working at the same time, and to remove the old structure only at the end.

> *Summary of Recommendations*:
> - You cannot avoid large refactorings when you give way to the simplest solution.
> - Try to isolate possible refactoring points by modularizing it from the rest of the software.
> - Perform large refactorings in small steps, running the tests after each one.

9.6 COMBINING TDD WITH OTHER DESIGN TECHNIQUES

Although TDD can be a consistent technique for software design, it does not target all existing design domains needed for an application. In other words, TDD is not effective enough as a design technique for all the needs of a software project. This section highlights the context where TDD is applicable and presents design domains that are out of TDD scope. It also presents how TDD can be combined with other design techniques and patterns to achieve other application modeling goals.

Based on what was presented on the previous sections, it is possible to conclude that the main focus of TDD is on API design. By creating a test that uses a class in order to execute some of its behavior, the main design effort is to define an API that is appropriate for that class and for that test scenario. The refactoring, which is a step on its basic cycle, and the incremental development also contributes to the internal class design, which is continuously refined during the process.

It is correct to state that TDD is a technique whose focus is on a single class or in a small group of classes. Although TDD can be applied in the development of a entire component, the definition of the design through the test happens mainly on the class that is the test target, which is usually the facade to the component functionality. Even when mock objects are used to define the dependences API, the main focus is on the collaborations needed by the class being tested, and not on the dependency itself.

Since TDD is a design technique that focuses on a small group of classes, it is not suitable for design domains where the set of classes and their relationships are more important. The next subsections present some design domains out of TDD scope and how TDD can be combined with other techniques to reach a suitable design for a software application.

Summary of Recommendations:
- Understand the role of TDD for design in the context of the project that is being used.
- Combine TDD with other design techniques with different scopes.
- Do not rely on TDD for all aspects of application design.

9.6.1 ARCHITECTURAL DESIGN

Software architecture cares about the general structure of the application, its layers and its constraints. For the architecture, it is also important to provide a structure that achieves the suitable quality attributes, such as performance and capacity, in order to fulfill the application requirements. The consistency on how the functionalities of software are implemented is an important characteristic of software architecture.

This general design of an application is out of TDD scope, since it does not care about the whole, but the focus is on a single class. Designing the application with TDD, but without architecture as a start point, can lead to bad consequences in the long term. Although the classes can be decoupled by using mock objects; the functionalities can be implemented with different approaches and by using distinct structures, hurting the design consistency. Following this approach, the application structure can be lead to chaos, made by a net of decoupled but inconsistent components.

There can be reports of software projects that used TDD successfully without an explicit architectural design. However, these applications usually follow well-defined reference architecture, such as Java EE or Ruby on Rails, in which the main component types, their roles and their relationships are already defined and clear to all developers (Fairbanks, 2010). By following reference architecture, it is possible to keep the design consistency by test-driven developing the architectural components following their roles and constraints.

On the other hand, after an initial architecture definition, the component details, their APIs, and their relationships can be designed individually by TDD. While the architectural design cares about how all the components fit together to achieve the application requirements, TDD can pick a single component in this context and work with more detail in its individual design.

In this context, the architectural information about the class that is being developed by using TDD is crucial for its design and development. The class role in the architecture is important in order to verify on the tests only the responsibilities that are assigned to it (Guerra et al., 2014). If the architecture defines that a type of component should collaborate with other in order to achieve some functionality, a mock object can be used on the test to explicitly define this separation of concerns. In other words, the class development and design will be driven by the tests. However, the tests will be created based on the existing constraints for its role on the architecture.

Summary of Recommendations:

- Use references for an initial architectural design.
- Consider architectural constraints of a class on TDD considering its role on the architecture.
- Consider using mocks to define low level details on the interaction of two explicit architectural components.
- Evolve the architectural design through the project.

9.6.2 DOMAIN MODELING

The domain modeling is a very important part of a software design. This model captures the knowledge from the domain, including the main concepts and their relationships. Also part of the domain model is the division of responsibilities among the domain classes, and how to collaborate on business scenarios to achieve the desired functionality. This kind of modeling translates the business concepts and processes into the software, representing on it the portion of the real world that is relevant for the application functionality.

With the arise of strong reference architectures, such as Java 2 EE (Alur et al., 2001), with the respective best practices and patterns (Fowler, 2002), the domain modeling was set aside at the expense of an emphasis on architectural modeling. This kind of practice, especially common on enterprise architectures, had bad consequences on applications that end up with a poor domain model, where domain classes are used only as value objects, in other words, to transport data between the database and the graphical interface.

With a poor domain model, the business rules are usually implemented on service classes or, worst, on controllers. That practice causes an overload of functionality on the service classes, duplication of functionality, and feature envy, since the logic that handles the data are defined in a separated class.

In this scenario, the Domain Driven Design (DDD) (Evans, 2003) was a design technique that brought back the focus to the domain modeling, highlighting its importance in the context of a software project. This technique, which is not the only one that can be used for domain modeling, presents patterns on how to identify the domain entities and how this structure should interact with the rest of the application. The usage of DDD is popular on agile teams, even being combined with TDD (Landre et al., 2007).

The domain modeling is also out of the scope of TDD as a design technique. According to the first TDD references (Beck, 2002; Astels, 2003) and patterns documented about it (Guerra et al., 2014), a list of test scenarios should be used as a reference to start the TDD section. Based on that, a reference from the application domain and class responsibilities is important to build this functionality list. In other words, it assumes the existence of a previous domain analysis.

The eXtreme Programming (Beck, 2004) was the first agile methodology to propose TDD as part of its set of practices. However, it also proposes the usage of CRC cards in order to enable a collaborative discussion about the application domain among the developers and the stakeholders. XP proposes the combination of TDD and CRC for the application design. In this context, CRC is used for a more abstract modeling about the classes, their collaborations and responsibilities, and after that definition TDD is used to develop each class modeling its API and refining it continuously.

TDD works fine with other design techniques for domain modeling. The domain modeling usually comes first by identifying the domain classes, their characteristics, collaborations, and responsibilities. Then, when TDD is used to develop that class, or a subset of its functionality, it uses the domain model as a reference. For instance, collaboration can be modeled defining a mock object and delegating part of the behavior for it.

Summary of Recommendations:

- Complement TDD with a technique for domain design, to have a broader view of the application domain.
- Create tests on a TDD session based on the domain class responsibilities.
- Create mock objects based on expected domain class collaborations.

9.6.3 DESIGN PATTERNS

Patterns can be considered a recurrent solution used to solve a problem in a given context (ale, 1977). The design patterns (Gamma et al., 1995) document solutions in the domain of object-oriented software design, providing several solutions that can be used to solve design problems. Each pattern contains forces and consequences that present the tradeoffs of adopting such solutions.

Design patterns are an important design knowledge base that can be used independent of the design technique adopted. If the design is performed with diagrams, the pattern solution can be expressed on them. Similarly, the same pattern can also be expressed by using the test, by defining an API suitable with the pattern implementation and mock objects consistent with the pattern collaborations. While on TDD the test is used to drive the implementation and design, the patterns can be used to define the direction of that guidance.

A recent article reported the usage of TDD to perform the design of a persistence framework (Guerra, 2014). In this framework, the pattern Visitor was adopted as a design solution to decouple the query definition from the query generation for a specific database. According to the paper, the Visitor implementation was driven by the tests, which pushed the code in the direction of the pattern. However, the author also states that the pattern knowledge was crucial to its adoption, and hardly the same solution would be adopted if it were not known.

On the context of TDD, another approach for implementing patterns is through refactoring (Kerievsky, 2004). One of the big advantages on applying patterns by refactoring is that you do not need to add it until it is really necessary, which can help to avoid over engineering. Usually, the patterns that are applied following this approach are to accommodate a crescent software structure, enabling the management of a large number of classes and behaviors.

Summary of Recommendations:

- Consider design patterns in the definition of the class interface in the test.
- Use patterns as targets to refactoring to solve design problems.
- Use the expected pattern relation to define mock behavior of a dependence.

9.7 PREPARING FOR TDD IN A SOFTWARE PROJECT

An important message from this chapter is that TDD is not enough to design an entire application. It is not viable to pick a set of requirements or user stories and jump straight to creating tests, without having a notion of how the architecture should be and how the domain entities relate to each other (Aniche and Gerosa, 2012). Sometimes this process is not formal or explicit, but that does not mean it does not exist. This section presents some activities that should be performed before the practice of TDD in order to improve the software quality as a whole.

In order to start a TDD session, the developer should know the scope of that session. In other words, he needs to know what should be developed. To define it, the developer should be aware of the functional requirements s/he needs to implement, what classes should be included in the context of this development, and the constraints based on the class role in the architecture. It is important to define these things with the team, either formally defining them in a document or by an informal discussion. Leaving these decisions for each developer can generate a lack of standardization in similar classes or layers, leading the production and test code to an unorganized structure.

To be able to understand the constraints of the class that is being developed, an envisioning of the architecture is necessary. The reference architectures play an important role on this issue, because they often can be used as this starting point for the architecture (Fairbanks, 2010). Based on them, the developers can start the development with a set of component types with their roles and constraints, without a formal architectural document. With more challenging requirements or when working to an application domain that is not well established in industry, an initial project that present solution proposals for the main architectural problems is advisable. By using this architectural definition as an initial reference, the team can refine and evolve it through the iterations.

To exemplify how the architectural constraints are considered in the TDD development, consider the development of a class from the business layer on a typical web-based information system. As constraints, the architectural definition states that it cannot access the database directly and that it should not retrieve information from the user session. Based on that, to develop this class by using TDD, the test needs to consider that this class needs collaboration from a class to persist an information. The API of the class being developed should also consider that if it needs information present on user session, it should be received somehow (for instance, as a method or constructor parameter).

Besides the architectural constraints, the TDD and testing approach that should be used to develop the target class should also be defined. Although the initial TDD sessions can be used to explore the possibilities, in the long term it is important to use the same approach to develop similar classes. For instance, it is desirable that classes from the same layer are developed using the same testing technique.

On a TDD session there are two scopes that should be defined: the test scope, and the development scope. The test scope includes which classes are verified by the tests and the development scope is the classes that are developed on the TDD session. They can be the same, for instance when the development uses unit tests, however existing classes may be involved on the tests but are not the target of that development session.

The standardization of how TDD should be used on each type of component of the application architecture is important for the success of TDD as a design technique in the context of the entire software. This process can help to define the scope of tests and TDD development for the application layers and the tools and frameworks that are going to be used in each one. Even more specific things, such as helper test classes (Meszaros, 2006) and test superclasses (Guerra and Kinoshita, 2012), can be developed to help on test code development. This practice is complimentary to the architecture definition, defining how each architectural component should be tested.

Even though TDD can be used as a personal development practice, for it to be effective on the context of a project as a design technique, the whole team should be aware of the application architecture and the TDD and test approach on its context. By having this preparation for TDD on the project, the team member can share the same understanding on how the software should be designed, enabling a synergy on the system evolution.

For instance, to use different tools and testing approaches to develop two components of the same layer, it would be like on a more traditional design approach to use different types of diagrams to model the same kind of behavior. This team shared understanding to talk the same design language when performing TDD enabling them to work together on the software evolution, even when working on separated artifacts.

Summary of Recommendations:

- Define the scope of the tests and of the TDD session before its beginning.
- Consider class constraints and known collaborations based on architecture design or domain model.
- Use the same test approach on TDD for the same kind of component.
- Encourage the reuse of common test routines to make test easier on further TDD sessions.

9.8 CONTINUOUS INSPECTION

Although TDD has refactoring as part of its cycle, that fact does not guarantee that the developers perceive all the problems in source code. Especially when the sessions use unit tests to develop a single class, it is hard to perceive a design problem with a broader scope. Because of that, the practice of continuous inspection (Merson et al., 2013) is important to provide a continuous feedback on the application design, allowing the detection of untimely problems, drawing the attention of the developers to that part of the source code.

The practice of continuous inspection uses static and dynamic analysis tools to retrieve information about important quality attributes from the source code, such as test coverage, complexity, and decoupling. SonarQube and Code Climate are examples of such tools. These tools are frequently executed on each source code version and the result of its execution is reported to the developers. Based on the information provided, the developers can draw their attention to a piece of code with a potential problem and consider its refactoring. Additionally, in the context of several project iterations, it is possible to perceive how the code is evolving, making possible to plan larger refactorings to the next iterations.

The feedback of the continuous inspection tools can happen at three different timings. The fastest one is in the developer IDE, showing warnings and errors based on the source code analysis, allowing the developer to rethink his current decisions. The second moment is at compile time on the developers' machine, when a broader analysis can be performed considering the entire application and even other components. Finally, the third moment is in a continuous integration server, when more complex and long analysis can be performed, even by executing the application to retrieve dynamic metrics.

There are several types of analysis that can be performed in the continuous inspection process. The most important ones based on the requirements should be chosen by the team, and can also be evolved based on the retrospectives. The quality analysis can retrieve metrics from the source code and compare the numbers to industry standards based on statistical thresholds (Lanza et al., 2005). Additional information, such as bad smells and bug detection can also be executed. Architectural conformance (Merson, 2013) and security verifications are other types of static analysis that can be executed on the source code. Additionally, dynamic analysis can be performed to measure other quality attributes, such as test coverage and performance.

Although tools can give an important feedback on quality attributes related to the source code, having the developers taking a critical looking at the project artifacts can also raise some important issues that were not detected by the tools. Because of that, it is important to have a time to stop and discuss the situation of the source code based on the tools report and the developers' point of view. The iteration retrospectives are a nice place to have this discussion, but the team can define when it should take place and the frequency that it should happen.

The practice of continuous inspection has the same value of evolutionary design as TDD. Since TDD introduces a simple design at first to evolve it through the iterations, the inspection reports can help to identify points where the design should evolve at the time that this need appears. In this sense, it complements TDD having a broader focus on the application design as a whole, covering that weak point of TDD to focus on the design of a small number of classes at a time.

Summary of Recommendations:
- Use the tools that focus on important aspects needed by the team.
- Evolve the Continuous Inspection process and verifications based on the team feedback and learning.
- Discuss on retrospectives actions based on the tools inspection.
- Encourage developers to give additional feedback.

9.9 CONCLUSIONS

TDD is a design and development technique that can have an important role in a software project. It brings important design values to the team, but its main focus is on the class' API and on its internal structure, which is far from being enough. The main weak point of TDD from the design perspective is that it does not consider the software as a whole and only looks at a small part of it. This chapter's goal was to present how TDD can be combined with other techniques to contribute to software quality in the long term.

Initially, this chapter presents TDD as a design technique, raising evidence from existing works about its contribution to software quality. After that it explained what are the design values adopted on TDD and how they are applied in practice based on the technique dynamics. The following section presented the mock objects and how TDD designs class and object relations; which is an important point on an object-oriented design. This presentation of TDD finishes with a section that presents why big refactorings are part of a normal TDD process if adopted in a software project.

After that, the chapter presented some design domains that are out of TDD scope, and how the use of other techniques can be combined with TDD. It was shown how a software project prepared for the TDD can be used as a team practice and to have a positive impact on software quality. Finally, continuous inspection is presented as a complimentary technique to enable the team to always keep an eye on how the design is evolving through the iterations.

As a final conclusion, it is important to recognize that TDD has a limited scope and should be combined with other techniques to be used as a team practice in a long-term software project. The weight for the entire application design should not be the responsibility of a single technique. If the support techniques for TDD are applied appropriately, it has a high potential to have a great impact on the software quality.

REFERENCES

Alexander, C., Ishikawa, S., Silverstein, M., 1977. A Pattern Language: Towns, Buildings, Construction, vol. 2. Oxford University Press.

Alur, D., Malks, D., Crupi, J., 2001. Core J2EE Patterns: Best Practices and Design Strategies. Prentice Hall PTR, Upper Saddle River, NJ.

Aniche, M., Ferreira, T., Gerosa, M., 2011. What concerns beginner test-driven development practitioners: a qualitative analysis of opinions in an Agile conference. 2nd Brazilian Workshop on Agile Methods (WBMA), Fortaleza, Brazil.

Aniche, M.F., Gerosa, M.A., 2012. How the practice of TDD influences class design in object-oriented systems: patterns of unit tests feedback. In: Software Engineering (SBES), 2012 26th Brazilian Symposium on, IEEE. pp. 1−10.

Astels, D., 2003. Test-Driven Development: A Practical Guide, segunda ed. Prentice Hall.

Beck, K., 2002. Test-Driven Development by Example, first ed. Addison-Wesley Professional.

Beck, K., 2004. Extreme Programming Explained, second ed. Addison-Wesley Professional.

Dogsa, T., Batic, D., 2011. The effectiveness of test-driven development: an industrial case study. Softw. Qual. J.1−19, <http://dx.doi.org/10.1007/s11219-011-9130-2>.

e Nat Pryce, S.F., 2009. Growing Object-Oriented Software, Guided by Tests, 1st ed. Addison-Wesley Professional.

Erdogmus, H., Morisio, M., Torchiano, M., 2005. On the effectiveness of the test-first approach to programming. IEEE Trans. Softw. Eng. 31, 226–237, <http://doi.ieeecomputersociety.org/10.1109/TSE.2005.37>.

Evans, 2003. Domain-Driven Design: Tacking Complexity in the Heart of Software. Addison-Wesley Longman Publishing Co., Inc., Boston, MA.

Fairbanks, G., 2010. Just Enough Software Architecture: A Risk-Driven Approach. Marshall & Brainerd.

Fowler, M., 1999. Refactoring: Improving the Design of Existing Code. Addison-Wesley Longman Publishing Co., Inc., Boston, MA.

Fowler, M., 2002. Patterns of Enterprise Application Architecture. Addison-Wesley Longman Publishing Co., Inc., Boston, MA.

Fowler, M., 2007. Mocks aren't stubs. <http://martinfowler.com/articles/mocksArentStubs> (last accessed 26.11.14.).

Freeman, S., Mackinnon, T., Pryce, N., Walnes, J., 2004. Mock roles, objects. In: Companion to the 19th Annual ACM SIG-PLAN Conference on Object-oriented Programming Systems, Languages, and Applications. ACM, New York, NY, pp. 236–246. <http://dx.doi.org/10.1145/1028664.1028765>.

Gamma, E., Helm, R., Johnson, R., Vlissides, J., 1995. Design Patterns: Elements of Reusable Object-oriented Software. Addison-Wesley Longman Publishing Co., Inc., Boston, MA.

George, B., Williams, L., 2003. An initial investigation of test driven development in industry. In: Proceedings of the 2003 ACM Symposium on Applied Computing. ACM, New York, NY, pp. 1135–1139. <http://doi.acm.org/10.1145/952532.952753>.

Guerra, E., 2014. Designing a framework with test-driven development: a journey. Softw. IEEE 31 (1), 9–14. Available from: http://dx.doi.org/10.1109/MS.2014.3.

Guerra, E.M., Kinoshita, B., 2012. Patterns for introducing a superclass for test classes. In: Proceedings of the 9th Latin American Conference on Pattern Languages of Programming. ACM, New York, NY.

Guerra, E.M., Yoder, J., Aniche, M., Gerosa, M.A., 2013. Test-driven development step patterns for handling objects dependencies. In: Proceedings of the 20th Conference on Pattern Languages of Programs. ACM, New York, NY.

Guerra, E.M., Aniche, M., Gerosa, M.A., Yoder, J., 2014. Patterns for preparing for a test driven development session. In: Proceedings of the 21th Conference on Pattern Languages of Programs. ACM, New York, NY.

Janzen, D., Saiedian, H., 2006. On the influence of test-driven development on software design. Proceedings of the 19th Conference on Software Engineering Education and Training (CSEET'06). Hawaii, US. pp. 141–148.

Janzen, D.S., 2005. Software architecture improvement through test-driven development. In: Companion to the 20th Annual ACM SIGPLAN Conference on Object-Oriented Programming, Systems, Languages, and Applications. ACM, New York, NY, pp. 240–241. <http://doi.acm.org/10.1145/1094855.1094954>.

Kerievsky, J., 2004. Refactoring to Patterns. Pearson Higher Education.

Landre, E., Wesenberg, H., Olmheim, J., 2007. Agile enterprise software development using domain-driven design and test first. In: Companion to the 22nd ACM SIGPLAN Conference on Object-Oriented Programming Systems and Applications Companion. ACM, New York, NY, pp. 983–993. <http://dx.doi.org/10.1145/1297846.1297967>.

Langr, J., 2001. Evolution of test and code via test-first design. <http://www.objectmentor.com> (last accessed 01.03.11.).

Lanza, M., Marinescu, R., Ducasse, S., 2005. Object-Oriented Metrics in Practice. Springer-Verlag New York, Inc., Secaucus, NJ.

Li, A.L., 2009. Understanding the Efficacy of Test Driven Development. Master's Thesis, Auckland University of Technology.

Mackinnon, T., Craig, P., Freeman, S., 2001. Endotesting: unit testing with mock objects. In: Succi, G., Marchesi, M. (Eds.), Extreme Programming Examined. Addison-Wesley Longman Publishing Co., pp. 287–301.

Madeyski, L., 2006. The impact of pair programming and test-driven development on package dependencies in object-oriented design—an experiment. In: Munch, J., Vierimaa, M. (Eds.), Product-Focused Software Process Improvement, Lecture Notes in Computer Science, vol. 4034. Springer, Berlin/Heidelberg, pp. 278–289.

Martin, R.C., 2002. Agile Software Development, Principles, Patterns, and Practices, primeira ed. Prentice Hall.

Merson P. (2013) Ultimate architecture enforcement: custom checks enforced at code-commit time. Hosking A.L., Eugster P.T. SPLASH (Companion Volume), ACM, 153–160, <http://dblp.uni-trier.de/db/conf/oopsla/splash2013c.html#Merson13>.

Merson, P., Yoder, J., Guerra, E., Aguiar, A., 2013. Continuous inspection—a pattern for keeping your code healthy and aligned to the architecture. In: Proceedings of the 3rd Asian Conference on Pattern Languages of Programs. ACM, New York, NY.

Meszaros, G., 2006. XUnit Test Patterns: Refactoring Test Code. Prentice Hall PTR, Upper Saddle River, NJ.

Muller, M., Hagner, O., 2002. Experiment about test-first programming. Softw. IEEE Proc 149 (5), 131–136. Available from: http://dx.doi.org/10.1049/ip-sen:20020540.

Siniaalto, M., Abrahamsson, P., 2008. Does test-driven development improve the program code? Alarming results from a comparative case study. Balancing Agility and Formalism in Software Engineering. Springer, Berlin Heidelberg, pp. 143–156.

Steinberg, D.H., 2001. The Effect of Unit Tests on Entry Points, Coupling and Cohesion in an Introductory Java Programming Course. XP Universe.

Architectural drift analysis using architecture reflexion viewpoint and design structure reflexion matrices

10

Bedir Tekinerdogan

Information Technology Group, Wageningen University, Wageningen, The Netherlands

10.1 INTRODUCTION

Each software architecture design is the result of a broad set of design decisions and their justifications, that is, the design rationale. To capture and communicate these architecture decisions a proper documentation of the software architecture is needed. The software architecture documentation as such can be used to serve as a guideline for the subsequent life cycle activities to realize and control the design decisions. Unfortunately, software systems are rarely static and need to evolve over time due to bug fixes or new requirements. This situation causes the so-called *architectural drift* problem which defines the discrepancy between the architecture description and the resulting implementation (Knodel and Popescu, 2007; Koschke and Simon, 2003; Murphy et al., 2001; Rosik et al., 2011). This architectural drift can be even introduced during the initial implementation of the architecture due to lack of knowledge about the architecture or stringent time-to-market constraints. The existence of discrepancies among the architecture description and its implementation is not a mere theoretical issue but it may directly lead to increased maintenance time and cost, because the original design goals have been lost. In the extreme cases, a system's architecture may even deteriorate to a degree where further development is not feasible, leading to a complete system re-implementation.

A successful technique that is used for architecture consistency checking is the reflexion modeling approach as proposed in the software architecture design community (Murphy et al., 2001; Babar et al., 2004; Browning, 2001). A reflexion model is the resulting model of the comparison of the architecture design with the derived abstract model of the code. Typically a reflexion model highlights the differences between the code and the architecture and as such defines the extent of the architectural drift problem. Based on the reflexion model, either the design or the architecture can be adapted to keep the consistency among both artefacts.

Although reflexion modeling seems to be relatively popular the architecture model for it has remained informal. In this chapter, we propose to enhance existing reflexion modeling approaches using architecture viewpoints. For this we introduce the architecture reflexion viewpoint that can be used to define reflexion model for different architecture views.

For large-scale software systems, the adoption of abstract visual models can soon become less practical and impede the architecture conformance analysis process. To represent the architecture using a more compact form, *design structure matrices* (DSMs) can be used (Danilovic and Sandkull, 2005). DSMs have been widely used outside the software engineering domain, and also in software engineering to assess the modularity of the design. We explore the adoption of DSMs in reflexion modeling to provide a common succinct representation of the architecture and code, provide powerful qualitative and quantitative analysis, and support the refactoring of the architecture and code. For this, we introduce the notion of *design structure reflexion matrices* (DSRMs) that are in essence DSMs indicating the inconsistencies as it is the case with abstract reflexion models. We present a generic architectural drift analysis approach based on these DSRMs. To cope with multiple architecture views, we provide also an approach for defining DSMs and DSRMs for architectural viewpoints. We discuss the key challenges in this novel approach and aim to pave the way for further research in DSM-based reflexion modeling.

The remainder of the chapter is organized as follows. In Section 10.2, we define the background on reflexion modeling. In Section 10.3, we present a feature model of design structure matrices and categorize the different DSMs. Section 10.4 discusses the notion of DSRM. Section 10.5 discusses the applicability and possible research directions for using DSRMs. Section 10.6 presents the conclusions.

10.2 REFLEXION MODELING

Architecture consistency implies that the architecture design elements can be mapped to the implementation elements. In case the relationships between the architecture and implementation do not correspond then these are called *architectural violations*. If the relations that are present in the architecture are also found in the implementation then this is *convergent relation*. In case the architecture relation is not present in the implementation then this is called an *absence relation*. Absence relations occur of course during the initial development of the system in which the architecture is defined but the implementation is not ready yet. As such, in the early phases of the development these absence relations might be a lesser concern. Finally, if the implementation includes relation that is not present in the architecture, then this is called *divergence relation*. Architectural violations are due to absence or divergence relations.

A successful design recovery technique that is used for architecture consistency checking is the *reflexion modeling* approach as proposed by Murphy et al. (2001).

Based on the literature, Figure 10.2 shows the activity diagram representing the reflexion modeling approach. In principle, a reflexion model allows a software developer to view the structure of a system's source through a chosen high-level (often architectural) view. To check the consistency between the architecture model and the code, an abstract model of the code is derived. The two models are then compared to each other with respect to earlier defined mapping rules between the code and the implementation. The results of the comparison are presented to the user through a *Reflexion Model*. The reflexion model explicitly represents the convergence, the divergence, and the absence relation. By analyzing the reflexion model, the architecture, the code or the mapping rules can be altered. Usually architecture conformance analysis approaches that apply reflexion modeling include tools for modeling the architecture, modeling the mappings, deriving the abstract model from the source code, the consistency analysis checker, and the generator of the resulting reflexion model.

10.3 REFLEXION MODELING USING SOFTWARE ARCHITECTURE VIEWPOINTS

Although reflexion modeling seems to be relatively popular the architecture model for it has been remained informal. A common practice is to model different architectural views for describing the architecture according to the stakeholders' concerns. A stakeholder is defined as an individual, team, or organization with interests in, or concerns relative to, a system. Each of the stakeholders' concerns impacts the early design decisions that the architect makes. An architectural view as such is a representation of a set of system elements and relations associated with them to support a particular concern. Because multiple concerns need to be taken into account when designing a system, multiple architecture views can help to separate the concerns and as such support the modeling, understanding, communication, and analysis of the software architecture for different stakeholders.

Architectural views conform to viewpoints that represent the conventions for constructing and using a view. In the literature, initially a fixed set of viewpoints have been proposed to document the architecture. Because of the different concerns that need to be addressed for different systems, the current trend recognizes that the set of views should not be fixed but multiple viewpoints might be introduced instead. The ISO/IEC 42010 standard (formerly IEEE 1471 Recommended Practice for Architectural Description; ISO/IEC 42010:2007, 2011) indicates in an abstract sense that an architecture description consists of a set of views, each of which conforms to a viewpoint realizing the various concerns of the stakeholders. The Views and Beyond (V&B) approach as proposed by Clements et al. is another multiview approach (Clements et al., 2010) that proposes the notion of architectural style similar to the notion of architectural viewpoint.

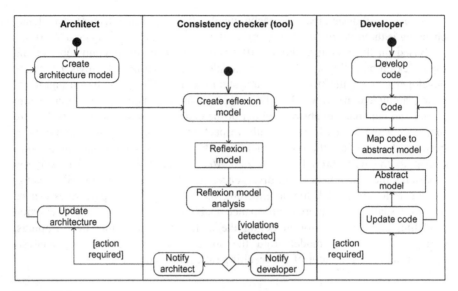

FIGURE 10.1

Activity diagram showing the steps in reflexion modeling for architecture-to-code conformance.

In alignment with the idea of multiple views for software architecture it is important that the reflexion modeling approach also considers views to identify inconsistencies between the code and the corresponding architecture views. As such the reflexion modeling of Figure 10.1 is enhanced to the process as shown in Figure 10.2. As it is shown in the figure, software architecture is now modeled using multiple views. On the other hand, code is abstracted to different abstract models that correspond to the architecture views. Finally, the reflexion model is also represented based on different architecture views. That is, for each architecture view a corresponding reflexion view will be required that shows the deviations with the code.

10.4 REFLEXION VIEWPOINT

Each architecture view can be analyzed with the code and result in a corresponding reflexion model. Hereby, the reflexion model will include the architecture elements as defined in the viewpoint. In addition, the reflexion model needs to be able to express the conformance, convergence and absence relations. Since these are not explicitly defined in the current architecture viewpoints we introduce the so-called *Architecture Reflexion Viewpoint*. Figure 10.3 shows the concepts related to the general notion of architecture viewpoints and the

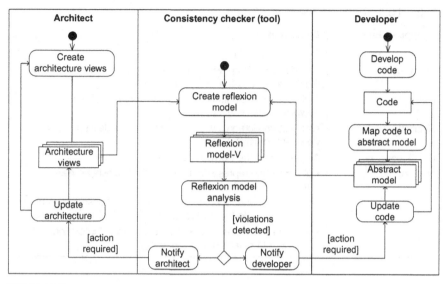

FIGURE 10.2

Activity diagram showing the steps in reflexion modeling for architecture-to-code conformance.

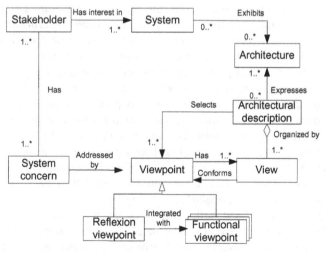

FIGURE 10.3

Conceptual model for architectural views based on ISO/IEEE/IEC standard.

Table 10.1 Reflexion Viewpoint Guide

Viewpoint Element	Description
Name	Reflexion viewpoint
Overview	This viewpoint is an abstract viewpoint that is used for defining the concrete reflexion viewpoints
Elements	Architecture elements which are elements as defined in the viewpoint to which it applies
Relations	Architecture elements which are relations as defined in the viewpoint to which it applies
Constraints	As defined by the viewpoint to which it is applied
Notation	• A solid edge represents an element/relationship present in both the A and the I (convergence)
	• A dashed edge represents an element/relationship present in the I, but not in the A (divergence)
	• A bold edge represents an element/relationship present in the A, but not present in the I (absence)

notion of reflexion viewpoint. The architectural description consists of a set of views that correspond to their viewpoints. Viewpoints aim to address the stakeholder's concerns. Functional concerns will define the dominant decomposition along architectural units that are mainly functional in nature. On the other hand, reflexion viewpoint is an abstract viewpoint that can be integrated with a functional viewpoint. Likewise we could have multiple different reflexion viewpoints based on the selected functional viewpoints.

The reflexion viewpoint that is based on the metamodel is shown in Table 10.1. As shown in Figure 10.3, the reflexion viewpoint can be applied to different viewpoints. Application of viewpoint means merging the elements of the reflexion viewpoint with the elements of the selected viewpoint. In this way reflexion mechanism are integrated to the selected viewpoint. Instantiating the reflexion viewpoint is therefore not directly possible but is performed indirectly over another viewpoint that defines the architecture components and connectors. If the reflexion viewpoint is applied to a particular viewpoint then in essence a customization of the corresponding viewpoint is defined. The resulting viewpoint is named *Reflexion−<Viewpoint Name>*. Simply, the term "Reflexion" is included as a prefix to the name of the viewpoint on which the reflexion viewpoint is applied. For example, if we apply the reflexion viewpoint to the Decomposition Viewpoint then the resulting viewpoint will be *Reflexion−Decomposition Viewpoint*.

Once the newly defined reflexion viewpoint has been defined then the corresponding architecture view with reflexion can be defined based on this viewpoint. Views that result from reflexion viewpoints represent in essence reference architecture from which different application architectures can be derived. The reference architectures are called *Reflexion Architecture Views*. In case of, for example, the merge

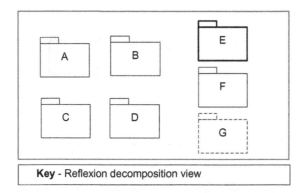

Key - Reflexion decomposition view

FIGURE 10.4

Reflexion decomposition view.

with the *Reflexion Viewpoint* with the *Decomposition Viewpoint*, a reflexion reference architecture view called *Reflexion Decomposition View* can be defined. Based on the reflexion architecture views, application architecture views are derived to represent the architecture of a particular application.

We can now present example instantiations of the reflexion viewpoint. For this we will select the decomposition, uses, and deployment viewpoints (styles) as defined in the V&B approach (Clements et al., 2010).

Figure 10.4 shows the application of reflexion viewpoint to the decomposition view. The view shows the decomposition of the system into different modules. The view is the result after comparison of the architecture with the implementation model. From the figure we can observe that module E is a module that appeared to be in the architecture decomposition view, but is missing in the implementation (absence). On the other module G seems to have been added to the implementation although this was not in the architecture decomposition view (divergence).

Figure 10.5 shows the application of reflexion viewpoint to the uses view. This view results from the comparison of the architecture uses view with the implementation and shows in addition to the modules also the differences in the uses relations. From the figure we can observe that the uses relation B to E (bold) is missing in the implementation although it was defined in the uses view (absence). The uses relations A to C, and G to B (dashed) is added to the imple-mentation although this was not present in the architecture (divergence).

Figure 10.6 shows the application of reflexion viewpoint to the deployment view. This view results from the comparison of the architecture deployment view with the implementation and shows in addition to the modules also the differences in the deployment view relations. From the figure we can observe that modules D that were deployed to the nodes in the nodes N2 and N3 (bold) are missing in the implementation although it was defined in the uses view (absence). Node N4 (dashed) is added to the implementation although this was not present in the architecture (divergence).

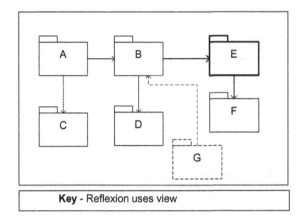

FIGURE 10.5

Reflexion uses view.

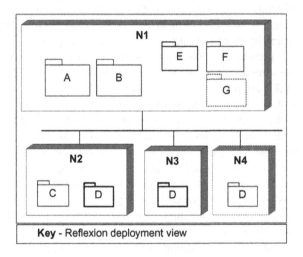

FIGURE 10.6

Reflexion deployment view.

10.5 DESIGN STRUCTURE MATRIX

As described in the previous section, a reflexion model is usually represented as an abstract visual model depicting the architectural elements and relations with the inconsistency results (convergence, absence, divergence). To provide an alternative more succinct representation of the architecture and the corresponding reflexion model, we further propose to adopt DSM. A DSM is simply a matrix in which the row and column elements represent the elements of the model that is analyzed

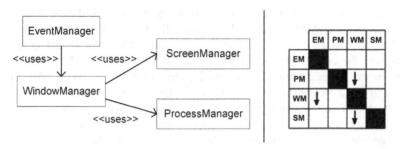

FIGURE 10.7

Example DSM representing a WMS system.

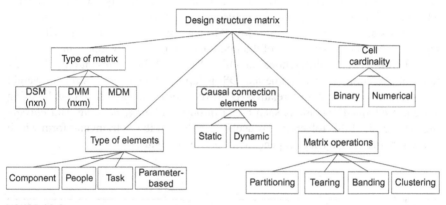

FIGURE 10.8

Feature model of design structure matrices.

(Browning, 2001; Danilovic and Sandkull, 2005; Sangal et al., 2005). The cells in the matrix represent the dependency relations among the elements. Figure 10.7 shows for example the DSM of a Window Management System architecture.

The acronyms EM, PM, WM, and SM represent *EventManager*, *ProcessManager*, *WindowManager*, and *ScreenManager*, respectively. The rows and columns represent subsystems and the arrow represents dependencies between architectural components. In the figure we can observe, for example, that *EventManager* depends on *WindowManager*.

The advantage of adopting DSMs is not only the succinct representation but also its support for qualitative and quantitative analysis. Analyzing the matrix either row wise or column wise provides us, for example, insight in the sensitive components of the architecture. DSMs can be also refactored to achieve a more preferable structure of the architecture. In fact we can distinguish among different types of design structure matrices. Figure 10.8 shows a feature diagram of design structure matrices that we have derived from the literature.

Three basic types of design structure matrices are described as DSM, domain mapping matrix (DMM), and MDM. Traditionally, the DSM is a square matrix that has been used in a variety of product, process, and organization modeling applications over the last 20 years. Complementary to DSMs, a DMM is used to map between two different project domains. Hereby, a DMM is a rectangular $(m \times n)$ matrix relating two different domains with element size m and n, respectively. Finally, MDM is a matrix that combines DSM and DMM into a complete system model. The elements that the design structure matrix can represent can be component, people, activity or parameter-based. In component-based relations among components are represented. Task-based DSMs are used for representing relations among tasks or activities. In people-based DSM the relation among people are defined. Finally, parameter-based DSM is similar to task-based DSM but at a lower level. DSMs can be either static or time-based. Static DSMs represent systems where all of the elements exist simultaneously. In time-based DSMs, the ordering of the rows and columns defines a flow through time, that is, earlier activities in a process appear in the upper-left of the DSM and later activities appear in the lower-right. DSMs can have different cardinalities. Binary DSMs represent only the existence of a relation, whereas numerical DSMs represent a numerical value or weight to represent the strength of a relation. DSM refactoring can be carried out by using several predefined operations such as *partitioning, tearing, banding*, and *clustering*. The result of this refactoring is usually a so-called lower-triangular form which helps to better reason about dependencies between modules.

10.6 DESIGN STRUCTURE REFLEXION MATRIX

Adopting DSMs in reflexion modeling can provide benefits for both analysis and refactoring of architectures. As stated before the software architecture is usually represented using multiple architecture views for addressing the stakeholders' concerns. After integrating views and DSM the resulted reflexion approach is shown in Figure 10.9. Here we assume that both the architecture views and the source code are mapped to corresponding DSMs. A DSM representing the architecture view V is called DSM-Arch-V, the DSM representing the source code from view V is called DSM-Code-V. The activity *Create Architecture Reflexion Views* compares the matrices DSM-Arch-V and DSM-Code-V and results in a *design structure reflexion model DSRM-V*. In this context, we could for example represent the decomposition view as *DSM-Arch-Decomposition*. Similarly, a corresponding *DSM-Code-Decomposition* will be derived from the code. Based on these two inputs the *DSRM-Decomposition* will be generated. In the activity *Consistency Analysis*, the generated DSRMs are analyzed and the architect and/or the developer is notified for changes.

An important challenge in this approach is the activity *Map Views to DSMs* whereby the visual architectural views are mapped to the corresponding DSMs. For this, each viewpoint will typically require its own specific implementation of

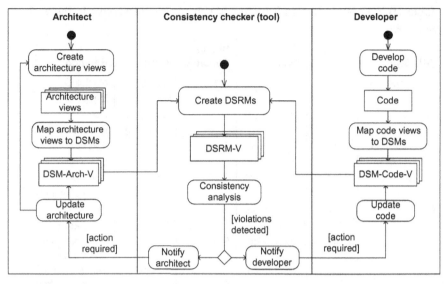

FIGURE 10.9

Activity diagram showing the architecture drift analysis using DSRMs.

the mapping process. To analyze the applicability of design structure matrix concept to architecture views, we have studied the viewpoints (styles) in the V&B approach (Demirli and Tekinerdogan, 2011; Clements et al., 2010). The analysis of all the views of the V&B approach is shown in Table 10.2.

The left column represents the different viewpoints, the column *Matrix Type* describes the possible type of DSM that we can apply. The column *Relation* describes the relations that are used in the viewpoints and as such in the matrix relations. Based on the table we can state that the viewpoints in the module style category, and component and connector style categories can be represented as DSMs, whereas the allocation styles can be represented as either DMM or MDM. The element types are in general components, but the allocation styles can also include people. In general, the styles can be represented as static DSM. The last column represents the relations of the style that also define the relations among the elements in the DSM. We have omitted the attributes *Matrix Operations* and *Cardinality* because in principle all operations can be applied to all matrices and both binary and numerical can be used.

Another challenge that we observe is the activity *Map Code Views to DSMs* resulting in the corresponding *DSM-Code-Vs*. Again for its viewpoint a specific implementation of the mapping process (reverse engineering) approach is needed. The implementation viewpoints of the V&B approach are the direct candidates for defining corresponding DSMs. The component-and-connector styles as well as the allocation styles require a more closer investigation on deriving the required views from the code, if possible.

Table 10.2 Possible Design Structure Matrix for the Viewpoints in the V&B Approach

V&B Style	Matrix Type	Element Type	Static/ Dynamic	Card.	Relation
Decomposition	DSM	Component	Static	Binary	Contains/ Is-part-of
Uses	DSM	Component	Static	Binary Numerical	Uses/ Is-used-by
Generalization	DSM	Component	Static	Binary	Parent-of/ Is-a
Layered	DSM	Component	Static	Binary Numerical	Can-use/ Can-be-used-by
Aspects	MDM DMM	Component	Static	Binary Numerical	Crosscuts/ Advised by
Data model	DSM	Component	Static	Binary	Aggregation and generalization
Pipe&filter	DSM	Component Task Parameter	Static/ Dynamic	Binary Numerical	Sends-data-to/ reads-data-from
Client-server	DSM	Component	Static	Binary Numerical	Server-of/client-of
Peer-to-peer	DSM	Component	Static	Binary Numerical	Attachment
Publish-subscribe	DSM	Component	Static	Binary Numerical	Subscriber-of/ publisher-of
Shared data	DMM	Component	Static	Binary Numerical	Data access
Deployment	MDM DMM	Component	Static/ Dynamic	Binary Numerical	Allocated-to/ contains
Install	MDM	Component	Static	Binary	Allocated-to/ contains
Work assignment	MDM	People Component	Static/ Dynamic	Binary	Allocated-to/ works-on
Implementation	MDM DMM	Component	Static	Binary	Allocated-to/ contains
Data stores	DMM	Component	Static	Binary	Allocated-to/ contains

The final challenge in the approach is the activity *Create DSRMs* in which the architecture and code DSMs for the corresponding views are compared, and the DSRM for the corresponding view is generated. Here we have to decide how to show the convergence, absence and divergence relations. In general,

Table 10.3 Reflexion Viewpoint with Design Structure Matrix notation

Viewpoint Element	Description
Name	Reflexion viewpoint
Overview	This viewpoint is an abstract viewpoint that is used for defining the concrete reflexion viewpoints represented as DSMs
Elements	Architecture elements which are elements as defined in the viewpoint to which it applies
Relations	Architecture elements which are relations as defined in the viewpoint to which it applies
Constraints	As defined by the viewpoint to which it is applied
Notation	Matrix notation whereby: • A *green cell* represents a relationship present in both the A and the I (convergence) • A *red* represents a relationship present in the A, but not present in the I (absence) • A *blue cell* represents a relationship present in the I, but not in the A (divergence)

reflexion modeling approaches do not provide completely new reflexion models for representing the architecture. Rather, these approaches adopt an existing architecture model and enhance the concrete syntax (notation) of these models with properties for convergence, absence and divergence. In its very basic form we have seen that different line formatting (e.g., solid, dashed, or dotted line) is used to distinguish among these properties. If we apply DSMs to reflexion modeling, we think that we can take a similar approach. For this we can identify various options including the use of colors: (i) A *green cell* represents a relationship present in both the A and the I (convergence). (ii) A *red cell* represents a relationship present in the A, but not present in the I (absence). (iii) A *blue cell* represents a relationship present in the I, but not in the A (divergence). In essence, this choice defines a new notation for the reflexion viewpoint that we have defined before (Table 10.3).

Figure 10.10 shows an example of the architecture uses view for a collaboration platform for patients who can share their health problems with other patients and doctors. Doctors can browse through the system, interact with other doctors, and provide recommendations to the problems of patients.

The application of the reflexion modeling approach to this case will compare the code with the architecture views and results in a set of DSRMs. In this context an example DSRM is shown in Figure 10.11 for the uses view.

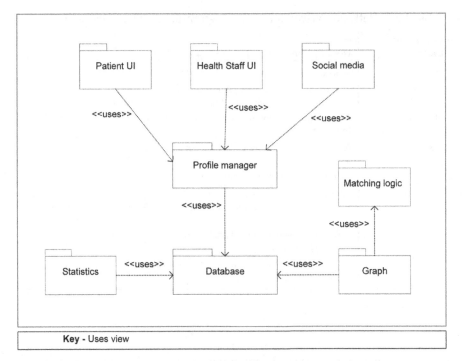

Key - Uses view

FIGURE 10.10

Decomposition view for E-Health system.

	1!	2!	3!	4!	5!	6!	7!	8!	9!	10
1! Web Based Collaboration System	■									
2! UI	0	■						2		
3! Patient UI		0	■					1		
4! Health Staff UI		0		■				1		
5! Database Connector	0				■		1	1	1	
6! Matching Logic	0					■		1		
7! Profile Manager	0	2	1	1			■			1
8! Graph Visualization	0							■		
9! Statistics	0								■	
10! Social Media Connector	0									■

FIGURE 10.11

Uses view represented as DSRM.

10.7 **POSSIBLE APPLICATIONS**

Using DSRMs in architecture conformance analysis leads to several interesting applications and challenges:

- *Architecture-to-Code Consistency Analysis*
    This is the approach that we have discussed in the previous sections. The architecture (view) and the code are mapped to a DSMs and the *Create DSRMs* generates a DSRM. Hereby, the DSMs and DSRMs do not only provide succinct representations of the architecture but also provide a means for analysis and refactoring.
- *Architecture-View to Architecture-View Consistency Analysis*
    The consistency analysis can be also carried out between selected views. In that case the consistency analysis checker will get as input DSMs that represent the selected architecture views. The resulting DSRM can be used to show the inconsistencies among the views.
- *Product Line Architecture to Application Architecture Consistency Analysis*
    In software product line engineering typically there are two distinct architectures, the product line architecture representing the architecture of a family of products, and application architecture representing the architecture of a single product. An important requirement in SPLE is that the application architecture should match the constraints that are defined in the product line architecture. In this case the input to the *Create DSRMs* activity will be the DSMs that represent the product line architecture and the application architecture. The resulting DSRM can be used to check the violations between the product line architecture and application architecture.
- *Code-to-Code Consistency Analysis*
    Hereby the input to the *Create DSRMs* activity are the DSMs from two different source codes. The output will be a DSRM that represents the differences among the two codes. This will be relevant for version control and configuration management systems.

10.8 **CONCLUSION**

In this chapter, we have proposed an approach for reflexion modeling which usually compares an abstract model of the code with the architecture model to identify the differences. We have proposed to enhance existing reflexion modeling approaches using architecture viewpoints and introduced the architecture reflexion viewpoint that can be used to define reflexion model for different architecture views. The approach has been illustrated for the architecture viewpoints of the V&B approach but can in principle be used for any viewpoint approach. In addition to the visual notation we have proposed the adoption of DSMs n reflexion modeling. DSMs have been used in different domains to cope with complexity and support the analysis of large scale systems. In particular, we have proposed the DSRM that shows the difference with the code and the architecture. We have discussed the important challenges and indicated several interesting applications of DSRMs. We believe that the identified possible applications of DSRMs can be valuable for coping with evolution of the architecture and/or the code. Based on the ideas in this chapter other challenges and applications could be identified as well. In our future work, we will detail the generic approach that we have defined in this chapter and develop the tool framework integrating reflexion viewpoints and DSRMs with reflexion modeling.

REFERENCES

Babar, M.A., Zhu, L., Jeffery, R., 2004. A framework for classifying and comparing software architecture evaluation methods. Proc. Australian Software Engineering Conference, 309−318.

Browning, T., 2001. Applying the design structure matrix to system decomposition and integration problems: a review and new directions. In: IEEE Trans. on Engineering Management, vol. 48. ACM Press, New York, NY, USA, pp. 292−306.

Clements, P., Bachmann, F., Bass, L., Garlan, D., Ivers, J., Little, R., et al., 2010. Documenting Software Architectures: Views and Beyond, second ed. Boston, MA, Addison-Wesley.

Danilovic, M., Sandkull, B., 2005. The use of dependency structure matrix and domain mapping matrix in managing uncertainty in multiple project situations. Int. J. Proj. Manage. 3, 193−203.

Demirli, E., Tekinerdogan, B., 2011. Software language engineering of architectural viewpoints. In: Proc. of the 5th European Conference on Software Architecture (ECSA 2011), LNCS 6903, pp. 336−343.

ISO/IEC 42010:2007, 2011. Recommended Practice for Architectural Description of Software-Intensive Systems (ISO/IEC 42010).

Knodel, J., Popescu, D., 2007. A comparison of static architecture compliance checking approaches. In: Proceedings of the 6th Working IEEE/IFIP Conference on Software Architecture, Mumbai, India, p. 12.

Koschke, R., Simon, D., 2003. Hierarchical reflexion models. In: Proceedings of the 10th Working Conference on Reverse Engineering, VIC, Canada.

Murphy, G., Notkin, D., Sullivan, K., 2001. Software reflexion models: bridging the gap between design and implementation. IEEE Trans. Softw. Eng. 27 (4), 364−380.

Rosik, J., Le Gear, A., Buckley, J., Babar, M.A., Connolly, D., 2011. Assessing architectural drift in commercial software development: a case study. Softw. Pract. Exp. 41 (1), 63−86.

Sangal, N., Jordan, E., Sinha, V., Jackson, D. 2005. Using Dependency Models to Manage Complex Software Architecture. In: OOPSLA '05, New York, NY, USA, pp. 167−176.

Tekinerdogan, B., Demirli, E., 2013. Evaluation framework for software architecture viewpoint languages. In: Proc. of 9th Int. ACM Sigsoft Conference on the Quality of Software Architectures Conference, Vancouver, Canada, June 17−21.

Driving design refinement: How to optimize allocation of software development assurance or integrity requirements

11

Ioannis Sorokos, Yiannis Papadopoulos, Martin Walker,
Luis Azevedo and David Parker

Department of Computer Science, University of Hull, Hull, UK

INFORMATION IN THIS CHAPTER

- System Design Refinement
- Optimal Allocation of Development Assurance Requirements
- Use of Metaheuristic Algorithms
- Case Study

11.1 INTRODUCTION

It is widely accepted that effective engineering of requirements is an important aspect of the software and system engineering lifecycle. The success of projects is often determined at early stages when requirements are elicited, because expensive errors or omissions at this stage often lead to system failures or expensive design iterations to correct problems identified later on. Although it is an important step, the correct elicitation of requirements is only part of an effective requirements engineering process. As the system design is elaborated and progressively refined, system-level requirements need to be translated to requirements for subsystems and components of the progressively refined system architecture. Requirements allocation is crucial in achieving effective refinement of design into smaller, more manageable elements, as well as providing traceability of how these elements combine to implement the system requirements by fulfilling their own.

We define the process as the "requirements allocation problem," that is, the problem of finding an effective translation of system-level requirements to

237

requirements for the elements of the system, in a scheme which guarantees that, when lower level requirements for elements are met, system level requirements are also met. In this chapter, we examine the problem in the context of safety critical systems such as those used in transport where safety requirements take the highest priority. The techniques we develop are specific to safety requirements but also shed some light into the more general problem of requirement allocation in complex software intensive systems.

In the case of safety critical systems, the elicitation and allocation of safety requirements is the focus of numerous safety assessment activities which aim at allowing safety properties to be controlled from the early stages of design. It is, indeed, increasingly considered important that safety should be controlled from the early stages of design rather than left to emerge (or not) at the end. This aspiration is embodied in all major safety standards, many of which provide an example of how this can be achieved. Specifically, the concept of Safety Integrity Levels, first introduced in the IEC61508 (SC 65-A, 2010) standard, provides a means of qualitatively describing and summarizing such requirements and assigning them across the system. This concept is shared across numerous domain-specific standards such as ISO 26262 (TC 22/SC3, 2011) for the automotive industry and ARP4754-A (S-18, 2010)/(EUROCAE, 2010) for the aerospace industry.

Although the standards do provide guidance as to how this allocation is to be performed in broad terms, applying the prescribed process in practice can be challenging, due to the impractically large number of possible allocations that need to be evaluated. Furthermore, selecting a particular allocation incurs a cost in development time and effort depending on the safety requirements assigned that need to be satisfied. Thus, there is an incentive to find an optimal allocation which minimizes the added development costs which poses an additional challenge that is impossible to be met using manual analyses. By automating this process, we believe that these challenges can be met.

Previous work on the automatic allocation of Automotive Safety Integrity Levels has provided support toward the ISO 26262 standard (Azevedo et al., 2014). In the work presented in this chapter, we will demonstrate an effective method of addressing the problem via automation, namely, automatic allocation of Development Assurance Levels (DALs), for the ARP4754-A standard. The structure of the chapter is as follows:

First, we discuss the elicitation and allocation of safety requirements as defined in the ARP4754-A standard. Second, we identify and discuss challenges in this process and formulate the research problem. Third, we present a method for automatic allocation of safety integrity requirements expressed as DALs and, finally, we present a case study of its application on an aircraft wheel braking system.

11.2 SAFETY REQUIREMENTS IN ARP4754-A

The Society of Automotive Engineers developed the Aircraft Recommended Practice set of standards in coordination with various regulatory bodies such as

Table 11.1 DAL to Hazard Severity Correspondence

DAL	A = 4	B = 3	C = 2	D = 1	E = 0
Hazard severity	Catastrophic	Severe-major	Major	Minor	No safety effect

the Federal Aviation Administration and the European Organization for Civil Aviation Equipment to provide generic guidelines toward the safety development of civil aircraft and their systems. ARP4754-A (S-18, 2010) provides general guidance in the safety development of aircraft functions and systems.

One of the fundamental aims of the standard is the mitigation of the negative impact of events on an aircraft or its occupants during its operation, such as that due to fire, engine failure and so on. The term "Failure Condition" (FC) (S-18, 2010, p. 11) describes the status of the aircraft when under such effects. Naturally, not all negative effects are equally devastating; for instance, loss of a single engine is less significant than loss of all engines. In accordance to this view, FCs are classified based on the severity of their impact in the worst possible case, as seen in Table 11.1, "Hazard Severity" row, from most to least severe.

To mitigate the effects of a FC, one must trace its root causes to the failure(s) of a particular element(s) of the architecture and then develop this element with increased care and architectural design considerations to contain and minimize the likelihood of their negative effects. This "increased rigor" as it is referred to in (S-18, 2010, p. 22) is summarized in the form of the DALs. In other words, allocating a particular DAL to an element means that the safety assessment process for both the subject and its contained elements (if any) must be conducted with an elevated level of effort, relative to the given DAL. There are five such levels and their correspondence to the FC severity classification can be seen in Table 11.1.

The role of the DALs is to provide an effective measure against systematic errors, errors which can occur due to design, implementation, or documentation errors (Capelle and Houtermans, 2006, pp. 2–3), including errors in the aircraft's architectural design but more significantly, software errors, which are exclusively systematic. This observation is noted in the standard; "the highly complex and integrated nature of modern aircraft... have highlighted concerns about the possibility of [systematic] errors... contributing to aircraft [FCs]" (S-18, 2010, p. 22) and under this view, software and hardware systems and components are naturally prime targets when allocating DALs.

Under the standard's view, the aircraft architecture can be separated into functions, systems, and items. Functions are at the highest level of the hierarchy, representing abstract aircraft functionality such as flight control and navigation. Systems are directly below them, with each system implementing one or several functions and containing in itself more elements. Finally, items are at the lowest end, elements which contribute toward the operation of their parent system and that cannot be further refined.

The allocation of DALs follows this hierarchy as a top–down process. Initially, when FCs have been determined, corresponding DALs are assigned to the functions based on their identified FCs.

Once DALs have been assigned to functions, and an architecture for the system has been defined, the rules defined in the standard for allocating DALs to items are applied. These rules utilize the concept of Functional Failure Sets (FFSs); these are sets that contain the minimum combinations of Functional Failures (FFs) that are necessary and sufficient to cause an overall system failure. The items whose failures are members of these sets will be allocated DALs. Given a FFS with a DAL of k, its members can be allocated a DAL based on two options:

- Option 1: A singular member is assigned a DAL of at least k and the other members of at least $k - 2$.
- Option 2: Two members are assigned a DAL of at least $k - 1$ and the other members of at least $k - 2$.

Note that in the case of a FFS with only one member, Option 1 is always taken.

The allocation rules effectively state that in a set of items which, by failing together, cause a system failure, either one of the items must be developed at the system DAL with the rest developed at two DALs below, or two items must be developed one DAL below the system DAL with the rest developed two DALs below the system integrity level.

11.3 THE ISSUE OF INDEPENDENCE IN ARP4754-A

In the standard, the concept of "Independence" is said to be "a fundamental attribute to consider when assigning Development Assurance Levels" (S-18, 2010, p. 41). The standard uses Independence as an attribute aiming to address the issue of common mode errors, which occur due to shared requirements amongst functions or development processes amongst items. Due to the apparent gravity that this concept garners in the standard (and the work mentioned above, amongst others) we feel that it is important to explain our views on this matter and how they support the methodology presented here. The standard introduces two forms of Independence: Functional and Item. The former refers to the presence of common causes of failure between separate functions or systems of the architecture, while the latter between separate items. In both cases, identification of such common causes falls within the purview of the Aircraft/System Common Cause Analysis (CCA) process. The CCA process identifies such causes and includes them in the failure analyses performed at subsequent stages such as Fault Tree Analysis (FTA). Failures derived in this way are treated as any other failure by our methodology; if the failure analysis determines that they indeed contribute toward the failure of an item, system or function, they will affect the DAL allocation. In our model-based approach, common causes either explicitly propagate through a system model from a single source to many sink components (e.g., failure of a common power supply or data source), or they can be declared as implicitly causing simultaneous failure of more than one components (e.g., electromagnetic interference). Therefore, our method captures correctly dependencies and therefore correctly allocates DALs while simultaneously addressing the issue of independence.

11.4 CHALLENGES IN REQUIREMENTS ALLOCATION—THE RESEARCH PROBLEM

The allocation of a specific DAL or a similar set of safety requirements to a function or item typically implies a development cost which increases as the DAL increases. Higher DALs imply a higher level of rigor, and therefore more expensive development and assurance activities. This is clear in the standards where one can see, for instance, that the higher the DAL for a software item, the higher the number of assurance objectives that must be achieved, as shown in Table 11.2 which is based on the guidelines given in DO-178B/ED-12B (SC-167, 1992). Note that the objectives "with independence" are required to be assessed twice by separate teams of safety developers, necessitating time and effort to be expended in this duplication of effort.

It is apparent that allocation schemes which can achieve the required integrity for the system by assigning lower DALs to more items would be more economical and translate into less effort and time spent on assurance activities. It is precisely those cost-optimal allocations that one is interested to find during the refinement of the architecture of a system under design. This problem can be more formally defined as a constrained optimization problem, with the decision variables being the DALs of each item, the constraints being the rules of allocation defined in the standard and the objective of the optimization to minimize the overall cost of the allocation on the development.

This description can be summarized in the following expressions:

$$\underset{X}{\text{argmin}} \sum_{i=0}^{n} Cost(X_i)$$

where

X_i: the ith allocated item DAL across all functions
Cost: the cost function, assigning each DAL a specific cost.

Table 11.2 Item DAL Cost (Nordhoff, p. 7)

Item DAL	A	B	C	D	E
Objectives	71	69	62	26	0
With independence	30	18	5	2	0

Therefore, we attempt to identify the allocation of item DALs across all functions which minimizes the total cost impact on the system.

Subject to:

$$\exists X_{ik} \in X_k : [(X_{ik} \geq k) \cap (\forall X_{jk} \in X_k \geq k - 2, i \neq j)]$$

or

$$\exists X_{ik}, X_{jk} \in X_k : \{[(X_{ik} + 1 \geq k) \cap (X_{jk} + 1 \geq k)] \cap (\forall X_{mk} \in X_k \geq k - 2, i \neq j \neq m)\}$$

where

X_{ik}: the ith allocated item DAL contributing to a function with a DAL of k

X_k: the set of DALs for items of a function with DAL of k.

The two inequalities used as constraints represent the two options available when allocating DALs. The first option allocates one member of the set of items contributing to the system failure with at least the system's DAL and the rest with at least two levels lower. The second option assigns two members of the aforementioned set with at least one level lower and the rest with at least two levels lower.

11.5 AUTOMATIC ALLOCATION OF DALs

Correct allocation of DALs hinges on establishing the contribution of item failures to the system failure. Therefore, by computing the causal relationship between item failures and system failure, we can automatically allocate overall system safety requirements as DALs of items. Towards this end, we have extended HiP-HOPS (Papadopoulos et al., 2011)—an advanced safety analysis tool—to compute the FFSs of a system and then allocate DALs using those FFSs.

11.5.1 HiP-HOPS

Hierarchically Performed Hazard Origins and Propagation Studies (Papadopoulos et al., 2011) is a state-of-the-art model-based safety analysis software tool that largely automates the synthesis of fault trees and FMEAs from system models. Model-based development is a design paradigm in which the nominal behavior of a system is developed using a common formal or semi-formal model of the system to facilitate communication of requirements and design between stakeholders in complex development processes. Model-based safety analysis extends this paradigm by enhancing the nominal behavior of the system described in the model with component failure logic (Sharvia and Papadopoulos, 2011). This allows safety analyses to be conducted synchronously with the rest of the development activities and provide feedback earlier and more efficiently. HiP-HOPS requires a model of the system that is annotated with local failure logic for each component from which the tool then automatically synthesizes fault trees. These fault trees represent the failure logic of the system in the form of a tree, with the root of the tree being the "top event" representing system failure and its leaves being base component failures.

These are linked through a series of logical connectors such as AND and OR gates. Once the fault tree synthesis stage is complete, the tool analyzes the trees to produce useful safety artifacts, such as the system's Minimum Cut Sets. These sets contain the combinations of basic failure events whose occurrence is both necessary and sufficient to cause the overall system's failure. These sets are equivalent to the standard's FFSs (S-18, 2010, p. 41), therefore we can use them to apply the DAL decomposition rules to allocate DALs onto the system's components. A more detailed description of HiP-HOPS can be found in Papadopoulos et al. (2011).

11.5.2 REDUCTION OF SEARCH SPACE

In practice, the options for allocation of function DALs to items of an architecture can be many, often too many to consider all exhaustively. An optimization algorithm that searches this space of potential allocations seeking a cost-optimal allocation would clearly benefit from a preprocessing step that reduces this search space, and in this section we propose how such reduction can be achieved. Due to the high severity of aircraft hazards, the rules for DAL allocation are stricter than those found in other standards, allowing DAL reduction of only two levels at most. This allows, when a model and the cost function exhibit certain properties, to reduce the possible allocations significantly by removing inefficient options, in some cases to the point of eliminating all options of allocation down to one. Even when there are still options remaining for optimization, the search space of the problem has been significantly reduced, thereby improving the effectiveness of optimization techniques employed afterwards. These series of option reductions can be applied when:

- The cost function of each element is nonlinear and strictly increasing with respect to the DALs of its FFs (see later)
- There exist N FFSs for all of the architecture's effects that, when sorted in descending order of their effect's DAL, exhibit the following "chain" property:
  - Let FFS_i of size n be followed by FFS_{i+1}, FFS_{i+2} and so on. The chain property holds for these FFSs if:
    - There exists a common FF that belongs to both FFS_i and FFS_{i+1}, one that belongs to FFS_{i+1} and FFS_{i+2} and so on
    - $|FFS_{i+1}| - |FFS_{i+2}| \leq 1$ and $|FFS_{i+2}| - |FFS_{i+1}| \leq 1$ and so on
- There exists a FFS amongst those satisfying the chain property with a single member.

A nonlinear, strictly increasing cost function is required in order for the algorithm to have only one option, the least expensive one, in cases where there are two variations of possible allocations.

The pseudocode for this reduction stage follows:

```
1) sizeCounter = 1
2) sort all FFSs in descending order of DAL
3) changesMade = true
```

```
4) while( changesMade )
    a. changesMade = false
    b. foreach FFS k
        i. if ( sizeCounter = k.size ) then
            1. if ( there is just one Member in k unassigned ) then
                a. assign it the lowest possible DAL
                b. changesMade = true
            2. end if
        ii. end if
    c. end foreach
    d. sizeCounter = sizeCounter + 1
5) end while
```

11.5.3 TABU SEARCH

There is a range of general optimization algorithms that could be adapted to solve the DAL allocation problem. We chose Tabu Search (Glover, 1986) for this study as a good candidate as it has already shown good performance in earlier work in allocation of automotive requirements (Azevedo et al., 2013). Tabu search is a meta-heuristic optimization technique, which owes its name to its memory structures, used to store recently evaluated candidate solutions. The candidates stored in these structures are not eligible for generation of further candidates and are thereby considered "Tabu" by the algorithm. By using these memory structures, the technique trades space for time and therefore accelerates the search for the optimal solution.

The memory structure used to store recent previous candidates is called the Tabu Tenure. A Tabu candidate can be selected for the iteration despite being Tabu if it meets certain Aspiration Criteria. These criteria are meant to allow exceptional candidates to be chosen more often than normal due to their desirable properties.

We have implemented a version of Tabu Search, where each candidate is an allocation of DALs over all FFs and the best candidates are those with the lowest overall DAL cost. The Aspiration Criterion employed here requires the candidate allocation to beat the Tenure's current best candidate in terms of overall DAL cost, thus being the best (i.e., cheapest) allocation in recent memory. When a candidate meets this criterion, it can be selected despite being Tabu (given no better non-Tabu candidates). The search method used to generate the next set of candidates produces a new candidate for each option of the current one that can be changed and not violate DAL decomposition rules. This means that DALs assigned by the reduction stage cannot be decreased, only increased.

The pseudocode for Tabu Search follows:

```
1) Generate a random allocation.
2) Set random allocation as the current choice.
3) Add the current choice to Tabu Tenure.
```

4) Repeat until iteration count or time limit are reached.
    a. Produce random alternative allocations from the current choice.
    b. Sort the produced allocations by DAL cost, ascending.
    c. Select the lowest cost allocation as the next choice.
    d. Repeat until a next choice has been selected or all alternative
        allocations have been examined.
          i.   If the next choice is not Tabu, select it to be the next choice.
          ii. If it is Tabu but aspiring, select it to be the next choice.
          iii. Otherwise, examine the next produced choice.
    e. If none of the produced allocations is either non-Tabu or aspiring,
        set the lowest cost one as the next choice.
    f. The next choice becomes the current choice.
    g. Add the current choice to the Tabu Tenure.
    h. Sort the Tabu Tenure by DAL cost, ascending.

The potential options per each FFS are placed in "Allocation Packs."
Generating a random allocation in Step 1 involves selecting a random option
from each Allocation Pack and then combining them with the nonoptional allocations from the reduction stage, as mentioned earlier.

Sorting the generated allocations for the next iteration means that after each
iteration the lowest cost—and ideally non-Tabu or aspiring—choice out of the produced candidates will have been made. To check if a candidate is Tabu, the fixed-
size Tabu Tenure is parsed to see if there's an identical allocation on it. If so, the
subject allocation is considered Tabu. An allocation is considered aspiring if its
cost is lower than each member of the Tabu Tenure. Thanks to the sorting of the
list in step 4b, a simple comparison with the first entry in the list is needed only.

We refer to a "partial allocation" as an allocation of DALs to only the members of an FFS. To produce the next set of alternative allocations, the process
described in the following pseudocode is performed:

1) Add into list Optional every 'optional' partial allocation.
2) Add into list IncreasableNonOptional every 'non-optional' partial
    allocation of DAL lower than 4.
3) For every partial allocation in the IncreasableNonOptional list,
    a. Select a random Allocation Pack affecting that partial allocation.
    b. Select a random partial allocation from that Pack which assigns a
        higher DAL than the current one.
    c. If none exist, continue to the next partial allocation.
    d. Else, use that selection to generate a new allocation and add it to
        the list of produced candidates.
    e. Repeat.
4) For every partial allocation in the Optional list,
    a. Select a random Allocation Pack affecting that partial allocation.
    b. Select a random partial allocation from that Pack which alters the
        current allocation.

    c. Use that selection to generate a new allocation and add it to the list
of produced candidates.

    d. Repeat.

5) Return the list of produced candidates.

Listed in this way for reasons of simplicity, note that steps 3 and 4 of the above pseudocode are almost (except for sub-steps b and c) identical—simply applied to a different list. The purpose of the two lists is to find all partial allocations due to options taken from Allocation Packs which can be altered. Sub-step b illustrates the difference between the two lists. Whereas in Optional, any partial allocation which alters the current allocation can be selected, in the IncreasableNonOptional list we can only choose a partial allocation, if any exist, which increases the DAL of the resulting allocation. As mentioned earlier, choosing such an option would not violate DAL allocation rules.

11.6 CASE STUDY: AIR WHEEL BRAKING SYSTEM

Our case study is based on an example aircraft wheel braking system from ARP4761, adapted by Sharvia and Papadopoulos (2011). The system is illustrated in Figure 11.1.

The purpose of the system is to provide safe braking during aircraft takeoff and landing. It features two primary hydraulic pumps, GreenPump and BluePump. The Brake System Control Unit (BSCU) forwards input from the brake pedals to the brakes, monitors input systems and states for correctness and provides feedback to other systems. The SelectorValve receives a constant stream of pressure from both pumps, relaying the pressure from the appropriate one (see

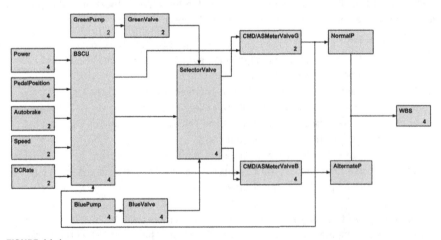

FIGURE 11.1

Allocation of DALs on model.

later) to the corresponding meter valve. The meter valves adjust the control the valve, outputting the required amount of pressure based on BSCU's commands.

The system features two modes of operation, Normal and Alternate. In Normal mode, GreenPump is used, sending pressure through the SelectorValve to ASMeterValveG. In Alternate mode, BluePump is used to send pressure through the SelectorValve to ASMeterValveB. Alternate mode is activated by BSCU when the pressure output falls under a certain threshold in Normal mode.

If braking fails while takeoff or landing, consequences could be catastrophic. The plane could fail to decelerate as expected or brake as it is about to take off, potentially causing the landing or takeoff to fail, causing a crash. We found this reasoning sufficient to test the allocation by assigning the overall DAL of the system output (WBS) to be A. We should note that this assignment is primarily used as an example and in practice the actual DAL assignment could be lower. However, this would not impact the allocation process described; a lower allocation can only potentially lead to a smaller number of potential allocations that need to be evaluated. Therefore, in this sense, we are demonstrating the worst case scenario with regards to the number of potential candidates that need to be evaluated.

For the purposes of the case study, the costs of Table 11.3 were used to approximate the cost each DAL would have on its component. A simple piecewise linearly decreasing function was chosen, with a higher cost jump between levels C and B. Naturally, other possibilities would be equally valid and per-component cost functions would also be justifiable.

Based on the FTA, the architecture's FFS are as follows:

- BSCU,
- Power,
- SelectorValve,
- AutoBrake AND PedalPosition,
- PedalPosition AND Speed,
- PedalPosition AND DCRate,
- BluePump AND CMD/ASMeterValveG,
- BluePump AND GreenPump,
- BluePump AND GreenValve,
- BlueValve AND CMD/ASMeterValveG,
- BlueValve AND GreenPump,
- BlueValve AND GreenValve,
- CMD/ASMeterValveB AND CMD/ASMeterValveG,
- CMD/ASMeterValveB AND GreenPump,
- CMD/ASMeterValveB AND GreenValve.

Table 11.3 Item DAL Cost

DAL	A = 4	B = 3	C = 2	D = 1	E = 0
Cost	50	40	20	10	0

The resulting allocation when the parent FC (WBS) assigned a DAL of A is shown in Figure 11.1 where DALs from A to E are numbered from 4 to 0 respectively:

The allocation algorithm was executed numerous times, each time producing a permutation of the allocation shown above (or the exact same) with the same overall DAL cost. This allocation was found to be optimal after exhaustively enumerating and evaluating all possible combinations of DAL allocations for this model. It should be noted that this was only possible due to the relatively small scale of the search space (531,441 possible allocations). Larger-scale models might require days, months or even longer periods of time to exhaustively search for their optimal solutions.

While we find the results of the exhaustive search sufficient to confirm our results, an explanation of the rationale behind this allocation should further illuminate its correctness.

Firstly, given the structure of the cost model used, it should be noted that the sum of the cost of a DAL A and DAL C allocation, which is 70, is lower than that of two DAL B allocations, which is 80. This observation explains the absence of level B DALs in the resulting allocation, as due to the two modes used for fault tolerance, the FFSs produced contain up to two members only, with a choice between choosing variations of A and C assignments or B and B assignments.

Secondly, in the case of the single-member FFS (first three in the list), these members can only be assigned the DAL of the parent FC, i.e., DAL A. Since they do not participate in other FFS, these members can be assigned immediately in the nonoptional allocation stage and not be considered further.

Thirdly, we notice that the rest of the FFS have common members between them: there are four groups containing PedalPosition, BluePump, BlueValve and CMD/ASMeterValveB. With the exception of the PedalPosition group, the other three groups also share their counterpart members as well. Therefore, we can deduce that an optimal allocation would revolve around assigning the highest of available DALs, which in this example is A, to as few of the common members as possible and the lowest, in this case C, to as many as possible. For instance, in the group of PedalPosition, it only makes sense to assign it DAL A and the rest of the members C since they do not affect any other members. For the other groups, finding the correct permutation manually is harder due to the interconnectivity and the answer given in the example's result is one of many possible.

Finally, the resulting allocation also illustrates the effect of the fault tolerant dual-mode architecture employed. Components common to both modes (e.g., BSCU, SelectorValve, etc.) have been assigned the DAL of the parent FC, which is DAL A. However, components in one mode (GreenValve, GreenPump, CMD/ASMeterValveG) have been chosen to have a reduced DAL, i.e., DAL C.

11.7 CONCLUSION AND REFLECTION

In the aerospace industry, dissemination of safety requirements across the system's architecture is a fundamental part of the safety development process described in ARP4754-A. Applying the guidance for this methodology provided by the standard is challenging, due to the often very high number of options that need to be evaluated, rendering this a combinatorial problem. Furthermore, finding a trivial allocation manually would not be ideal, as each allocation has a different impact on development costs. Therefore, there is a significant incentive in determining the optimal allocation automatically.

We have demonstrated that it is possible to allocate DALs to a given system architecture automatically, optimally and efficiently by applying this method to an example system. This development confirms that the possibility of automation of safety development processes is common between multiple standards and we feel confident that further automation is possible in this direction.

That being said, the method we have provided here is still at an early stage of development. The Tabu Search implementation has further room for improvement, the first obvious step for improvement being the incorporation of longer-term memory structures. Said structures would allow for an enhanced capability for intensifying toward better local candidate solutions rapidly and diversifying toward different regions of the search space when getting stuck in local solution "plateaus." Furthermore, although Tabu Search has proven effective, a plethora of other optimization techniques exist, as mentioned in (Bieber et al., 2011). The question of which technique maximizes efficiency and at what cost still remains.

Despite this early stage of implementation, tool support for the method has been established, via extension of the HiP-HOPS reliability analysis tool. The method has been applied on a variety of abstract system models so far, the most significant of which is the aircraft wheel braking system presented here, based on the example found in the standard itself. We aim to apply the approach in a greater range of systems—especially in case studies of systems direct from the industry—to further gauge the utility of both the method and the tool.

The issue of selecting an appropriate cost function at both the system and the individual component level was presented within the scope of this work. Further research toward developing such cost heuristics would be beneficial, as their structure can directly influence both the results and the computational difficulty of the optimization, as demonstrated.

Finally, this work should be seen as partially addressing a more general problem of optimal requirement allocation. In the future, we hope that this research could be extended with algebras and optimization techniques that can address allocation of other types of requirements beyond those of safety and integrity.

REFERENCES

Azevedo, L.S., Parker, D., Walker, M., Papadopoulos, Y., Araujo, R.E., 2013. Automatic decomposition of safety integrity levels: optimization by tabu search. In: Workshop CARS (2nd Workshop on Critical Automotive Applications: Robustness & Safety) of the 32nd International Conference on Computer Safety, Reliability and Security, Toulouse, France.

Azevedo, L.S., Parker, D., Walker, M., Papadopoulos, Y., Araujo, R.E., 2014. Assisted assignment of automotive safety requirements. IEEE Software 31 (1), 62–68. Available from: http://dx.doi.org/10.1109/MS.2013.118.

Bieber, P., Delmas, R., Seguin, C., 2011. DALculus—Theory and tool for development assurance level allocation. In: Proceedings of the 30th International Conference on Computer Safety, Reliability and Security, Naples, Italy. Springer, Berlin, Heidelberg, pp. 43–56.

Capelle, T.V., Houtermans, M.J., 2006. Functional Safety: A Practical Approach to End-Users and System Integrators. HIMA Paul Hildebrandt GmbH Co. KG, Germany. Available from: <https://www.researchgate.net/publication/228620983_Functional_safety_a_practical_approach_for_end-users_and_system_integrators> (retrieved 8.2.14.).

EUROCAE, 2010. ED-79A—Guidelines for development of civil aircraft and system. In: EUROCAE (retrieved 2014).

Glover, F., 1986. Future paths for integer programming and links to artificial intelligence. Comput. Oper. Res. 13 (5), 533–549.

Nordhoff, S., n.d. DO-178C/ED-12C—The New Software Standard for the Avionic Industry: Goals, Changes and Challenges. Available from: <www.sqs.com/uk/_download/DO-178C_ED-12C.pdf>.

Papadopoulos, Y., Walker, M., Parker, D., Rude, E., Hamann, R., Uhlig, A., et al., 2011. Engineering failure analysis and design optimisation with HiP-HOPS. Eng. Fail. Anal., 590–608.

SC 65-A, 2010. IEC61508—Functional Safety of Electrical/Electronic/Programmable Electronic Safety-Related Systems. International Electrotechnical Commission, Geneva, Switzerland.

SC-167, 1992. DO-178B—Software Considerations in Airborne Systems and Equipment Certification, first ed. RTCA Inc.

Sharvia, S., Papadopoulos, Y., 2011. IACoB-SA: an approach towards integrated safety assessment. In: IEEE International Conference on Automation Science and Engineering. IEEE, Trieste, Italy, pp. 220–225.

S-18, SAE, 2010. ARP4754-A guidelines for development of civil aircraft and systems. SAE Int. Available from: <http://standards.sae.org/arp4754a/> (retrieved 2013).

TC 22/SC3, 2011. ISO 26262—Road Vehicles—Functional Safety. International Organization for Standardization.

Model-based dependability analysis: State-of-the-art, challenges, and future outlook

12

Septavera Sharvia, Sohag Kabir, Martin Walker and Yiannis Papadopoulos

Department of Computer Science, University of Hull, Hull, UK

INFORMATION IN THIS CHAPTER

- Failure Logic Synthesis and Analysis
- Behavioral Fault Simulation
- Towards Integrated Approaches
- Challenges and Future Outlook

12.1 INTRODUCTION

Integrated and effective dependability analysis has become increasingly important as modern safety-critical systems become more heterogeneous and complex. Dependability can be defined as the "the ability of an entity to perform one or several required functions under given condition" (Villemeur, 1991). The study of system dependability covers four properties: safety, reliability, availability, and maintainability. Safety is the ability of the system to avoid causing hazards for people and the environment. Reliability is the ability of the system to perform its intended functions satisfactorily for a given time interval. Availability studies the readiness of the system to perform its function at a given instance of time. And maintainability is the ability of the system to be maintained or restored to a state in which it can perform its function, when maintenance is performed as specified. In this chapter, emphasis is placed on safety and reliability due to the context of safety-critical systems in which many of the techniques are situated. However, references are made to work within these techniques to address availability and maintainability (e.g., as in Papadopoulos et al., 2010). The integration between analysis techniques and advanced system engineering and modeling is also beneficial for the functionality, accessibility, and usability dimensions of the system development.

Dependability assessment should begin early in the design phase so that potential problems can be identified and rectified early to avoid expensive changes in the later phase of the system life cycle. Traditional dependability analysis techniques like fault tree analysis (FTA) (Vesely et al., 2002) and Failure Modes and Effects Analysis (FMEA) (US Department of Defense, 1980) are well-established and widely used during the design phase of safety-critical systems. FTA is a deductive analysis technique which utilizes graphical representation based on Boolean logic to show logical connections between different failures and their causes. FMEA is an inductive technique which tries to infer the unknown effects on the system of known component failure modes.

These techniques are typically applied manually and often performed on an informal system model which may rapidly become out of date as the system design evolves. This presents challenges in maintaining the consistency and completeness of the assessment process.

Over the past 20 years, new developments in the field of dependability engineering have led to a body of work on model-based assessment and prediction of dependability. Model-based techniques offer significant advantages over traditional approaches as they utilize software automation and integration with design models to simplify the synthesis and analysis of complex safety-critical systems. These techniques can be applied from early stages of expressing requirements and until detailed architectural design.

Emerging model-based dependability analysis (MBDA) techniques can be conceptualized and classified according to different criteria. In Aizpurua and Muxika (2012), classification criteria include the type of traditional limitations overcome by new techniques, recovery strategies, and the approach to design verification. Classical FTA and FMEA are static in nature and do not take into consideration the time or sequence dependencies. They are also traditionally manual processes which rely heavily on the analysts' skills and are susceptible to human errors. Certain MBDA techniques have been developed to address the temporal and dynamic limitations, while other techniques focus on making the analysis process more manageable. Different techniques may also employ different recovery strategies, including heterogeneous redundancies, homogeneous redundancies, shared redundancies, graceful degradation, and implicit redundancies. Techniques have also been classified based on the type of design verification, that is, whether it is based on fault injection or an integrative approach. In Lisagor et al. (2011), MBDA are categorized based on the model provenance and the engineering semantics of the component interfaces. Model provenance categorizes techniques based on the construction of a safety model and its relationship with the system design. Safety analysis models can be defined either through extension to the design model, or as a dedicated model defined by safety engineers. Regarding the engineering semantics of components, categorization is possible with respect to the type of modeling of component dependencies. These dependencies can be captured in terms of either deviations from design intent, or abstracted nominal flow (e.g., energy, matter, and information).

The classification of MBDA techniques in this chapter is based on the general underlying formalism and the types of analysis performed. Based on this, model-based techniques typically gravitate towards two leading paradigms. The first paradigm, termed Failure Logic Synthesis and Analysis (FLSA), focuses on the automatic construction of predictive system failure analyses, such as fault trees or FMEAs, on the basis of information stored in the system model. These approaches are typically compositional, where the system-level models of failure propagation can be generated from component-level failure logic and the overall topology of the system. This compositionality lends itself well to automation and reuse of component failure models across applications, and this is beneficial to dependability analysis in ways similar to those introduced by reuse of trusted software components in software engineering. Techniques which follow this approach include Hierarchically Performed Hazard Origin and Propagation Studies (HiP-HOPS), Component Fault Trees (CFT), State-Event Fault Trees (SEFT), and the Failure Propagation and Transformation Notation and Calculus (FPTN and FPTC).

The second paradigm, termed Behavioral Fault Simulation (BFS), automatically analyzes potential failures in a system and the development has led to a group of formal verification based techniques. These generally work by injecting possible faults into simulations based on executable, formal specifications of a system and studying the effects of those faults on the system behavior. The results are then used by model checking tools to verify whether system dependability requirements are being satisfied or whether violations of the requirements exist in normal or faulty conditions. Techniques in this category include AltaRica, The Formal Safety Analysis Platform/New Symbolic Model Verifier (FSAP-NuSMV), Safety Analysis Modeling Language (SAML), and Deductive Cause Consequence Analysis (DCCA).

Much of this recent work on dependability analysis has a natural synergy with a wider trend towards model-based design, particularly domain-specific languages. In many industries, particularly transport and aerospace, designers are increasingly adopting Architecture Description Languages (ADLs) to encapsulate both architectural and behavioral information about the system. Such ADLs may not only represent the system itself, but also the functional and nonfunctional requirements and properties of the system; they may also provide facilities for the refinement of the system throughout the design life cycle, showing how the requirements are being met at each stage. One key aspect of such ADLs is to represent the safety requirements and the failure logic of the system, and these areas have often seen integration with MBDA techniques. For instance, recent work has demonstrated that dependability analysis of automotive EAST-ADL models is possible via HiP-HOPS while dependability analysis of aerospace AADL (Architecture Analysis and Design Language) error models is possible via conversion to classical artefacts, e.g., combinatorial and temporal fault trees or

Generalized Stochastic Petri Nets (GSPNs). The integration of the comprehensive behavioral and architectural data offered by ADLs with model-based analysis engines also makes new forms of analysis possible. This has subsequently led to techniques that allow automatic optimization of system attributes—such as dependability, cost, and performance—by means of meta-heuristics that can efficiently explore the huge design spaces involved.

This work complements previous less-detailed discussions on classification and overview of model-based analysis techniques presented in Lisagor et al. (2011) and Aizpurua and Muxika (2013). We extensively explore various prominent techniques and study their recent updates and developments. The aim of this chapter is not to define strict classification of techniques, but to review the state-of-the-art in this field, explaining the fundamental concepts involved and comparing the key techniques that have been developed in terms of their features, achievements, applicability, and scalability. We also discuss the current challenges faced by these techniques, including representativeness and completeness of models, modeling and analysis structure, the scalability of models and analyses, and obstacles in practicability and uptake of this work. We conclude with a discussion on the future outlook of this work, looking at how these challenges may be addressed and how research is already being developed to address new problems, including separation of hardware/software concerns in embedded systems, and efficient multiobjective optimization of different system attributes.

The remainder of this chapter is structured as the following: Section 12.2 discusses a number of prominent FLSA techniques. Section 12.3 discusses a number of techniques employing BFS. As techniques mature, further development tends to blur the lines of categorization, and techniques often extend into a hybrid or integrated approach. Section 12.4 studies a number of emerging integrated techniques and challenges, while Section 12.5 concludes and outlines future outlook.

12.2 FAILURE LOGIC SYNTHESIS AND ANALYSIS

In FLSA, system failure models are constructed from component failure models using a process of composition. System failure models typically comprise, or can be automatically converted into, well-known dependability evaluation models such as fault trees, stochastic Petri Nets and Markov chains. These types of techniques therefore model the deviation from the design intent rather than nominal (normal) behavior of the system.

Techniques based on FLSA include the FPTN, FPTC, HiP-HOPS, CFT, and SEFT. ADLs have been widely adopted in the recent years to support the integration between analysis models in FLSA and system design models expressed in the language. An introduction to an ADL called AADL is therefore included in this section.

12.2.1 FAILURE PROPAGATION AND TRANSFORMATION NOTATION

FPTN (Fenelon and McDermid, 1993) is among the pioneering MBDA methods designed to address limitations of FTA and FMEA in specifying system failure behavior. It was developed as part of the Software Safety Assessment Procedures (SSAP) project. It uses a modular, hierarchical notation to describe the propagation of faults through the modules of system architecture. FPTN module is represented as a box with a set of inputs and outputs, which can be connected to other modules. To form a hierarchical structure, each module can contain a number of sub-modules. Failures can be propagated or transformed from one type to another. The relation between the inputs and outputs is expressed by a set of logical equations equivalent to the minimal cut-sets (smallest and necessary combination of failures which cause a higher-level fault) of the fault trees describing the output failure modes of the module. Therefore, each module represents a number of fault trees describing all the failure modes for that module. These equations can also contain more advanced constructs, allowing FPTN to represent recovery mechanisms and internal failure modes. This type of notation enables FPTN to be used both inductively (to create an FMECA) and deductively (to create an FTA).

FPTN is designed to be developed alongside the design of the system. Information collected can then be used to identify potential flaws and problems in the system design so that they can be eliminated or compensated for in the next design iteration. In its classical form, FPTN is limited to static analysis, but recent work on Temporal-FPTN (Niu et al., 2011) extended FPTN with temporal information to allow dynamic analysis by using Failure Temporal Logic to specify failure relationship, and produces Minimal Cut-set Sequences. However, although FPTN provides a systematic and formal notation for representing the failure behavior of a system (a distinct improvement on traditional *ad hoc* approaches), it lacks full automation, and the fact that each analysis must be conducted manually hampers the opportunity for it to be used in an iterative design process.

12.2.2 FAILURE PROPAGATION AND TRANSFORMATION CALCULUS

FPTC (Paige et al., 2008) is a method for the representation and analysis of the failure behavior of the software and hardware components of a system. It allows annotation of an architectural model of a system with concise expressions describing how each component can fail; these annotations can then be used to compute the failure properties of the whole system automatically.

FPTC is primarily designed for real-time software systems where a statistically schedulable code unit is considered as the primary unit of the architectural description. The data and control flow behavior of the system is defined by connecting these units using communications protocols like handshakes and buffers. FPTC assumes that all the threads and communications are known in advance and are not created or destroyed dynamically during the system operation. FPTC also offers the capability to describe the allocation of these units and their

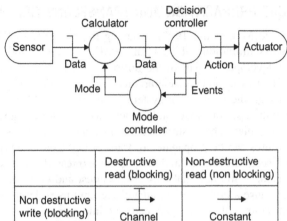

FIGURE 12.1

Example of FPTC representation in RTN (Walker et al., 2008).

communications to different physical processing devices and networks. This makes it possible to describe how, for example, one faulty processor can affect all software units running on it.

FPTC represents the system architecture using a RTN (Real-Time Network) style notation, consisting of a graph of arcs and nodes representing hardware and software units and the communications between them. Communications are typed according to protocol (e.g., blocking/nonblocking). RTN offers significant capabilities, including the ability to refine graphs hierarchically, to define code units as state machines, and to automatically generate Ada code from the design. An example RTN graph and associated key to some communications protocols are illustrated in Figure 12.1.

Similar to FPTN, components may respond to failures in one of two ways: by propagating the failure or by transforming the failure. Components may also initiate or terminate failures, e.g., by failing silent or by detecting and correcting failures. These failures are typed similarly to FPTN, e.g., timing, value, omission failures, but the types are not fixed and can be extended as required. "Normal" is also a type, indicating the lack of a failure.

The reaction to failure is described by a simple pattern-based notation. Once components are annotated with FPTC expressions, the resulting RTN graph can then be thought of as a token-passing network in which failure tokens flow from one node to another, being created, transformed, and destroyed along the way. Each arc in the graph can then be further annotated with the set of possible failures that may propagate along it. This is done by "running" each expression in reaction to the "normal" type and listing the resulting output failures on the output communication arcs; each component is then re-run in response to any new input failure types. The process terminates when no more new output failures are generated and all possible input/output combinations have been considered.

One advantage of FPTC is the fact that it uses the full architectural models used for developing the software code and can adapt much more readily to changes. This helps ensure the FPTC model is synchronized with the design and offers significant advantage compared to FPTN which is annotated according to *known* failures, and so any new failure to be added requires the whole model to be manually reannotated. It also handles cycles in architectures by using fix-point calculations. There is also support for model transformation from AADL and SysML models through Epsilon (Paige et al., 2008). Recently, a probabilistic type known as FPTA was proposed by Ge et al. (2009). This method links architectural models with probabilistic model checkers specified in PRISM and allows FPTC to capture nondeterministic failure behavior. FI^4FA (Gallina and Punnekkat, 2014) is the most recent extension of FPTC which allows FPTC to consider more types of failure behavior, e.g., incompletion, inconsistency, interference and impermanence, and also analysis of mitigating behaviors. The primary disadvantage of FPTC is the necessity of performing a different analysis for each failure or combination of failures to be considered. Each originating failure must be specified at a component and then the model must be re-analyzed to determine how this failure will propagate through the system and what failure modes will be communicated to critical components.

12.2.3 COMPONENT FAULT TREE

CFTs (Kaiser et al., 2003) is an extension to traditional fault trees which aims to provide better association between the hierarchy of faults and the architectural hierarchy of the system components. Although traditional fault tree allows modularization, it provides little information on the hierarchical decomposition of the physical system. CFTs define smaller fault trees for each component, thus incorporating the fault trees as part of the hierarchical component model of the system. Like traditional fault trees, CFTs use basic events, logical gates as well as input and output ports. The fact that CFTs are still logical structures linking output failures to input causes means that they can be analyzed qualitatively and quantitatively using standard fault tree algorithms.

CFTs differ from traditional fault trees in the sense that they allow multiple top events and by representing repeating (or common cause) failures only once. CFTs also form directed acyclic graphs called Cause Effect Graphs (CEGs), as illustrated in Figure 12.2, instead of traditional tree structure. The use of CEGs

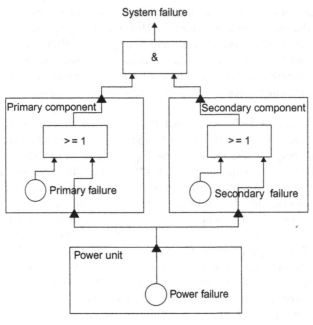

System failure

FIGURE 12.2

Example of CFT (Kaiser et al., 2003).

makes the CFTs smaller and easier to analyze, both significant benefits when modeling large systems. It also makes the diagrams clearer, as the fault tree nodes can be displayed as part of their components.

The main advantage of CFTs is its capability of hierarchical decomposition of systems to manage the complexity of modern systems. CFTs create smaller fault trees for each of the components and neatly capture the hierarchical system architecture. Consequently, different parts of the system can be developed and stored separately as part of the component definition in a library, and this facilitates greater degree of reusability. Conceptually, this hierarchical decomposition also makes it possible for the failure behavior of the system to be modeled at different levels, for example, for the top-level subsystems first, and then once the design has been refined further, for the subcomponents as well.

A windows-based tool, ESSaReL (ESSaRel, 2005) is available to perform minimal cut set analysis and probabilistic evaluation of CFTs. Recently another tool called ViSSaAn (Visual Support for Safety Analysis) (Yang et al., 2011) has been developed based on a matrix view to allow improved visualization of CFTs and efficient representation of information related to minimal cut-sets of CFTs. Adler et al. (2011) have developed a metamodel to extract reusable CFTs from the functional architecture of systems specified in UML.

12.2.4 **STATE-EVENT FAULT TREE**

One of the limitations of FTA is its inability to adequately account for the temporal order of events, whether in terms of a simple sequence or a set of states and transitions. This limits the capability to analyze complex systems, particularly real-time embedded and software based systems. Fault trees are fundamentally a combinatorial technique and are not well suited to modeling the dynamic behavior in such systems. SEFTs (Grunske et al., 2005) are developed to address this limitation by combining elements from fault trees with State charts and Markov chains. This is done by adding states and events to fault trees, allowing the use of system state-based models as the basis for the analysis, as well as enabling the use of more sophisticated analysis methods (e.g., Markov chains). SEFTs can also be seen as an evolution of CFTs in that they allow decomposition and distribution across the components of the system, and represent inputs and outputs as visible ports in the model.

SEFTs make a distinction between causal transition and sequential relation, and therefore provide corresponding separate types of ports. A sequential transition applies to states which specify a predecessor or successor relation between states, whereas a causal transition applies to events which define a causal (trigger/ guard) relationship between events. Because events are explicitly represented (and do not always have to be state transitions), it is also possible for one event to cause another event. These events can also be combined using traditional fault tree gates (e.g., AND and OR) so that a combination of events is necessary to trigger another event. SEFTs also offer more advanced features for modeling timing scenarios. For example, events can be assigned deterministic or probabilistic delays by means of Delay Gates and SEFTs also allow the use of NOT gates. Sequential and causal modeling is further refined by means of History-AND and Priority-AND gates, which can check whether an event has occurred in the past and in what order it occurred, and other gates are also possible, for example, Duration gates to ensure that a state has been active for a given amount of time.

In SEFTs, a state is graphically represented as a rounded rectangle and considered as a condition that lasts over a period of time whereas an event is graphically represented as a solid bar and considered as an instantaneous phenomenon that can cause state transition. Each component has its own state space and each component can only be in one state at any point in time (the "active state"). For the purposes of quantitative analysis, probabilities can be assigned to each state to reflect its chance of being the active state at any time. Similarly, events may be assigned probability densities for quantitative analysis.

SEFTs follow the same general procedure as standard FTA in the modeling of system failure behavior. Analysts begin with the occurrence of a system failure and trace it back through the components of the system to determine its root causes. SEFTs offer a greater level of detail during this analysis, for example, by considering the effect of states in fault propagation. SEFTs also allow a greater degree of reuse than traditional fault trees because pre-existing state charts from the design can be used, as can Markov chains, which can be similarly integrated into the SEFTs.

Unlike CFTs, SEFTs can no longer be analyzed using traditional FTA algorithms. The inclusion of states and the different modeling of events means that different techniques are needed, such as the conversion to Petri Nets, to allow for the calculation of probabilities of system failures. Steiner et al. (2012) have proposed a methodology to create and analyze SEFTs based on the ESSaRel tool (ESSaRel, 2005). SEFT models are converted to Deterministic Stochastic Petri Nets (DSPNs) (Marsan and Chiola, 1987), then the analysis of the DSPN models can be performed using a DSPN analyzer like TimeNET (German and Mitzlaff, 1995). The conversion process requires the consideration of the entire system, which can lead to an explosion of state-spaces and thus performance problems for larger system models. This issue can be alleviated to some degree by using both combinatorial FTA-style algorithms and dynamic state-based algorithms to analyze different parts of the system, for example, using the faster techniques for simple, static subsystems and using slower but more powerful techniques for the dynamic parts of the system. The effectiveness of this dual-analysis technique will depend heavily on the type of system being analyzed.

12.2.5 HIERARCHICALLY PERFORMED HAZARD ORIGIN AND PROPAGATION STUDIES

HiP-HOPS (Papadopoulos and McDermid, 1999) is one of the pioneering MBDA techniques, and amongst the well-supported advanced compositional safety analysis techniques. It provides a greater degree of automation compared to CFT or FPTN. HiP-HOPS also supports automatic optimization of designs (Adachi et al., 2011; Papadopoulos et al., 2011) which can be employed for selection among alternatives for components and subsystems as well as for optimal decisions on the level and location of replicated components. Recently HiP-HOPS has also been extended with capabilities for top-down automatic allocation of safety requirements in the form of Safety Integrity Levels (SIL). The latter automates some of the processes for Automotive SIL (ASIL) allocation as specified in the safety standard ISO 26262.

HiP-HOPS works in conjunction with commonly used system modeling tools, for example Matlab Simulink or Simulation X. Failure editors are integrated into these modeling tools to allow system designers to annotate components with failure information. This failure information includes failure modes (internal malfunction) and output failure expressions, and describes how the component fails and its relationship with other component failures, that is, whether and how the component responds or not to effects of failure received at the component inputs. HiP-HOPS takes this information and examines how the component failures propagate through the system topology, producing sets of interrelated fault trees and eventually an FMEA. This approach also enables the hierarchical structure of the system to be captured neatly in the fault trees.

There are three main phases in HiP-HOPS: model annotation, fault tree synthesis, and fault tree and FMEA analysis phase.

The model annotation phase provides information to HiP-HOPS on how the component can fail. It takes the form of a set of expressions which are manually added. These local failure expressions describe how failures of the component outputs can be caused by a combination of failures received at the component's inputs and/or by internal malfunctions of the component itself. Common cause failures are also supported, as are failures propagated via other means, for example, from allocated components. In this way it is possible to model more sophisticated scenarios—for instance, the effects on a software function, and consequently the software architecture, when the processor shown in the hardware architecture to be executing that function fails.

The synthesis phase produces an interconnected network of fault trees which link system-level failures (i.e., failures of the system's output functions) to component-level internal failures by using the model topology and component failure information. These fault trees show how component failures propagate from one component to another and how ultimately they may affect the wider system, whether individually or in combination with other component failures.

In the analysis phase, the synthesized fault trees are analyzed via automated algorithms to generate minimal cut-sets. Minimal cut-sets describe the necessary and sufficient combination of events which lead to the undesired events. Eventually the data is combined into a multiple FMEA which shows both direct effects of failure modes on the system, as well as the further effects of the failure modes caused in conjunction with other failure modes occurring in the system. The resultant FMEA is presented in tables which are conveniently displayed through a web browser. These main phases of HiP-HOPS are illustrated in Figure 12.3.

Quantitative data can also be entered for the component to estimate the probability of internal failures occurring and the severity of output deviations. This data can then be used in the quantitative analysis phase to calculate the unavailability, that is, failure probability, of the top event. HiP-HOPS assists reusability by enabling failure-annotated components to be stored in a library. This allows other components of a similar type to reuse failure data, and avoids the designer having to enter the same failure data multiple times. Recently, HiP-HOPS has also been extended with advanced features, including the capability to accommodate temporal analysis and perform multiobjective optimization.

12.2.5.1 Temporal analysis in HiP-HOPS using Pandora

HiP-HOPS fundamentally inherits the static nature of FTA and this includes the lack of capability to capture time information or sequence-dependent behavior. While the compositional failure model may be sufficient to describe the systems' behavior in many scenarios, it may not be adequate to describe the complete behavior of complex systems. This drawback is particularly limiting in a system where functions and failure modes change according to different states. In addition to this, the ability to understand and capture the order of failures can be

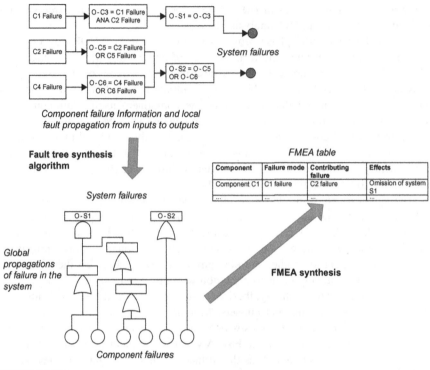

FIGURE 12.3

Main phases in HiP-HOPS.

important in producing an accurate failure model. Pandora (Walker et al., 2007; Walker, 2009) was proposed to extend traditional fault trees with dynamic analysis capability by introducing new temporal gates and temporal logic. This technique can be used to obtain minimal cut sequences (the smallest necessary sequences of events to cause the top events) of temporal fault trees. Pandora is based around the redefinition of the long-established Priority-AND (PAND) (Fussel et al., 1976) gate and aims to solve the ambiguities in the original PAND gate whilst maintaining the simplicity and flexibility of FTA. It allows the temporal ordering of events to be represented as part of the fault tree structure, and uses temporal logic gates Priority-AND (PAND), Priority-OR (POR), and Simultaneous-AND (SAND) to represent the temporal relations.

Pandora provides better modeling for precise failure behavior of dynamic systems than ordinary FTA. Because Pandora is designed to integrate with existing Boolean logic, it can be used in existing tools such as HiP-HOPS, extending it with additional dynamic FTA capabilities. The solution proposed by Merle et al. (2010) is used as an analytical solution to Pandora's PAND gate. Quantitative analysis of Pandora is discussed in Edifor et al. (2012) and Edifor et al. (2014).

12.2.6 ARCHITECTURE ANALYSIS AND DESIGN LANGUAGE

AADL (Feiler and Rugina, 2007) is a domain-specific language developed for the specification and analysis of hardware and software architectures of performance-critical real-time systems. AADL enables an array of modeling capabilities including structural description of the system as an assembly of software components mapped onto an execution platform, functional description of interfaces to components, and performance description of critical aspects of components. AADL allows both architectural modeling and error modeling. Architectural modeling describes the nominal architecture of the system, including the components, and their connections and interactions. Interactions show structural and behavioral aspects without considering the presence of faults. In contrast, error modeling captures the behavior of components in the presence of internal faults, repair events, as well as external propagations of faults from other components.

An AADL error model consists of a model type and, at least, one error model implementation. The form of error models is described in the AADL error model annex, which was intended to support the qualitative and quantitative analysis of dependability attributes. The error model is a state machine that can be associated with an AADL element, that is, component or connection, in order to describe its behavior in terms of logical error states in the presence of faults. The error model can be associated with software (e.g., process, data, thread), hardware (e.g., processor, memory, device) and composite component (e.g., system) component and connection (Feiler et al., 2006). In AADL, systems may be represented as collections of components, hierarchies of components, or systems of systems. Therefore an AADL error model extends from system to subsystem to component, and the system error model is a composition of the error models of its subsystems or components. This captures hazards at system level, risk mitigation architecture at subsystem level and FMEA models at component level.

Each AADL error model can be stored in a library and can be reused for different AADL components. Propagation of errors between components is determined by their interdependencies and the AADL Error Model Annex has defined a set of dependency rules (Feiler and Rugina, 2007) to define interdependencies between components. For example, propagations may occur from a component to any outgoing connections and between all subcomponents of the same process which is conceptually similar to Papadopoulos's dual approach to propagations in his integration of HiP-HOPS and Matlab Simulink models (Papadopoulos and Maruhn, 2001).

One limitation of the language lies in the incomplete support, at least in its core concepts, of analysis of the runtime architectures. This is compensated by extensions to accommodate analysis specific notations that can be associated with components. Error modeling for instance is supported through an annex that has been added to the standard. AADL error models can be analyzed through an automated translation into a standard fault tree (Joshi et al., 2007), or by generating GSPNs from error model specifications and using a GSPN tool for quantitative analysis (Rugina et al., 2007).

12.2.7 SYSTEM DYNAMICS AND TEMPORAL CONSIDERATIONS

A number techniques have been developed to address the temporal and dynamic limitation of classical FTA and FMEA. The Dynamic Fault Tree (DFT) (Dugan et al., 1992) approach introduced new gates and temporal notions to account for ordered events and handle probabilistic timed behavior in fault trees. Some techniques which are based on Monte Carlo Simulation (MCS) (Rao et al., 2009) offer alternatives by modeling temporal failure and repair through state-time diagrams. Dynamic Reliability Block Diagram (DRBD) (Distefano and Puliafito, 2007) model component failures and repairs based on their dependencies using state machines, while colored Petri Nets have been used to analyzed DRBD in Robidoux et al. (2010). Other researchers like Hura and Atwood (1988) and Helmer et al. (2007) have used Petri Nets to solve classical fault trees. The combination of state and event based formalisms has been adopted in Boolean Logic Driven Markov Processes (Bouissou, 2007) and SEFT. The temporal extension to HiP-HOPS which is implemented through Pandora also aims to address temporal dynamics.

12.3 BEHAVIORAL FAULT SIMULATION

In BFS, system failure models are produced by injecting faults into executable formal specifications of a system, thereby establishing the system-level effects of faults. This fault injection technique was developed in the ESACS (Bozzano et al., 2003) and ISAAC (Akerlund and Bieber, 2006) projects. As opposed to the dedicated analysis model commonly used in FLSA, BFS uses an extended model which is automatically constructed from a system design model. The extended model typically contains both the nominal input flow as well an input related to the fault, which is taken into consideration when activated. System behavior is observed when faults are activated. The fundamental analysis of this approach is similar to the exhaustive search through activation of all possible combinations of failures.

Model checking is often used to verify the system safety properties in the extended model. Model checking performs exhaustive exploration to check whether a safety property—which is usually expressed in temporal logic—holds. The tool produces counterexamples when safety properties do not hold to show traces of simulation on how the breaching condition is reached.

12.3.1 FORMAL SAFETY ANALYSIS PLATFORM—NEW SYMBOLIC MODEL VERIFIER

The FSAP/NuSMV-SA (Bozzano and Villafiorita, 2003) consists of a set of tools including a graphical user interface tool, FSAP, and an extension of model checking engine NuSMV. The aim of this platform is to support formal analysis and safety assessment of complex systems and allows failure injection into the system. The effects of that failure on the system behavior are then observed.

The FSAP/NuSMV-SA platform has different modules to perform different tasks. The central module of the platform is the SAT Manager which controls the other modules of the platform. It stores all the information related to safety assessment and verification which includes the extended system model, failure modes, safety requirements, and analyses. System models are described as finite state machines using the NuSMV language as plain text. A model can be a formal safety model or a functional system model and the user has the flexibility to use their preferred text editor to design or edit the system model. The Failure Mode Editor and Fault Injector modules allow the user to inject failure modes in the system model to create an extended system model. The expressions of the failure modes can be stored in a library to provide greater degree of reusability. The system model is then augmented with safety requirements in the Safety Requirement Editor. Temporal logic is used to express the safety requirements and can also be stored in a library to facilitate future reuse. The Analysis Task Manager defines the analysis tasks that are required to be performed, that is, specification of the analyses. The next step is to assess the annotated system model against its functional safety requirements. This task is done based on the model checking capability incorporated in the NuSMV-SA Model Checker module. This module also generates counterexamples and safety analysis results by means of fault trees. The Result Extraction and Displayer modules process all the results generated by the platform and present to the user. The fault trees can be viewed in the Displayer that is embedded in the platform or using commercial tools, and counterexamples can be viewed in textual or graphical or tabular fashion.

Although the FSAP/NuSMV-SA platform provides multiple functionalities; it does also have some limitations, especially in handling fault trees. Fault trees generated by this toolset show the relation between top events and basic events. However fault trees are flat and don't show propagation of failure which could make the fault trees for complex systems unintuitive. The tool enables qualitative FTA, but it does not have the ability to perform probabilistic evaluation of FTs. Like other model checking based approaches, this platform also suffers from state space explosion while modeling large or complex systems.

12.3.2 ALTARICA

AltaRica (Point and Rauzy, 1999) is a description language designed to be able to formally describe complex systems. AltarRica allows systems to be represented as hierarchies of components and subcomponents and models both events and states. Unlike FSAP/NuSMV, AltaRica uses dedicated safety models. AltaRica models can be analyzed by external tools and methods, e.g., for the generation and analysis of fault trees, Petri nets, and model checking (Bieber et al., 2002).

In AltaRica, components are represented as nodes, and each node possesses a number of states and variables (either state variables or flow variables). The

```
node block
        flow
              O : bool : out ;
              I, A : bool : in ;
        state
              S : bool ;
        event
              failure ;
        trans
              S |- failure -> S := false ;
        assert
              O = (I and A and S) ;
              extern initial_state = S = true ;
    edon
```

FIGURE 12.4

Small example of AltaRica node.

values of the state variables are local to the node they are in, and change when an events occur, i.e., events are triggering state transitions, thus changing the values of state variables. Flow variables are visible both locally and globally and are used to provide an interface to other nodes in the model.

Each basic component is described by an interfaces transition system, containing the description of the possible events, possible observations, possible configurations, mappings of what observations are linked to which configurations, and what transitions are possible for each configuration. A small example of AltaRica node is shown in Figure 12.4.

The behavior of a component (node) is defined through assertions and transitions. Assertions specify restrictions over the values of flow and state variables whereas transitions determine causal relations between state variables and events, consisting of a single trigger (event) and a guard that constraints the transition; guards are assertions over flow and state variables. In the example, the node "block" contains three flow variables (O, I, A) and one state variable (S). There is one event, failure, that causes the state to transition to false. The assertion links the flow variables such that output only occurs when input is present, an active signal is present, and the component is functioning (i.e., S = true, which is the initial state).

After defining the nodes, these can be organized hierarchically to reflect system decomposition and architecture. The top-level node represents the system itself, and it consists of other lower-level nodes. Nodes can communicate either through interfaces or though event dependencies. The first process is done by specifying assertions over interfaces and the second one is done by defining a set of *broadcast synchronization vectors*. These broadcast synchronization vectors allow events in one node or component to be synchronized with those in another node. Vectors can contain question marks to indicate that an event is not obligatory (e.g., a bulb cannot turn off in response to a power cut if it is already off). Additional constraints can be applied to the vectors to indicate that certain combinations or numbers of events must occur, particularly in the case of these "optional" events, e.g., that at least one of a number of optional events must occur, or that k-out-of-n must occur.

Two main variants of AltaRica have been designed so far. The primary difference between the variants is how the variables are updated after firing of transitions. In the original AltaRica (Arnold et al., 2000), variables are updated by solving constraints, and thus consume too much computational resource. Therefore, this approach is not scalable for industrial application although it is very powerful. To make AltaRica capable of assessing industrial scale applications, AltaRica Data-Flow (Boiteau et al., 2006) is introduced where variables are updated by propagating values in a fixed order, and the order is determined at compile time. This approach takes fewer resources, however, it cannot naturally model bidirectional flows through a network, cannot capture located synchronization, and faces difficulties in modeling looped systems. Recent work on AltaRica 3.0 (Batteux et al., 2013) is under specification. It improves the expressive power of the second version without reducing the efficiency of assessment algorithms. The main improvement is: it defines the system model as a new formalism—that of Guarded Transition Systems (GTS)—which allows modeling systems with loops, and can easily model bidirectional flows. AltaRica 3.0 provides a set of assessment tools, e.g., a Fault Tree generator, a Markov chain generator, and stochastic and stepwise simulators.

12.3.3 SAFETY ANALYSIS MODELING LANGUAGE

The SAML (Güdemann and Ortmeier, 2010) is a tool-independent modeling framework that can be used to construct system models with both deterministic and probabilistic behavior. It utilizes finite state automata with parallel synchronous execution capability with discrete time steps to describe system models consisting of hardware, software components and environment inputs. In the state automata, transitions can be defined both as probabilistic and nondeterministic. From a single SAML model both qualitative and quantitative analysis can be performed.

A SAML model consists of at least one module description and declarations of zero or more constants and formulas. Figure 12.5 shows an example of SAML model.

This example has two modules (A and B), four constants, and one formula. The modules are declared as state automata, so every module has at least one state variable and at least one rule to update the state variable. Every state variable is represented as a range of integer values and initialized with a value. Every update rule defines either at least a probabilistic assignment or at least one nondeterministic choice of assignments, and they are conditioned on a Boolean activation condition.

SAML models can be transformed automatically to the input format of other model-based safety analysis techniques. Therefore SAML can work as an intermediate language for MBDA techniques, i.e., if models designed in any other higher-level language can be converted to SAML models (extended system

```
constant double P_A := 0.1;
constant double P_B1 := 0.2;
constant double P_B2 := 0.3;
constant double P_B3 := 0.5;
formula CASE_3 := V_A=0& !
(V_B1=0&V_B2=0|V_B1=1&V_B2=1)

module A
V_A:[0..2] init 0;
V_A=0&V_B1=0&V_B2=0 ->
choice (P_A:(V_A'=0)+(1-P_A):(V_A'=1));
V_A=0&V_B1=1&V_B2=1 -> choice (1:(V_A'=2));
CASE_3 -> choice (1:(V_A'=1));
V_A=1 -> choice (1:(V_A'=1));
V_A=2 -> choice (1:(V_A'=2));
endmodule

module B
V_B1:[0..1] init 0;
V_B2:[0..1] init 0;
true -> choice (P_B1:(V_B1'=0)&(V_B2'=0) +
P_B2:(V_B1'=1)&(V_B2'=0) +
P_B3:(V_B1'=1)&(V_B2'=1)) +
choice (1:(V_B1'=1)&(V_VB2'=1));
endmodule
```

FIGURE 12.5

Example of SAML model.

models) then the resultant models can be transformed to input format of other targeted analysis tools, and, thereby analyzed with different targeted tools.

Güdemann and Ortmeier (2011) have shown ways of transforming SAML model into the input language of probabilistic model checker PRISM (Kwiatkowska et al., 2011). In the same work, the above researchers have also shown ways of transforming SAML modules to NuSMV although the former supports both nondeterministic and probabilistic update rules whereas the later one supports only nondeterministic update rules. In addition to being a high-level modeling and specification language, SAML can also be used as an intermediate language. Its formal qualitative and quantitative semantics allows different analyses to be performed in the same model. Software-intensive Systems Specification Environment (S^3E) was introduced in Lipaczewski et al. (2012) to support SAML.

12.3.4 DEDUCTIVE CAUSE CONSEQUENCE ANALYSIS

DCCA (Ortmeier et al., 2005) is a formal method for safety analysis which uses mathematical methods to determine whether a given component fault is the cause of a system failure. It is a formal generalization of FMEA and FTA, but it is more formal than FTA and more expressive than FMEA. DCCA represents the system model as finite state automata with temporal semantics using Computational Tree Logic (CTL). It assumes that all the basic component failure modes are available, and then defines a set of temporal properties that indicate whether a certain combination of component failure modes can lead to system failure. This property is known as *criticality* of a set of failure modes which are analogous to cut-sets of classical fault trees. Similar to FTA, DCCA aims at determining the minimal critical sets of failure modes which are necessary and sufficient to cause the top event (system failure).

DCCA also faces state explosion problem because to determine minimal critical sets it has to consider all possible combinations of component failure modes. This problem can be alleviated to some extent by using results from other informal safety analysis techniques like FTA which are believed to be generating smaller but good initial guesses for solutions. However, by doing this, DCCA also inherits the shortcomings of FTA, i.e., inability of capturing dynamic behavior where order of events is important. Deductive Failure Order Analysis (Güdemann et al., 2008) is a recent extension which enables DCCA to deduce temporal ordering information in critical sets. In this extension, Pandora style temporal gates like PAND and SAND are used to capture temporal behavior. Temporal logic laws are also provided to make the temporal ordering deduction process automated.

12.4 TOWARDS INTEGRATED APPROACHES

This section explores the strengths and limitations often shared by different techniques within the FLSA and BFS fields. There has been a paradigm shift in recent years where research work and efforts have been channeled into extending and integrating different techniques to address identified limitations.

12.4.1 APPLICABILITY AND CHALLENGES OF FLSA

FLSA techniques generally use a dedicated model developed for the purpose of the analysis (or annotations that augment the design model), which makes it easier to analyze the effect of failures on the system. This allows safety engineers to modify level of details avoiding unnecessary complexity while ensuring that the model is sufficient for dependability analysis purposes. Unintentional interactions (e.g., short circuits of electrical systems) can also be taken into consideration.

The true benefits of this type of approach are most apparent when used as part of an iterative design process. As the failure behavior of the system components is modeled in a compositional fashion, it is easier to determine the effects of design changes. This is particularly true for automated or partly automated techniques, which speed up the analysis process and make it possible to rapidly evaluate speculative changes to the design. This efficient nature of FLSA also means that valuable analysis can be started early in the design process when concrete system details are still scarce. FLSA produces safety artefacts which are familiar to safety engineers (e.g., FTA and FMEA).

However, dedicated models also mean that additional effort is required to create these new models or extend any normal system model with the required information, and further effort may be required to harmonize these disparate models. This may also hamper the traceability between design and analysis models.

Another limitation of FLSA is the lack of support for formal verification. FLSA are also fundamentally static analyses, which do not take into consideration the changes in system states and are therefore limited in their ability to capture dynamic behavior (although this limitation is, to a certain extent, addressed by some extended techniques as previously mentioned).

12.4.2 APPLICABILITY AND CHALLENGES OF BFS

The strength of BFS lies in its ability to facilitate automated formal verification and capture the system dynamic behaviors. It is also possible to distinguish between transient and permanent failures and model the temporal ordering of failures. However, the fault simulation techniques have a number of limitations. The valuable safety artefacts such as fault trees (which are obtained through model checking) tend to have a "flat structure," representing disjunction of all minimal cut-sets. This may hamper the understanding of the fault trees. Model checking based techniques are computationally expensive, inductive in nature, and therefore suffer from state-space explosion problems. The exhaustive assessment of the effects of combinations of component failures is not feasible in large systems.

Fault injection is also typically applied to executable design models, which are typically produced at a later development process stage when design changes are costly to implement. The analysis results therefore often lose the opportunity to drive the design process itself. While the construction of the extended model supports the consistency of the safety analysis, it may impose constraints on the safety analysis as explained in Lisagor et al. (2011). Extended models are inadequate in covering failures resulting from unintentional interactions or unintended dependencies between seemingly unrelated components. The techniques also rely on the set of predefined failure modes to be injected, and therefore the completeness of the analysis depends on the completeness of the failure list, which is difficult to guarantee.

12.4.3 TOWARDS INTEGRATED APPROACHES

As MBDA techniques develop and mature, various extensions are introduced to address the limitations identified. One of the increasing trends in integrated approaches is that between ADLs and FLSA techniques. FLSA techniques aim to overcome the problems associated with a "pure" dedicated model by automatically or semi-automatically constructing the dependability analysis model (by partially utilizing the architecture of the design model). Translations from high-level ADLs to FLSA techniques allow tighter integration between the design and analysis process, and therefore a better traceability between design and analysis models. Recent work on FPTC in Paige et al. (2008) uses a metamodel to support model transformations from SysML and AADL models. Metamodels have also been developed in Adler et al. (2011) to obtain CFT models from architectural models specified in UML. HiP-HOPS has been integrated with Matlab Simulink and Simulation X for many years (Papadopoulos and Maruhn, 2001). Recent integration work between HiP-HOPS and EAST-ADL is discussed in Chen et al. (2013) and Sharvia et al. (2014), and model transformation between HiP-HOPS and AADL is presented in Mian et al. (2014).

Another trend on integration aims to enable the verification capabilities in FLSA. A number of integrated approaches have emerged where compositional FLSA techniques are merged with fault injection approaches. In this integrated approach, system structure and behavior (nominal and failure) is expressed using a compositional model of architecture, and model transformation is performed to obtain a model which can be formally verified (verification model). The transformation can be carried out through direct transformation rules, or through an intermediate transformation where the intermediate model is used to achieve consistency and traceability between different design, analysis and verification approaches. The outline of this structure is illustrated in Figure 12.6. With the use of the intermediate transformation, high-level models can be reused for different target approaches. Counterexamples which are obtained from fault injection techniques can also be transformed back into dependability analysis models, for example, as minimal cut-sets of fault trees. FPTA (Ge et al., 2009) links FPTC architectural models with probabilistic model checkers specified in PRISM. This enables FPTC to capture nondeterministic failure behavior, and perform verification. Combined application between HiP-HOPS and NuSMV is described in Sharvia and Papadopoulos (2011). This work describes how dependability analysis results from HiP-HOPS can be used to systematically guide the construction of verification models specified in NuSMV, allowing early verification of functional behavior and formulation of system degradation states.

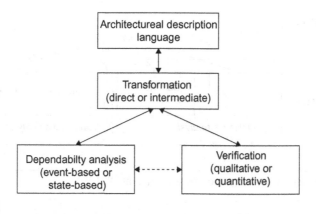

FIGURE 12.6

Model-based integrated approach (Aizpurua and Muxika, 2013).

Integration through direct transformation is used in COMPASS project (COMPASS, 2013) which utilizes the System Level Integrated Modeling (SLIM) language (Bozzano et al., 2011). SLIM semantics covers nominal and error behavior of AADL, and contains an extended model which allows verification via model checking. ESA support toolset is available internally.

SAML is an example of an integrative approach via intermediate transformation. This is illustrated in Figure 12.7. Specification can be written in high-level CASE tool like SCADE or Matlab Simulink, transformed into a SAML model, and verified using NuSMV or PRISM. However, work on this is still in progress and there are transformation-related issues which need to be addressed (e.g., implementation of high level to intermediate level model transformation). Another example is the Topcased project (TOPCASED, 2013) which transforms SysML, UML and AADL models into an intermediate model specified in FIACRE language (Berthomieu et al., 2008).

Challenges in these integrated approaches include the state-space explosion problem due to the size of verification model. There is also need to find an efficient way to feed the analysis results into the design model in order to maintain consistency, and a need to construct a user friendly toolset due to the range of models and analyses.

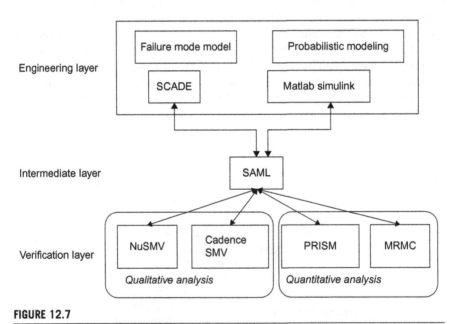

FIGURE 12.7

SAML as an intermediate language (Güdemann et al., 2012).

The following table summarizes the approaches discussed in this chapter:

Technique	Features	Limitations	Tool Support	Extension/ Integrated Work
FPTN	Formal notation for system behavior; temporal extension	Lack of full automation	SSAP toolset	N/A
FPTC	Integration with probabilistic model checker	Manual identification of all potential failure modes of interest	Epsilon	AADL, SysML, PRISM
CFT	Associations between fault and architectural hierarchies	Lack of dynamic behavioral analysis	ESSaRel tool	UML
SEFT	Capture system dynamic behavior	Conversion to state-based models for analysis; state explosion	ESSaRel, TimeNET	N/A
HiP-HOPS	Automated dependability analysis; temporal extension; multiobjective optimization	Lack of mature dynamic behavioral analysis	HiP-HOPS tool	EAST-ADL, AADL, Simulink, Simulation X, NuSMV
FSAP/ NuSMV	Formal verification; library of failure modes	Flat fault tree structure; state explosion	FSAP/ NuSMV	N/A
AltaRica	Formal verification; timed automata and GTS extension	State explosion	AltaRica tools	AADL
SAML	Captures deterministic and probabilistic behavior	Manual extension of nominal model	S^3 tools	NuSMV, ADL (ongoing)
SLIM	Integrated formal verification and dependability analysis	Manual extension of nominal model; state explosion	ESA toolset (internal)	ESA toolset (internal)

12.5 CONCLUSIONS AND FUTURE OUTLOOK

Various MBDA techniques have been developed over the past 20 years, and these techniques tend to gravitate towards two different paradigms. This chapter discussed the characteristics of both paradigms, and reviewed a number of prominent techniques, exploring their working mechanism, strengths, limitations, and recent developments. These techniques have also evolved with recent extensions and integrations (as discussed in Section 12.4.3) and utilize different strengths to address various challenges outlined earlier. In line with the increasing adoption of ADLs which encapsulate both architectural and behavioral information of the system, recent work has seen a number of model transformations between pioneering MBDA techniques and ADL models to enable greater analysis capabilities and consistency between design and analysis. This addresses the challenges arising from the use of dedicated model and improves the traceability between design and analysis models. Other types of integration aim to extend the analysis capabilities of the MBDA technique itself, particularly to enable verification in conjunction with dependability analyses. With the increasing popularity of model-driven engineering, metamodels for techniques have also been constructed to assist automation of code generations and model transformations.

Future trends are likely to yield more robust integrations between existing paradigms and techniques. Efforts should also be placed into exploring ways to utilize different strengths in a complementary manner. The dependability community will also benefit from integrated automated tools to support adoptions of various techniques with minimum overhead caused by disjoint and dysfunctional tool chains. Separation concerns for hardware and software within design of complex embedded systems have, to a certain extent, been supported through the integration of analysis techniques with ADLs. Concerns still exist about traceability between models and analysis and focus should be given to feeding analyses effectively back to the design. The state-space explosion problem, which is inherently part of state-based techniques, can be addressed with abstraction techniques (although this is a largely complex subject in itself).

Advanced capabilities to support the development and design decision of safety-critical systems are also important, particularly in a modern competitive engineering environment. The design of dependable systems must often address both cost and dependability concerns. The availability of different component alternatives and architectural configurations means that the task to find optimal or near optimal solutions is not a trivial one. It is also possible that no architectural configuration is able to meet all design requirements. In this case, the optimal trade-offs between dependability and cost need to be established. This opens the field to multiobjective optimization. MBDA techniques like HiP-HOPS have been extended with multiobjective optimization capabilities to assist design decisions (Adachi et al., 2011); and Eclipse-based tool, ArcheOpterix, allows evaluation techniques and optimization heuristics for AADL specifications (Aleti et al.,

2009). Other works which look into the use of reconfigurable architectures for fault tolerant design and recovery strategies are discussed in Aizpurua and Muxika (2013) and Papadopoulos et al. (2011). There is also opportunity for model-based allocation of dependability requirements to be used as a tool for driving design refinement itself. This topic is, for example, studied in recent works within HiP-HOPS (Azevedo et al., 2013) where the automated allocation of safety requirements in the form of SIL is investigated.

REFERENCES

Adachi, M., Papadopoulos, Y., Sharvia, S., Parker, D., Tohdo, T., 2011. An approach to optimisation of fault tolerant architecture using HiP-HOPS. Softw. Pract. Exp. 41 (11), 1202−1327.

Adler, R., Domis, D., Hofig, K., Kemmann, S., Kuhn, T., Schwinn, J., et al. 2011. Integration of component fault trees into the UML. In: Workshops and Symposia at MODELS, pp. 312−327.

Aizpurua, J.I., Muxika, E., 2012. Design of dependable systems: an overview of analysis and verification approaches. In: DEPEND'12: Fifth International Conference on Dependability. IARIA, pp. 4−12.

Aizpurua, J., Muxika, E., 2013. Model-based design of dependable systems: limitation and evolution of analysis and verification approaches. Int. J. Adv. Sec. 6 (1&2), 12−13.

Akerlund, O., Bieber, P., 2006. ISAAC, a framework for integrated safety analysis of functional, geometrical, and human aspects. In: 3rd European Congress on Embedded Real Time System (ERTS), Toulouse, France.

Aleti, A., Bjornander, S., Grunske, L., & Meedeniya, I., 2009. ArcheOpterix: an extendable tool for architecture optimization of AADL models. In: MOMPES'09, Vancouver, Canada.

Arnold, A., Point, G., Griffault, A., Rauzy, A., 2000. The Altarrica formalism for describing concurrent system. Fundamenta Informaticae 40 (2), 109−124.

Azevedo, L., Parker, D., Walker, M., Papadopoulos, Y., Araujo, R., 2013. Assisted assignment of automotive safety requirements. IEEE Softw. 31 (1), 62−68.

Batteux, M., Prosvirnova, T., Rauzy, A., Kloul, L., 2013. The AltaRica 3.0 Project for Model-Based Safety Assessment. INDIN. 741−746.

Berthomieu, B., Bodeveix, B., Farail, M., Garavel, H., Gaufillet, P., Lang, F., et al. 2008. Fiarce: an intermediate language for model verification in topcased environment. In: ERTS'08.

Bieber, P., Castel, C., Seguin, C., 2002. Combination of fault tree analysis and model checking for safety assessment of complex system. In: Proceedings of the 4th European Depting Conference on Dependable Computing, pp. 19−31.

Boiteau, M., Dutuit, Y., Rauzy, A., Signoret, J., 2006. The AltarRica dataflow language in use: modeling of production availability of a multi-state system. Reliab. Eng. Syst. Saf. 91 (7), 747−755.

Bouissou, M., 2007. A generalization of dynamic fault trees through Boolean Logic Driven Markov Processes (BDMP). In: Proc. ESREL'07, pp. 1051−1058.

Bozzano, M., Villafiorita, A., 2003. Improving system reliability via model checking: the FSAP/NuSMV-SA safety analysis platform. In: International Conference on Computer Safety, Reliability, and Security, Edinburgh. pp. 49–62.

Bozzano, M., Villafiorita, A., et al., 2003. ESACS: an integrated methodology for design and safety analysis of complex systems. In: ESREL '03.

Bozzano, M., Cimatti, A., Katoen, J., Nguyen, V., Noll, T., Roveri, M., 2011. Safety, dependability, and performance analysis of extended AADL models. Comput. J. 54 (5), 754–775.

Chen, D.-J., Mahmud, N., Walker, M., Feng, L., Lonn, H., Papadopoulos, Y., 2013. Systems modeling with EAST-ADL for fault tree analysis through HiP-HOPS. In: 4th IFAC Workshop on Dependable Control of Discrete Systems. 4 (1), 91–96.

COMPASS, 2013. Correctness, Modeling, and Performance of Aerospace Systems. Retrieved from <www.compass.informatik.rwth-aachen.de>.

Distefano, S., Puliafito, A., 2007. Dynamic reliability block diagram VS dynamic fault trees. In: Proceedings of Reliability Availability Maintainability Safety 2007, pp. 71–76.

Dugan, J., Bavuso, S., Boyd, M., 1992. Dynamic fault tree models for fault tolerant computer systems. IEEE Trans. Reliabil. 41 (3), 363–377.

Edifor, E., Walker, M., Gordon, N., 2012. Quantification of priority-OR gates in temporal fault trees. Comput. Saf. Reliabil. Secur. SE, 99–110.

Edifor, E., Walker, M., Gordon, N., Papadopoulos, Y., 2014. Using simulation to evaluate dynamic systems with weibull or lognormal distributions. In: Proceedings of the 9th International Conference on Dependability and Complex Systems, pp. 177–187.

ESSaRel, 2005. Embedded Systems Safety and Reliability Analyser. Available from: <http://essarel.de> (retrieved 3.9.14.).

Feiler, P., Rugina, A., 2007. Dependability Modeling with the Architecture Analysis & Design Language (AADL). Tech. Rep. Software Engineering Institute, Carnegie Mellon University, Pittsburgh, US.

Feiler, P., Gluch, D., Hudak, J., 2006. The Architecture Analysis & Design Language (AADL): An Introduction. Tech. Rep. Software Engineering Institute, Carnegie Mellon University, Pittsburgh, US.

Fenelon, P., McDermid, J., 1993. An integrated toolset for software safety analysis. J. Syst. Softw. 21 (3), 279–290.

Fussel, J., Aber, E., Rahl, R., 1976. On the quantitative analysis of Priority-AND failure logic. IEEE Trans. Reliabil R-25 (5), 324–326.

Gallina, B., Punnekkat, S., 2014. A formalism for incompletion, inconsistency, interference and impermanence failures' analysis. In: Proceedings of the 37th EUROMICRO Conference on Software Engineering and Advanced Applications, pp. 493–500.

Ge, X., Paige, R., McDermid, J., 2009. Probabilistic failure propagation and transformation analysis. In: International Conference on Computer Safety, Reliability, and Security (SAFECOM), pp. 215–228.

German, R., Mitzlaff, J., 1995. Transient analysis of deterministic and stochastic Petri Nets with TimeNET. In: Proceedings of the 8th International Conference on Computer Performance Evaluation, Modeling Techniques, and Tools and MMB, pp. 209–223.

Grunske, L., Kaiser, B., Papadopoulos, Y., 2005. Model-driven safety evaluation with state-event-based component failure annotations. In: 8th international conference on Component-Based Software Engineering (CBSE'05), pp. 33–48.

Güdemann, M., Ortmeier, F., 2010. A framework for qualitative and quantitative formal model-based safety analysis. In: Proceedings of the 12th International Symposium on High-Assurance System Engineering (HASE), pp. 132−141.

Güdemann, M., Ortmeier, F., 2011. Towards model-driven safety analysis. In: 3rd International Workshop on Dependable Control of Discrete Systems (DCDS), pp. 53−58.

Güdemann, M., Ortmeier, F., Reif, W., 2008. Computation of ordered minimal critical sets. In: Proceedings of the 7th Symposium in Computer Safety, Reliability, and Security.

Güdemann, M., Lipaczewski, M., Struck, S., Ortmeier, F., 2012. Unifying Probabilistic and Traditional Formal Model Based Analysis. In: MBEES'12.

Helmer, G., Wong, J., Slagell, M., Honavar, V., Miller, L., Wang, Y., Wang, X., Stakhanova, N., 2007. Software fault tree and coloured Petri net − based specification, design and implementation of agent-based intrusion detection systems. Int. J. Info. Comput. Secur. 1 (1), 109−142.

Hura, G., Atwood, J., 1988. The use of Petri Nets to analyze coherent fault trees. IEEE Trans. Reliabil. 37 (5), 469−474.

Joshi, A., Vestal, S., Binns, P., 2007. Automatic generation of static fault trees from AADL models. In: DSN Workshop on Architecting Dependable Systems.

Kaiser, B., Liggesmeyer, P., Mackel, O., 2003. A new component concept for fault trees. In: Proceedings for the 8th Australian Workshop on Safety Critical Systems and Software (SCS'03). vol. 33, pp. 37–46.

Kwiatkowska, M., Norman, G., Parker, D., 2011. PRISM 4.0: verification of probabilistic real-time systems. In: Proceedings of the 23rd International Conference on Computer Aided Verification (CAV'11), pp. 585−591.

Lipaczewski, M., Struck, S., Ortmeier, F., 2012. SAML goes eclipse—Combining model-based safety analysis and high-level editor support. In Proceedings of the 2nd International Workshop on Developing Tools as Plug-Ins (TOPI), pp. 67−72.

Lisagor, O., Kelly, T., Niu, R., 2011. Model-Based Safety Assessment: Review of Discipline and its Challenges. In: 9th International Conference on Reliability, Maintainability and Safety (ICRMS), pp. 625–632.

Marsan, M., Chiola, G., 1987. On Petri nets with deterministic and exponentially distributed firing times. In: Advances in Petri Nets, 266, pp. 132−145.

Merle, G., Roussel, J., Lesage, J., Bobbio, A., 2010. Probabilistic algebraic analysis of fault trees with priority dynamic gates and repeated events. IEEE Trans. Reliabil. 59 (1), 250−261.

Mian, Z., Bottaci, L., Papadopoulos, Y., Sharvia, S., Mahmud, N., 2014. Model transformation for multi-objective architecture optimization of dependable systems. In: Dependability Problems of Complex Information Systems, 91−110.

Niu, R., Tang, T., Lisagor, O., McDermid, J. A., 2011. Automatic safety analysis of networked control system based on failure propagation model. In: IEEE International Conference on Vehicular Electronics and Safety, pp. 53−58.

Ortmeier, F., Reif, W., Schellhorn, G., 2005. Deductive cause-consequence analysis. In: Proceedings of the 6th IFAC World Congress, pp. 1434−1439.

Paige, R., Rose, L., Ge, X., Kolovos, D., Brooke, P. J., 2008. FPTC: automated safety analysis for domain specific languages. In: Proceedings of Workshop on Non Functional System Properties in Domain Specific Modeling Languages, pp. 229−242.

Papadopoulos, Y., Maruhn, M., 2001. Model-based synthesis of fault trees from matlab simulink models. In: International Conference on Dependable Systems and Networks (DSN), pp. 77−82.

Papadopoulos, Y., McDermid, J., 1999. Hierarchically performed hazard origin and propagation studies. In: International Conference on Computer Safety, Reliability and Security, pp. 139–152.

Papadopoulos, Y., Nggada, S., Parker, D., 2010. Extending HiP-HOPS with Capabilities of Planning Preventative Maintenance, Strategic Advantage of Computing Information Systems in Enterprise Management, editiors. Majid Sarrafzadeh Volume containing revised selected papers from International Conference in Computer Systems and Information Systems 2009-2010, pp. 231–245, ISBN: 978-960-6672-93-4.

Papadopoulos, Y., Walker, M., Parker, D., Rude, E., Hamman, R., Uhlig, A., et al., 2011. Engineering failure analysis & design optimization with HiP-HOPS. J. Eng. Fail. Anal 18 (2), 590–608.

Point, G., Rauzy, A., 1999. AltaRica: constraint automata as a description language. Eur. J. Autom. 33 (8–9), 1033–1052.

Rao, K., Durga, V., Gopika, V., Sanyasi, R., Kushawa, H., Verma, A., et al., 2009. Dynamic fault tree analysis using Monte Carlo simulation in probabilistic safety assessment. Reliabil. Eng. Syst. Saf. 94 (4), 872–883.

Robidoux, R., Lu, H., Xing, L., Zhou, M., 2010. Automated modeling of dynamic reliability block diagrams using coloured Petri Nets. IEEE Trans. Syst. Man, Cybernatics 40 (2), 337–351.

Rugina, A., Kanoun, K., Kaaniche, M., 2007. A system dependability modeling framework using AADL and GSPNs. In: Architecting Dependable Systems IV, pp. 14–38.

Sharvia, S., Papadopoulos, Y., 2011. IACoB-SA: an approach towards integrated safety assessment. In: Proceedings of 7th IEEE International Conference on Automation Science and Engineering, Trieste, Italy. pp. 220–225.

Sharvia, S., Papadopoulos, Y., Walker, M., Chen, D., Lonn, H., 2014. Enhancing the EAST-ADL error model with HiP-HOPS semantics. In: Athens ATINER Conference Paper Series.

Steiner, M., Keller, P., Liggesmeyer, P., 2012. Modeling the effects of software on safety and reliability in complex embedded systems. Comput. Saf. Reliabil. Secur., 454–465.

TOPCASED, 2013. The Open Source Toolkit for Critical System. Available from: <www.topcased.org> (retrieved 9.11.14.).

US Department of Defense, 1980. Procedures of Performing a Failure mode, Effects, and Criticality Analysis. Washington, DC.

Vesely, W., Dugan, J., Fragola, J., Minarick, J., Railsback, J., 2002. *Fault Tree Handbook with Aerospace Applications.* Tech. rep., NASA office of safety and mission assurance, Washington, DC.

Villemeur, A., 1991. Reliability, Availability, Maintainability and Safety Assessment: Methods and Techniques. John Wiley & Sons, Chichester.

Walker, M., 2009. Pandora: A Logic for the Qualitative Analysis of Temporal Fault Trees PhD Thesis. University of Hull.

Walker, M., Bottaci, L., Papadopoulos, Y., 2007. Compositional temporal fault tree analysis. In: Proceedings of the 26th International Conference on Computer Safety, pp. 106–119.

Walker, M., Mahmud, N., Papadopoulos, Y., Tagliabo, F., Torchiaro, S., Schierano, W., Lonn, H., 2008. ATESST2: Review of relevant Safety Analysis Techniques. Tech. Rep, 1–121.

Yang, Y., Zeckzer, D., Liggesmeyer, P., Hagen, H., 2011. ViSSaAn: visual support for safety analysis. In: Daastuhl Follow-Ups, pp. 378–395.

Influences of architectural and implementation choices on CyberInfrastructure quality—a case study

13

Emilia Farcas, Massimiliano Menarini, Claudiu Farcas, William G. Griswold, Kevin Patrick, Ingolf Krueger, Barry Demchak, Fred Raab, Yan Yan and Celal Ziftci

University of California, San Diego, La Jolla, CA, USA

13.1 INTRODUCTION

While the E-Health IT ecosystem includes many complex platforms, such as EHRs for Electronic Health Records used by clinicians and PACS for the Picture Archiving and Communication System used by radiologists, essentially all of them are part of the standard systems used in hospitals and other clinical environments. Extending their reach to the "last mile" (i.e., the patients or individuals in the community) is still in its early stage, with modest attempts to allow patients to see parts of their health data records being hamstrung by both technical issues and institutional policies and regulations. As such, modern E-Health research focuses on novel methods that leverage cutting-edge technologies to advance approaches to personalized healthcare and population health by bringing patients and individuals into the mix.

CyberInfrastructures (CIs) have been successfully developed in other scientific fields such as earth-sciences and oceanography for earthquake and wave monitoring, and weather forecasting; yet, their development did not have to navigate the myriad policies, regulations, and standards of the healthcare domain. Here, significant challenges stem from the inaccessibility of patient-data silos at each institution; lack of standardization or—even worse—multiple, competing, incompatible standards; minimal technical proficiency of end users; difficulty in ascertaining the sensitivity of data; and a lack of maturity of the information technology used in the field. In our experience, E-Health CIs span many organizational, geographical, and technological boundaries. They exist in a complex socio-technical-economic environment that is inherently difficult to describe, design, implement, and evaluate.

CI is a term that is often overloaded. In some contexts, the CI definition covers technical elements that are typical of the deployment layer of a system's architecture. Other times, it encompasses software elements all the way to user facing applications. Nevertheless, two key elements common to all definitions of CIs are: (i) they should support all aspects of data management, such as acquisition, processing, integration, and visualization and (ii) they cross the boundaries of different authority domains, such as different intuitions, companies, and the Internet. These two characteristics—data management coupled with different authority domains—make CIs both technological and sociological solutions. Their goal is to connect people from different domains to data in an efficient and privacy preserving way.

From a technical standpoint, the CIs we describe in this chapter are platforms that encompass both the basic technological infrastructure (servers, networks, operating systems, databases, etc.) and a set of software services. We distinguish between CI services and application services. The software services we consider part of the CI are the ones needed to deal with the specific goals of CIs: the manipulation and sharing of data across different authority domains. In particular, we consider the specific constraints and regulations of the medical field when designing E-Health CIs. According to our definition, CIs are really platforms that support connecting people—in our context these are often researchers, medical doctors, patients, and other individuals participating in research studies—to data. Different applications use the CI to share and process data according to the protocols, constraints, and regulations of the specific application.

We have designed, implemented, and deployed multiple successful E-Health CIs at the University of California, San Diego (UCSD), including CYberinfrastructure for COmparative effectiveness REsearch (CYCORE) (Patrick et al., 2011; Peterson et al., 2013) for cancer clinical trials, Personal Activity Location Measurement System (PALMS) (Demchak et al., 2012; Demchak and Krüger, 2012) for studying human activity patterns, and CitiSense (Nikzad et al., 2011, 2012) for sensing air quality. These three CIs were developed independently of each other; each CI evolved while also developing the specific applications and user interfaces (UIs) that use the CI. Furthermore, we also designed the CI of the NIH-supported National Center for Biomedical Computing—Integrating Data for Analysis, Anonymization, and SHaring (iDASH), which serves the biomedical community with both privacy-preserving computational capabilities using a private cloud and a secure HIPAA-compliant repository for research data.

These CIs have served their communities well with respect to their projects' goals and durations. For example, during 2012–2013, the CYCORE CI (detailed in Section 13.3.3) was successfully used in cancer feasibility trials at the M. D. Anderson Cancer Center (MDACC), University of Texas, in three populations: advanced colorectal cancer patients, head and neck cancer patients, and cancer survivors who were smokers. The clinical trial for detecting dehydration in head and neck cancer patients (Peterson et al., 2013) was highly successful: 96% of the enrolled patients completed the study, and more than 90% of patients rated their ease, self-efficacy, and satisfaction regarding use of the sensor suite as extremely favorable. In addition, clinicians reported a high degree of satisfaction with using CYCORE to monitor their patients during radiation treatment.

The development process for these research-oriented CIs focused on meeting both E-Health customer needs and at the same time experimentation with different architectures and implementation strategies to advance our computer science research. Therefore, there are significant differences in how these CIs were designed and implemented in each project. In this chapter, we extract generic CI requirements that crosscut each E-Health application, and we analyze the trade-offs of development and deployment choices and their impact on quality attributes. The main questions we try to answer are: *How can we compare the quality of these CIs? How can we improve the quality of future CIs by capitalizing on lessons learned, the best architectural and implementation choices, and reusing elements from all these existing systems?*

Moreover, there is often a tension between the customers' quality requirements (e.g., usability, privacy, security, performance, and reliability) and developers' quality requirements (e.g., maintainability, operability, and reusability). Due to the nature of academia, developer turnover is high and funding is unstable; thus, making it difficult to maintain projects long term to support the user community after the initial funding period. As such, for the analysis in this chapter, long-term sustainability requirements take precedence, and we place greater emphasis on the quality requirements most relevant for the development and support team. Grounding this work, we apply the lessons learned to a new project, namely Data E-platform Leveraged for Patient Empowerment and Population Health Improvement (DELPHI), where we are evaluating what to develop, reuse, or integrate in its new CI. Our long-term goal is to create a generic E-Health CI to support all of our applications.

In the following, we give an overview of the E-Health domain along with several concepts, basic services, and challenges in this field. Then, we explain the quality perspective and goals for the evaluation in this chapter. A detailed outline can be found at the end of Section 13.1.

13.1.1 CONCEPT OF OPERATION

The E-Health domain revolves around patient and person-level data and novel ways of capturing more relevant data, analyzing it with a multitude of algorithms, and providing the results to interested parties. These results, used for research or clinical applications, will ultimately help in making better decisions for personal care.

Figure 13.1 shows the main data flow in our typical E-Health application. Study participants, many of whom are patients, use sensors in their homes or while out in the community. Data collected by these sensors reaches the CI in various ways depending on the project: manually uploaded through a web

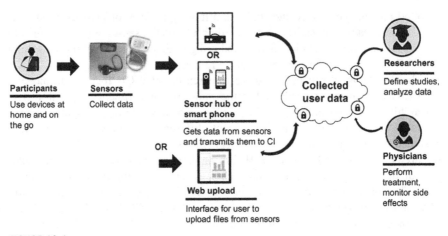

FIGURE 13.1

Data flow from participants to researchers or physicians.

interface (PALMS); automatically transmitted from the sensors to a sensor hub (CYCORE) that sends data to the CI back-end; or sent by mobile phones to the CI (CitiSense and CYCORE). Once data reaches the CI, it is stored, processed, and relayed to users, researchers, or clinicians according to the policies in place.

As an example from CYCORE, consider the scenario of a cancer patient, Alice, who has just completed a radiation session and is now home. CYCORE allows for home-monitoring of her vital signs such as blood pressure and heart rate, and these data are then shared with her physician, Frank. Alice also uses a smartphone to record videos of herself doing exercises as instructed by Frank and to answer dietary intake- and symptoms-based questionnaires. Frank can monitor these diverse data daily and determine if changes in Alice's treatment should be made. According to an IRB-approved protocol, researchers can use the CI to enroll patients in clinical trials and collect, store, process, and visualize their patients' data.

13.1.2 E-HEALTH SERVICES

The main challenge in developing E-Health systems is to integrate a variety of distributed components to serve the heterogeneous and evolving requirements of a diverse stakeholder community, while meeting the specific quality constraints of the domain. At the same time, building the corresponding system-of-systems requires an architecture that achieves a coherent integration of these capabilities and that manages the lifecycle of all resources, while addressing crosscutting concerns, such as security, policy management, and logging.

For this purpose, we combine techniques from service-oriented architecture (SOA) (MacKenzie et al., 2006) and development (SOD) with Model-Driven

Architecture® (MDA®) (Object Management Group® [OMG], 2003) and design (MDD). We have created the Rich Services (RS) architecture blueprint (Arrott et al., 2007), which complements the OASIS SOA Reference Model (MacKenzie et al., 2006) and W3C Web Services Architecture (Booth et al., 2004) by providing an architectural style particularly suitable to integrating crosscutting concerns. In a nutshell, the RS architecture integrates application services (which provide core application functionality) with infrastructure services (which transform messages defined by the application services, providing the underlying mechanisms to inject crosscutting concerns). The related development process (Demchak et al., 2007) briefly described in Section 13.3.1 helps us organize complex systems in a hierarchical fashion so that we can manage distributed capabilities that may be under the control of different ownership domains.

All CIs discussed in this chapter use the logical RS architecture, but they vary to the extent this architecture is used in several components of the system, interactions between components, and its actual implementation in code. In particular, E-Health systems have requirements for privacy and security, and depending on the type of data collected, these systems could be subject to regulations such as the Health Insurance Portability and Accountability Act (HIPAA) (1996) and the Federal Information Security Management Act (FISMA) (2002). HIPAA provides standards for ensuring the security and privacy of Protected Health Information (PHI), which is an individual's health information that is created or received by a healthcare provider and that can identify the individual. FISMA requires each federal agency to implement a costly agency-wide program to provide information security for the information and systems that support its operations and assets. The purpose of this chapter is not to discuss such security aspects in detail; instead, we will discuss security strategies in the context of maintainability and operation.

Figure 13.2 shows the basic set of capabilities that are found in E-Health systems: (i) multiple ways to collect data from internal and external sources, including integration adapters that create interfaces with external systems across organizational or geographical boundaries; (ii) data distribution mechanisms that deliver data artifacts at the necessary service endpoints; (iii) data transformation such as filtering, conversions, and quality control that support the numerous types of data used by its stakeholders; (iv) data preservation with indexes of participants and record locators that enable retrieval of data of interest; (v) analytics processes and workflows that make sense of the data, including event detection/notification services; (vi) portals for data access, both for providers and participants; and (vii) streamlined infrastructure support for privacy, security, and information assurance.

13.1.3 GOALS FOR THE QUALITY REVIEW

In this chapter, we focus on software quality assurance from the developers' perspective. We focus on supporting maintenance and portability of the system; we

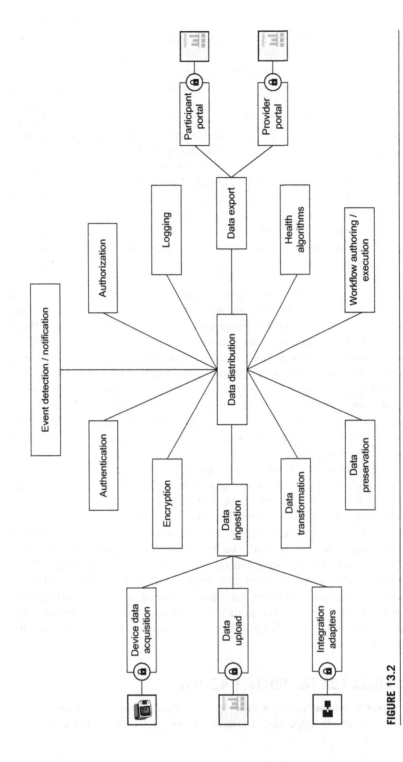

FIGURE 13.2

E-Health services.

do not cover security in detail, but we mention how it affects maintainability and portability. The complexity of modifying or adding new code to an application is an important consideration in projects that often evolve substantially over their lifetime, such as our research applications.

During the development process, we used rapid prototyping for system development, and most prototypes have been incorporated and refined in successive iterations within each project's duration. Throwaway prototypes, built to evaluate high risk items and then discarded, were used sparingly due to timeline and economic reasons.

The goal for the quality review in this chapter is to learn from the experience in developing each of these CIs and to improve the quality of future systems. The research objective is to define a framework for analyzing our CIs and to identify successful architectural or implementation choices from each CI. We created a framework based on the model from (Deissenboeck et al., 2007), which is an activity-based model specific for assessing maintainability. The model distinguishes between activities and characteristics (i.e., facts) of the system to maintain—a generic impact matrix expresses how each fact affects each activity. In order to determine the maintainability of each system, we evaluate all facts for each project. We limited our analysis to activities and facts relevant to our case studies.

We created an impact matrix, and then we added one more dimension to the model: besides evaluating each fact for the overall system, we also evaluate how a set of architectural or implementation choices increase or decrease the fact metric. Consequently, we are able to assess the impact of each choice on the system quality. (Note that we do not evaluate separate components, but focus on separate decisions that crosscut components.)

While our analysis is specific to the E-Health domain, we believe that the same analysis process is applicable to any other domain. The facts and activities are generic enough to be valid in many domains; additional facts should be elicited from the requirements particular to a domain under study. Our goal was not to create a comprehensive methodology, but to define a framework for our own case study. This is a first attempt at such an analysis and subsequent work will refine the framework.

When discussing quality characteristics for the scope of this chapter, we use the following terminology and definitions from ISO 25010 (ISO, 2011) standard:

- Maintainability—The ability to make modifications to the system to improve it, correct a fault, or adapt it to changes in environment or requirements.
  - Modularity: The degree to which a change to one component has minimal impact on other components.
  - Reusability: The degree to which an asset can be used in more than one system.
  - Analyzability: The effort needed for assessing the impact of an intended change, diagnosing the root cause of failures, or identifying the parts to be modified.

- Modifiability: The degree to which a system can be modified without introducing defects or degrading existing quality.
- Testability: The effort needed for establishing test criteria and performing tests to validate the modified system.
- Portability—The ability of software to be transferred from one environment to another.
  - Adaptability: The degree to which a system can be adapted to new hardware, software, or other operational or usage environments.
  - Installability: The effort needed to install the software in a specified environment.
  - Replaceability: How easy it is to change a software component (i.e., plug and play) within a specified environment.
- Security—Degree to which a system protects information so that data access for an entity is appropriate to its level of authorization.
  - Confidentiality: ensures that data are accessible only to those authorized
  - Integrity: prevents unauthorized access or modification of programs or data
  - Non-repudiation: actions or events can be proven to have taken place
  - Accountability: actions of an entity can be traced uniquely to the entity
  - Authenticity: the identity of a subject or resource can be proved to be the one claimed.

13.1.4 OUTLINE

In the introduction, we gave an overview of the E-Health domain, basic services, and challenges in the field and outlined our goals for quality review. We continue in Section 13.2 with related work on quality definitions, models, and evaluation.

In Section 13.3, we explain the development process used to engineer our CIs and provide an overview of all projects we compare in this chapter. Each project had different stakeholders, and developed its own independent CI and applications based on the set of elicited requirements, which evolved during the life cycle of the project. We used variations of the same development process in all our projects; thus, we can evaluate the same activities related to maintenance, portability, and security.

In Section 13.4, we analyze the requirements and identify common requirements to all of our CIs, some being generic to any domain and some being specific to the E-Health domain. We also identify differences in the application requirements and quality requirements that have driven the development of each application. Identifying common requirements gives us a good basis to compare the quality of the resulting systems, and it allows us to establish quality in the context of the requirements the application must fulfill. Separating CI requirements from application requirements also allows us to determine that it is feasible to implement one CI to support all applications, which would greatly help with maintenance efforts.

Then, in Section 13.5 we explain our framework for the evaluation and present the activities, the facts, and the impact of facts on the maintenance, portability, and security activities. We also evaluate facts about each E-Health CI and the impact of several architectural and implementation choices on the facts, and consequently on the system quality. Section 13.6 summarizes the lessons learned and outlines decisions we identified that impacted negatively or positively our projects. We also present a summary of the recommendations to improve the quality of future E-Health systems. As an example, we discuss the new DELPHI CI we are currently developing based on these recommendations and how this will be the basis for the generic CI that will support the evolution of our previous applications.

Our main contributions reside in Sections 13.4−13.6 and consist of requirements analysis for E-Health, evaluation framework, applying the framework to three CIs as case studies, and extracting recommendations for further CIs.

13.2 BACKGROUND ON QUALITY ASSURANCE

Software Quality Assurance is a widely researched topic, beginning with fundamental work in the 1970s and with periodic advances in the context of major trends, such as functional programming, object orientation and services and web architectures. In this section, we provide an overview of definitions, models, metrics, processes, and evaluation methods that are relevant for our domain and CIs.

13.2.1 QUALITY DEFINITIONS

Discussions of quality improvement must start with defining what quality means, which is nontrivial because quality is a multidimensional concept (Garvin, 1984) and has both objective and subjective dimensions (Shewhart, 1931). We focus on the two main perspectives on quality: (i) conformance to specification and (ii) customer satisfaction.

In the conformance to specification view, quality is defined in terms of measurable characteristics satisfying a specification. Crosby defines quality as "conformance to requirements," implying that requirements must be clearly stated and "quality problems become nonconformance problems" (Crosby, 1979). Juran defines quality as "fitness for use" (Juran and Gryna, 1970, 1988), referring to both the quality of design (determining requirements and specifications) and quality of conformance to design. In practice, requirements change quite often and they are not articulated as clearly as expected by such early definitions. More recently, ISO 9001 standard (International Organization for Standardization [ISO], 2000) defines quality as "the degree to which a set of inherent characteristics fulfills requirements."

In the customer satisfaction view, quality is defined in terms of meeting customer expectations, explicit or not. For example, Feigenbaum defines quality based upon "the customer's actual experience with the product or service, measured against his or her requirements—stated or unstated, conscious or merely sensed, technically operational or entirely subjective" (Feigenbaum, 1983). Ishikawa further emphasizes that requirements change and, thus, quality is a dynamic concept (Ishikawa, 1985). Deming defines quality as translating "future needs of the user into measurable characteristics" (Deming, 1986).

Our view on quality during the development process is in terms of customer satisfaction. Therefore, all CIs were designed and developed to meet customers' needs, which were mostly about functional requirements with a few specific quality requirements. However, for the purpose of this review, we are interested in evaluating how the architectural and implementation choices taken in these CIs affect the quality requirements relevant for the development and support team with respect to maintainability, operability, reusability and, ultimately, the overall sustainability of these projects.

13.2.2 QUALITY MODELS

Quality models build a hierarchical structure starting from high-level quality perspectives further detailed into a set of factors or intermediate-level characteristics, which are related to a set of quality criteria or primitive characteristics. Taxonomy decomposition and vocabularies differ from model to model. McCall's quality model (McCall et al., 1977) has three perspectives for quality: product revision (ability to undergo changes), product transition (adaptability to new environments), and product operations (its operation characteristics). Boehm's model (Boehm et al., 1976, 1978) has the following high-level characteristics: as-is utility (i.e., how well the system can be used as it is), maintainability (i.e., how easy it is to understand, modify, and retest), and portability (i.e., ability to change the environment). The FURPS (Grady, 1992) model uses the categories: functionality, usability, reliability, performance and supportability. These can be used for functional (F) or nonfunctional (URPS) requirements as well as in quality assessment. Dromey builds the quality model bottom-up (Dromey, 1995) starting from the product characteristics and their relationships to quality attributes. ISO 9126 "Software Product Evaluation: Quality Characteristics and Guidelines for their Use" standard (ISO, 2001) is based on McCall and Boehm models, and it specifies six quality factors: functionality, reliability, efficiency, maintainability, portability, and usability. ISO 25010 (ISO, 2011) is ISO's 9126 successor and adds two new characteristics: security and compatibility.

The idea of quality models is that the quality factors (e.g., maintainability) represent the *external* view of the system and the qualities expected from the system; and its quality criteria (e.g., modularity, self-descriptiveness, and conciseness) describe the *internal* view of the system and represent the basis for defining quality metrics. Therefore, each primitive characteristic contributes to the overall quality level; the values determined by the metrics for the primitive characteristics can be aggregated towards the root of the hierarchy to obtain a quality evaluation for the higher levels. This method is called the Factor-Criteria-Metric (FCM) approach.

These quality models are valuable, but they have some limitations that limit their acceptance in practice, such as: (i) limiting the number of model levels makes it hard to break down quality characteristics to a list that can actually be evaluated by a metric; (ii) variations in vocabulary and the inconsistency in the definitions of quality factors lead to ambiguous application of the models; (iii) the list of properties do not include organizational issues and many other properties that cannot be evaluated automatically; (iv) most models do not include suggestions for how to actually measure the quality characteristics; and (v) aggregating numbers in the hierarchy to produce a value for a high-level complex quality characteristic is a heuristic process with little benefit.

Moreover, as identified in Deissenboeck et al. (2007) most models mix two types of nodes: activities and characteristics. For example, in Boehm's model, modifiability (an activity) is broken down into augmentability (an activity) and structuredness (a characteristic). This mixture leads to semantic ambiguity, problems in evaluating metrics, and in aggregating values. It comes to no surprise that several attempts in the literature to compare quality models side by side differ significantly in their results, confirming the ambiguity of the models. Therefore, in this chapter we will use the model from Deissenboeck et al. (2007), which distinguishes between activities and characteristics (i.e., facts about the situation) as we show in Section 13.5.

13.2.3 METRICS

In general, various measurement scales can be applied for evaluating quality characteristics: (i) nominal scale (i.e., classification); (ii) ordinal scale (i.e., classification into ordered categories with little to no information on the magnitude of the differences between elements) such as the five-point scales; (iii) interval scale (i.e., indicates the exact difference between measurement points, requiring a well-defined unit of measurement for the scale and allowing the mathematical operations of addition and subtraction); and (iv) ratio scale (i.e., an interval scale with a nonarbitrary zero point, allowing all mathematical operations including division and multiplication).

Well-known metrics for assessing maintainability include the number of bugs or defect rate, lines of code, function points, Halstead volume (Halstead, 1977), and McCabe's Cyclomatic Complexity (McCabe, 1976). Some metrics are often combined by using weights, which are determined statistically. More details on metrics can be found in Kan (2002).

Such metrics provide insight into quality aspects of a system, but they are limited by focusing on syntactic aspects that can be measured automatically, whereas many quality aspects are semantic in nature. In general, metrics are neither sufficient not necessary to indicate quality. Furthermore, the variety of languages, frameworks, and tools available make such metrics irrelevant in practice when comparing different systems. Therefore, in this chapter, we focus on evaluating quality by manual inspection of the design and code, and we typically use ordinal scales. While such analysis can be subjective (e.g., depending on the expertise of each reviewer), it covers both syntactic and semantics aspects with more insightful outcomes that can be leveraged for refactoring existing code or developing new systems.

13.2.4 PROCESS MODELS

Process-based approaches to software quality such as the ISO 9001 standard (ISO, 2000) and the Software Engineering Institute's (SEI) Capability Maturity Model (CMM) (Humphrey, 1989; Paulk et al., 1995) and its successor Capability Maturity Model Integration (CMMI) (SEI, 2001a, 2001b) cover the organizational aspects, the overall quality management system for the organization, and the reproducibility of the development process, each of which have direct impact on the quality of the software product. (Note that ISO 9001 is a process standard, whereas ISO 9126 is a product standard). The debate regarding which process standard to use was resolved by declaring that ISO 9001 and CMMI are complementary, and that having ISO 9001 certification can help in achieving the higher maturity levels of CMMI (Dache, 2001). CMMI defines five levels of process maturity and the levels are hierarchical. CMMI provides assessments methods and a road map for the organization to understand its processes and improve quality in successive stages.

However, a quality process does not guarantee quality products, as the relationship between process and product is complex and not well understood. Heavyweight, rigorous processes with junior developers often backfire and are perceived as burdensome. Agile processes can also be perceived as lacking strategic planning that lead to prototypes or immature products. Ultimately, the quality of the generated product depends on the actual team structure, skills, development schedule, requirements, quality criteria, system architecture, and tools used during development, to mention just a few. The quality of the process, people, and technology combined determine the quality of the product.

For the development of our E-Health CIs, we used an iterative development process (detailed in Section 13.3.1) that leverages the spiral model (Boehm, 1988). Such development process applies to software development, whereas quality processes, such as CMMI, deal with the maturity of the organization's processes, regardless of the development process used. In this chapter, we do not focus on the maturity of the process, but on the impact of architectural and implementation choices on CI quality.

13.2.5 ARCHITECTURE EVALUATION FRAMEWORKS

There are a number of architectural evaluation frameworks available, including the Software Engineering Institute's Architecture Tradeoff Analysis Method (ATAM) (Clements et al., 2002) and the Cost Benefit Analysis Method (CBAM) (Kazman et al., 2001, 2002); the Tiny Architectural Review Approach (TARA) (Woods, 2011), the Lightweight Architecture Alternative Assessment Method (LAAAM) (Carriere, 2009), and Scenario-based Peer Reviews (Bachmann, 2011). In the following, we discuss their applicability to this domain.

ATAM is a complex, rigorous process that helps with prioritizing and refining requirements and promotes shared understanding between stakeholders. Its greatest value is in active projects where it clarifies the architectural approaches available and identifies risks and non-risks from the business perspective. However, a significant shortcoming is that in step 4 "Identify architectural approaches" it stops too short and does not consider the details of the design and their associated costs, especially considering the workforce skillset, and turnover rates in academia (e.g., graduating students). Another drawback is that it places too much emphasis on well-developed documentation, adequate architecture and support teams, and on the long-term perspective, which are unfortunately hard to maintain when using agile methods in a fast-moving field such as academic E-Health research. For our use case, the application of this method for the analysis of the existing CIs has little benefits as the risks and non-risks are already known, and the stakeholders already have a running system that meets their needs. The method does not help with identifying winning strategies or technical guidance for future integration projects. We foresee it being valuable during the development of other projects where the application requirements drive significant changes to CI.

CBAM helps with reducing the uncertainty around architectural choices and provides mechanisms to analyze their economic tradeoffs. While increasing the quality and quantity of the communications between stakeholders, it is perceived as subjective, heavy-weight, prone to confirmation bias, and highly impractical in this domain. One of the main drawbacks is the consideration of the quality attributes as "atomic" (i.e., they can be discussed in isolation and can be developed or addressed independently). However, in this domain and other fast-moving research areas, focusing on even just one characteristic (such as performance or security) has drastic impacts on the architecture and technology choices of the project. Furthermore, using an agile approach and then trying to divide the requirements for these quality attributes into pieces manageable within an iteration is very challenging. For our particular use case, the cost-benefits tradeoffs are already known for the developed Cis, and instead we want to synthetize the lessons learned into actionable knowledge for future projects in this field.

Going further, more lightweight approaches (such as LAAAM and TARA) are better suited for both developing quick-turnaround systems and evolving small-to-medium scale architectures. Using domain models to bring shared understanding of key entities and their interactions is very valuable and speeds up the consensus reaching process for requirements elicitation. We have previously described an economic perspective on these approaches (Farcas et al., 2014).

13.2.6 TECHNICAL DEBT

Technical debt is an often overlooked aspect critical for long term software evolution and project sustainability. Decisions on strategic maintenance, infrastructure, or other long term impact choices are not part of a typical agile process, with little valuation given to re-architecting, optimizing, or improving the odds of future sustainability. Instead the emphasis is on customer-facing functional requirements implementation and near-term gains, following a basic YANGNI (you are not going to need it) principle. Scaling such agile practices (Leffingwell, 2007) without consideration for the technical debt can lead to large cost overruns and significant quality issues down the road. This is one of the reasons for our quality evaluation. Given that we know the business case for each project, the architecture of the corresponding CIs, we want to evaluate how the technical choices influenced the associated costs and whether any of the encountered issues can be avoided in the future.

There are a number of approaches for measuring technical debt, such as a simple cost–benefit analysis (Guo et al., 2011; Seaman and Guo, 2011), portfolio management (Markowitz, 1952; Guo and Seaman, 2011) popular within the financial world, and an analytic hierarchical process (Saaty, 1982). The cost–benefit analysis is rather problematic to apply in our case as the projects we detail here span multiple technologies, both at the implementation and deployment levels. Furthermore, these technologies had various maturity levels and were often part of the research agenda. An exploration of the technology portfolio can thus be influenced by both quality attributes (such as performance) and research directions (such as a novel storage strategy).

Refactoring (Fowler et al., 1999) addresses code-level technical debt; yet, the projects we detail here span multiple technologies, both at the implementation and deployment levels. Static code analysis tools designed to detect code smells, spaghetti code, god classes, and cyclomatic complexity are very limited and target mostly Java code. Complex, distributed systems with components leveraging multiple languages or frameworks are simply beyond the capabilities of the vast majority of tools.

Looking at the architectural level, the technical debt is even harder to evaluate, especially for an ongoing project with frequently changing requirements and high developer turnover rates. For instance, some approaches rely on the implementation cost (Ci) and rework cost (Cr) (Nord et al., 2012). While Ci is relatively easy to obtain, the Cr is very difficult to estimate because changing a developer, technology, or deployment option for the same set of requirements leads to widely different numbers. Moreover, the Cr estimation is not driven by *deliberate*, *reckless* actions (Fowler, 2009) such as unskilled labor or poor technology choices. Instead, this factor is primarily driven by funding or research direction constraints inherent in this field. It is also extremely difficult to compare the tradeoffs between each pair of quality attributes in isolation. Therefore, our analysis in Section 13.5 covers a wide range of parameters that ultimately lead to the recommendations and lessons learned from Section 13.6.

13.3 OVERVIEW OF CIs

In this section, we introduce the E-Health CIs designed and implemented in our group, with their goals, external dependencies, and stakeholder roles. We discuss the logical architecture and capabilities supported, identifying the capabilities or challenges unique for each project. Then, we discuss the technical architecture and implementation choices in terms of programming language, integration technologies, and Web frameworks used.

13.3.1 DEVELOPMENT PROCESS

All E-Health CIs in our group evolved continuously through successive iterations that involve activities from requirements elicitation to physical network deployment. We used an iterative, service-oriented development process (Demchak et al., 2007; Farcas et al., 2014) that leverages the spiral (Boehm, 1988) model of agile development methodologies (Boehm and Turner, 2003). During development of our CIs our target objectives were to understand the domain and needs in E-Health and provide a CI with quick turnaround time and minimal cost, while researching/experimenting and evaluating new architectural and technology choices. Typical iterations spanned 2–6 weeks, depending on the stage of the project and stakeholders' goals. At the end of the each iteration, the architecture of the system was refined according to new insight into the user or system requirements discovered during that iteration.

Our process has three phases that repeat in a cyclical fashion: service elicitation, logical architecture, and system architecture definition. Each phase is further divided into stages that can also be iterated for incremental refinement. In the service elicitation phase, we identify requirements, express them as use cases (Cockburn, 2000), identify crosscutting concerns, construct a domain model of the system, and identify service roles and interaction patterns. In the logical architecture phase, we create the logical decomposition of the system into RS. The system architecture definition focuses on the actual implementation aspects, network analysis, and physical deployment.

Our perspective of quality has been customer satisfaction while meeting timeline and budget constraints. Therefore, we used the perspective from value-based software engineering (Boehm, 2006; Boehm and Jain, 2006) to integrate value considerations within the software engineering activities. Our value-based development process (Farcas et al., 2014) emphasizes stakeholders' involvement and negotiating requirements to arrive at mutually satisfactory agreements regarding what the exact requirements are and which are their values. Another part of requirements negotiation is to establish priorities based on value and cost in order to address the conflict between a long wish list for requirements and a reduced set of resources available for implementation. The cost evaluation comes from the choice implementation.

This process has worked well to produce successful systems for the goals of the projects. Most requirements from our users have been functional requirements, with quality requirements focusing in the area of security, usability, and reliability. However, developer concerns (such as maintainability) received less priority due to accelerated delivery schedules and lack of development resources. When evaluating the cost of a choice design or implementation, the cost did not include the maintenance cost to support the system long term because funds could not be allocated past the awarded project period—contingency plans for retaining the initial workforce remain an unending battle in the academia.

13.3.2 PALMS

PALMS (Demchak et al., 2012; Demchak and Krüger, 2012) merges data from physical activity sensors (e.g., accelerometers and heart rate monitors) with GPS data to construct a detailed picture of a participant's day: travel patterns, locations, durations, and levels of physical activity and sedentary periods. PALMS supports the research of a worldwide community of exposure biologists who study human health as a function of geographical location and ambient conditions. Thus, PALMS employs a number of principle investigators, each defining distinct studies involving study participants, data collection, and analysis. Each study is unique as to content, funding agency requirements, and personnel organization.

13.3.2.1 Architecture

The PALMS CI follows the Rich Service architectural pattern. In particular, it exposes different sets of services for authorization and authentication, data repository access, data processing, study configuration, and CI configuration. The CI uses an Enterprise Service Bus (ESB) architecture where all services are accessed using standardized XML messages. The front end UI of PALMS runs in the web browser as a JavaScript application leveraging the Google Web Toolkit (GWT) technology. It communicates with a Tomcat web server using an internal RPC protocol defined by GWT. The web server transforms the UI requests into CI requests via a standard SOAP web service interface exposed by PALMS' CI. These requests are then converted into XML messages and sent to the proper services in the CI. Each service request is authenticated, and a policy engine is used to enforce policies defined by study researchers. The PALMS system is essentially a batch processing system. It supports uploading data in batches

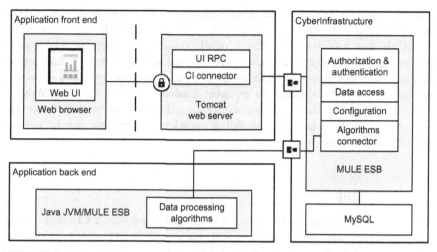

FIGURE 13.3

PALMS overview.

from the web UI. Each data element is then processed using study-defined algorithms that run in the Java Virtual Machine (JVM) and connect to the rest of the CI using a service interface. All data is persisted in a relational MySQL database.

Services in the CI use the following pattern, where each service has three parts: (i) one interface that defines methods to call; (ii) a proxy that implements the interface, converts each service request to a standard XML message, and dispatches the message using the MULE ESB; (iii) the actual implementation of the service as another Java class. The ESB infrastructure processes the XML messages generated by the proxy (ii) and calls methods defined by the implementation class (iii) as specified in a configuration file. This approach has several benefits. For example, all requests can easily be redirected to remote machines, and additional services can be injected and manipulate all service requests—we use this ability to enforce policies. The price to pay is more complexity in debugging the code and having to write more classes for each service (Figure 13.3).

13.3.2.2 Implementation

The front end is a web interface. We developed it using GWT, a Java-based framework that compiles Java code to JavaScript that executes natively inside web browsers. The main benefit is that this approach enables programmers to share some code with the back end (also written in Java) and enables us to use just one language for developing all parts of PALMS, thus limiting the need of having developers with different skills. To simplify the front end development, we decided to connect the Web UI to the web server using the RPC protocol supported natively by GWT and to translate these requests in service requests to the CI using SOAP. The CI uses MULE, a Java based ESB. The version 1.4 of MULE that was available during development has limitations that lead to developing very verbose code. Newer MULE versions improve on this aspect but require extensive changes of older code. A set of repository services encapsulate all data access—they abstract the concrete database used, in this case MySQL. The use of these services enables data access and storage to be treated like any other service of the platform, supporting complex policies that can be defined on each data element.

13.3.3 CYCORE

CYCORE (Patrick et al., 2011; Peterson et al., 2013) provides a CI for collection and analysis of home-based physiological, behavioral, social, and environmental data from patients undergoing cancer treatment. Previously, these essential data have been largely either unmeasured or self-reported. Thus, CYCORE revolutionizes clinical trials in cancer research by allowing new data sources to be captured and integrated. The CI provides data about symptoms, quality of life, performance status, and physiological parameters that signal how well participants are doing with their treatment and provide key information for cancer prevention and control research.

The suite of wireless devices that send data to a sensor hub include weight scales, blood pressure monitors, heart rate monitors, accelerometers (which measure the number of walking and running steps), carbon monoxide monitors, and global positioning systems (GPS). Video and self-report data from a questionnaire/response application are delivered via smartphone.

13.3.3.1 Architecture

CYCORE's CI uses the RS architectural pattern to separate application services from infrastructure services. The CI is a message-based system and uses a Router/Transformer component to inject behavior. The RS pattern is hierarchical; however, in CYCORE CI it has a flat structure with services such as Data Ingestion, Data Preservation, and Algorithms placed at the same level. These services are further decomposed, but their decomposition does not follow the same RS pattern with a message-based infrastructure inside them. This means that policy is injected when data is transferred between RS, but does not apply to what happens inside a service.

The CI supports user roles such as patients, researchers, clinicians, policy makers, sensor operators, and cyber operators. The CI provides role-based access and tailors different views for each role. The policy model is simple, as all users with the same role have the same rights.

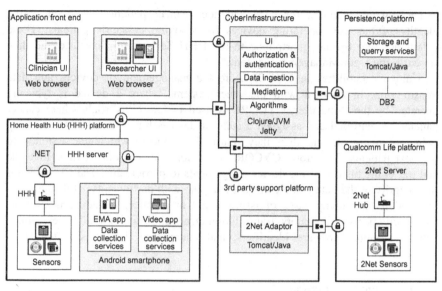

FIGURE 13.4

CYCORE overview.

Acquisition Servers and Data Preservation are components separate from the CI, with well-defined interfaces between them, but volatility of requirements also affects these interfaces (Figure 13.4).

CYCORE has several data acquisition servers. First, we had one team specialized in hardware devices that built a sensor hub, called Home Health Hub (HHH). The HHH is the physical device that aggregates sensor data collected by the patient and relays these to the HHH Server over an available Internet connection—the HHH Server subsequently notifies the CI of new data events. Second, CYCORE integrated the 2net platform from Qualcomm Life, where we do not have control on the hub communication, but we receive notifications directly from 2net servers. We used the *Adaptor pattern* to build a 2net Adaptor that deals with the specific 2net communication and relays data to CI in the same format as HHH Server. Third, CYCORE integrated external systems developed at MDACC for patient surveys on smartphones, called Ecological Momentary Assessments (EMA). The HHH server provides an interface for ingesting bulk data. We used this interface for receiving EMA data from the smartphone app and the related configuration information from the EMA Web manager, thereby avoiding creating another acquisition server or adapter at ingestion site. However, the adapter had to be implemented in the Data Preservation system to make sense of the EMA semantics and convert EMA data into the data model used in CYCORE. Fourth, we developed a smartphone app to record videos of participants, which were required to monitor adherence to swallowing exercises for head and neck cancer patients, or to check the identity of the user operating devices for smoking cessation patients. These videos are sent by the smartphone to the HHH Server bulk interface and then stored in the Data Management system.

Unique capabilities in CYCORE are the management of devices and data transmission. In contrast with the other systems where a device is typically operated by the same user, CYCORE is used in feasibility trials where cancer patients are enrolled and assigned a suite of devices for a period of time during radiation treatment, and then they return the devices, which are assigned to the next patients. Therefore, CYCORE transitions devices during their lifecycle and tracks the history of the device assignments to participants. The CI maintains the integrity of the data and the correct mapping with participants, while appropriately addressing many cases of issues found in practice, including user errors from participants or operators, transmission errors and caching on devices, simple sensors without hardware identifiers, and unexpected data outside the study protocol.

13.3.3.2 Implementation

Due to the distribution of the responsibilities in the team and reusing already-available components in each team, CYCORE used several programming languages and technologies. HHH Server is developed in .NET, whereas the 2net Adapter is a Java servlet.

The CI is implemented in Rich Hickey's Clojure, which is a functional language executed on top of the JVM. Clojure provides us with the benefits of built-in lock-free concurrency support, high-performance immutable data structures, late-binding capabilities, and excellent Java interoperability. The web server is based on Clojure web framework Compojure and web application library Ring. The UI is developed using HTML, CSS, and Javascript.

The CYCORE data architecture employs a 2-tier approach where a MongoDB implementation is used for kinetic data, along with a relational data model for the persistence layer. The Data Preservation system implements the persistent layer using Java classes mapped to tables in IBM's DB2 relational database.

The communication between all components is based on web service REST APIs and uses HTTPS to ensure encrypted transmission. Standard XML/JSON serialization/deserialization techniques are used for processing inputs and outputs. The Data Management system provides REST web services for CRUD operations on persistent classes, as well as services for supporting complex queries based on application requirements.

13.3.4 CITISENSE

CitiSense (Nikzad et al., 2011, 2012) uses sensors placed in the environment and carried by users to collect data about city pollution (such as ozone and carbon monoxide) along with mobile phones to send the collected data to the back end infrastructure, which stores the data and serves it to the outside world. CitiSense uses the data to provide real-time feedback to users and allows them to make healthier choices about where they live, work, and play. The data can also be shared within the CI for further processing and modeling, helping other stakeholders better understand how diseases such as asthma develop and coordinate efforts within a user's community to improve conditions.

A substantial difference between this project and the other discussed above is that in this case we developed our own hardware sensors. The air pollution sensors developed in this project use Bluetooth to connect to Android smartphones that collect the measurements and relay them to the back end system for storage and processing. The sensors and mobile application work together to minimize the power consumption of the mobile platform, thus making CitiSense a viable technology.

13.3.4.1 Architecture

CitiSense CI encompasses (i) the back end that supports data acquisition and processing, (ii) a web front end used by researchers to analyze the data collected, (iii) a mobile phone app that collects data and provides real time information on air quality to users, and (iv) machine learning algorithms to infer general pollution information from the data captured (Figure 13.5).

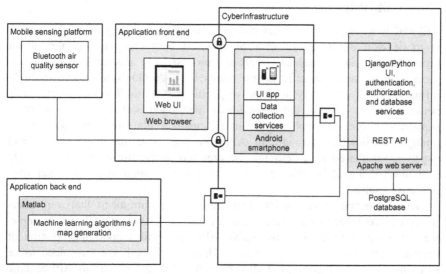

FIGURE 13.5

CitiSense overview.

In this project, we developed a set of core services following the Rich Service architectural pattern in the phone application. Services are there to (i) receive the data from the Bluetooth sensor, (ii) store them locally, (iii) run some local processing, and (iv) upload them in batches to the back end system. The back end is implemented using Django, a Python-based platform, running under the Apache web server. The storage relies on a PostgreSQL database. The benefit of using this COTS platform is that much of the standard services to store and browse data via a web interface are already in place. Additional services where developed and made accessible to both the phone and Matlab data analysis algorithms by means of standard REST calls. Each night, a separate Matlab module runs complex computations on all data collected.

13.3.4.2 Implementation

In developing CitiSense, we selected different languages and platforms for each component. This choice contrasts with the approach in PALMS, where everything was written in Java. The rationale was to minimize the development of new components, and reuse platforms and libraries that were available for specific services (e.g., UI, data processing), at the cost of needing programmers with different skill sets and minimizing reuse of code between the different parts of the system. The code for the Bluetooth sensor platform was written in C; Java was used for the mobile Android application; the code on the web server was written in Python; JavaScript drives the UI in the web browser; lastly, the algorithms that analyze all data collected and generate air quality maps run in Matlab.

13.3.5 DELPHI

DELPHI is an ambitious project currently in progress. The goal of the project is to develop an advanced data platform to help clinicians, public health professionals, and researchers collect and process large amount of data and use them to both target specific health issues for individuals that have multiple influences, and, ultimately, to improve population health. The major difference between this project and those previously mentioned is that the goal is not to support one specific application, but to create a platform that can support multiple applications through an API. We are using the requirements and experience gathered in developing the previous applications and CIs to create a platform that will be able to support all previous applications together with new case studies.

To achieve the vision for DELPHI, all quality requirements that were afterthought in the other projects become a key element of the new CI. For example, we will need to have clear and stable APIs that will support the creation of diverse applications by multiple teams. Thus, the CI will not only need to be extensible and maintainable, but also the usability of the CI and its API become an important factor in defining requirements. Moreover, because we envision multiple projects and applications using the same CI, we need to ensure proper performance and reliability characteristics. Therefore, in defining the architecture and the implementation technologies for DELPHI, we are leveraging the results of the research presented in this chapter.

13.3.6 IDASH

The NIH National Center for Biomedical Computing—integrating Data for Analysis, Anonymization, and Sharing (iDASH) (Ohno-Machado et al., 2012) is completely different from all the projects above. It acts as an umbrella across multiple scientific projects in areas as diverse as Medical Imaging, Natural Language Processing, Privacy, and Genomics. As such, it targets a much broader community with a wider range of stakeholders. Its main purpose is to facilitate collaboration in the biomedical field through data, tools, and algorithms sharing, while addressing the privacy and security aspects related to human subjects data. At the organizational level, it provides an excellent model for DELPHI regarding future collaborations and community engagement.

13.3.6.1 Architecture

Relevant for the CIs discussed above is the iDASH Compute & storage eLastic On-demand, User-friendly Data analysis environment (CLOUD). Implemented at the IaaS level, this environment leverages mature commercial solutions with enhancements and customizations to achieve HIPAA compliance and support the security and privacy of research on human data. Multiple iDASH projects are already hosted in this environment. We plan to move all the above CIs into the iDASH CLOUD.

Furthermore, iDASH implemented the Safe HIPAA-compliant Annotated Data Deposit box (SHADE), a domain-independent repository of data with role-based access control and two-factor authentication for researchers to share their data. A legal framework based on Data Use Agreements between the institutions exchanging data (along with the necessary IRB approvals) safeguards the privacy of the data deposited in this repository.

Both CLOUD and SHADE provide service interfaces to integrate with other systems. Yet, the mix of technologies involved does not conform to a single architectural pattern.

13.3.6.2 Implementation

The iDASH CLOUD uses industry proven VMware vCloud software customized for the E-Health domain and our particular implementation. The SHADE repository uses open-source MIDAS software with enhancements for two-factor authentication and stronger security. Leveraging their REST APIs, additional tools were developed for both these platforms to enable researchers to record scientific workflows as recipes, share, and reuse them with other data.

13.4 REQUIREMENTS

In this section, we take a closer look at the requirements of each E-Health CI developed in our group. We reviewed the documentation available in terms of requirements documents, use case descriptions, domain models, development tasks from the management tracking system, and code documentation. All of this documentation was created incrementally during the iterative development process for each CI.

Comparing requirements between projects was difficult because of (i) different terminologies; (ii) different granularity; and (iii) a different mix of application and infrastructure requirements. A first step when reviewing requirements was to understand the vocabulary of each project and to bring requirements into a common terminology. Glossaries and domain models have helped in clarifying the language of each system. However, the level of detail varied from one requirement to another even inside the same project. In fact, we followed an agile process. Many requirements were elicited during the process, but only a subset was detailed and implemented in each iteration, leaving aside a "wish list" for refinement in the future. Thus, for the purpose of this chapter, we selected key high-level user requirements that exemplify the main usage scenarios for the system. Also for reasons of brevity, we sometimes combine several requirements in the same line, when in fact they could be broken down into several sub-items.

The last step of the analysis was to separate requirements into infrastructure and application concerns. Because each had a separate funding source, development team, and development lifecycle, all of these CI projects have been designed from scratch without prior assumptions or knowledge about what CI services were needed for E-Health. Requirements gathering and engineering followed an iterative process carried out independently during the implementation phase for each project. Therefore, the resulting CIs were tailored to the specific application domain. At this point, we ask the question: *what is needed to create a common CI to support all of these applications*? To answer this question, we identified overlapping requirements and separated them into four categories:

1. generic CI requirements, which are not related to a specific application
2. E-Health CI requirements, which are still infrastructure concerns, but they are tailored to E-Health needs
3. common requirements across applications, which are more specific than CI requirements because they relate to application management concerns
4. specific requirements for each application (e.g., data visualization).

In Section 13.5.2, we refer to these requirements through their ID with regard to the impact of their implementation choice on the quality of the system.

13.4.1 CI REQUIREMENTS

In the following, we present the infrastructure requirements, some of them are generic enough to be present in other domains, and some are specific to the E-Health domain.

The projects we analyzed have several common needs expressed by the set of generic CI requirements from Table 13.1. These include the importing, processing, and exporting of multiple types of data subject to various access policies. Looking at other application domains, a CI implementing these requirements has great potential for reuse. At the same time, details such as the data formats and metadata elements remain application specific.

Table 13.1 Generic CI Requirements

ID	Requirement	PALMS	CYCORE	CitiSense	DELPHI
I01	The CI shall support ingestion of data from multiple sources, such as physical devices, external systems, as well as processes (algorithms)	H	H	H	H
I02	End-to-end data integrity from devices to storage shall be guaranteed	–	H	H	H
I03	The CI shall support the storage of both raw and derived data	H	H	H	H
I04	Messages within the CI, and between CI and connected services shall be time-stamped	H	H	H	H
I05	Data archived should be easily recoverable	H	H	H	H
I06	Exporting data to external formats (e.g., CSV files) shall be supported	H	H	L	H
I07	Creation and modification of metadata (e.g., video comments) shall be supported	–	H	–	M
I08	The association of metadata with resources shall be supported	H	H	L	H
I09	The CI shall support email alerts when an event is triggered or to notify researchers when batch processing is completed	H	H	L	L
I10	The execution of processes across the network shall be supported	M	M	–	H
I11	The CI shall enforce role-based access to data. The system shall provide or refuse access to capabilities depending on the identity authorizations	H	H	H	H
I12	The integration of external data analysis and visualization tools shall be supported (e.g., plugins and/or standardized inputs/ outputs)	–	L	H	H

Table 13.2 E-Health CI Requirements

ID	Requirement	PALMS	CYCORE	CitiSense	DELPHI
H01	Participant data shall be transmitted and stored securely	H	H	M	H
H02	All resources shall have an identity	H	H	H	H
H03	All data shall be archived according to policy	H	H	H	H
H04	Current and historical status information for all resources shall be provided (e.g., history of device assignments to participants)	–	M	–	M
H05	The CI shall support ingestion of algorithms that run on the incoming data stream to filter data or to detect events (e.g., dehydration events)	H	H	H	H
H06	Capabilities to track data access, subject to policy, shall be provided	L	H	–	H
H07	An interface to define policy shall be provided (e.g., via XML)	M	L	H	H
H08	The CI shall support basic device registration and lifecycle and association of devices to studies	H	H	H	H

The requirements in Table 13.1, as well as all tables in Section 13.4, use the following notations:

- Stakeholder value priority for a requirement is listed as high (H), medium (M), low (L), or not applicable (–) for each project. This represents the agreed upon value of a requirement for all stakeholders after negotiating different perspectives on value propositions as needed. The value priorities were updated from one iteration to another; hence, the tables reflect the status at the end of each project.
- Implemented requirements are marked with a dark background. The implementation priority was determined based upon both the value priority and cost in resources and time. Because the DELPHI project is currently under development, the table does not indicate which requirements have been implemented so far.

Table 13.2 shows CI requirements that emerge from specific privacy and security requirements in E-Health.

13.4.2 APPLICATION REQUIREMENTS

In the following, we present the application requirements, which are more specific than CI requirements because they relate to application management concerns, which could be similar across applications or very different from one system to another.

Table 13.3 Common Requirements Across E-Health Applications

ID	Requirement	PALMS	CYCORE	CitiSense	DELPHI
Study Management					
C01	Management of studies by researchers (create, edit, list) and enrolling participants in a study shall be supported, subject to access permissions	H	H	H	M
C02	A study shall be associated with a set of researchers or other domain specialists	H	H	M	M
C03	The system shall allow researchers to access only the studies to which they are given access	H	H	M	M
C04	The CI shall allow researchers to select the sensor types used in the study	H	H	L	H
Data Visualization					
C05	Data visualization shall support tabular view and graphs, and aggregated view per device or per participant	H	H	H	M
C06	Data visualization shall allow for specifying date ranges and value filtering criteria (filter values above or below a threshold)	H	M	M	M
C07	The system shall visualize location data on a map	H	–	H	M
Device Management					
C08	A web interface for participants/researchers to manually upload data files from devices shall be supported. Also batch upload shall be supported	H	L	L	M
C09	The system shall support data acquisition from sensors via a Hub or smartphone	L	H	H	M
C10	The system shall support video acquisition via a smartphone app	–	H	–	M
C11	The system shall support participant input of self-reported data via an assessment app for smartphone	L	H	L	M

As the projects are in the same E-Health domain, Table 13.3 reveals shared requirements revolving around domain-specific concepts, such as studies, researchers, and visualization options. Note that each application might have different implementation of these requirements that best fits the technology stack used by the project.

What ultimately distinguishes the projects are the application-specific requirements. In Table 13.4, we provide a snippet of such requirements that apply specifically to one or more projects. For instance, the concept of clinicians and the associated requirements are specific to the CYCORE project, whereas the notion of location data applies to all projects to various degrees.

Table 13.4 Application-Specific Requirements

ID	Requirement	PALMS	CYCORE	CitiSense	DELPHI
Data Visualization and Access					
A01	Collaborative resource use for multiple studies shall be supported (e.g., a sensor can be shared between studies, but is used only by one participant in one study at a time)	–	H	H	–
A02	For video data, the system shall display only metadata information. Only a subset of researchers (with video assistant role) shall be authorized to view videos	–	H	–	–
A03	The system shall allow researchers to assign clinicians (physician, nurse, etc.) to participants	–	H	–	–
A04	The system shall allow clinicians to access only data from their patients	–	H	–	–
	The system shall provide a clinician view customized for each study to display only the data expected per the study protocol. The view should allow for easily recognition of trends	–	H	–	–
A05	The system shall provide a feature to mark that data has been reviewed for the current day	–	H	–	–
Data Analysis/Algorithms					
A06	The system shall filter aberrant data as defined by the user	H	H	L	–
A07	The system shall support a web interface to customize the built-in algorithms for the query criteria and algorithm parameters	H	M	–	–
A08	The web interface shall allow researchers to define processing workflows on data and the actions to be taken when an event is triggered	L	M	–	–
A09	Algorithms shall be provided to correlate location data with sensor data and/or symptoms	H	M	H	–
A10	A web interface for uploading of external data (e.g., from medical records) shall be supported	H	L	–	–
Device Management					
A11	A UI to monitor activity and status of each device shall be provided (to identify transmission problems vs. missing data)	–	H	M	
A12	The system shall manage the lifecycle of devices (sensors, hubs, phones) from registration until decommissioning. The assignment of available devices to participants shall be supported	M	H	M	
A13	The system shall allow defining the study period for each participant; the system shall filter out data collected by any device outside of the study time period	–	M	–	–

Table 13.5 Quality Requirements

ID	Requirement	PALMS	CYCORE	CitiSense	DELPHI
CyberInfrastructure					
Q01	Functional suitability	H	H	H	H
Q02	Security	H	H	H	H
Q03	Reliability	L	M	L	H
Q04	Usability	L	L	L	H
Q05	Performance efficiency	L	M	H	H
Q06	Maintainability	H	M	H	H
Q07	Portability	L	L	L	H
Q08	Compatibility	H	L	L	H
Q09	Extensibility	H	L	L	H
Applications					
Q10	Functional suitability	H	H	H	–
Q11	Security	H	H	H	–
Q12	Reliability	H	H	M	–
Q13	Usability	H	H	H	–
Q14	Performance efficiency	L	M	L	–
Q15	Maintainability	L	M	M	–
Q16	Portability	L	L	L	–
Q17	Compatibility	L	M	L	–
Q18	Extensibility	L	H	L	–

13.4.3 QUALITY REQUIREMENTS

In Table 13.5, we present an overview of the quality requirements for these projects, as prioritized during the project development when most articulated customers' needs addressed functional requirements. Customers also identified a few specific quality requirements typical for E-Health, such as usability and security. In particular, maintainability, portability, and extensibility were rather low priority, and became more important in the next generation of each project.

We separate requirements for the CI and for application, and we use the list of quality factors from the ISO 25010 standard (ISO, 2011): functional suitability, security, reliability, usability, performance efficiency, maintainability, portability, and compatibility. Extensibility is covered under maintainability, but we list it separately as it is particularly relevant for sustainability. The functional suitability characteristic refers to the appropriateness, correctness, and completeness of the functions of the software, and thus, we list it in the table although we have already discussed functional requirements in previous sections.

We do not mark which requirements have been implemented as we did in the prior three tables for functional requirements because the evaluation for quality requirements is more complex and cannot be expressed as either implemented or not. As the purpose of this chapter is to evaluate sustainability with its maintainability and portability aspects, the details of the analysis can be found in Section 13.5.2.

The distinction of requirements between CI and application leads to several interesting observations. For example, the usability of the actual CI in terms on how to monitor and reconfigure it has been considered low priority, whereas the usability of the application has always been a high priority for customers. Furthermore, reliability at the level of the application refers to maintaining the integrity of the data and not losing any data from sensors to storage, whereas the reliability of the CI refers more to availability and limited down-time. Given the limited budget available, there has been little investment in a reliable infrastructure for these CIs; yet, iDASH will provide the stable infrastructure for our CIs in the future.

13.5 QUALITY EVALUATION

In this section, we evaluate how each project achieves quality attributes of maintainability and portability. We discuss rationale and tradeoffs, and propose a strategy for the next generation of CIs.

13.5.1 EVALUATION METHODOLOGY

The approach to evaluate our CIs is based on the two-dimensional quality model from Deissenboeck et al. (2007), which maps facts about a development situation to maintenance activities. Therefore, in our review process we follow these steps, detailed further in this section:

1. Define activities that we want to evaluate.
2. Define facts about the system and organization that affect these activities. The facts are tuples of entities and attributes described in the format: Entity | ATTRIBUTE.
3. Define the impact of facts on activities. We depict this in a quality matrix, where we link atomic facts with atomic activities. We indicate the impact as positive (+) or negative (−) in the cells. Steps 1−3 are generic.
4. Identify a set of architectural or implementation choices for each project and evaluate how these choices increase (↑) or decrease (↓) each fact metric for that project. Based on the impact of that fact on quality (step 3), we also determine if this choice and this fact have a positive or negative impact on overall quality.

5. Evaluate facts overall for each project, using High, Medium, and Low, and determine if this fact has a positive or negative impact on overall quality.

Steps 4−5 are specific to our projects. Most of these fact assessments cannot be automated and the evaluation is subjective to some degree. Our evaluation was done in a group review with system architects based on analyzing documentation about requirements, architecture, code, and issue tracking/bug reports and from inspecting and running the actual code. The tables reflect the values after we reached consensus.

6. Based on the facts evaluation, we identify successful architectural and implementation choices.

13.5.1.1 Activities

Starting with the definitions from ISO 25010 (ISO, 2011) standard presented in Section 13.2, we identify the main activities involved in maintenance: analysis, modification, testing, and reuse. System modularity is a fact and not an activity, so we discuss it in Section 13.5.1.2. We ensure the high quality of our systems by testing thoroughly at different levels. As E-Health CIs are typically distributed systems-of-systems, one of the most complex activities in which we are interested is integration testing, where we test how the different parts developed by different teams work together. Thus, we list integration testing as an activity, and we evaluate as facts the coverage of unit test and the existence of debugging tools.

The main activities involved in portability are installation, configuration, and replacing one component with another. To evaluate adaptability, we define as facts the complexity of machine configuration and software configuration, and the degree the code depends on the machine.

For security, the activities we consider are end-to-end data tracing and security configuration for access control. Tracing data end-to-end from the source to the consumers is very important in our domain because data go across multiple systems and networks. For security audits and debugging of issues where users cannot access data, we must be able to trace every step on the pathway. We do not cover details related to authentication, but we include a series of facts related to authorization in the following section.

Finally, we also evaluate a separate activity for scaling up, which involves aspects from maintainability, portability, and security all together. While our CIs initially support small groups of users, as time goes by more participants are enrolled and more research studies are launched, thus requiring the CI to scale up to support this new workload. Key technological and architectural choices influence how well such CIs can scale.

Therefore, the list of high-level activities evaluated in our review is the following:

- Analysis: code understanding, debugging, identification of elements to modify, impact analysis for a proposed modification
- Modification: changing existing code
- Integration testing: integrating subsystems and testing their aggregate end-to-end

- Reuse: applying the system to a different application/set of requirements
- Installation and configuration: initial installation and further upgrades to the operating system, software, or library versions—includes software configuration and machine configuration
- Replacing: substituting one component with another
- End-to-end tracing of data acquisition/access: showing flow of data through the system, with all actions logged and all entities identified
- Access control configuration: security management at the machine level such as setting up firewalls and SSL certificates
- Scaling up: accepting greater loads due to more end users or more data for each user.

Each activity can be further decomposed, and each subactivity can be evaluated separately. A lower granularity is especially useful when different teams are involved in subactivities. It is important to see how the system quality affects their work. We focus on high-level activities as our goal is to evaluate different architectural and implementation choices and how they impact overall quality.

13.5.1.2 Facts

- From the requirements and context for our E-Health CIs, we selected the following facts that impact the quality attributes:
  - Organization
    - Stakeholder I DIVERSITY—number of different scientific fields of the stakeholders
    - User I BUY IN—acceptance of the system's capabilities
    - Requirements I VOLATILITY—how often requirements change
    - Schedule I CONSTRAINED—external pressure for features in a tight schedule
    - Iteration I FREQUENCY—the cycling rate of spiral development process
    - Funding I SUFFICIENCY—the degree to which the funding resources are appropriate for realizing the system
    - Team I DISTRIBUTION—such as decoupling efforts for various system entities
    - Developer I CONFORMANCE—conformance to architecture and guidelines when implementing
    - Developer I TURNOVER—rate of changing developers because of skill, funding, or other reason.
  - System
    - Architecture
      - Communication between UI and CI I EFFICIENCY—overhead imposed by the chosen technology stack to CI–UI interaction
      - Services exposed by CI to UI I GRANULARITY—how granular are the services exposed by the CI that the UI uses. High granularity

represents many fine-grained services while low granularity indicates fewer coarse-grain services

- Services internal to CI | GRANULARITY—similarly this represents the set of services that can be called by other services inside the CI
- System | MODULARITY—degree to which the system is decomposed into logical/functional constituents
- Logging | INTEGRATION—if logs are integrated between components to show one system view on the status of all components
- Policy model | COMPLEXITY—amount of work necessary to express a policy using the model
- Policy enforcement | GRANULARITY—the level of policy enforcement points. High granularity policy enforcement enables policies to be evaluated between any service call or data access in the system. Low granularity enforcement can usually enforce policies only between subsystems calls
- Data transfer | EFFICIENCY—how efficient is to transfer data from one entity to another (affected by marshaling/unmarshaling, policy checks, etc.).
- Implementation
  - Bugs | FREQUENCY—how often bugs occurred during the operation of the system
  - Code | SELF-DESCRIPTIVENESS—how easy is it to understand the code for an inspector that did not author the code
  - Code generation | COVERAGE—how much code is generated compared to manually written
  - Entity | VERBOSITY—in respect to number of classes or other entities (depending on programming language)
  - Data access | SPEED—how fast are queries processed between UI to the DB
  - Unit test | COVERAGE.
- Documentation
  - Documentation | COMPLETNESS—the coverage of the documentation
  - Documentation | UPDATED—how recent the documentation is.
- Infrastructure
  - Technology | MATURITY—years on the market, number of entities/ groups using the technology in real-world applications
  - Software configuration | COMPLEXITY—how difficult is it to configure all tools needed by the system
  - Debugging tools | EXISTENCE—the availability of tools for debugging the system for each component/language
  - Machine security | INTEGRITY—protection from unauthorized access to machines

- Machine configuration | COMPLEXITY—how difficult is it to configure the machines that host the system in regard to firewalls rules, ports allowed for communication, VPN restrictions for login, etc.
- Machine | DEPENDENCE—if the code depends on the machine setup.

Most of these facts require manual review and cannot be automated by tools.

13.5.1.3 Impact matrix

In this section, we present the impact that entity/attribute pairs have on the different activities we perform during the life cycle of E-Health systems. In Section 13.5.2, we further use this impact analysis to evaluate the impact that the different pairs have on the quality of each of our applications.

Table 13.6 has two columns containing entities and attributes identified in Section 13.5.1.2, followed by separate columns for the activities identified in Section 13.5.1.1.The impact is defined as negative (−), positive (+), or neutral (empty cell). The impact is identified depending on the attribute evaluation as high. For example, a high system modularity has a positive impact on most activities, except integration testing because more modules imply more effort spent on integration testing to make sure changes in one do not affect others.

The last column "Total Quality Impact" summarizes the total impact of each entity/attribute pair on the overall software quality by averaging the impact on all activities. As we use a three-point scale, the Total Quality Impact reflects how the majority of the activities under analysis are influenced when the attribute for the given entity evaluates to high. We use this parameter in our evaluation of the choices in the various projects. We do not analyze organizational factors in our comparative analysis of the different CIs quality because all projects had similar organizational constraints.

13.5.2 EVALUATION

Our goal in this section is to identify technological and architectural choices that improve quality attributes when the software development follows the agile process outlined in Section 13.3.1 and the project is subject to the typical constraints of the health sciences domain in academia. We evaluate the facts we collected for each project and try to identify key architectural and implementation choices that affected the attributes. We believe this exercise has a general validity and helps in improving the software quality of future projects in a given domain.

Organizational factors have a great impact on the quality of software applications being developed. However, we do not focus on these factors in our analysis, because the different projects followed a similar development process and had many similar organizational constraints, including diverse stakeholders, volatile requirements, high customer involvement and buy in, tight schedules, frequent iterations, limited funding and availability of developers, and high turnover once students graduated. One difference worth noting here is that CYCORE

Table 13.6 Influence of High Entity Attributes for Typical Activities of Software Development and Maintenance in E-Health Applications

Entity	Attribute	Analysis	Modification	Integration Testing	Reusing in New Applications	Installation and Configuration	Replacing Components	End-to-End Tracing	Access Control	Scaling-up	Total Quality Impact
Organization											
Stakeholder	DIVERSITY	-			-				-	+	-
User	BUY IN	-			+				+	-	+
Requirements	VOLATILITY		+	-					-		-
Schedule	CONSTRAINED					-			-		-
Iteration	FREQUENCY		+	+	-	-			+	+	+
Funding	SUFFICIENCY			-	+						+
Team	DISTRIBUTION										-
Developer	CONFORMANCE	+	+	+	+	-	+		+		+
Developer	TURNOVER	-	-	-		-	-		-		-
Architecture											
Communication between UI and CI	EFFICIENCY	+	+	+	-		-		-	+	+
Services exposed by CI to UI	GRANULARITY	+	+	-	+		+	-		-	-
Services internal to CI	GRANULARITY	+	+	-	+		+	+	+	+	+
System	MODULARITY	-	-	+		+	-	+	-		+
Logging	INTEGRATION			+				+	+		+
Policy model	COMPLEXITY		-								-
Policy enforcement	GRANULARITY	-	+					+	+		+
Data transfer	EFFICIENCY							+		+	+

(Continued)

Table 13.6 Influence of High Entity Attributes for Typical Activities of Software Development and Maintenance in E-Health Applications *Continued*

Entity	Attribute	Analysis	Modification	Integration Testing	Reusing in New Applications	Installation and Configuration	Replacing Components	End-to-End Tracing	Access Control	Scaling-up	Total Quality Impact
Implementation											
Bugs	FREQUENCY	−	−	−	−				−		−
Code	SELF-DESCRIPTIVENESS	+	+		+						+
Code generation	COVERAGE		+		+		+				+
Entity	VERBOSITY	−	−								−
Data access	SPEED										+
Unit test	COVERAGE		+	+	+					+	+
Infrastructure											
Technology	MATURITY		+		+					+	+
Software configuration	COMPLEXITY		+	−	−	+	−				−
Debugging tools	EXISTENCE	+	+	+	+		+	+			+
Machine security	INTEGRITY								+		+
Machine configuration	COMPLEXITY				−	−	−		−		−
Machine	DEPENDENCE				−		−			−	−

The last column evaluates the effects on the overall system quality.

is a multi-institution project where users come from different oncology domains and the developer team is distributed, making collaboration and integration more challenging.

An interesting result of our analysis is that the RS architecture—and indeed many software architectures—suffer from the potential for *architectural mismatch;* not so much at the component level, but at the social-technical level. In particular, each of our domain-specific CIs is embedded in the context of the modern web, which has its own architecture. With this architecture comes a set of highly developed technologies including programming languages, databases, and frameworks. Along with this technical infrastructure comes a highly developed social infrastructure as well, including a skilled workforce, educational system, and socially networked collaboration environments. This technical and social infrastructure complicates the deployment of novel system architectures. For starters, there are, at least initially, no existing tools to aid the development and deployment of that architecture. Compounding this issue is not only the lack of familiarity developers have with the architecture, but also their predisposition to see and solve problems in their traditional ways. Even when initially successful, staff turnover is a recurring problem. As a result, the development of a novel architecture is slow and fraught with imperfections.

13.5.2.1 PALMS architecture and implementation quality analysis

Table 13.7 summarizes our analysis of how key architectural and implementation choices affected the quality of the PALMS CI. We selected a set of entities/attributes that influence the quality of the CIs under consideration. For each pair, the column "Attribute Evaluation" identifies how the entity attribute is evaluated in the overall PALMS system: high (H), moderate (M), or low (L). The column "Impact on Quality" identifies how this has a positive (+), negative (−), or no significant ( ) effect on the software quality—the impact is computed from the Attribute Evaluation and the impact matrix summary (see Section 13.5.1.3). If the Attribute Evaluation is H, then the impact is the same as from the impact matrix; if the evaluation is L, then the impact is the opposite. The other columns identify how different implementation and architectural choices affected the quality tuple.

Furthermore, Table 13.7 details the results of our analysis of six architectural and implementation choices we made in developing PALMS. The six columns under "PALMS Choices Evaluation" uses arrows up and down and plus and minus signs, to summarize how each choice affects the given factor. An arrow up (↑) means that the choice made the entity attribute increase, while a down arrow (↓) indicated that the choice made the attribute decrease. Next to the arrow we also put plus (+) or minus (−) symbols to specify if the change (increase or decrease) of the given attribute for the entity affects the system quality in a positive or negative way based on the matrix from Section 13.5.1.3.

Responding to requirements with ID I01, I04 (see Section 13.4 for requirements tables), a first fundamental architectural choice was to define a standardized message format to send every service request and data element on the

Table 13.7 Quality Analysis of Architectural and Implementation Choices for PALMS

Quality Factors		PALMS Choices Evaluation						PALMS Overall	
Entity	Attribute	ESB Services with Standard Messages	UI and CI SOAP Façade	Policy enforced on every message	Front end GWT/RPC	Uniform Java Language	MULE 1.4.3\GWT	Attribute Evaluation	Impact on Quality
Architecture									
Communication between UI and CI	EFFICIENCY		−↓		−↓			L	−
Services exposed by CI to UI	GRANULARITY	+↑	+↑					L	+
Services internal to CI	GRANULARITY	+↑	+↑					H	+
System	MODULARITY	+↑	+↑					H	+
Logging	INTEGRATION	−↑		+↑				H	+
Policy model	COMPLEXITY	+↑		−↑				H	+
Policy enforcement	GRANULARITY	+↑		+↑				H	−
Data transfer	EFFICIENCY	−↓	−↓	−↓	−↓			L	−
Implementation									
Bugs	FREQUENCY	−↓	−↓		−↓	+↓	−↓	H	−
Code	SELF-DESCRIPTIVENESS	−↓	+↓		−↓	−↑	−↓	L	−
Code generation	COVERAGE		−↓		+↑	−↓	+↓	M	+
Entity	VERBOSITY	−↓	−↓		−↓	−↓	−↓	H	−
Data access	SPEED	−↓		−↓	−↓			L	−
Unit test	COVERAGE	+↑	−↓		−↓	+↑	−↓	M	−
Infrastructure									
Technology	MATURITY		−↓			+↑	−↓	L	−
Software configuration	COMPLEXITY	+↑	−↓			+↓	+↓	L	+
Debugging tools	EXISTENCE	+↑	−↑	+↑		+↑	−↓	H	+
Machine security	INTEGRITY		−↓				−↓	M	−
Machine configuration	COMPLEXITY		+↓			+↓		L	−
Machine	DEPENDENCE					+↓	+↓	L	+

MULE ESB. This choice lead to many benefits for the overall software quality, but also a few drawbacks. One benefit was a fine granularity of CI services and high level of modularity. Logging what happens in the system (requirements I02, I09–11, H02, H04, H06, H07) is then simply a matter of analyzing message queues and interpreting the messages. This choice also simplified defining and enforcing policies with a high level of granularity (requirements I02, I04, I05, I07, I08, I09, I11, H02, H03, H06, H07). In fact, policies can be defined to easily analyze messages as they appear on the message bus and modify them as needed. Also, testing services becomes as easy as recording a set of messages, replaying them, and observing the message output. Messages in a standard format can be easily debugged and their content can be sanitized if needed to prevent data leakage. Drawbacks resulted when data transfer rate and access latency were negatively impacted due to formatting messages as XML, which resulted in large serialization/deserialization overhead and increased the amount of data to send for each message (requirements I01–I08, I10, H04, H07). Also, because of the technology choices made in implementing the system, developers had to write a lot of code to explicitly convert method calls to XML messages (e.g., requirements I10, I12).

The second choice we analyze is the use of a SOAP-based façade to isolate the UI from the CI. In this case, the benefits where in exposing a smaller set of services to the UI, which simplifies its development and increases the modularity of the system. Moreover, the use of standard web technologies such as SOAP made it possible to generate a lot of the boilerplate code needed for implementing the services automatically and made the system easy to configure and debug. On the other hand, the cost of introducing this façade was high both in term of performance and in terms of bugs in converting data from the internal messages used in the CI to SOAP messages. The first problem is determined by the choice of translating messages, whereas the second was caused by the fact that the libraries used in the implementation were not mature enough.

The choice of enforcing policies on every message was great for configurability and security, but it slowed down the data transfer and access substantially. While this can partially be attributed to the choice of XML and XPATH technologies to implement the policy engine, a more coarse policy definition and enforcement schema is necessary for high-performance applications.

We chose to use the RPC schema supported by the GWT framework for the communication with the browser application to simplify the UI development (requirements C01–C11, A06–A11, A12). This choice turned out to be detrimental in many aspects. In fact, while we gained some benefit from the code generation supported by GWT, we ended up introducing yet another format that required the translation of our request to access the façade, further slowing down the data access speed. Moreover, we introduced verbose code that replicated data structures already defined in the CI and introduced additional bugs in translating all our requests in three different formats. The problems introduced by this choice definitely outweighed the benefits.

The choice of selecting a single mature language, such as Java was a good one. The availability of mature tools and libraries for many tasks, and availability of expert Java programmers helped the quality of the resulting software. On the other hand, using appropriate domain-specific languages would have made the code more self-descriptive, potentially improving the maintainability of PALMS.

Finally, the implementation frameworks we used (e.g., MULE ESB) helped generate parts of the code and simplified the configuration of the resulting systems. But they were not as mature as we would have liked. Compared to modern incarnations of the same frameworks, the version we used had many bugs and required verbose configurations and additional code to perform tasks that are automated in more recent frameworks. In particular, they did not have good support for debugging and presented bugs that could lead to the instability of the CI. A lot of time and effort was required to work around these limitations.

13.5.2.2 CYCORE architecture and implementation quality analysis

Table 13.8 summarizes our analysis of CYCORE architectural and implementation choices, and our evaluation of how they affected the overall system quality.

Working from similar CI requirements with PALMS (I01−I18), a key architectural decision was to decouple the CI from the Data Preservation system (DP), and to use a REST API to access data persistence services. The advantage was that a dedicated team specialized in data management could develop these services in parallel with the CI development. Moreover, CYCORE CI uses an internal NoSQL database, namely MongoDB, for kinetic data. The data management system provided the same interface to access data as MongoDB, which allowed for a uniform access from the CI and for easily swapping one database to another when needed (e.g., during unit testing). However, separating CI and DP had significant negative impact on maintainability for several reasons: (i) data had to be serialized/deserialized each time a query was performed; (ii) the data model had to be replicated in the CI and in the DP (in fact, there were differences in the data models and data had to be converted from one model in another); (iii) any changes in the model lead to a cascade of changes from UI to application services to DP services to the actual database; and (iv) DP used a relational database (DB2), which was mapped to Java classes and then to web services providing a MongoDB interface. All of these impacted performance by not taking advantage of the strengths of relational databases for advanced queries.

Another architectural choice in CYCORE was to have separate acquisition servers to receive data from devices (via HHH or Qualcomm's 2net). This was a good choice as it separates data acquisition pathways and specific issues of each set of devices. The security can also be enforced locally as each acquisition server knows what kind of data it expects and from where. The disadvantage is that the machine configuration becomes more complex, and the acquisition code depends on the specific ports to which the devices push data.

Separating CI, DP, and acquisition servers lead to separate logging capabilities inside each system, without any integration to provide an end-to-end view of the

Table 13.8 Quality Analysis of Architectural and Implementation Choices for CYCORE

Quality Factors		CYCORE Choices Evaluation						CYCORE Overall	
Entity	Attribute	REST API between CI and DB	Separate Acquisition Servers; REST API	UI Generated as HTML	Role-Based Access	Clojure for CI and UI	Multiple Languages: Clojure, Java, .NET	Attribute Evaluation	Impact on Quality
Architecture									
Communication between UI and CI	EFFICIENCY	→		→ −		→ −		L	−
Services exposed by CI to UI	GRANULARITY	← +	← +	← −		← −		H	−
Services internal to CI	GRANULARITY	← +	← +				→	H	+
System	MODULARITY	← −	← −	→ −		→ −		H	+
Logging	INTEGRATION				→ +	← +		L	−
Policy model	COMPLEXITY				← +	← +		L	+
Policy enforcement	GRANULARITY	→ −				← +		L	−
Data transfer	EFFICIENCY	→ −	← +	→		← +	−	H	+
Implementation									
Bugs	FREQUENCY	←		← −	→ +	← −	← −	L	+
Code	SELF-DESCRIPTIVENESS	−		← −		→ −	→ −	L	−
Code generation	COVERAGE			→ −		→ −	− −	L	−
Entity	VERBOSITY				← +	← +	← −	M	
Data access	SPEED			→ −		+	← −	L	−
Unit test	COVERAGE					← −	−	L	−
Infrastructure									
Technology	MATURITY	→ −				→ −	← −	L	−
Software configuration	COMPLEXITY	← −	← +		← +	→ +	→ −	M	−
Debugging tools	EXISTENCE		← −			← −	→ −	L	
Machine security	INTEGRITY	→ +	← −			← +	← −	M	
Machine configuration	COMPLEXITY						−	H	−
Machine	DEPENDENCE					→	← +	L	+

data pathway from device to storage to user. This made debugging quite hard, especially as the main source of problems in CYCORE is data acquisition and its integrity (requirement I02). CYCORE had relatively few bugs during operation, as problems were often not related to the quality of the code, but due to issues with the devices themselves. Thus, handing requirements I01–I09, each time our users failed to find expected data in the system or when data appeared differently than expected, it was a quest to debug each component and figure out if the problem was in our system to begin with or somewhere upstream where we got data from. Note that it is not enough to debug acquisition servers to troubleshoot data acquisition problems because, for security reasons, acquisition servers have a limited view on data without any knowledge to what participant it belongs or how it is interpreted at the data management and application layers.

We mentioned that bugs were infrequent during operation; however, bugs were frequent during integration testing because of the duplications of models from CI and DP, and tight coupling of UI and CI. Using Clojure for CI has many advantages; yet using Clojure for UI to implement requirements C01–C11, A01–A13 and writing the entire UI as HTML plus Javascript was not a wise choice. The code generation, unit testing, and debugging support was very limited for the UI component, which went through many iterations due to ever changing requirements to meet the usability needs for the research and clinical team. The UI uses the Model-View-Controller pattern; yet, the unit tests cover only for models in the form of pre and post conditions; most of the UI was tested manually.

In contrast with the PALMS results, towards the end of the CYCORE project, using separate programming languages for the acquisition servers, CI, and DP revealed a significant negative impact on quality as seen from the table, especially in light of reduced development effort and high turnover.

13.5.2.3 *CitiSense architecture and implementation quality analysis*

Table 13.9 summarizes our analysis of how key architectural and implementation choices affected the quality of CitiSense. The table follows the same schema of the ones before.

We again analyze six key architectural and implementation choices that affected the quality of CitiSense. The first important decision was to develop a Bluetooth air quality sensor in house in response to requirements A01 and A09. This was due both to the inability to find an off-the-shelf alternative and also to experiment with power efficient sensing solutions. The choice of connecting the sensor to a phone via Bluetooth in order to relay data to the CI improved the efficiency of the data transfer. In fact, part of the CI runs on the phone, so immediate processing and presentation of data to the user is possible even if the phone is not connected to the CI back end (requirements A09, A11, A12). Moreover, this approach makes it possible to create a sensor that is not specifically tied to CitiSense and that can be easily replaced (requirements C01–C04, C09, C11, A01). The main drawback of using a phone as a proxy between the sensor and the rest of CitiSense is that each sensor needs to be paired to a specific phone

Table 13.9 Quality Analysis of Architectural and Implementation Choices for CitiSense

Quality Factors		CitiSense Choices Evaluation						CitiSense Overall	
Entity	Attribute	Develop CitiSense Bluetooth Sensor	Native Android App Interface with Sensor	Traditional Web-Based Back end	Different Programming Languages	Batch Machine Learning in Different Process	Django Framework	Attribute Evaluation	Impact on Quality
Architecture									
Communication between UI and CI	EFFICIENCY		↑ +	↓ −		↓ −		L	−
Services exposed by CI to UI	GRANULARITY		↑ −	↓ +		↓ +	↓ +	L	+
Services internal to CI	GRANULARITY		↓ −	↓ −		↓ −		L	−
System	MODULARITY		↑ +	↑ +		↑ −	↓ +	H	+
Logging	INTEGRATION	↓ −	↓ −	↓ +		↓ −	↓ +	L	−
Policy model	COMPLEXITY		↓ −	↑ +		↓ −		M	
Policy enforcement	GRANULARITY		↓ −					L	−
Data transfer	EFFICIENCY	↑ + ↓	↑ +	↑ +		↓ −	↑ +	H	+
Implementation									
Bugs	FREQUENCY		↓ +		↓ +	↓ +	↓ +	L	+
Code	SELF-DESCRIPTIVENESS				↑ +		↓ −	H	+
Code generation	COVERAGE						↑ +	H	+
Entity	VERBOSITY				↓ +	↓ +	↓ +	L	+
Data access	SPEED						↓ +	L	−
Unit test	COVERAGE		↑ +			↓ −		M	
Infrastructure									
Technology	MATURITY		↑ +	↑ +	↓ −	↑ +	↑ +	H	+
Software configuration	COMPLEXITY		↑ +			↓ −	↓ −	H	−
Debugging tools	EXISTENCE		↑ +	↑ +		↑ +	↑ +	H	+
Machine security	INTEGRITY		↓ −	↓ +		↑ +	↓ +	H	+
Machine configuration	COMPLEXITY	↑ −	↓ −				↓ +	H	−
Machine	DEPENDENCE	↓ +		↑ +	↑ −		↓ +	L	+

(adding to the configuration complexity). To simplify the development, we did not develop capabilities to remotely debug and fix problems (such as loss of calibration) and it is often necessary to examine the sensor manually and discover problems that commercial sensors could simply report to a centralized log.

A second choice was to develop an Android app to connect the sensor to the rest of CitiSense. The application has both a CI part and a UI part. The CI part is in charge of receiving the sensor data, caching it, running certain computations locally, and forward data to the back end. The UI portion of the app displays important data to the user. The main benefit of this choice is that the communication between the UI and CI is extremely efficient; in fact, data can be processed and presented to the user as soon as received from the sensor. Even if the phone is disconnected from the Internet, the app can still present data collected by the local sensor. Moreover, the communication between the phone and the server can be optimized to improve the bandwidth and power efficiency. Android is also a mature platform with good debugging tools, so it was a great choice as a platform for CitiSense. On the other hand choosing to develop a phone app for connecting the sensors to the CI forces all CitiSense users to have an Android phone, making CitiSense dependent on such devices. Furthermore, the configuration complexity of the system increased because we have to pair every sensor with phones and keep track of user to phones/sensors mapping. Additionally, policy definition and enforcement become more complex because they are distributed between the back end and all the phone systems.

Developing the back end based on standard web technologies proved to be an excellent choice. It made the system modular, ensured that services are exposed to clients with the right granularity, simplified the configuration of the system, and guaranteed a certain independence from the selected hardware system. One drawback is that, because the CI is distributed, phones and external algorithms use REST services to communicate with the back end. This means that the granularity of services offered between the different parts of the CI is also low, making it impossible to move some computations outside the back end. Furthermore, the web UI follows the traditional pattern of generating HTML content inside the server, and is not as efficient in manipulating large dataset as a more modern AJAX-based application.

The choice of using different programming languages, each to support specific parts of the system, helped to minimize how much code needed to be written and to improve its quality. The resulting code has less bugs, is more self-descriptive, and less verbose. However, the price to pay is a more complex configuration of the software and the need to have different skill sets in the development team. As encountered in the other projects above, the choice of development languages and frameworks must be carefully evaluated with respect to their maturity, availability of talent in the development team, and long term financial support for that team.

We chose to develop most of the back end services using the mature Django web framework. The main benefit is that most of the low level services to define, access, and present data are already in place. Moreover, it supports access to data services both via REST interface and via web views. This minimized the development effort improving the overall quality of the implementation. Moreover, the framework supports an administrative site out of the box. The real drawback of this choice is that you cannot easily deploy services that scale to process large amount of data.

Therefore, we had to make a key choice regarding the execution of data analysis jobs within a different process running a Matlab script (requirements I09, I10). The main benefit was to have the domain scientist work with a mature tool optimized for the job, improving the modularity and decreasing the amount of bugs in the computation. On the other hand, this choice further increased the complexity of the system configuration. The current implementation of this CitiSense computation exchanges data with the CI back end by sharing text files through the local storage. This is clearly not a portable and general way to access CI services.

13.6 RESULTS AND LESSON LEARNED

In the previous section, we analyzed the main architectural, implementation, and infrastructure choices made during the development of three e-Health CIs. Our analysis identified how these choices affected maintenance and portability of the resulting systems. We did not consider these activities while defining the requirements for the three CIs. In fact, each CI was a part of an effort to create a specific system to support a relatively short-lived research effort. However, how a system supports these activities influences the overall quality of any software product. This is even more important when the goal is to develop a reusable CI supporting multiple applications and research efforts—the goals of our DELPHI CI.

In this section, we summarize the lessons learned from our pervious systems and provide recommendations on which architecture, implementation, and infrastructure to choose to achieve high quality CIs.

Table 13.10 summarizes key differences between decisions, both architectural and implementation, taken in the different projects. For each decision, we identify a recommendation that in our experience leads to a better quality CI. We discuss the tradeoffs involved with each choice and explain each recommendation below.

The first decisions we discuss are which types of sensors to use, and how to connect these sensors to the CI. For example, in CitiSense we developed our own in-house sensor nodes and connected them directly to the CI. In CYCORE, on the other hand, we purchased commercial sensor nodes that were connected to an external data collection platform. Finally, in PALMS we manually uploaded sensor data files.

Our first recommendation (Rec 1) is to choose commercial sensor nodes if possible. The work required to develop and maintain the sensor nodes is

Table 13.10 Recommended Decisions

#	Decision	Recommendation
Rec 1	Developing *ad hoc* sensors vs. using existing sensors	*Favor existing sensors* Use existing ones if you have a choice. If not, try to integrate your sensors in existing nodes
Rec 2	Connecting sensors directly to the CI vs. using a separate collection framework	*Favor a separate framework* Both have pros and cons. It depends on when they need to be available. A dedicated collection module makes sense
Rec 3	Using a web-based back end vs. implementing services on an ESB	*Favor ESB* ESB can expose some services using standard web protocols
Rec 4	Using a single programming language vs. using different languages for different parts of the system	*Use a sensible choice of multiple languages* and frameworks
Rec 5	Separating data processing components in different OS processes vs. using a single OS process for all data processing	*Support both* You need multiple processes for maximum flexibility (languages/ frameworks). Important to have coarse granularity of services in different processes
Rec 6	Developing the UI using a traditional web framework vs. developing *ad hoc* AJAX Applications that communicate with a service layer	*Develop UI services that both can use*
Rec 7	Using the same technology for UI services and CI services vs. supporting different technologies	*Support different technologies*
Rec 8	Supporting policy definition and enforcement on each internal service call vs. supporting them only on the data layer and/or UI service layer	*Favor policy on data layer* but retain ability to apply arbitrary policies between subsystems
Rec 9	Accessing databases using native libraries vs. using a standard REST API to access databases	*Use native libraries.* They are more efficient and your code is more compact

substantial. Moreover, while you get more control over how the data is moved from sensors to CI and over how a sensor is calibrated, in general the process of deploying and maintaining in-house sensors adds substantial complexity to the system, and can lead to a suboptimal user experience. The only valid reasons to go for in-house sensors are (i) the sensors are the focus of the research, or (ii) there is no commercial sensor that supports the measurements needed in the project.

Our second recommendation (Rec 2) is to keep the ingestion of sensor data on a separate subsystem. The existence of an external platform simplifies the deployment of the sensors and the configuration of the system. However, it also introduces a dependency on an external system that could be outside the project control and limits the choices of the system architect in how to move data within the system. For applications that do not require real-time data analysis, it is better to rely on a dedicated data collection platform. An external platform can accommodate even manual upload of sensor data files, increasing the modularity of the system. Sometimes applications need more fine-grained control over sensors and their data. In this case, a good option is connecting each sensor directly to a device that communicates with the CI. This approach trades the complexity and dependency on specific hardware for the configurability and real-time data access capability. We still recommend that both the external collection platform and each node that connects a sensor to the CI use a uniform set of services. This simplifies the global architecture as we can consider each node connected to sensors as an independent data collection platform.

Another result of our analysis is that the quality of the user experience changes depending on the technology and architecture chosen for the UI. All of our projects have web-based interfaces; in addition, CitiSense has a native phone application. While more complex to develop, the native phone App has the benefit of an immediate interaction with the user and the ability to easily deploy parts of the CI near the user. On the other hand, web interfaces provide portability and independence from specific hardware and software. We also experimented with traditional web pages (where the server generates HTML pages for each request) and AJAX applications (where a JavaScript UI runs of the browser). The main benefit of the AJAX approach is that the data manipulation is more efficient—only changes are sent between browser and server. We can also use a unified service interface for the UI and other parts of the system that interact with the CI, making the system more maintainable and uniform. However, AJAX applications are much more complex to develop and troubleshoot, and rely heavily on modern browsers and powerful hardware.

With respect to the UI, our first recommendation (Rec 6) is to focus on the creation of a technology agnostic UI service layer. This layer should strike the right balance between coarse granularity (to support efficient communication between layers and application of access policies) and functionality to support UI requests (to simplify the development of different UIs). In our experience, we often ended up adding features to the CI to minimize the work in the UI or maximize code reuse. It is our conclusion that the best way to simplify the development of UI should be to provide UI libraries that give additional functionalities on top of the services provided by the CI to UI layer. The concrete web technology to use really depends on the goal of the UI. In general, traditional frameworks are simpler to use and less subjected to security issues than AJAX applications. However, AJAX applications provide better user experience. Given the current state of technology, AJAX is a viable solution, as frameworks are now mature and make it relatively easy to make secure applications without too much overhead. However, traditional web apps are still a good candidate for systems that do not require too much interaction with the data.

We advocate this approach for two reasons. First, the library does not pay the cost of communication incurred when accessing CI services. This means that by using libraries, we can expose finer granularity services on the UI platform while potentially increasing responsiveness and minimizing bandwidth requirements. Second, providing a well-designed service library for the developers of the UI can potentially minimize the development effort and increase the quality of the UI. In fact, a library would abstract from the details of accessing a standard technology (such as REST API based on JSON messages, which is used in our latest CI) and focus the developer's attention on the presentation of the data to the user.

We found out that using a single language for all parts of E-Health CIs and applications is problematic. While we get some organizational benefits by not needing programmers with vastly different skillsets, we discovered that code tends to be less self-descriptive and more verbose. An important factor that leads to this result is the choice of programming frameworks used in developing the system. While a given programming language can be concise per se, the key element to take into account when choosing it is the availability of application and CI-appropriate frameworks for that language. Often such frameworks are not good or mature enough to support all features needed by E-Health applications. Choosing a single language, therefore, leads to selecting suboptimal frameworks, decreasing the reuse of mature code and increasing the amount of new code written, all of which can add bugs and increase costs.

In CYCORE, we used Clojure to develop both the CI services and to generate web pages. In PALMS, we developed both CI and UI in Java using GWT to compile Java to a Javascript AJAX application. Finally, CitiSense used Django and Python to develop the Web UI and part of the CI, Java to develop the phone UI and parts of the CI running on mobile devices, and other languages, including Matlab for AI algorithms and Unix shell scripts. In general, our recommendation (Rec 4) is to support multiple languages in different parts of the CI. In particular, we should support different technologies and frameworks. In fact, we noticed a substantial increase in productivity by using the best tool for the job.

An implementation decision tightly coupled with the language decision is whether we implement UI and CI using the same technology and framework or we use distinct languages and frameworks. Our recommendation (Rec 7) is to support multiple languages and frameworks also for the UI. However, we advocate the use of a uniform service layer that all UI modules access. This uniform layer simplifies applying permissions in a uniform way to different UIs and is independent of the chosen UI technology.

We also learned that different choices in implementing access control policies have profound implications on systems' quality. We found out that, while a flexible policy enforced on every service call in the CI can be extremely powerful, it makes the system slow and makes developing new policies or updating policies a daunting task. On the other hand, role-based access policies meet most of the requirements for E-Health applications. Because many role based access systems already exist, a good compromise is to reuse an existing access system (such as the ones implemented in many off-the-shelf databases). One shortcoming of using role based access in databases is that while a generic policy system supports adding arbitrary functionalities to the system at runtime, the role based access does not support this unless significant effort is devoted to implementing workarounds at the application level. Therefore, to address the remaining requirements of E-Health applications, we suggest integrating such systems with a limited set of policies, enforced only on services with coarse granularity, such as the services exposed at the boundaries of different subsystems. Thus, our recommendation on the subject (Rec 8) is to favor policy definition and enforcement on the data layer, but retain the ability to apply arbitrary policies on services exposed to different subsystems (that usually have a coarse granularity). An easy way to achieve this is to use a message-based ESB architecture.

A key factor that influences the quality of a CI is the technology used for implementing its services. We experimented with (i) two types of web service technologies, SOAP and REST; (ii) using methods or functions of the programming language to represent services; and (iii) using an ESB instead of direct calls. The use of web technologies to expose services has many benefits because such technologies implement a standard; therefore, many mature frameworks exist and can provide and consume services based on these standards. This means that these technologies promote machine and software independence, and reuse many services already implemented. On the other hand, web services have substantial cumulative overhead compared to using native methods; therefore, they are a good choice for façades and long running services where their overhead is offset by inherent service latencies. ESBs, especially if supported by modern frameworks, are a good solution because they support multiple ways to expose the same service implementation. An ESB can transparently expose a function as a web service to be called by different processes and subsystems, or it can expose it as a method call that is directly invoked by code running in the same process and subsystem. Therefore, our recommendation is to use ESBs whenever possible (Rec 3).

In our CIs, we also experimented with performing all data processing in a single OS process and in splitting the processing in different OS processes. Sometimes, splitting a computation into different processes is required, for example, when part of the computation is implemented in different languages or frameworks. However, this can introduce substantial overhead when a single request must be processed by a pipeline of different OS processes. For applications where a single request passes through different processes, we need to make sure that the granularity of the interprocess communication is coarse enough to avoid substantial overhead. However, separating computation into different processes has a beneficial influence on the security and privacy of the CI. In summary, we recommend (Rec 5) to support both models: (i) single process whenever possible, and (ii) multiple processes based on the language, frameworks, or security requirements.

Our last recommendation pertains to the database interface, where we experimented with different abstractions. We tried using libraries and frameworks supported by our programming languages, or creating and using REST APIs to communicate with the database. The result of our experiments is that there is no reason to try to apply a standard based but inefficient way to interact with the database over the network when each database provides optimized network interfaces and standard libraries to access data in most languages. The only place where it would make sense to access the data via standard REST and JSON is in web-based UI. However, these interfaces do not access the database directly but present data mediated by the services of the CI. Thus, our recommendation (Rec 9) is to use native interfaces and leverage the standard libraries of the programming language to access databases.

13.7 CONCLUSIONS

The ever-changing and growing E-Health domain poses significant challenges to research CI development. These include limited and unsecure funding; high developer turnover rates; maturity (or lack thereof) of available technologies; diversity of data types and their corresponding standards; policies regarding handling sensitive human-subjects data; complexity of the interactions involved; and diversity and number of stakeholders. All of these factors significantly impact the architectural and implementation choices for developing quality CIs for health related research. While the CIs presented in this chapter are highly successful from the point of view of their customers, to sustain them will require significant effort to maintain and to adapt to the rapidly changing requirements of this field.

An important part of our contribution is the set of recommendations presented above. We are following these recommendations in implementing DELPHI, the reusable CI we are currently developing. This CI will support follow-up projects to CitiSense, PALMS, and CYCORE. By using a common CI and developing three different applications, we will be able to validate that the recommendations presented in this section lead to higher quality products. In fact, a second contribution is the set of actions and facts we have identified and the process we follow to assess the quality of our E-Health CIs. After DELPHI is completed and the three new applications are in use, we will perform the same analysis we performed on the old systems and assess how much the quality improved.

An additional contribution is the identification of core requirements for E-Health CIs. Having distinguished generic CI requirements from E-Health specific ones, and common E-Health application requirements from specific application requirements, our requirement organization paves the way to more general purpose E-Health CIs and frameworks that will enable rapid development of E-Health applications. DELPHI is the first stepping stone in this direction.

ACKNOWLEDGMENTS

This work was supported in part by the National Institutes of Health (NIH) PALMS grant U01-CA130771; NIH/NCI CYCORE grants RC2CA148263, R01CA177914, and R01CA177996; National Science Foundation (NSF) Cyber-Physical Systems CitiSense grant CNS-0932403; NSF MetaSense: Calibration of Personal Air Quality Sensors in the Field — Coping with Noise and Extending Capabilities grant CNS-1446912; the NIH Roadmap for Medical Research iDASH program grant U54HL108460; and the NSF "Information & Intelligent Systems" grant #1237174.

REFERENCES

Arrott, M., Demchak, B., Ermagan, V., Farcas, C., Farcas, E., Krüger, I.H., et al., 2007. Rich services: the integration piece of the SOA puzzle. In: Proceedings of the IEEE International Conference on Web Services (ICWS). IEEE Computer Society, Salt Lake City, UT, pp. 176–183.

Bachmann, F., 2011. Give the Stakeholders What They Want: Design Peer Reviews the ATAM Style. CrossTalk.

Boehm, B., 1988. A spiral model of software development and enhancement. Computer 21 (5), 61–72, IEEE Computer Society.

Boehm, B., 2006. Value-based software engineering: overview and agenda. In: Biffl, S., Aurum, A., Boehm, B., Erdogmus, H., Grünbacher, P. (Eds.), Value-Based Software Engineering. Springer, Berlin, pp. 3–14. (Chapter 1).

Boehm, B., Jain, A., 2006. An initial theory of value-based software engineerin. In: Biffl, S., Aurum, A., Boehm, B., Erdogmus, H., Grünbacher, P. (Eds.), Value-Based Software Engineering. Springer, Berlin, pp. 15–37. (Chapter 2).

Boehm, B., Turner, R., 2003. Balancing Agility and Discipline: Guide for the Perplexed. Longman Publishing Co, Boston, MA.

Boehm, B.W., Brown, J.R., Lipow, M., 1976. Quantitative evaluation of software quality. In: Proceedings of the 2nd International Conference on Software Engineering. IEEE Computer Society Press Los Alamitos, CA, pp. 592–605.

Boehm, B.W., Brown, J.R., Kaspar, H., Lipow, M., McLeod, G.J., Merritt, M.J., 1978. Characteristics of Software Quality. TRW Series of Software Technology, vol 1 North Holland, Amsterdam.

Booth, D., Haas, H., McCabe, F., Newcomer, E., Champion, M., Ferris, C., et al., 2004. Web Services Architecture. W3C Working Group Note. Retrieved from: <http://www.w3.org/TR/2004/NOTE-ws-arch-20040211/>.

Carriere, S.J., 2009. Lightweight Architecture Alternative Assessment Method. <http://technogility.sjcarriere.com/ 2009/05/11/its-pronounced-like-lamb-not-like-lame/>.

Clements, P., Kazman, R., Klein, M., 2002. Evaluating Software Architecture: Methods and Case Studies. Addison Wesley, Boston, MA.

Cockburn, A., 2000. Writing Effective Use Cases. Addison-Wesley, Boston, MA.

Crosby, P.B., 1979. Quality is Free: The Art of Making Quality Certain. McGraw-Hill, New York, NY.

Dache, G., 2001. IT Companies will gain competitive advantage by integrating CMM with ISO9001. Qual. Syst. Update 11 (11).

Deissenboeck, F., Wagner, S., Pizka, M., Teuchert, S., Girard, J.F., 2007. An activity-based quality model for maintainability. In: Proc IEEE International Conference on Software Maintenance (ICSDM'07). IEEE Press, New York, NY, pp. 184–193.

Demchak, B., Krüger, I., 2012. Policy driven development: flexible policy insertion for large scale systems. In: 2012 IEEE International Symposium on Policies for Distributed Systems and Networks. IEEE Computer Society, Chapel Hill, NC, pp. 17–24.

Demchak, B., Farcas, C., Farcas, E., Krüger, I., 2007. The treasure map for rich services. In: Proceedings of the 2007 IEEE International Conference on Information Reuse and Integration (IRI). IEEE, Las Vegas, pp. 400–405.

Demchak, B., Kerr, J., Raab, F., Patrick, K., Krüger, I., 2012. PALMS: a modern coevolution of community and computing using policy driven development. In: 45th Hawaii International Conference on System Sciences (HICSS), Maui, Hawaii.

Deming, W.E., 1986. Out of the Crisis: Quality, Productivity and Competitive Position. Cambridge University Press, 507 pages.

Dromey, R.G., 1995. A model for software product quality. IEEE Transactions on Software Engineering 21 (2), 146–163, IEEE Press Piscataway, NJ.

Farcas, E., Farcas, C., Krüger, I., 2014. Successful CyberInfrastructures for E-Health. In: Mistrik, I., Bahsoon, R., Zhang, Y., Kazman, R. (Eds.), Economics-driven Software Architecture. Elsevier, Waltham, MA, pp. 259–296. , ch. 12.

Federal Information Security Management Act of 2002, Title III, E-Government Act of 2002, P.L. 107_347.

Feigenbaum, A.V., 1983. Total Quality Control. McGraw-Hill, New York, NY.

Fowler, M., 2009. Technical Debt Quadrant, Oct. Available from: <http://www.martinfowler.com/bliki/TechnicalDebtQuadrant.html> (accessed March 2012).

Fowler, M., Beck, K., Brant, J., Opdyke, W., Roberts, D., 1999. Refactoring: Improving the Design of Existing Code. Addison-Wesley Longman Publishing Co., Inc, Boston, MA.

Garvin, D.A., 1984. What does product quality really mean? MIT Sloan Manage. Rev. 26 (1), 25–43.

Grady, R.B., 1992. Practical Software Metrics for Project Management and Process Improvement. Prentice-Hall.

Guo, Y., Seaman, C., 2011 A portfolio approach to technical debt management. Presented at the 2nd Workshop on Managing Technical Debt, Honolulu, HI.

Guo, Y., Seaman, C., Gomes, R., Cavalcanti, A., Tonin, G., Da Silva, F.Q.B., et al., 2011. Tracking technical debt—an exploratory case study. In: 27th IEEE International Conference on Software Maintenance (ICSM'11), Williamsburg, VA, pp. 528–531.

Halstead, M., 1977. Elements of Software Science. Elsevier Science Inc., New York, NY.

Health Insurance Portability and Accountability Act of 1996. P.L. 104_191.

Humphrey, W.S., 1989. Managing the Software Process. Addison-Wesley, Reading, MA.

Ishikawa, K., 1985. What Is Total Quality Control?: The Japanese Way. Prentice-Hall.

ISO, International Organization for Standardization, 2000. ISO 9001:2000, Quality Management Systems—Requirements.

ISO, International Organization for Standardization, 2001. ISO 9126-1:2001, Software engineering—Product Quality, Part 1: Quality Model.

ISO, International Organization for Standardization, 2011. ISO/IEC 25010:2011: Systems and software engineering—Systems and Software Quality Requirements and Evaluation (SQuaRE)—System and Software Quality Models.

Juran, J.M., Gryna, F.M., 1970. Quality Planning and Analysis: From Product Development Through Use. McGraw-Hill, New York, NY.

Juran, J.M., Gryna, F.M., 1988. Juran's Quality Control Handbook. McGraw-Hill, 1872 pages.

Kan, S.H., 2002. Metrics and Models in Software Quality Engineering, second ed. Addison-Wesley.

Kazman, R., Asundi, J., Klein, M., 2001. Quantifying the costs and benefits of architectural decisions. In: Proceedings of the 23rd International Conference on Software Engineering (ICSE'01). IEEE Computer Society, Toronto, Ontario, Canada, pp. 297–306.

Kazman, R., Asundi, J., Klein, M., 2002. Making Architecture Design Decisions: An Economic Approach (CMU/SEI-2002-TR-035, ESCTR-2002-035). Software Engineering Institute, Carnegie Mellon University, Pittsburgh, PA.

Leffingwell, D., 2007. Scaling Software Agility: Best Practices for Large Enterprises (The Agile Software Development Series). Addison-Wesley Professional.

MacKenzie, C., Laskey, K., McCabe, F., Brown, P., Metz, R., 2006. Reference Model for Service Oriented Architecture 1.0. OASIS Standard. Retrieved from: <http://docs.oasis-open.org/soa-rm/v1.0/soa-rm.pdf>.

Markowitz, H., 1952. Portfolio selection. J. Finance 7, 77–91.

McCabe, T.J., 1976. A complexity measure. IEEE Trans. Softw. Eng. 2 (4), 308–320.

McCall, J.A., Richards, P.K., Walters, G.F., 1977. Factors in Software Quality, The National Technical Information Service (NTIS), Vols. 1, 2 and 3.

Nikzad, N., Ziftci, C., Zappi, P., Quick, N., Aghera, P., Verma, N., et al., 2011. CitiSense—Adaptive Services for Community-Driven Behavioral and Environmental Monitoring to Induce Change, Tech. Rep. CS2011-0961. University of California, San Diego, CA.

Nikzad, N., Verma, N., Ziftci, C., Bales, E., Quick, N., Zappi, P., et al., 2012. CitiSense: Improving Geospatial Environmental Assessment of Air Quality Using a Wireless Personal Exposure Monitoring System. Wireless Health (Best Paper).

Nord, R.L., Ozkaya, I., Kruchten, P., Gonzalez-Rojas, M., In search of a metric for managing architectural technical debt. In: 2012 Joint Working IEEE/IFIP Conference on Software Architecture (WICSA) and European Conference on Software Architecture (ECSA), pp. 91, 100, 20–24 August 2012.

Object Management Group, 2003. Model Driven Architecture (MDA) v1.0.1. omg/03-06-01, OMG.

Ohno-Machado, L., Bafna, V., Boxwala, A.A., Chapman, B.E., Chapman, W.W., Chaudhuri, K., et al., 2012. iDASH: integrating data for analysis, anonymization, and sharing. J. Am. Med. Inform. Assoc.: JAMIA 19 (2), 196–201. Available from: http://dx.doi.org/10.1136/amiajnl-2011-000538.

Patrick, K., Wolszon, L., Basen-Engquist, K., Demark-Wahnefried, W., Prokhorov, A., Barrera, S., et al., 2011. CYberinfrastructure for COmparative effectiveness REsearch (CYCORE): improving data from cancer clinical trials. J. Transl. Behav. Med. Practice, Policy, Research 1 (1), 83–88. Available from: <http://dx.doi.org/10.1007/s13142-010-0005-z>.

Paulk, M., Weber, C.V., Curtis, B., Chrissis, M.B., 1995. The Capability Maturity Model: Guidelines for Improving the Software Process. Addison-Wesley.

Peterson, S.K., Shinn, E.H., Basen-Engquist, K., Demark-Wahnefried, W., Prokhorov, A. V., Baru, C., et al., 2013. Identifying early dehydration risk with home-based sensors during radiation treatment: a feasibility study with head and neck cancer patients. J. Natl. Cancer Inst. Monograph 47, 162–168, Oxford University Press, http://dx.doi.org/10.1093/jncimonographs/lgt016.

Saaty, T.L., 1982. Decision Making for Leaders: The Analytical Hierarchy Process for Decision in a Complex World. Lifetime Learning Publications, Belmot, CA.

Seaman, C., Guo, Y., 2011. Measuring and monitoring technical debt. Adv. Comput. 82, 22.

SEI, Software Engineering Institute, 2001a. Capability Maturity Model Integration (CMMI), Version 1.1, CMMI for Systems Engineering and Software Engineering (CMMI-SE/SW, V1.1), Continuous Representation. Carnegie Mellon University, CMU/SEI-2002-TR-001.

SEI, Software Engineering Institute, 2001b. Capability Maturity Model Integration (CMMI), Version 1.1, CMMI for Systems Engineering and Software Engineering (CMMI-SE/SW, V1.1), Staged Representation. Carnegie Mellon University, CMU/SEI-2002-TR-002.

Shewhart, W.A., 1931. Economic Control of Quality of Manufactured Product. D. Van Nostrand Company, New York, NY.

Woods, E., 2011. Industrial architectural assessment using TARA. In: Ninth Working IEEE/IFIP Conference on Software Architecture (WICSA).

Exploiting the synergies between SQA, SQC, and SPI in order for an organization to leverage Sarbanes Oxley internal control budgets

14

I. Fleming

SQA.net, USA; SugarCRM Inc., Cupertino, CA, USA

14.1 TOTAL QUALITY MANAGEMENT ROLE DEFINITIONS FOR QUALITY RELATED ACTIVITIES

The following is an overview of Total Quality Management (TQM; Martínez-Lorente et al., 1998), which provides the framework under which the quality assurance, quality control, and process improvement roles are defined in manufacturing and from which their software counterparts are derived.

As part of Japan's post war reconstruction efforts, led by the allied occupied forces, W. Edwards Deming (Deming, 1986) was invited by the Japanese Union of Scientists and Engineers to train engineers, managers, and scholars in concepts of quality that included the application of Statistical Process Control (SPC; Tennant, 2001) based on Walter Shewart's earlier work: "Economic control of quality of manufactured product" (Shewhart, 1931). A number of Japanese manufacturers later applied these techniques and experienced significantly increased levels of quality and productivity that the West would later emulate. This period of history in the quality movement marked the beginning of what later became known as Total Quality Management, that encompassed management ownership of quality as well as a more analytical perspective on quality control and process improvement.

Based on SPC concepts, TQM seeks to break down the manufacturing production process into discrete steps. Each discrete step has an output or component that has a required specification, e.g., measurement, weight, etc. Throughout the production cycle the process step outputs are continually sampled and verified for being within their required specifications.

14.1.1 DEFINITION OF SOFTWARE QUALITY CONTROL, DERIVED FROM ITS MANUFACTURING COUNTERPART WITHIN TQM

The activity, within TQM, of verifying that throughout production the process step outputs conform to specifications is what Juran (1999) refers to as the *narrow meaning of Quality Control*. Under this definition the term quality control refers to defect prevention during the manufacturing process, rather than *after-the-fact inspection*. It is from this manufacturing definition of narrow quality control that the following definition of Software Quality Control (SQC) is derived.

Software Quality Control: The function of software quality that checks that the project follows its standards, processes, and procedures, and that the project produces the required internal and external (deliverable) products (NASA, 2009).

14.1.2 DEFINITION OF SOFTWARE PROCESS IMPROVEMENT, DERIVED FROM ITS MANUFACTURING COUNTERPART WITHIN TQM

In addition to a more effective and efficient method of discovering process issues early in the production process, TQM also contains an element of process improvement (Houston, 1988). Given a repeatable set of process steps that are producing components within specified requirements the capability of a process can be known and documented. By measuring and benchmarking process capability, alternative process steps can be proposed and evaluated for potential process improvement. In this way the complete production cycle is continually monitored for meeting the process specifications and the whole process is subjected to continuous process improvement. Software Process Improvement (SPI) is the adoption of manufacturing process improvement methodologies in TQM.

14.1.3 DEFINITION OF SOFTWARE QUALITY ASSURANCE, DERIVED FROM ITS MANUFACTURING COUNTERPART WITHIN TQM

Quality assurance in the sense of adherence to processes, procedures, and standards, is pivotal to TQM in terms of ensuring usage of the specified procedures and providing reliable baseline product metrics for both process control and process improvement. Without having confidence that a given process had been followed to produce known results, any comparison of results would be meaningless for either process control or process improvement. Software

Quality Assurance (SQA) is the adoption of manufacturing quality assurance in TQM and is defined as:

Software Quality Assurance: The function of software quality that assures that the standards, processes, and procedures are appropriate for the project and are correctly implemented (NASA, 2009).

14.2 TQM FOR SOFTWARE DEVELOPMENT—CMMI®

Following the impressive results achieved by manufacturers worldwide in product quality (including cost reduction) using TQM, Watts Humphrey (Humphrey, 1987) and others began applying TQM to software development. The Software Engineering Institute (SEI) formalized these TQM based concepts as the Capability Maturity Model for Software (Software CMM). Version 1.0 of the model was published in 1991 (Paulk et al., 1991). The "I" in CMMI® stands for Integration, as over the years various models have been integrated to form the current offerings from the CMMI® Institute, the organization that is now responsible for maintaining and publishing the CMMI® models.

The basic premise underlying the SEI's work on software process maturity embodies TQM principles, namely that the quality of the software product is largely determined by the quality of the software development and maintenance processes used to build and maintain it.

Within CMMI® for software development the core engineering process capabilities, project management capabilities and process management capabilities are presented alongside SQA, SQC, and SPI (as previously defined) to form a comprehensive TQM based approach to the development of software.

It is the CMMI® framework that will be used as a reference model for the motivation and explanation of a proposed Quality Process Team (QPT), organizational unit, that seeks to exploit the synergies between SQA, SQC, and SPI.

14.3 OPPORTUNITIES AND CHALLENGES ADDRESSED BY FORMING A CONSOLIDATED QPT

14.3.1 OPPORTUNITY: SYNERGY AND OVERLAPS BETWEEN THE SQA AND SQC ROLES AND RESPONSIBILITIES

In order to understand potential synergies between SQA and SQC an examination of the procedure of Software Requirements Specification (SRS; IEEE, 1984) review is presented. The SRS review is the formal scrutiny of the SRS in order to determine whether or not it meets its purpose in terms of completeness and correctness.

Prior to the SRS review itself; a documented set of standards and procedures would be in place to make certain that the SRS review procedure was repeatable and conformed with current best practices. In addition baseline metrics

(ISO 9126-2, 2001) would have been defined in order to evaluate the SRS review procedure and in turn subject it to continuous improvement. Metrics for measuring the SRS review process would include identifying software defects that could be attributed to an ambiguous SRS, or customer needs that were not present in the software, and not caught in the SRS review.

Given the above SRS review process and prerequisite documented standards and procedures, the SQA and SQC roles can be defined.

The role of SQA is to verify that the SRS document, and the procedure that produced it, follows the appropriate documented standards.

The role of SQC is concerned with the verification via inspection and review of the SRS itself in terms of:

- Does the SRS include all known customer needs?
- Do any requirements conflict with, or duplicate, other requirements?
- Is each requirement in scope with the Project?

As can be seen, SQC needs to have a deeper knowledge of the content of the SRS in terms of fitness for purpose whilst SQA needs only to ensure that the document standards and procedures used are appropriate for the task and have been correctly followed.

A given person performing the SQC role against the SRS can efficiently perform SQA on the document and procedures as the two roles require a slightly different perspective on essentially the same activity: that is, reading and reviewing the documentation. It is important to note that in the case of the SRS review, the document itself has been produced by a individual outside of SQA and SQC so that the review of procedures and standards is targeted at a third party's work.

This example, of the SRS review, is typical of the opportunity for overlapping the roles of SQC and SQA. Design reviews, code reviews, configuration management audits, test documentation review, and requirements traceability reviews are other examples of where this synergy work well.

14.3.2 OPPORTUNITY: SYNERGY AND OVERLAPS BETWEEN THE SQA AND SPI ROLES AND RESPONSIBILITIES

The synergy and overlaps between SQA and SPI are concerned with tasks related to understanding the extent to which a given process is repeatable, compliant, and performing within its specified quality objectives.

SPI is concerned with making sure that processes are behaving consistently with regard to defined process measures and instigating, then managing, process improvement initiatives when appropriate. In order to determine whether or not a process is behaving consistently measurements such as number of times an SRS revision is made, using the pervious SRS review example, need to be taken and recorded.

One of the roles of SQA is to record noncompliant issues, which are occurrences of the appropriate standards and procedures not being followed. A single person within the QPT group can efficiently do the recording of noncompliant issues, an SQA activity, and process quality measurements that is an SPI activity. In addition, an understanding of noncompliance, or the extent to which a given process is repeatable, is essential for any process improvement analysis.

QPT team members performing both SQA and SPI would also be well positioned to characterize the given process in terms of its repeatability, noncompliance issues, quality measurements and being a suitable candidate for potential process improvement.

14.3.3 OPPORTUNITY: LEVERAGING INCREASED SQA CAPABILITIES REQUIRED FOR EXTERNAL REGULATIONS

Although CMMI® is targeted at all organizations developing software, only 4.36% of the total successful CMMI® appraisals, from January 1, 2007, to March 31, 2014, were for organizations performing "Application development for in-house use" (SEI CMMI® Maturity Profile Report, 2014).

Whilst the percentage of CMMI® appraisals for organizations developing in-house applications is relatively small, the basic SQA function has increased significantly since the year 2000 within many large organizations due to increased government, state, and industry regulations. These regulations include Sarbanes Oxley (SOX; SOX, 2002) that contains Section 404 which mandates:

All publicly traded companies must establish internal controls and procedures for financial reporting and must document, test, and maintain those controls and procedures to ensure their effectiveness.

Given the increase in personnel fulfilling basic SQA and SQC roles, to satisfy regulations such as SOX (Coates IV et al., 2014), an opportunity exists to leverage those individuals for process improvement.

14.3.4 COMMON CHALLENGE: THE ESSENTIAL DIFFICULTIES OF WORKING WITH THE CONCEPTUAL STRUCTURES OF THE SOFTWARE PRODUCT

All software construction involves essential tasks, the fashioning of the complex conceptual structures that compose the abstract software entity.

In his paper Brooks (Brooks, 1975) defines the essential difficulties of working with software, a nonphysical medium. These essential difficulties of software include invisibility, changeability, and complexity. In software there are no physical measurements (weight, dimensions, tensile strength, etc.) that can be specified and measured to facilitate SQA, SQC, and SPI in the quantitative manner that their counterparts can do with a physical manufactured product.

Being able to usefully define and measure desired attributes of the abstract software entity is a common challenge for SQA, SQC, and SPI. By combining SQA, SQC, and SPI personnel into a single group, a center of excellence can be established to address the essential difficulties of defining and measuring the abstract software entity.

14.3.5 COMMON CHALLENGE: MUTUAL REQUIREMENT OF INDEPENDENCE OF SQA AND SQC FROM ENGINEERING

For independent software verification (SQC) and enforced compliance to standards (SQA) to take place the SQC and SQA manager(s) need to be at a peer with their engineering counterparts. Organizationally SQA and SQC have the same independence requirements from engineering. SPI, however, could be managed by engineering or project management but given the SPI synergies already outlined with both SQA and SQC an *independent* group consisting of SQA, SQC, and SPI will prove effective for implementing a process improvement framework such as CMMI®.

14.4 OVERVIEW OF THE CMMI® MODEL AND DOCUMENT STRUCTURE

CMMI®'s purpose is for modeling and building process improvement systems. CMMI® for Development (CMMI®, 2010) is a presentation of goals and practices pertinent to software development that can be defined in terms of maturity and then subjected to process improvement. CMMI® process maturity follows the basic TQM, using SPC techniques, path of defining repeatable processes that have capabilities that are within the required specifications and then subjecting those processes to continuous improvement. The five levels of maturity in CMMI® are:

- Initial—Process unpredictable, poorly controlled, and reactive
- Managed—Process characterized for projects and is often reactive
- Defined—Process characterized for the organization and is proactive
- Quantitatively managed—Processes managed and controlled
- Optimizing—Focus on process improvement.

CMMI® is documented as a set of goals and practices within process areas that are relevant for software development, within a process improvement framework. The goals and practices within the key process areas specify what is required rather than how to achieve them. There are 22 process areas in total and these are subdivided by the following process area groups:

- Process management
- Project management
- Technical solution
- Support (processes that support other processes).

By way of example, of the CMMI® structure, *Elicit needs* is a specific practice for the *Develop customer requirements* specific goal within the Requirements

Development process area, which is a part of the Technical solution group of process areas.

In addition to specific goals and practices, which are pertinent to a given process area, there are also generic goals and practices which relate to the achievement of a given level of process maturity. For example *"The process is institutionalized as a defined process"* is a generic goal, broken down by generic practices, for achieving a level three maturity, which is "Defined."

14.5 PROPOSED QPT'S ROLES AND RESPONSIBILITIES WITHIN CMMI®

The following section lists the QPT's core roles and responsibilities (SQC, SQA, and SPI) with the related CMMI® process areas. For each role a short responsibility assignment matrix RAM (PMI, 2010) presentation is made in order to define the QPT roles and responsibilities within the context of CMMI®. In addition recommended skills, tools, and techniques that would be relevant to a QPT center of excellence, for CMMI®, are presented.

14.5.1 SQC WITHIN CMMI®

There are two process areas in CMMI® that exclusively contain SQC goals and practices and these are Validation and Verification.

Validation (Andriole, 1986) refers to *the correct product being built,* whilst Verification refers to *the product being built correctly.* In this way the question of validation is one of the product meeting is requirements when placed in its operational setting, whilst verification refers to meeting the specifications and following correct standards and procedures as the software product is being built.

Validation and verification are essentially testing activities; testing being defined as both dynamic and static where dynamic testing involves running some code whilst static testing involves code or document reviews.

The scope of the verification and validation is not just functionality but includes other software quality attributes (Boehm et al., 1978), for example:

- Usability
- Performance.

14.6 QPT RESPONSIBILITIES FOR VALIDATION AND VERIFICATION

QPT management should be accountable and responsible for the goals and practices within these two process areas, given they are core to SQC. QPT personnel should perform validation and verification activities within the development organization where independent SQC is required, for example, system or acceptance testing (Cimperman, 2006). Developers, writing automated unit tests (JUNIT, 2014) or conducting peer code reviews (Cohen, 2006), can also perform SQC (validation and verification activities) during product development where independence is not a requirement.

14.7 QPT CENTER OF EXCELLENCE SKILLS, TOOLS AND TECHNIQUES RECOMMENDATIONS FOR VALIDATION AND VERIFICATION

The following center of excellence recommendations for Validation and Verification is a subset of the possible tools, techniques, and skills (IEEE, 1990) that can be used and serves as further clarification of the roles and responsibilities for QPT personnel performing SQC within a CMMI® implementation:

- White box testing (Tester has knowledge of the internal structure)
- Black box testing (Tester has no knowledge of the internal structure)
- Automated GUI testing
- Automated API testing
- Performance (load) testing
- Usability testing.

14.7.1 SQA WITHIN CMMI®

In CMMI® the Process and Product Quality Assurance (PPQA) process area contains the goals and practices of SQA.

A Process Asset Library (PAL) is first established, as part of the goals and practices of the Organizational Process Definition (OPD) process area, referenced in the later *SPI within CMMI®* section. The PAL documents standards, processes, and procedures that the organization has deemed appropriate, in terms of their usefulness for achieving project or process goals, and these are subjected to formal SQA (PPQA).

The selection, and definition, of the contents of the PAL is made on the basis of the value of following or not following a given standard, process or procedure and this selection decision is a group one made by project management, engineering and the QPT.

14.8 QPT RESPONSIBILITIES FOR PPQA

QPT management should be accountable and responsible for the goals and practices within the PPQA process area. QPT personnel should perform PPQA activities although not exclusively. A peer code review (Cohen, 2006), where one developer reviews another's code is an example of a PPQA evaluation that could be performed by non-QPT personnel.

For large software organizations an independent group, such as the QPT being described, from engineering and project management should be established to ensure objectivity during PPQA product and process audits.

In addition to objectively evaluating processes and work products for compliance, PPQA in CMMI® includes goals and practices for documenting and resolving noncompliance issues. Noncompliance issues can be examined to determine if there are any quality trends that can be identified and addressed. This practice by PPQA overlaps with SPI practices identified in the following *Software Process Improvement within CMMI®* section and has been discussed in the previous *Synergy and overlaps between the SQA and SPI roles and responsibilities* section. The presence, and trend, of noncompliance issues is one of the first indications that processes are not repeatable or processes are not being managed effectively.

14.9 QPT CENTER OF EXCELLENCE SKILLS, TOOLS AND TECHNIQUES RECOMMENDATIONS FOR CMMI® PPQA

The PPQA activity, in terms of evaluating whether or not processes and work products are compliant, is essentially an audit activity. In some cases it is not possible to audit all processes and work products so sampling and the use (and knowledge) of statistical sampling techniques from SPC (Tennant, 2001) would be required. SPC knowledge would also be needed for the identification of noncompliance trends, and the identification of potential process areas for improvement.

14.9.1 SPI WITHIN CMMI®

There are six CMMI® process areas that are relevant to SPI in terms of defining, managing and improving a given organizations processes, these process areas are:

- Organizational Process Definition (OPD)
- Organizational Process Focus (OPF)
- Organizational Performance Management (OPM)
- Organizational Process Performance (OPP)
- Measurement and Analysis (MA)
- Causal Analysis and Resolution (CAR).

There is overlap between OPM/OPP and OPF process areas as they are targeted at different CMMI® process performance maturity levels. The following breakdown does not include OPP and OPM, although the discussion on OPF is applicable for the roles and responsibilities of both OPM and OPP.

14.10 ORGANIZATIONAL PROCESS DEFINITION

The OPD process area defines the key practices for establishing and maintaining documentation for process, procedures, and standards. This process area forms the centerpiece for both SPI and SQA by providing documented procedures, contained in a PAL that must be complied with. In addition the OPD contains practices for defining and maintaining product and process measures, contained in the Organizations Measurement Repository (OMR), that are related to the organization's set of formal processes, procedures, and standards contained in the PAL.

14.11 ORGANIZATIONAL PROCESS FOCUS

The goals and practices of the OPF are concerned with process improvement, based on the processes defined in the OPD and using the measurements defined in the OMR. OPF has goals and practices for:

- Establishing process needs
- Identifying potential process improvements
- Establishing process improvement action plans
- Implementing process improvement action plans
- Monitoring the potential process improvement
- Updating the PAL.

14.12 MEASUREMENT AND ANALYSIS

Both OPD and OPF practices make use of goals and practices defined in the MA process area.

The MA process area contains the following practices:

- Establish measurement objectives
- Specify measures
- Specify data collection and storage procedures
- Specify analysis procedures
- Obtain measurement data
- Analyze measurement data
- Store data and results
- Communicate results.

MA is considered a support process area within CMMI® as its goals and practices support both project management and process management process areas.

14.13 CAUSAL ANALYSIS AND RESOLUTION

The CAR process area is, similar to the MA process area, considered a support process area in that its goals and practices are to support project and process management *to identify causes of selected outcomes and take action to improve process performance.*

14.14 QPT RESPONSIBILITIES FOR CMMI® SPI RELATED PROCESS AREAS

QPT management should be accountable and responsible for the goals and practices within the organizational process management areas of:

- Organizational Process Definition (OPD)
- Organizational Process Focus (OPF)
- Organizational Performance Management (OPM)
- Organizational Process Performance (OPP).

QPT management should also be accountable and responsible for the goals and practices of the following two *support* process areas when they relate to process management:

- Causal Analysis and Resolution (CAR)
- Measurement and Analysis (MA).

When tasks performed in the above two process areas are supporting project management then project management could choose to either delegate or retain responsibility for the goals of the CAR and MA process areas.

For all six CMMI® process areas related to SPI it is advised that QPT form and maintain a center of excellence for the required knowledge of skills, tools, and techniques of those process areas' practices.

14.15 QPT CENTER OF EXCELLENCE SKILLS, TOOLS AND TECHNIQUES RECOMMENDATIONS FOR CMMI® SPI RELATED PROCESS AREAS

Six Sigma (Tennant, 2001) is a set of tools and techniques, developed by Motorola in 1986, which seek to improve the quality of process outputs by minimizing variability and identifying and removing the cause of defects.

Six Sigma's tools and techniques are a good match for use within the CMMI® process improvement related process areas as both Six Sigma and

CMMI® are based on the concepts of TQM. The following is a list of Six Sigma tools and techniques related to the SPI relevant process areas of CMMI®.

- 5 Whys: An approach to root cause analysis
- Control charts: Determine whether or not a process is stable
- Design of experiments: Formal experiments to determine cause and effect
- Fishbone diagram: High-level root cause analysis
- Pareto charts: Uses include charting the most common sources of defects
- Process mapping: Used to analyze process flows for issues and process improvement
- Sampling/data: Statistically based techniques for sampling
- Value stream mapping: Determine which activities add value in the process map
- Variation: Techniques to identify and classify variation for process control.

14.16 POTENTIAL CMMI® ROLE CONFLICTS OF INTEREST FOR A COMBINED SQC, SQA, AND SPI TEAM

All process areas are potentially subjected to PPQA and this includes those processes that are related to SQC and SPI. Any individual from the QPT team cannot SQA his or her own work so peer SQA, similar to peer code reviews between developers, is recommended. In this way a QTP team member could verify, SQC, a given software component but a peer QTP team member would perform SQA on the verification activity itself. These roles could then be reversed for other verification and SQA activities so that the QPT team member performs both verification SQC and SQA but never on their own work.

14.16.1 WHO QUALITY ASSURES QUALITY ASSURANCE?

As with all processes in CMMI® the PPQA (SQA) process area itself has documented procedures and is itself subjected to PPQA (SQA).

Peer SQA reviews could be performed as outlined for the SQA of SQC and SPI related process areas. In this way QPT team members could audit each other in terms of performing SQA activities. QPT management could also perform hands-on SQA solely for this purpose, that is to review the QPT teams PPQA activities in terms of conforming to agreed standards and guidelines.

14.17 CONCLUDING REMARKS

All software development organizations will have some form of SQA and many IT organizations are subjected to federal, state, or industry governance. Compliance with agreed critical processes, such as requirements documentation, program specifications, source revision control, etc., is essential for basic management and control of the development process as well as for the satisfaction of external regulations. In addition all software organizations will have some form of SQC, which could range from performing dynamic testing to the review of all intermediate work products, such as requirements, specifications, and code.

SPI will also be present in most organizations although it is less likely to be a formalized process, as it is not considered *essential*. Combining SQA (including regulation compliance activities), SQC, and SPI into a separate QPT will allow organizations to address the common problems of measuring, controlling, and improving software production. Aligning and addressing the difficulties and required knowledge of all software audits, reviews, and measurements can facilitate an effective process improvement framework implementation, such as CMMI®.

REFERENCES

Andriole, 1986. In: Andriole, S.J. (Ed.), Software Validation, Verification, Testing, and Documentation. Petrocelli Books, Princeton, NJ.

Boehm, B.W., Brown, J.R., Kaspar, H., Lipow, M., McLeod, G., Merritt, M., 1978. Characteristics of Software Quality. North Holland Publishing, Amsterdam, the Netherlands.

Brooks, 1975. The Mythical Man Month. Addison-Wesley, Reading, MA (Chapter 14).

Cimperman, R., 2006. UAT Defined: A Guide to Practical User Acceptance Testing. Pearson Education, New York City NY, (Chapter 2) ISBN 9780132702621.

CMMI®, 2010. CMMI Product Team: CMMI for Development, Version 1.3 (CMU/SEI-2010-TR-033). Carnegie Mellon University, Software Engineering Institute, Pittsburgh, PA.

Coates, IV, J.C., Srinivasan, S., 2014. SOX after ten years: a multidisciplinary review (January 12, 2014). Accounting Horizons. Available at SSRN: <http://ssrn.com/abstract=2379731>.

Cohen, J., 2006. Best Kept Secrets of Peer Code Review (Modern Approach. Practical Advice.). Smart Bear Inc., Somerville, MA, ISBN 1-59916-067-6.

Deming, W.E., 1986. Out of the Crisis. MIT Center for Advanced Engineering Study, Cambridge, MA.

Houston, A., 1988. A Total Quality Management Process Improvement Model. Navy Personnel Research and Development Center, San Diego, CA.

Humphrey, W.S., 1987. Characterizing the Software Process: A Maturity Framework. CMU/SEI-87-TR-11. Carnegie Mellon University, Software Engineering Institute, Pittsburgh, PA.

IEEE, 1984. Guide to Software Requirements Specifications. ISBN 0-7381-4418-5, IEEE Computer Society Press, Los Alamitos, CA.

IEEE, 1990. IEEE Standard Glossary of Software Engineering Terminology" (IEEE Std 610.12-1990). IEEE Computer Society Press, Los Alamitos, CA.

ISO 9126-2, 2001. DTR 9126-2: Software Engineering—Software Product Quality Part 2—External Metrics. ISO /IEC JTC1/SC7 N2419, 2001, International Organization for Standardization, Geneva, Switzerland.

JUNIT, 2014. Retrieved from <http://junit.org> (October 2014).

Juran, 1999. Juran's Quality Handbook, fifth ed. McGraw-Hill, New York, NY, ISBN 0-07-034003-X.

Martínez-Lorente, A.R., Dewhurst, F., Dale, B.G., 1998. Total quality management: origins and evolution of the term. The TQM Magazine. MCB University Publishers Ltd, Bingley, UK.

NASA, 2009. NASA software assurance definitions. Retrieved from <http://www.hq.nasa.gov/office/codeq/software/umbrella_defs.htm> (October 2014).

Paulk, M.C., Curtis, B., Chrissis, M.B., Averill, E.L., Bamberger, J., Kasse, T.C., et al., 1991. Capability Maturity Model for Software. CMU/SEI-91-TR-24. Carnegie Mellon University, Software Engineering Institute, Pittsburgh, PA.

PMI, 2010. A Guide to the Project Management Body of Knowledge (PMBOK Guide). PMI Standards Committee, Project Management Institute, Newtown Square, PA, ISBN 1-933890-66-5.

SEI Cmmi® Maturity Profile Report, 2014. CMMI Maturity Profile Report. Carnegie Mellon University, Software Engineering Institute, Pittsburgh, PA, Retrieved from <http://cmmi®institute.com/wp-content/uploads/2014/05/Maturity-Profile-Ending-March-2014.pdf> (October 2014).

Shewhart, 1931. Economic Control of Quality of Manufactured Product. D. Van Nostrand Company, New York, NY, ISBM0-87389-076-0.

SOX, 2002. Public Law 107-204—Sarbanes-Oxley Act of 2002.

Tennant, G., 2001. Six Sigma: SPC and TQM in Manufacturing and Services. Gower Publishing Ltd, Farnham, UK, ISBN 0-566-08374-4.

Glossary

Acceptable Quality Minimum expected quality (combination of different quality parameters with expected values) of the product/service at which customer of the product/service is willing to use the product/service.

Accessibility The degree to which a software product can be used by persons with special needs.

Accident A catastrophic failure of a software system resulting in substantial financial loss or physical harm.

Agile Development Process A lightweight software engineering process that promotes iterative development and close collaboration between developers and customers.

Agile Methods A method for software development that follows the principles of the Agile Manifesto.

Appraisal Costs Cost of technical review activities, testing and debugging the software, data collection, and metrics evaluation.

Architectural Choice Choices typically taken by software architects regarding some aspects of the design of a software system. Typical choices involve technologies and design or architectural patterns.

Architectural Technical Debt (ATD) Immature architecture artifacts caused by architecture decisions that consciously or unconsciously compromise system quality attributes, particularly maintainability and evolvability.

Architectural Trade-Off Analysis The process of analyzing pros-cons of alternative architectures based on a set of formal, well-defined, clear, and measurable criterion.

Architectural Violation The discrepancy between the architecture and implementation.

Architecture Conformance Analysis The process for checking the consistency between an architecture description and the corresponding implementation.

Architecture Decision Design decision affecting the architecture design space for a target software system. An example architecture decision is the adoption of a specific architecture pattern in a software system.

Architecture Reflexion Viewpoint Architecture viewpoint that can be used to define reflexion model for different architecture views.

Asset An asset is a computing resource (data, bandwidth, process use, privacy) whose loss incurs signification damage (financial or physical).

ATD Item A unit of architectural technical debt in a software system. An ATD item is characterized by multiple elements such as name, version, status, priority, intentionality, compromised quality attribute, rationale, benefit, cost, principal, interest, and related change scenarios.

ATD View Architecture view expressing the architecture of a software system from the perspective of specific concerns on architectural technical debt. An ATD view conforms to the definition of a specific ATD viewpoint.

ATD Viewpoint Architecture viewpoint framing specific concerns about architectural technical debt.

Attack Attempts to damage software system resources or render them inaccessible to authorized users.

Attributes Characteristics of software products or processes.

Automated Testing The use of software tools (separate from the software being tested) to control the execution of tests and the comparison of actual outcomes with predicted outcomes.

Behavioral Fault Simulation (BFS) An MBDA paradigm which focuses more on behavioral simulation of system models, and produces the failure model of a system by injecting faults into the executable formal specifications of the system, thereby establishing the system level effects of faults.

Capability Maturity Model Integration (CMMI) A process improvement training and appraisal program and service administered and marketed by Carnegie Mellon University and required by many Department of Defense and Government contracts, especially in software development.

Capacitated Task Allocation Problem A common name for task-resource mapping problems in a limited resource environment.

Change Management The process of managing requests for system modification which include determining their feasibility, evaluating their impact, planning, implementing, and assessing their success.

Class Encapsulates the data and methods used to create the declaration for an object in a programming language.

Cloud Computing Focuses on maximizing the effectiveness of the shared resources in particular virtual data storage and web services.

Code-Smells Bad design choice that can have a negative impact on the code quality which could introduce defects.

Cohesion The extent to which a module's individual parts are needed to perform the same task.

Component Fault Trees (CFT) An extension to traditional fault trees which aims to provide better association between the hierarchy of faults and the architectural hierarchy of the system components.

Compositional Traceability Extension of traceability to include compositional equivalence between specification and collection of elements that address the specification. While Traceability identifies the relationship between specification and elements that address them, compositional traceability includes analysis that the elements collectively meet the specification.

Context The degree to which a software product is able to modify its behavior based on characteristics of its user or the environment in which it is used.

Cost of Quality Costs incurred by all quality-related activities pursued by the development tram plus the downstream costs that can be demonstrably related to lack of quality.

Coupling The degree of interdependence between the different modules in a system.

Crowd Sourcing The process of obtaining needed services by soliciting contributions from a large group of people in an online community.

Customer Person who will ultimately buy a software product or service created to meet a targeted market need.

Customer Satisfaction Ensuring that a software product does what the customer expects to with an appropriate amount of effort.

CyberInfrastructure Socio-technical-economical systems supporting the efficient delivery, processing, and visualization of data across different communities. CyberInfrastructures deal both with technical problems such as data encryption and scalability of data delivery and processing, and with social and organizational problems such as privacy concerns and organizational control over shared data.

Deductive Cause Consequence Analysis (DCCA) A formal method for safety analysis which uses mathematical methods to determine whether a given component fault is the cause of a system failure.

Defect Any deviation from the specification mentioned in software product's functional specification document.

Defect Analysis Done by the development team, in order to decide what defects should be assigned, fixed, rejected, or deferred to be dealt with later.

Deployment Alternative Each one of alternative approaches for assigning a set of tasks to the available resources.

Design Pattern A recurrent solution to solve a software design problem used on several context.

Design Structure Matrix (DSM) A matrix in which the row and column elements represent the elements of the model that is analyzed. The cells in the matrix represent the dependency relations among the elements.

Design Structure Reflexion Matrix A design structure matrix that represents the reflexion model as a result of architecture conformance analysis.

Development Assurance Level (DAL) One of five levels which summarizes the level of rigor necessary to assess the safety of an aircraft's architectural element.

Domain Design A subset of software design that cares about on how the business domain is represented on the software.

Effective Quality Management (EQM) Method to help software quality managers to negotiate acceptable quality targets with input from a minimum set of stakeholders.

Efficiency The hardware, software, and programming resources required by a program to perform its function.

E-Health The practice of applying electronic communication and processing to the health-care domain.

Fact Facts describe the situation for a software system, which includes organizational concerns, the development process, architecture, implementation, or operation of a software system. Facts are tuples of Entities and Attributes, where entities specify the elements we observe (e.g., documentation and code), and attributes specify the properties of the entity under evaluation (e.g., consistency and completeness).

Failure Inability of a software product to perform a required function within its specified performance requirements.

Failure Costs Costs incurred to repair the defect as well as those to ensure that the repair has not introduced additional defects.

Failure Logic Synthesis and Analysis (FLSA) An MBDA paradigm which focuses on the automatic construction of predictive system failure analyses, and where the system failure models are constructed from component failure models using a process of composition.

Failure Modes and Effects Analysis (FMEA) A well-known safety analysis method which reviews components, sub-systems to identify failure modes, and their causes and effects in the system behavior.

Failure Propagation and Transformation Calculus (FPTC) A method for determining and modeling failure behavior of both hardware and software components of systems.

Failure Propagation and Transformation Notation (FPTN) A modular and graphical MBDA method to specify failure behavior of systems with complex architectures.

Fault Tree Analysis (FTA) A widely used dependability analysis method that utilizes graphical representation based on Boolean logic to show logical connection between different faults and their causes.

Federal Information Security Management Act (FISMA) A US law passed in 2002 that requires each federal agency to implement an agency-wide program to provide information security for the information and systems that support its operations and assets. This law requires all government agencies to adhere to a set of security standards defined by the National Institute of Standards and Technology (NIST).

Flexibility Effort required to modify an existing software system.

Formal Methods Mathematically based approach to program modeling and design verification that relies on using mathematical proof of correctness.

Formal Safety Analysis Platform/New Symbolic Model Verifier (FSAP-NuSMV) A safety analysis tool based on the NuSMV2 model-checker which allows the user to inject particular failure modes into the system and then observe the effects of that failure on the system behavior.

Guidelines Alternate patterns of activities to achieve an objective.

Hazard A risk that if realized can lead to the failure of a software system to satisfy its safety requirements.

Health Care Health care (or healthcare) is the diagnosis, treatment, and prevention of disease, illness, injury, and other physical and mental impairments in human beings.

Health-Related Social Networking Sites (SNSs) Online communities that enable the connection of users and facilitate the exchange of health experiences, outcomes, advice, and support among them.

Hierarchically Performed Hazard Origin and Propagation Studies (HiP-HOPS) An advanced and well supported model based dependability analysis tool which allows automatic dependability analysis and multiobjective optimization of system models.

Hierarchically Performed Hazard Origins Propagation Studies (HiP-HOPS) A software model-based reliability analysis tool and methodology which allows automatic failure analysis of a given system model.

High-Level Module (HLM) A grouping of explicit programming structures— packages and/or directories, that cumulatively demonstrate high modularity.

Health Insurance Portability and Accountability Act (HIPAA) A US law passed in 1996 and defining standards for ensuring the security and privacy of Protected Health Information (PHI).

Implicit Requirements Requirements supposed to be part of the design phase, but not formally expressed and/or discussed by the contractual parts.

Information Hiding The decomposition of a system into modules such that difficult design decisions or design decisions that are likely to change are hidden from other modules.

Inheritance Allows the specialization of class behavior by reusing some parts of the parent class when defining a new sub class.

Integrity The extent to which access to data and software by unauthorized persons is controlled.

Interoperability Effort required to use software on more than one system.

Lines of Code (LOC) Metric based on the number of executable statements in the source code used to implement a software product.

Maintainability The effort required to locate and fix program defects.

Mean-Time-Between-Failure (MBTF) Metric that measures the average time a system is available and operating, excludes the time spent on repair.

Mean-Time-to-Failure (MTTF) Metric that describes the average expected time to failure for a non-repairable system.

Mean-Time-to-Repair (MTTR) Metric that measures the average time a system is down following a failure.

Metric Quantitative measure of a degree to which a software system or process possesses some property.

Model Based Dependability Analysis (MBDA) An emergent dependability analysis paradigm where formal system models are used in the analyses and the syntheses are performed automatically.

Model-Driven Development A software development approach that is based on developing—generally visual—models instead of plain text coding. Since the developed model will be used for deriving the actual system, it shall be as detailed as an equivalent executable code.

Nonfunctional Requirements (NFR) Nonfunctional requirements for a software/software system describe operational requirements like portability, performance, scalability, etc.

Object An entity in a software system that represents an instance of a real world entity or the instance of a class.

Phase Activities segregated as per professional knowledge domain in a process.

Polymorphism Allows object-oriented programmers to assign different meanings to a name variable or function based on its context of use.

Portability (1) ease with which a system or component can be transferred from one hardware or software environment to another (ISO/IEC/IEEE 24765:2010 Systems and software engineering—Vocabulary) (2) capability of a program to be executed on various types of data processing systems without converting the program to a different language and with little or no modification (ISO/IEC 2382-1:1993 Information technology—Vocabulary—Part 1: Fundamental terms, 01.04.06) (3) degree of effectiveness and efficiency with which a system, product, or component can be transferred from one hardware, software or other operational or usage environment to another (ISO/IEC 25010:2011 Systems and software engineering—Systems and software Quality Requirements and Evaluation (SQuaRE)—System and software quality models, 4.2.8) (4) property that the reference points of an object allow it to be adapted to a variety of configurations (ISO/IEC 10746-2:2009 Information technology—Open Distributed Processing—Reference Model: Foundations, 15.4.1) Syn: transportability See Also: machine-independent.

Portability Effort required to transfer a program from one computing platform or operating environment to another.

Postmortem A mechanism to allow a development team to extract the lesson learned following the completion of a software product.

Practices Locally discerned patterns of activities. Here, locality is with respect to project, or scope of professional work.

Prevention Costs Costs associated with management and planning of quality activities, along with the technical activities to verify and validate the requirements and design models.

Privacy Privacy refers to the user's ability to control when, how, and to what extent information about themselves will be collected, used, and shared with others.

Process Engineering A discipline including various techniques and methods to design, operationalize processes to meet quality of the outcome of a process.

Process Improvement Identification of current state-of-the-practice for software development within an organization and making it better.

Process Metric Measure of a characteristic of specific software engineering tasks (e.g., defect removal rate).

Process Quality While every process is carried out, it has certain properties like time in which it is carried out, costs associated, etc. Process quality is combination of values of such properties of the process.

Process A process is a set of activities that performed in an organized manner produces a desired outcome (product/service) with acceptable quality under a set of constraints.

Product metric Measure of an attribute possessed by the software product itself (e.g., lines of code).

Product/Outcome Quality Qualities of the outcome of a process (which can be a product or a service).

Professional Responsibility Professional responsibility associated with a process step or set of steps is the contribution towards the intended outcomes of the process from that step or set of steps that must be satisfied by the actor performing the step or set of steps.

Progress of a Process The progress of a process is manifest through the Goods and / or Services (Outcome of the Process) with perceivable aspects of acceptable quality that every activity has as its outcome.

Protected Health Information (PHI) An individual's health information created or received by a health-care provider and that can identify the individual.

Publish-Subscribe Architecture The software architecture that provides abstraction among data producers and consumers. This architecture enables development of more scalable, modular and dynamic distributed systems.

QF^{2}D—QFD by QF (Quality Factor) A QFD tailoring using the QF (Quality Factor) technique.

Quality Assurance Assuring that the process of outcome design will result in desired or intended Quality, and that the process of outcome production ensures this.

Quality Control Checking or testing the outcome for desired Quality, after the fact.

Quality Function Deployment (QFD) A software development process that attempts to prioritize the development priorities (including quality attributes) based on stakeholder's perception of customer's needs.

Quality Metric Measures extent a software product rates on a specific quality characteristic (e.g., reliability).

Quality Pattern A description of the quality problem and the essence of its solution to enable the solution to be reused in different settings.

Refactoring Changes that aim to improve the internal structure of a software without changing its external behavior.

Reflexion Model The resulting model of the comparison of the architecture design with the derived abstract model of the code. Typically a reflexion model highlights the differences between the code and the architecture and as such defines the extent of the architectural drift problem.

Reliability The extent to which software completes its intended task without failure in a specified environment.

Requirement Conformance Ensuring that a software product as built matches its specification.

Requirements Creep Refers to uncontrolled changes or continuous growth in a project's scope, sometimes called scope creep.

Requirements Elicitation (1) process through which the acquirer and the suppliers of a system discover, review, articulate, understand, and document the requirements on the system and the life cycle processes (ISO/IEC/IEEE 29148:2011 Systems and software engineering—Life cycle processes—Requirements engineering, 4.1.18) (2) the use of systematic techniques, such as prototypes and structured surveys, to proactively identify and document customer and end-user needs (ISO/IEC/IEEE 24765:2010 Systems and software engineering—Vocabulary).

Retrospective To allow the development team the time to step back and reflect on what went right or wrong on a recently completed product iteration.

Reusability Extent to which software components can be used in new applications.

Reviews Meeting during which a software product is examined by any interested stakeholders for comment or approval.

Root Cause Analysis Process of identifying the factors that resulted in the failure of a software product to deliver the correct behavior nature and to identify the lessons to be learned to achieve of better consequences in the future.

Safety Software quality assurance process that focuses on the identification and assessment of potential hazards that may affect software negatively and cause an entire system to fail.

Safety Analysis Modeling Language (SAML) A tool-independent modeling framework that can be used to construct system models with both deterministic and probabilistic behavior.

Safety Case Evidence collected during system development and testing to ensure that a product conforms to its safety requirements.

Scope Management (project) Scope management includes the processes required to ensure that the project includes all the work required, and only the work required, to complete the project successfully. (A Guide to the Project Management Body of Knowledge (PMBOK(R) Guide)—Fifth Edition).

Security The degree to which assets (data, bandwidth, processor use) of value are protected from attacks that will result in their loss.

Security Assurance Process whose intent is to ensure the design and implementation of software systems that protect their data and resources from attack.

Security Controls Security controls are safeguards or countermeasures to avoid, counteract, or minimize security risks relating to personal information, or any organizational information. Selecting proper controls and implementing those will initially help an organization to bring down risk to acceptable level.

Security The practice of protecting the confidentiality, integrity, and availability of data from those with malicious intentions.

Security Policy Framework The security policy framework is a set of high-level policies on security, mainly affecting the policy makers and stakeholders.

Security Policy Security policy is a set of policies issues by an organization to ensure that all information system users within the system comply with rules and guidelines related to the security of the information stored digitally in the system.

Security Threat A security threat is a possible danger that might exploit a vulnerability to breach security and thus cause possible harm.

Separation of Concerns A design principle for separating a computer program or any system into different parts so that each part address separate concerns when a concern is set of information or particular problem domain.

Social Media Computer-mediated tools that allow people to create, share or exchange information in virtual communities and online networks.

Software Architecture View A representation of a set of system elements and relations associated with them to support a particular concern. Having multiple views helps to separate the concerns and as such support the modeling, understanding, communication and analysis of the software architecture for different stakeholders.

Software Architecture The conventions for constructing and using an architecture view.

Software Architecture A subset of software design that cares about the nonfunctional requirements and issues that affect the software as a whole.

Software Design A discipline on software development that cares about how to structure the software to fulfill its requirements.

Software Evolution A discipline on software development that study the way that the software evolves through time.

Software Maintenance The "modification of a software product after delivery to correct faults, to improve performance or other attributes, or to adapt the product to a changed working environment."

Software Measurement "The process by which numbers or symbols are assigned to attributes of entities in the real world in such a way as to define them according to clearly defined rules."

Software Metric "An objective mathematical measure of software that is sensitive to differences in software characteristics. It provides a quantitative measure of an attribute which the body of software exhibits."

Software Modularity The "degree to which a system or computer program is composed of discrete components such that a change to one component has minimal impact on other components."

Software Process Activities involved from understanding what "customer needs" intended software must satisfy to deploying the software for the customer.

Software Product Quality* Capability of a software product to satisfy stated and implied needs when used under specified conditions.

Software Product Set of computer programs, procedures, and possibly associated documentation and data. [ISO/IEC 12207].

Software Quality How well a software product conforms to its functional and nonfunctional requirements and how well it satisfies user expectations.

Software Quality Assurance (SQA) The function of software quality that assures that the standards, processes, and procedures are appropriate for the project and are correctly implemented.

Software Quality Characteristic Category of software quality attributes that bears on software quality. Software quality characteristics can be refined into multiple levels of subcharacteristics and finally into software quality attributes. [ISO/IEC 25000].

Software Quality Control (SQC) The function of software quality that checks that the project follows its standards, processes, and procedures, and that the project produces the required internal and external (deliverable) products.

Software Quality Management (SQM) Comprises of processes that ensure that the software project meets its goals and meets the clients' expectations.

Software Quality Requirement Requirement that a software quality attribute be present in software. [ISO/IEC 24765].

Software Quality "Conformance to explicitly stated functional and performance requirements, explicitly documented development standards and implicit characteristics that are expected of all professionally developed software."

Software Quality Qualities of the resultant software/software system from software development efforts. ISO 25010 can be taken as guidance for various quality parameters.

Stakeholder Any individual, team, or organization with interests in, or concerns relative to, a system.

Stakeholder Any individual, team, or organization having an interest in the development and deployment of a software system.

Standards Enforceable patterns of processes that must be complied with.

State-Event Fault Trees (SEFT) An extension of classical fault trees that added the capabilities for representing states and events to the fault trees.

Statistical Software Quality Assurance The use of statistical tools and techniques are applied in an attempt to trace defects to their root causes and focus on correcting the defects with greatest impacts on the system.

Tabu Search An optimization technique which exploits memory structures to explore a search space of potential solutions.

Testability Effort required to create the test cases and procedures necessary to ensure software performs its required functions.

Test-Driven Development A development and design technique in which the test code is developed before the production code, alternating among each other and in small steps.

Testing The process of executing a software product with the intent of finding software defects.

Threat Conditions or events that may be used to damage system resources or render them in accessible to authorized users.

Total Quality Management (TQM) Consists of organization-wide efforts to install and make permanent a climate in which an organization continuously improves its ability to deliver high-quality products and services to customers.

Trust Indicates the level of confidence that one entity (system, organization, person) can rely on another.

Trust Assurance Process of verifying the level of confidence that entities (systems, organizations, persons) can rely on one another.

Usability The effort required to learn, use, enter data, and interpret program output.

User Experience (UX) All aspects of the user's interaction with a software product, service, or environment.

User Story Used in agile development to capture a description of software functionality from an end-user perspective.

Validation Ensures that the product actually meets the user's needs and that the specification was correct in the first place.

Verification Ensuring that a product has been built according its requirements and design specifications.

Work Breakdown Structure A hierarchical representation of the process clearly showing contribution to system and sub-systems of the product resulting from the process.

Author Index

Note: Page numbers followed by "*f*" and "*t*" refer to figures and tables, respectively.

357

Subject Index

Note: Page numbers followed by "*f*" and "*t*" refer to figures and tables, respectively.